KILLING *the* MESSENGER

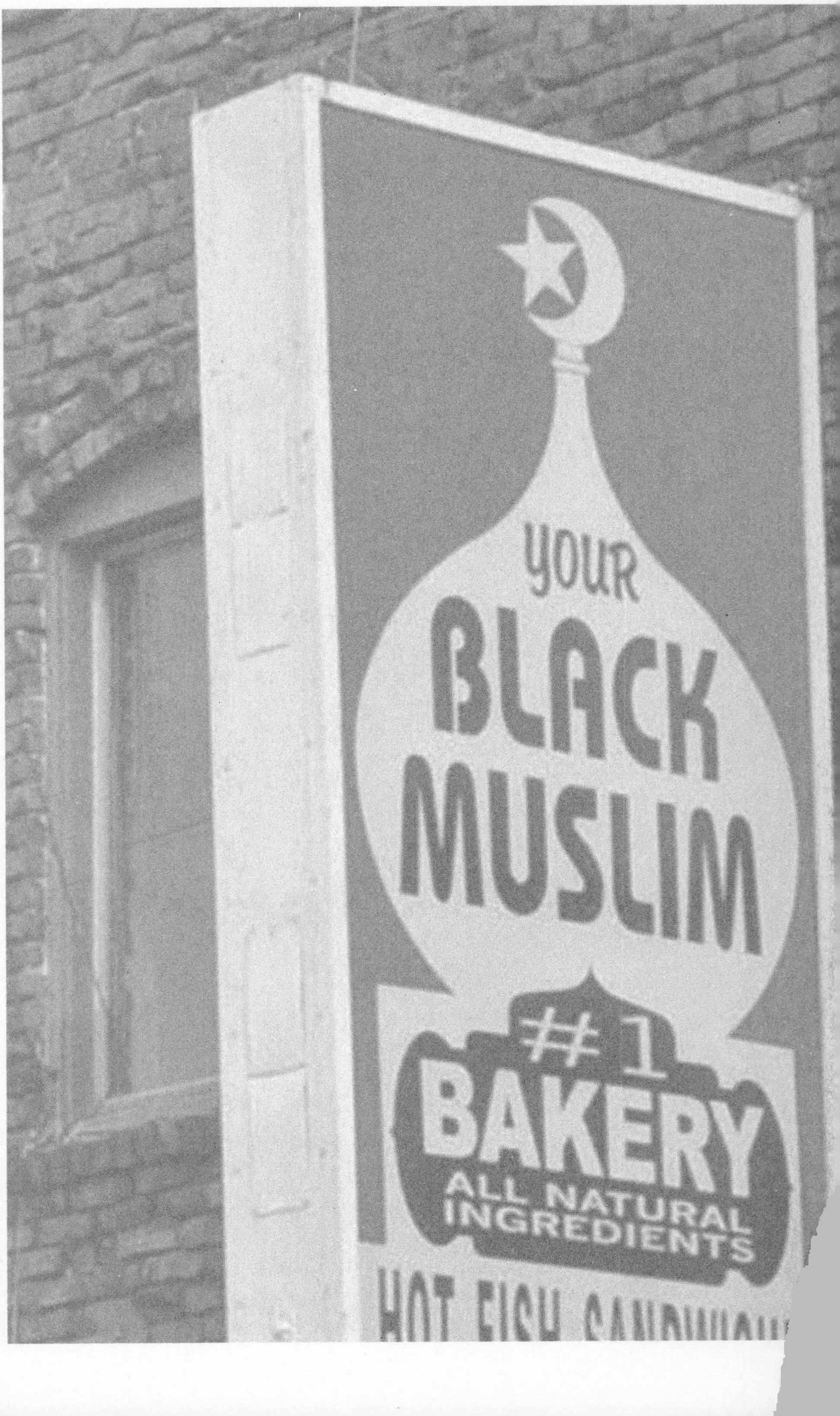
YOUR
BLACK
MUSLIM
#1
BAKERY
ALL NATURAL
INGREDIENTS

KILLING *the* MESSENGER

A story of radical faith,

racism's backlash, and

the assassination of a journalist

THOMAS PEELE

CROWN PUBLISHERS

New York

Copyright © 2012 by Thomas Peele

Published in the United States by Crown Publishers, an imprint of the Crown Publishing Group, a division of Random House, Inc., New York.
www.crownpublishing.com

CROWN and the Crown colophon are registered trademarks of Random House, Inc.

Library of Congress Cataloging-in-Publication Data
Peele, Thomas.
    Killing the messenger : a story of radical faith, racism's backlash, and the assassination of a journalist / by Thomas Peele. — 1st ed.
        p.   cm.
    Includes bibliographical references and index.
    1. Bailey, Chauncey, 1949–2007.   2. Murder—California—Oakland—Case studies.   3. Black Muslims—Press coverage—California—Oakland—Case studies.   4. Corruption—Press coverage—California—Oakland—Case studies.
I. Title.
    HV6534.O23P55 2011
    364.152'3092—dc23   2011029542

ISBN 978-0-307-71755-9
eISBN 978-0-307-71757-3

PRINTED IN THE UNITED STATES OF AMERICA

Jacket design by Ben Gibson
Jacket photography by Karl Mondon

10 9 8 7 6 5 4 3 2 1

First Edition

For Mary Sayre Frazee

You inherit the sins, you inherit the flames

BRUCE SPRINGSTEEN, "Adam Raised a Cain"

Contents

Author's Note on Usage

This work spans periods of American history when Americans of African descent were commonly called Negroes, Colored, then Blacks, and eventually African Americans. I have attempted to stay true to the context of the time, using, as have other authors, the word "Negro" to describe African Americans during the *Plessy v. Ferguson* and civil rights eras. "Colored" and "Black" are used from the midsixties through the eighties, when the preferred phrase "African American" became more common. Much of this book is set in Oakland, California, home at one time to the Black Panthers. It is a city where the word "Black" remains in popular use to describe African Americans. In specific Oakland references, "Black" is used to describe people and events as late as 2011.

The slur "nigger" is never an easy word to write. I use it primarily in quoted dialogue, as I use the slur "darkie," to fully illustrate the state of mind of the speaker.

The phrase "Black Muslim" is frequently employed in reference to followers of W. D. Fard and Elijah Muhammad. It is the phrase that the primary subjects of this book, Yusuf Ali Bey and his followers, use in self-description. Historically, it is used to describe members of the Nation of Islam through the mid-1970s, but it also describes Bey's followers and descendants in the text through 2011. At no time should the reader interpret "Black Muslim" or "Muslim" in the text to refer to traditional followers of the Prophet Muhammad, who are referred to hereafter as Orthodox Muslims for clarity.

Dramatis Personae

Numerous characters in this book are referred to by more than one name, largely because of their evolution through the Black Muslim faith. There are also numerous characters in this book with the surname "Bey." For the sake of clarity, many are referred to on second reference by their first name or by their common name, which is sometimes a number.

To aid the reader, following are the full names of prominent characters along with their names commonly used in the text.

Yusuf Ali Bey, founder of Your Black Muslim Bakery: Joseph Stephens, Joseph X Stephens, and sometimes Daddy

Billy Stephens: Billy X Stephens and Billy and sometimes Abdul Rabb Muhammad

Theron Stephens: Theron

Farieda Bey: Farieda

Yusuf Ali Bey IV: Fourth and occasionally Bey IV

Yusuf Ali Bey V: Fifth

Antar Bey: Antar

Joshua Bey: Joshua

Akbar Bey: Akbar

Waajid Aljawwaad: Waajid

Alaia Bey: Alaia

Saleem Bey: Saleem

Antoine Mackey: Mackey and occasionally Ali

Devaughndre Broussard: Broussard and occasionally Catfish

Robert Harris: Sometimes referred to as Karriem in chapters 6 and 7

Elijah Muhammad: Elijah; sometimes referred to as Elijah Poole in chapter 7

Malcolm X: Malcolm

W. D. Fard: Wallace D. Ford, Walli Fard, Wallace Davis-el, Master Wallace D. Fard Muhammad

I have given pseudonyms to several people who were victims of Yusuf Bey's rapes and other abuses. "Jane," "Nancy," "Timothy," "Tammy," "Alice," and "Vincent" are pseudonyms out of respect to the victims they represent. Tammy is referred to a few times by Yusuf Bey IV as "Mommy." A woman kidnapped and tortured in 2007 by Yusuf Bey IV and others has been given the pseudonym "JoAnne." The pseudonym "Cheryl Davis" has been given to a woman who worked at Your Black Muslim Bakery at the time of Chauncey Bailey's murder.

Introduction
A Murmur of Growing Intensity

On the morning of August 2, 2007, I drove my then-usual commute from an apartment, not far from the eastern shore of San Francisco Bay in the city of Alameda, to a newsroom nearly twenty miles away in the East Bay suburbs. The route took me in and out of the city of Oakland through tunnels—the first passing beneath a shipping channel, the second carving its way through cumbersome hills. Oakland was little more than the place I passed through to get anywhere—to work, to pick up my wife at her job in San Francisco, to visit friends.

That bright, sunny morning seemed like just another day. I had moved to California seven years earlier and had only recently committed to staying longer, having just turned down a good newspaper job in New Jersey. That summer I was in the throes of finishing a graduate writing program, and my mind was stuck on a looming thesis deadline. The radio was off, and as I drove I dictated ideas into a little recorder about how to finish that tome. As I entered Oakland, I didn't know that a horrible murder had occurred an hour or so earlier just blocks away—a man had been gunned down on a busy city street by a masked killer.

I had worked for newspapers of various sizes since 1983, pulling myself upward from the traditional starting places of municipal-government and police beats, and now carried the somewhat overblown title of "investigative reporter." I liked to dig, to get to the bottom of things, to find their roots, their causes. As sort of a subspecialty, I had also carved out a niche writing about the First Amendment, censorship, and press rights. People, I had come to believe, were often ignorant of journalists' struggles to adequately serve them, the roadblocks we overcome, the daily fights to be watchdogs of the public interest. As I parked my car in the lot next to the long, flat, nearly windowless building that housed the *Contra Costa Times,* slung a bag over my shoulder, and grabbed my ubiquitous cup of black coffee, I had no idea that three booming reports of a shotgun in Oakland earlier that morning had signaled the convergence of many of my interests.

I walked into a newsroom in transition. The newspaper industry had not yet been rocked the way it would be a few years later, with massive layoffs and closures, but it was starting to tremble. The *Contra Costa Times,* once a part of the venerable Knight Ridder chain, had recently been put up for sale and bought by MediaNews, the same company that owned the nearby *Oakland Tribune.* A painful consolidation of news staffs that had competed for years was under way. Everyone, it seemed, was leery of losing their jobs.

As I entered, there was a commotion around the desks where the police reporters sat among an array of scanners and radios, a wall-mounted television dangling over their heads. Even to a skeptical veteran such as me, the buzz seemed different, a real story developing with a murmur of growing intensity about it.

"What's going on?" I asked.

"Someone shot the editor of the *Oakland Post,*" a reporter told me.

"Dead?"

"Very," she deadpanned, glancing up from a computer, a hand briefly covering the mic on her telephone headset.

A journalist? Really? I knew the *Post* was a small weekly that covered Oakland's African American community, but I had no idea who was its editor.

"Chauncey Bailey," the reporter told me and turned away to continue her call.

I knew the name, but only vaguely. Bailey had worked for the *Tribune* once and had gotten fired for some sort of ethical lapse. I asked an editor if anyone knew yet who had killed Bailey or why. He said no. I felt an immediate frustration. Before the merger, our newsroom would have mobilized to cover the story, but now Oakland was strictly the *Tribune*'s territory, and I could do nothing. And though I worked primarily on long investigative pieces that often took months, I wanted in on *this* breaking story. A journalist. Murdered. If someone had killed him over his work, then the implications were boundless.

A few minutes later my phone rang. It was a source I had developed in Oakland a few years earlier, a minor official who often proved helpful with information.

Two theories about the murder were raging across the city, he said, both fueled by rumors concerning Bailey's personal life—he had been killed either by a jealous husband or boyfriend or by someone seeking retribution over an unpaid debt, a loan shark or shylock. My source had strong credibility, and his leads that Bailey's slaying had to do with something other than journalism brought me a tinge of relief. It seemed overly dramatic anyway, I realized, to suggest that the editor of a weekly newspaper had been killed for reasons directly related to his job. The last local print reporter killed in the United States was Don Bolles of the *Arizona Republic,* who was investigating ties between business leaders in Phoenix and the Mafia in 1976 when he suffered fatal wounds in a car bombing. The little *Oakland Post* was not prone to the type of reportage that provoked anyone. I returned to an analysis of government pay data I'd been working on for months, thinking the Bailey story would blow over in a few days.

Half an hour later, my source called back.

"Bailey was working on a story about the Black Muslim Bakery," he said.

"Holy shit," I said out loud, as if I were playing a reporter in a B movie.

That phone call changed everything.

If a journalist was going to get killed in Northern California over any story, then Oakland's Your Black Muslim Bakery, run by a defiant, violent, polygamous cult under the leadership of the Bey family, was a likely topic. A few years earlier, a gutsy reporter named Chris Thompson of the weekly *East Bay Express,* had written several long exposés about the Beys. Consequently, he received death threats, the windows of the *Express*'s office were smashed, and Thompson spent several weeks in hiding. The Beys were demonstratively dangerous people. Their belief system didn't just approve of violence—it encouraged it as the default mode to deal with any and all problems they encountered.

Unconfirmed reports of a Bey connection to Bailey's slaying soon overwhelmed the story. A colleague came to me and suggested what I was already thinking: If Bailey *had* been killed over a story, the journalistic community needed to rally the way it had following Bolles's murder, by banding together to answer the assassination with a show of force in finishing his work. The response to Bolles's death, known as the Arizona Project, was journalistic legend—two dozen reporters had descended on Phoenix and dug into the corruption Bolles had been investigating in a way that he never could have working alone. Their message was clear: A story could not be killed by killing a journalist.

A legendary investigative reporter for *Newsday,* Bob Greene, pitched the project to journalists around the country, writing that a communal response to Bolles's death would cause "the community and other like communities [to] reflect on what has happened and hopefully would think twice about killing reporters. For all of us—particularly newspapers with high investigative profiles—this is eminently self-serving. As individuals we are buying life insurance on our own reporters. If we accomplish only this, we have succeeded."

That a similar effort—eventually known as the Chauncey Bailey Project— would occur in this case became clear early the next morning, August 3, when police raided the Beys' North Oakland compound, an operation planned for weeks in response to two *other* murders and the kidnapping and torture of a woman that cult members were suspected of committing months earlier. That raid had come too late to save Bailey's life. In less than a day, a nineteen-year-old Bey "soldier" admitted to police he had killed Bailey to stop a story he was writing about the bakery.

The confession made clear that Bailey's work had to be completed, that a clear message had to be sent by other journalists: Killing a reporter would result in far more journalistic scrutiny than a single reporter could have achieved. It didn't matter that the *Post* was a small weekly on the margins of journalistic credibility, or that Bailey was, at fifty-seven years old, caught in a downward career spiral. What had happened to him was far bigger than that. The free press on which the public depends to keep it informed had been attacked. If Chauncey Bailey could get killed over a story, a reporter anywhere in the country could get killed over a story. A week after the murder, his former editor at the *Detroit News,* where Bailey had worked for many years, summed it up best: The assassination "was an attack on the American way of life."

The Chauncey Bailey Project, born of newspapers, nonprofit journalism organizations, radio and television stations, freelance and retired reporters, and journalism students and professors at two universities, began a few weeks later through a series of chaotic gatherings. As my own company's consolidation went forward, I moved to the *Tribune*'s office in Oakland, where much of the work was based. Along with a handful of other reporters who had to quickly learn to work together, trust one another, and share sources, I became part of a team that would investigate the Beys and Bailey's murder for more than four years. We remained, over that time, driven by a common purpose—to get to the bottom of what happened.

To call Chauncey Bailey a flawed journalist is to imply that there is such a thing as an unflawed one. Journalism is an incredibly human endeavor. Bailey's reputation, at the end of a career that had taken a long fall to the *Oakland Post,* was one of hasty reporting, poor writing, and questionable ethics. But none of those things made him less of a First Amendment martyr when he was killed because the subject of his story objected to its publication.

That subject was a young man named Yusuf Ali Bey IV, who had taken over leadership of the cult, which worshipped the teachings of Nation of Islam founder Elijah Muhammad. But while clinging to the Nation's early dogma, the Beys had long since broken away, acting independently, answering to no one other than their leader and their God. Other than Chris Thompson's extraordinary work in the *Express,* they had largely gone without scrutiny for decades. The Oakland Police Department's indifference to—or outright fear of—the cult members was legendary. Politicians kowtowed to them, praised them, loaned them taxpayer money that went unrepaid. Even when the cult's patriarch, Bey IV's father, Yusuf Ali Bey, was found through DNA evidence to have raped girls as young as thirteen years old, he was still heralded as a community leader. That he died in 2003 before the charges were proven in court only added to his followers' belief that he was a victim of persecution.

As the days following Bailey's death turned into months and then years, questions about the Beys mounted. What did they really believe, and where did it come from? Was there any sincerity to their dogma about a desire to promote only African American self-help, or was it all hokum and exploitative self-aggrandizement meant only to enrich them? Were they true believers or hucksters who used religion to hide a criminal organization?

How did they manage to find an endless wellspring of converts to their hate-based cosmology? And how did they come to intersect so violently with Bailey, a minor journalist who always seemed to work on the edge of advocacy, who himself believed strongly in the self-determination of African Americans?

This book, a further endeavor to provide a full accounting of what happened, is an attempt to explore those and other questions.

Killing *the* Messenger

part one

"You don't know my name?"

Your Black Muslim Bakery on San Pablo Avenue in North Oakland, the base of power for Yusuf Bey and, eventually, his sons Antar and Yusuf Bey IV. *Photo by Bob Larson/ Contra Costa Times, courtesy of the Bay Area News Group*

That Will Teach Them . . .

Chauncey Bailey awoke near dawn that fateful Thursday summer morning. By six thirty he was hurrying around his little apartment near the western edge of Oakland's Lake Merritt, folding a silver pocket square into a point before tucking it into his jacket, stuffing papers into the gym bag he used as a briefcase. Newspaper work was never much of an early-morning profession, at least for reporters, but a busy day lay ahead and Bailey wanted to get at it. He took a moment to check his suit—a suit he had bought in a thrift store because at fifty-seven, after spending his entire adulthood in journalism, he had long accepted the frugal realities of the news business. But in spite of his finances, he took great care in how he appeared, often lamenting to friends that too many African Americans dressed badly. "The only men a lot of Blacks see in ties are detectives and preachers," he once told his brother. Throughout his career he had both witnessed and been the subject of constant racism inside and outside of newsrooms. To combat it, Bailey clung tightly to his self-respect, and that meant dressing well. He was by no means an overly talented reporter or writer, but he remained a hardened and gritty adherent to his basic craft—an editor once described his strength

as the ability to "get it down and get it in." He was good with the facts on
deadline. Bailey dressed fancy. He wrote plainly.

Bailey knotted a gray tie and stuffed a jury summons in his pants pocket.
He needed to mail it back; it was just one more bother. His civic duty wasn't
in a jury box; it was at his desk, putting out a newspaper. A few weeks
earlier, Bailey had been named editor of the *Oakland Post,* a tiny, giveaway
weekly that served the city's African American community. It printed just
about anything written by anyone—press releases, community notices,
rambling columns. Its main source of income was competing pastors, who
were always trying to outdraw each other on Sunday mornings—and thus
fill their collection plates—by heralding their coming sermons in display
ads. The paper even carried a biblical quote in its banner, Proverbs 29:18:
"Where there is no vision, the people will perish . . ."

But Bailey had his own vision for the *Post.* He wanted to shape it to address
minority issues head-on, with blunt, aggressive reportage in the long tradition of the Black press. That challenge, he'd confided to friends in recent
weeks, had righted him after a time spent listing and being adrift. He was,
quite simply, happy to be working and determined to turn the *Post* into
an intricate slice of Oakland's life. At the same time, Bailey's often stormy
personal life seemed to be calming. He had recently reunited with his father after a long estrangement. He had a young son in Southern California,
Chauncey Wendell Bailey III, and despite the geographic distance, he was
doing all he could to help raise him. His son's visits to Oakland were nothing short of a joy for Bailey; people said the child brought out the best in
him. Hidden behind his tough reporter persona was a soft spot for children.
When he had lived in Detroit years earlier, he and his then wife had taken
in and raised her sister's two daughters, creating an instant family that Bailey loved. Although friends said he was loath to admit it, he wanted those
closest to him to be proud of his new job title: editor.

But at a small paper like the *Post,* which ran on a thin budget, his assignment encompassed almost all editorial functions. He wrote stories, took
photographs, laid out pages, sometimes even carried copies over to Oakland's ornate city hall and handed them out.

The paper crammed Bailey's days with meaningful work, and August 2, 2007, arrived as if it would be no different. First on his list that morning was to get downtown to the *Post*'s cramped offices in the old Financial Services Building at Fourteenth and Franklin streets and finish a story about an Oakland cult of Black Muslims with a long history of crimes and violence.

The story nagged at Bailey. He had written it—gotten it down, gotten it in—only to have the *Post*'s publisher, Paul Cobb, a longtime Oakland activist and politician, spike it. The Black Muslims that were the story's subject—a sprawling family with the surname Bey—owned a business called Your Black Muslim Bakery in the North Oakland ghetto that served as a community center and makeshift mosque. Its founder and patriarch, Yusuf Ali Bey, had died four years earlier. A blood feud had followed for control of the strange business, which Oaklanders simply called "the bakery." It was now in the control of one of Bey's many children, twenty-one-year-old Yusuf Ali Bey IV, who was one of five sons upon whom Bey had bestowed his own name. Most people thought that because of the bakery's name, the Beys were members of the Nation of Islam, the Black separatist sect of Elijah Muhammad, Malcolm X (before he rejected its teachings), and Louis Farrakhan. They weren't, though. While the Beys preached with unrelenting zeal the Nation's original dogma of Black racial superiority, hatred of inferior blue-eyed devils, and salvation though devotion and work, they and their followers were an independent sect. But despite their bombastic evangelism and frequent violence, the Beys were widely credited—even admired—for giving jobs to those others would not: ex-convicts, recovering drug addicts, the poor and uneducated, those with nowhere else to go.

Bailey had reported on the Beys for years, and he headed out the door that August morning wanting to tell another chapter about them. The previous month, he had run into a man who had been driven out of the bakery during the struggle for control of the business. Bailey—who had always admired the Beys' arguments for African American self-determination—had listened to how the bakery had fallen into chaos and bankruptcy and recognized an important story in the man's tale. Based on information from this single source, Bailey had hammered out a short piece. But Cobb had spiked it, saying it needed better attribution. Bailey had fumed, but Cobb had won the argument. The Beys were not to be treated lightly. If the *Post* was going to print a critical story about them, it needed better sourcing than one person with fears about his name being used. At least that's what Cobb had insisted. Bailey, though, had confided to people that he thought Cobb was scared of the Beys and was just making up excuses.

But Bailey also knew well the level of violence that radicalized Black Muslims could commit. In 1974, as a young reporter for the *San Francisco Sun Reporter,* he'd written about a handful of Black Muslims who became known as both the Zebra Killers and the Death Angels. For months they terrorized San Francisco, randomly shooting whites, justifying killings through the sect's early teachings that salvation could be achieved by the slaying of "white devils." Bailey had been one of the first journalists to report—weeks before arrests—that those gunmen were likely Black Muslims. He also made a provocative link between the San Francisco slayings and similar shootings in Oakland and other East Bay cities, suggesting a connection. But before he could probe any deeper, he left the Bay Area for the East Coast and a new job. The nexus between the San Francisco murders and those across the bay remained largely ignored.

The sun had barely peeked above the brown Oakland hills when Bailey stepped outside, the bag slung over his left shoulder. Atop the peaked roof of his gray stucco building, someone had stationed a pair of plastic owls to scare away the Lake Merritt seagulls that were the neighborhood's bane. But they didn't work: The winged pests were everywhere, doing whatever they wanted, sometimes even sitting atop the fake owls' heads.

Bailey headed downtown.

During the past thirty-five years, Oakland had grown both numb to and afraid of the Beys. Their bakery was part health-food store, part ministry, and part front for wide-ranging criminal enterprises run by its patriarch, a former hairdresser born Joseph Stephens who had reinvented himself as Dr. Yusuf Ali Bey. The surname was one that followers of a 1920s Chicago-based sect, the Moorish Science Temple of America, which practiced a fictive version of Islam, had used as a suffix. But rather than be Stephens-Bey in the Moorish tradition, he was just Bey, a title once used by Egyptian and Turkish dignitaries.

Bey was blessed with the quicksilver tongue of a natural minister. He also possessed a predator's ruthless soul. To many of his followers and children he was godlike; to an objective observer of his organization, he was a cult leader that Oakland had let flourish in its midst. Each week, on a television show called *True Solutions,* which he paid to have broadcast on local cable stations, Bey repeated the Black Muslims' basic beliefs: In 1930, Allah, in the person of a man named W. D. Fard, traveled from the Holy City of Mecca to Detroit, arriving on July 4 and announcing that he had come to find what he called the Lost Tribe of Shabazz in the wilderness of North America and lead its members to salvation through their true religion, Islam. Fard's messenger was the Honorable Elijah Muhammad, who led the Nation of Islam for forty-one years, demanding complete segregation of the "so-called Negroes" from the rest of American society.

With images of Fard and Elijah behind him and stoic young men in dark suits and bow ties standing rigidly at his side, Bey railed against "tricknology," which Black Muslims defined as a science of deception whites used to deceive and suppress people of other races. He referred to people of color collectively as "Asiatics," a group that included Native Americans, Africans, and Asians. He spewed anti-Semitism and claimed the Holocaust paled when compared to the treatment of African slaves and their descendants in the Americas. Christianity, he said, was nonsense, a "spook religion."

Like Elijah Muhammad before him, Bey often babbled about a mad scientist named Big-Headed Yakub who created the devils—Caucasians and Jews—through a series of grafting experiments 6,600 years earlier, or how a mile-wide "mother plane" orbited the earth, forever preparing to annihilate the devils in an apocalypse that would restore Asiatics to their rightful place as humankind's masters. The devils were "snakes of the grafted type," or skunks, or "cavies," short for cavemen.

Bey was also unambiguous about his willingness to employ violence to enforce his will or retaliate against those who crossed him, positions he articulated weekly on television.

"We don't turn no other cheek. You turn a fire hose on my mother, I will kill you 'til I die. If you think I am going to let you put a hose on my mother, put dogs on my mother, so I can sit in a toilet next to you, you are out of your cotton-picking mind," he said in a 2002 sermon. "You're not just ordinary people. Black is dominant. The Caucasian is the scientist for evil."

Bey had never really moved beyond the rigid Black Muslim dogma of the early 1960s, and much of what he preached was rhetoric long dismissed as ignorant fables from another age. Although he wasn't part of the Nation of Islam, Bey was among the last true believers in its original, racist message that was, itself, a backlash to centuries of white oppression.

Thousands of African Americans had migrated to Oakland during World War II for shipyard jobs, and they found in the ensuing decades that the deed covenants that kept them segregated in ghettos were as much a part of racism in California as the Klan was in the South. They found, too, that suburban flight and lack of postwar jobs had slipped an economic noose around their necks. It was Oakland where the Black Power movement took root, where screeds seemed to forever blare from scores of storefront churches of thin repute, and where Bey hacked out a niche.

When he started in the early seventies, attention was focused on the gun-toting Black Panthers, not the little baker in a kufi hawking banana cakes and fish sandwiches. Panther leader Bobby Seale twice ran for mayor of Oakland and Bey supported him, but he was more concerned at the time about his own business ascent than about elective politics. That would come. Attention paid to the Panthers gave Bey the cover to establish his business largely unnoticed, and the enabling environment of the Black Power movement made him seem like just one more minority trying to get ahead. By the time the Panthers flamed out a few years later, Bey was entrenched in North Oakland, his bakery an institution.

Parroting Elijah Muhammad, he sought out poor, uneducated African Americans, most of them male ex-offenders eager to hear they were not inferior, as paternalistic, racist America insisted, but were in fact *superior* beings with larger brains and God-given righteousness. Bey converted the weak and vulnerable into indentured servants, the angry into his warriors. He gave them bakers' aprons and beds and preached self-respect and self-sufficiency. They returned unwavering loyalty. Bey also built his own version of the Nation's shadowy paramilitary, the Fruit of Islam, calling his men soldiers, drilling them relentlessly. To those who pleased him, worshipped him, and did his bidding without question, he was a benevolent yet stern father. To become a spiritually adopted son of Yusuf Bey, to shed one's "slave name" and take his surname in exchange for idolatry, was the status to which all his male followers aspired.

Bey also capitalized on public ignorance about who the Blacks Muslims were and what they believed. Few seemed to fully understand that there was little correlation between the kind of Islam that he practiced—it is best called Fardian Islam—and the teachings of the Prophet Muhammad. Orthodox Muslims do not profess racial superiority or larger brains or believe a mad scientist created Caucasians and Jews. Following Elijah Muhammad's death in 1975, most African American Muslims denounced his teachings and joined Orthodox Muslim communities. But not Bey. He continued to preach that Fard was God in the flesh and that God is thus a man, which Orthodox Muslims consider blasphemy. Bey, like Elijah Muhammad, created a false legitimacy based on the illusion that the Black Muslim and Orthodox Muslim faiths were much more similar than they are.

There is no question that Yusuf Bey sometimes helped people. He employed and sheltered men fresh from prison whom others shunned. He counseled them that they mattered, that to find themselves they had to shed the ugly vestiges of four hundred years of stereotypes and live virtuous lives free of alcohol, drugs, and slothfulness, that they could manifest their own destiny with the very hands that they extended, palms upward, to Allah in prayer.

If only he had stopped there.

While a large majority of people rejected Bey's rants, few actually challenged him, and even detractors bought his food. Police saw that crime around the bakery was significantly lower than elsewhere in Oakland and left Bey's soldiers to patrol the neighborhood, enforcing their own brand of justice. (Bey often touted the fact that the bakery had never been robbed or burglarized as a sign of how much respect he had in the area. That his men would have killed anyone foolish enough to try such a thing remained unsaid.) He railed against drugs and alcohol enough to be considered a community leader.

Even those who kept their distance admired how he drove new luxury cars and how he seemed to have no end of solemn young men in suits and bow ties at his side. Bey's followers called him Dr. Bey, adding to his mystique the allure of educational credentials—and a title of high honor in African American culture—where none existed. It stuck. Even though Bey's highest educational achievement was a cosmetology certificate, all of Oakland called him Dr. Bey.

When the *Oakland Tribune* hired him to cover African American affairs in 1992, Chauncey Bailey soon found that Yusuf Bey made good copy. Bailey wrote positively about the mini empire Bey had built in the name of self-determination. If Bailey noticed that Bey used his platoons of young men for intimidation, that he was, by nearly any definition, a thuggish charlatan with a goon squad, he chose to ignore it. Bailey sometimes confided to friends that he found it difficult to write what he deemed "negative" stories about those he commonly called "Black folks."

But in *East Bay Express* stories on the Beys, Chris Thompson had raised the truths that Bailey and others largely ignored: that Bey was a psychopath and that his followers were, by any applicable definition of the word, a "cult." Bey's men used violence and torture to enforce their agenda, which largely consisted of acquiring wealth. Dozens of women around the bakery, their heads wrapped in colored scarves, their eyes always averted downward, openly referred to themselves as Bey's wives. Bruises and cuts frequently appeared on their faces. Fists, feet, telephones, pans, plates, even sidewalk concrete were used to batter them. The women all had multiple children whom Bey embraced as his own, despite the fact that no father was identified on their birth certificates. The women, despite living in his compound and working in his bakery, all received public assistance.

For four years following Bey's 2003 death, his followers engaged in a battle for control of his empire. The victor was Bey IV, known as "Fourth," who promised a new regime of Black Muslim activism in his father's name.

In the summer of 2007, when Chauncey Bailey ran into the man who would eventually be his anonymous source for a story about the bakery, most of what he had to say was about Fourth. What he told Bailey was a frightening truth for Oakland: All that the city had tolerated and ignored from Yusuf Bey and his minions for the past three and a half decades in the name of religious freedom and self-determination had been but a haunting prologue for what had come under Fourth's leadership.

Several buses ran past Bailey's building. He sometimes jumped on the AC Transit 40 line to get downtown. But August 2, 2007, was emerging as a thing of beauty, the cloudless sky matching Bailey's powder-blue shirt. He had worked for a decade in Detroit and had grown to hate the winters there, how people bundled up and ignored one another on the frigid streets. He never grew tired of California sunshine. Even though he was in a rush, he decided to walk. On such a splendid day, he never knew whom he might meet on the way to work.

Bailey hurried around the corner to the northern edge of central Oakland's finest attribute, Lake Merritt, which had been created from a drained swamp in the 1860s. Jogging trails ringed its 155 acres; to the east, luxury homes dappled the hills. From the corner of Lakeshore and First avenues, Bailey looked out over the water rippling in the morning breeze. The sun was above the hills now, joggers and dog walkers squinting in its light. Soon, small sailboats would be out on the water and the oars of a crew or two would slice at the surface. At moments like these, Oakland could fool one into thinking it was a bursting metropolis, clean and bright and pointed forward.

But Lake Merritt's flaws, like the rest of the city's, were easily seen. Bailey crossed a culvert through which water flowed out toward San Francisco Bay. At low tide, the spot reeked of rotting mussels ripped open by hungry gulls. The concrete walkway on which Bailey hurried was faded and decaying, chunks of it falling away and lying in the brown mud below. He passed a large wooden sign describing lakeshore improvement projects under way. It was covered with a thick, curling tangle of black graffiti, the symbols unintelligible to all but those who knew the language of the gang that marked its territory. A long line of four-foot-high orange plastic blocks that created a bike lane along the lake's edge was tagged with similar markings. Even the asphalt was graffitied every few feet. The streets around the western end of the lake divided central and East Oakland and formed a half oval, with lanes crossing one another on short overpasses. Eastbound Fourteenth Street dipped below the westbound lanes, a poorly kept median dividing them.* It proved a perfect place for a homeless encampment, filled with old furniture, shopping carts, even a couple of grills that were often aflame. Underground walkways had been built to give people in East Oakland easy access to Lake Merritt, but they were chained shut, garbage littering their steps.

Oakland is an old city. Its three major highways, the Nimitz, the Mac-Arthur, and the Warren, are named for past heroes most residents probably couldn't identify. Its civic infrastructure is antiquated, perhaps none more so than the Rene C. Davidson Courthouse looming in front of Bailey as he hugged the lakeshore, its white concrete walls awash in sunlight. Bailey rarely went into the courthouse. There was always too much else for him to do, and he was not the type of reporter to spend time digging and research-ing. Yet if he had looked at the ever-growing files of criminal allegations against Bey IV, Bailey would have found plenty of documentation to ap-pease Paul Cobb's desire for attribution. But Bailey didn't have the patience to read through stacks of legal papers.

Bailey stopped for coffee at a McDonald's, then hurried up Fourteenth Street. He was just three blocks from the *Post* with plenty of time to take another pass at the bakery story before his deadline.

Somewhere along the way a battered white minivan passed him.

Suddenly a tall, lean man dressed in a black sweatshirt and pants ran across the street toward Bailey, a ski mask covering his face. His gloved hands were wrapped around a pistol-grip, 12-gauge shotgun, its barrel only eighteen inches long, tilted to port arms. Bailey turned to his right, the masked gunman right on top of him, leveling the weapon just before it erupted.

A few hours later, a young man more certain of his power and destiny than ever before watched a television news report about the murder, the victim identified only as a prominent Oaklander. The young man beamed and

*A large reconstruction of the area began in 2009, greatly altering it.

laughed, as if a huge burden had been lifted from him. Mission accomplished. He didn't need a newscaster to tell him who was dead. Another of the enemies and devils was gone. He was certain there would be no public accountability for what his soldiers had carried out on his order. His father had killed with impunity for nearly forty years. So would he. There was no question now of his omnipotence. Oakland was his city, and anyone who challenged that fact would die.

The man called Fourth summoned a young woman to a television set in his bathroom above Your Black Muslim Bakery. On the screen a solemn reporter stood just outside the cordoned-off crime scene. Fourth pointed at the picture and loudly proclaimed words that surely would have made his late father proud: "That will teach them to fuck with me."

There Goes Lucifer

"Why do I recall, instead of the order of seed bursting in springtime, only the yellow contents of the cistern spread over the lawn's dead grass? Why? And how? How and why?"
—RALPH ELLISON, *Invisible Man*

Several times a day, Yusuf Bey IV would make a hard U-turn on San Pablo Avenue at Fifty-ninth Street and gun his black BMW 745i toward downtown Oakland. He drove by no known rules, swinging in and out of lanes, accelerating, ignoring red lights, other cars, whatever stood in his way. He couldn't go anywhere without scaring people, and he was always going somewhere, a cell phone pressed to his ear as the BMW coursed through the city's streets, three or four impassive young men whom he called his soldiers dressed in cheap dark suits piled in with him. He'd speed away from the fading red and black brick walls of the compound that housed Your Black Muslim Bakery, away from the frenzied pit bull and mastiffs that guarded it, away from the steaming industrial ovens, assault rifles leaning against them, spent cartridges and banana clips scattered on the rat shit–flecked kitchen floor.

Beneath the bakery's signature black star-and-crescent sign looming over the street was an awning with words printed on it in block letters: TASTE OF . . . THE HEREAFTER. That the kind of Islam—or what they called Islam—that the Beys and their followers practiced was based on teachings that rejected belief in an afterlife escaped most passersby. Despite those words, Black Muslims didn't believe in heaven. "I have no alternative than to tell you that there is no life beyond the grave," Elijah Muhammad once wrote. "There is no justice in the sweet bye and bye. Immortality is NOW, HERE. We are the blessed of God and we must exert every means to protect ourselves."

The now, here for Yusuf Bey IV was the sagging, blood-splattered ghetto.

Fourth referred to himself as the bakery's chief executive officer, as if that meant much for someone who had barely graduated from high school thanks only to social promotion and administrators' unrelenting desire that he be gone. He lacked even basic business skills. But as prosecutors would one day lean over lecterns and impress upon jurors, the bakery was much more than a bakery, so he had much more to do than just keep shop anyway. Sure, the Beys churned out sugarless cakes and sold tofu burgers on whole-grain buns. But they also churned out scores of converts to their cause who helped them run innumerable criminal enterprises. Many of those people had worshipped Fourth's father, Yusuf Bey, as God, and those who remained were ready to follow his son's commands to their deaths.

By late 2005, a few months before his twentieth birthday, Fourth stood at the head of the remnants of his father's cult. He claimed that his ascension to leadership and greatness at such a young age had been prophesied in the book of Genesis. Allah had chosen him—and him alone—for greatness. The correct interpretations of the Bible and the Holy Qur'an made plain his destiny.

The facts of his life, though, seemed to destine him for something else.

Fourth grew up as one of the last believers in W. D. Fard's divinity. Despite claims dating to 1930 that followers of Fard and the man who claimed to be his messenger, Elijah Muhammad, simply sought freedom, justice, and equality, the Nation of Islam they founded had largely collapsed under the weight of hate and violence that equaled those of Klansmen and Fascists. Its more well-known members, Malcolm X, Muhammad Ali, and Elijah's son, Wallace Muhammad, had renounced and abandoned its rhetoric for Orthodox Islam. The Nation had been left, since 1980, under the leadership of Louis Farrakhan, a man of frequent, incoherent rants whose former spokesman, Khalid Abdul Muhammad, had called for Hitleresque mass slaughters of whites and Jews. But despite Farrakhan's occasional feints toward moderation, the Black Muslims had, by the end of the twentieth century, become an afterthought, a bizarre, fading fringe group.

Yet in Oakland, Yusuf Bey had clung to their rhetoric and preached their radical faith to his breakaway sect. From behind brick redoubts at his compound in the city's northwest corner, he ruled a small, cloistered cadre of believers with inviolable authority.

Fourth, the third-oldest child and second son of a woman who had borne Yusuf Bey eight children, had grown up in a compound where his father bellowed about self-determination yet held absolute power over his followers, controlling when they worked, ate, and spoke, when and where they slept, what they wore, where they went. Through ridicule and beatings or pretenses of love and praise, he convinced them to give themselves totally to him. Many were but indentured servants, working only for room and board. In that compound, on any given day, Bey could point to a dozen or more women and say that each, under his fictive version of Islam, was his wife; those women were taught that their lives were but the floor upon which their leader walked. In that compound children were forced to work endlessly; some were kept from school and lived in constant terror of what Bey did to them when he got them alone. Guns were omnipresent and violence was the routine way to deal with even the most minor transgression; hate was preached continuously, as was the inferiority of other races, especially whites and Jews, who were devils created by the mad scientist Big-Headed Yakub. So was the idea that the mother plane was always on the brink of launching Armageddon.

As his father's son, Fourth was raised to believe that he was among the last true Black Muslims. He was told he was entitled to whatever he wanted and should obtain it by any means necessary, that his value was based upon how much money he had in his pocket at any moment and what he could make others do for it. It was instilled in him that his father was a God-king, and so he called himself "the prince of the bakery."

Those who feared Fourth called him something else.

When he drove away from the compound, he sometimes banged a quick left or right from San Pablo and cruised along residential streets, passing a mishmash of yardless, vinyl-sided houses that made up North Oakland, iron grates covering nearly every window and door. When he wasn't on the phone, music thumped from the car, Usher, Tupac, 50 Cent. People had long since accepted that living near the bakery meant being under the constant dint of vigilantism and terror. They would hear the blaring hip-hop, inch curtains aside, recognize the BMW's twenty-two-inch, five-thousand-dollar rims, and mutter the name no one dared call Fourth to his face. "There goes Lucifer," they'd say.

When Fourth stayed on San Pablo Avenue, North Oakland's main drag, he rolled past coin laundries, check-cashing joints, and neon-glowing liquor stores, street-corner drug hawkers and prostitutes scurrying into the darkness when they saw or heard the BMW approach. It would be just like Fourth to swing sharply to the curb, doors flying open before the car stopped, his soldiers swarming, kicking, beating, filling their pockets with money, sometimes tossing tiny glass vials of rock cocaine or heroin in the gutter and grinding their feet over them, sometimes, depending on Fourth's whim and the girth of his own roll of bills, stealing them so they could be sold elsewhere.

Railing about drugs—they were but the devil's way of suppressing and destroying Blacks—had always been a cornerstone of the mantra that enabled the Beys to control North Oakland. It was Hoover, Fourth's father would preach, *that motherfucking devil J. Edgar Hoover and his motherfucking FBI,* who first enabled the flow of heroin (he pronounced it "hair-on") into Black communities to push them further toward destruction, knowing that the already hopeless conditions that African Americans faced made narcotics a desperate form of escapism. Regardless of his theories (and history has proven that Hoover's clandestine campaigns had few limits), Bey's antidrug screeds helped bolster his image as an iron-willed civic reformer.

Bey's soldiers frequently attacked drug sellers, beating them senseless in the name of Allah. They were unlikely to steal their wares, though. To them, it was about righteousness: They would leave cheap, clip-on bow ties on the blood-speckled cement as calling cards: The Beys were here.

Fourth aspired to that same image, but if he had a chance to sell drugs stolen on the street, or to dispatch his soldiers to do muscle work for those who sold them wholesale, he would sidestep his self-righteous spiels in favor of what mattered most to him: money.

Fourth drew his *superbia* from the fealty of the grim-faced young men, their suits freshly pressed, their hair shaved in military crops, who flanked him at every turn. They lived on his largesse, nearly begging for his attention and approval. Inside the bakery, he ordered them to salute him like privates passing a general. They did little without his authority. If a drug dealer was beaten and robbed, it was because Fourth wanted that drug dealer beaten and robbed. Soldiers follow orders. Yet Fourth knew that keeping his charges close to him meant his own conduct stood under constant scrutiny. The highest disgrace a Black Muslim could face was being labeled a hypocrite. Fourth had to be careful about who was around when he ordered drugs stolen. He needed his men as close to him as intimate brothers, but he couldn't let the exposure corrode his authority, lest his followers learn his true nature: Just like his father, Fourth falsely claimed to be motivated only by a desire to help his people, when his true obsessions were greed and power.

Fourth and his men had little to fear from police. If an officer happened past and saw Fourth's men blitzing a corner, that officer was likely to keep driving. If the cocaine or heroin being stolen ended up being sold elsewhere, it would probably be way out in East Oakland, where it became another officer's problem. To the cops, they were just punks beating up other punks. Maybe luck would prevail and someone would get shot; one less scumbag to worry about.

Oakland's police department was chronically understaffed despite the city's soaring crime rates—higher per capita than Detroit, New York, or Los Angeles—mostly because voters rejected property-tax levies to pay for more cops, landing the department in a perpetual catch-22: It needed more money for additional officers and better equipment with which to fight crime, but because it did a poor job of fighting crime in the first place, voters lacked the faith to provide more resources.

To many cops, the job was simply about racking up overtime, collecting paychecks, and surviving. In 1999, then-governor Gray Davis signed laws that doled out the most lucrative law-enforcement pensions in the country to California's police officers and prison guards. Ostensibly, Davis's plan was designed to attract and retain better-qualified and better-educated applicants to law-enforcement by providing a back-loaded incentive. A cop who retired at fifty could then embark on a second career knowing that hefty government checks were a monthly certainty for life. But, as in nearly all of his dealings, Davis was mostly motivated by the quid pro quo of campaign cash and union endorsements.

In urban areas with soaring crime and diminishing police resources, such as Oakland, the golden pension plan simply encased many officers' feet in clay. Most cops could recite the exact number of years, months, and days to retirement, even if it was more than a decade away. As a result, many Oakland cops didn't act unless they had no choice. The department investigated public crimes and responded to most calls for service, but initiative on the street wasn't just frowned upon, it was considered suicidal. If a cop saw Fourth and his henchmen, the assumption was that they were armed, that a shotgun, a high-caliber pistol, or an assault rifle was stashed in the BMW. Police can find probable cause to stop and search a vehicle for almost any reason—rolling through a stop sign, having a busted taillight, not signaling a lane change—but Oakland cops employed a "don't search, don't find" policy when it came to the Beys because finding something meant nothing but trouble. Where the Beys were concerned, unless a gun was in plain sight, unless someone had been shot, there was no reason to act. The unwritten department policy on the Beys was nonconfrontation, an officer would eventually testify, and a senior commander would say, "Everything related to the bakery was handled differently. *Everything.*"

So rather than flinch when a patrol car approached, Fourth became emboldened, growing more demonstrative. If anything, a passing cop simply increased Fourth's magnetism to his men. Look how scared those motherfuckers are. Sometimes a cop might shine a searchlight over a corner before moving on. Fourth would turn away if it illuminated his face, not from fear but because he loathed the acne that covered his cheeks. Tall, lean, and otherwise good-looking, Fourth was embarrassed by his pubescent pimples.

But other than the whiteheads and pocks, he believed himself flawless. He did what he wanted when he wanted with no fear of reprisal or account-ability. He was the scion of a great man. Such was the weight of his name in Oakland.

Like his siblings and half siblings, Fourth had called his father Daddy. And there was no question that Daddy had been strong, righteous, and infallible. If he wasn't, why did the devils seek his favor? As Fourth grew up, he had seen the politicians come, both African American and white, asking for Daddy's blessing—even a former governor who had twice contended for president of the United States climbed the stairs to Yusuf Bey's private study seeking approval.

In 1998, Jerry Brown, who had sought the Democratic presidential nomination in 1976 and 1992, wanted to become Oakland's mayor. He was fifteen years removed from the governor's office, but Brown had mapped out a route to recapturing California's leadership—two terms as mayor, one as state attorney general, and a successful gubernatorial bid in 2010. But first he needed to win in Oakland. By 1998, Yusuf Bey's beliefs—white devils, mad scientists, bloodsucking Jews—were well exposed. But politi-cians called him Dr. Bey anyway. Brown knew his path was more easily navigated if Bey, who had run for mayor himself in 1994, didn't oppose him. So Brown paid a visit to Your Black Muslim Bakery. Bey, despite label-ing Caucasians as his oppressors, took the meeting and later invited Brown back to give a stump speech.

If Brown saw the children in bakers' whites laboring in Bey's indus-trial kitchen in violation of the law, he said nothing, at least not officially, and ordered no investigation when he easily became mayor months later. If Brown saw women with faces full of bruises or young girls swollen with pregnancy, he said nothing publicly and took no action. If Brown learned as mayor that Bey had defaulted on a city loan of one million dollars, there is no record he did anything to recover the money.

As a youngster watching the politicians come and go, Fourth looked smart and tidy in his after-school kitchen whites, a red bow tie peeking out above his apron as he tended to trays of cookies and muffins. When he wasn't learning to bake, Fourth spent his youth in his father's Sunday and Wednesday meetings, listening as Daddy deconstructed tricknology and boasted of superiority.

"You have a God in you, a natural God that no other people have," his father preached. "You have to understand who you are. You are not ordinary people. You are superior."

When he urged them to use violence to attain their ends, his eyes often fell on his attentive, doting sons. "If you don't have a gun, get a chair. If you don't have a chair, use your fingernails."

Fourth watched as his Daddy built a small empire. Bey won government deals to sell food at Oakland's sports stadium and airport and rented stores across the bay in San Francisco, the stoners and hippies in the Haight-Ashbury district lining up daily to buy bean pies. But Bey also propped up his businesses and legitimacy with vast frauds, exploiting government programs, dodging bills, cheating wherever and whomever he could. His sons were learning all about that too.

They also observed how their father radiated power wherever he went. On Saturdays, Yusuf Bey made a show of visiting his retail stores like a king or president inspecting an embassy in some far-flung place. A motorcade of dark cars would speed across the San Francisco Bay Bridge, little star-and-crescent flags snapping above the doors. They raced from store to store, skidding to stops, double-parking, bodyguards surrounding Daddy like Secret Service agents, soldiers spilling out onto crowded sidewalks, captains and lieutenants ordering them to attention and then barking out drill commands, the men putting on bizarre displays of discipline and physical skill. Fourth and his brothers, in suits they would soon outgrow, did their best to keep up. Back in Oakland after such a day, Yusuf Bey would sometimes invite his sons into his study in the afternoon as he counted endless bags of money and jotted down notes for his next sermon, reminding himself what he wanted to say about devils, those "damn Jews and faggots," and especially those "weak-hearted, turn-the-other-cheek so-called Negro Christians," the people who would only find salvation when they awoke and listened to him. Daddy told his sons that they, like him, would grow to be infallible. This was especially true, he taught them, when it came to women, who were preordained by God to submit to whatever demands a man made of them.

On the night of April 28, 2006, Fourth rounded up his best soldiers, ordered them into the BMW, and sped into the darkness. Much blood had spilled at Your Black Muslim Bakery in the two and a half years since Yusuf Bey had died, and Fourth was now in charge. The heavy mantle of leadership bore down upon him, the constant pressure to live up to his name. While prophecy dictated his divinity, how he ruled was up to him. And so he intended to lead not just the bakery and his family but all of Oakland. He would be its savior, a figure so young yet so strong and absolute in his authority and belief in his own abilities that he would convince scores of Blacks to abandon their "spooky" Christian beliefs and join him. If he had to break laws to do it, they were just the devil's laws, meant only to suppress him. If he stole, it would be the devil's money he stole. If he killed, it would only be devils and their "house niggers"—those too weak to ever find salvation in themselves—who died.

The Honorable Elijah Muhammad, messenger of Allah in the person of W. D. Fard, had prophesied several dates when the mother plane would launch its bombers to destroy the devils in Armageddon's fires. Those dates had passed uneventfully every decade or so beginning in 1934. But Fourth was beginning to understand why those days had come and gone with no hellfire. It was so he could live his very destiny. Daddy hadn't wavered over or liberalized the words of W. D. Fard or the messenger; he hadn't become a heretic like that hypocrite Malcolm, and neither would Fourth. Those who attempted to move Black Muslims toward Orthodox Islam were weak, victims of tricknology. It was one of the reasons Daddy had shunned the Nation in favor of his independence. It had become soft; hands were wrung rather than fists clenched. He, Fourth, was the strong one, the natural one. Perhaps it was even in Allah's plans for him to become a national—or, better yet, international—leader of his people.

The young men with him in the car were among his most loyal followers. As the city raced by the windows, they would follow him anywhere, go anywhere he wanted, do anything he asked. They knew he would conquer Oakland and more. Fourth was virtuous; he would destroy those who opposed him. And those who followed him would live in salvation when the

Apocalypse eventually wiped the devils from the earth as the Honorable Elijah Muhammad had said it would.

As the BMW sped on, none of the young men inside could have suspected that the next few hours would alter the course of Fourth's life and the lives of others. It was just a night out, a chance to relax, to be among men. Fourth deserved a diversion. So much of his time was focused on prophecy and what Allah meant for him to achieve.

The BMW streaked through the approaches to the Bay Bridge and began the long ascent up its skyway and into a night that would set in motion the events that would eventually define Fourth. But Fourth just wanted what was across the bay, what they all had talked about incessantly since he told them where they were headed. They were after the one thing so primal that it could make a man forget Allah and act in implosive, desultory ways, no matter what prophecy held for him: sex.

2

You're a Baker?

"Nothing is more despicable than respect based on fear."
—ALBERT CAMUS

The Tenderloin and Polk Gulch weren't the best districts in San Francisco to leave a $75,000 BMW, but what could a man and his posse do when they wanted white stripers? Besides, Fourth knew no one would mess with his ride, not with its DR BEY custom license plates letting the world know who he was. Or so he thought.

Some called the Tenderloin "the wine country" for all the empty Thunderbird bottles broken in its gutters; it was San Francisco's skid row, a downtown slum of residential hotels, flophouses, old speakeasies and dives, liquor stores on every corner, streetwalkers milling around in miniskirts. In another time, Dashiell Hammett made it Sam Spade's neighborhood in *The Maltese Falcon.* Yusuf Bey had briefly opened a Tenderloin storefront in the 1990s, but the drunks and junkies didn't make good customers for wholesome cookies or incendiary rhetoric.

On its western edge, the Tenderloin ran up against Polk Gulch, the city's first gay quarter. Long after that scene had moved to the Castro, the neighborhood remained sketchy and threadbare, home to hipsters, toothless meth heads, the occasional hustler still trolling for johns. Strip clubs and peep shows had been ensconced in the area for decades.

Fourth and his crew walked by a bar and a hookah lounge and down Larkin Street past a Motel 6. They had shed their suits for casual attire, Fourth in designer blue jeans, a white leather jacket, and a white dress shirt. They could have been five college guys out for the night.

The purple and yellow marquee above the New Century Theatre advertised its weekly amateur contest. Posters near its door billed "First Class XXX Entertainment" and described "over 100 naughty hotties" inside. Because it featured nude dancers, the club was banned from selling alcohol. But that meant anyone eighteen or older was allowed in. Since Fourth observed the strict Black Muslim prohibition against alcohol and was barely twenty years old, the New Century was perfect for him and his coterie. San Francisco took them out of their element, but Oakland had no all-nude clubs, and given the strict, conservative rules of conduct between the sexes that was part of his faith, it was better to go out of town for a night like this.

At the bakery, Fourth tried to keep up the limits on interaction between males and females that his father had enforced to contribute to the public luster of piety about his people. Women kept their heads covered; members of the opposite sex spoke to each other only when necessary—"brother" this, "sister" that, men initiating most conversations in polite but condescending tones. Women knew their place and what would happen if they didn't keep it. If they smiled or flirted at a brother or started conversations about anything other than work, they risked a beating. Subservience was absolute. Women simply obeyed, even when their leader ordered their submission to men to whom he owed a favor or wished to accumulate favors owed to him. Fourth planned a polygamous life like his father's. He wanted multiple wives to bear him dozens of children. He already referred to a young woman as his first wife and had identified three other young women as potential multiple wives.

Fourth forked over $150 for what was billed as a private VIP room on the club's second floor. He expected the nude dancers would readily satisfy his needs and those of his men. Like his father, Fourth found power in forcing women to perform oral sex, and he sometimes urinated in their mouths afterward to complete his domination.

The first complaint from the young men from Oakland was that their VIP room was empty.

"The fuck we get for $150?" Fourth asked the floor manager.

"You just get the room," he replied.

"The fuck are the girls?"

"Oh, you want girls too?" the manager replied in the bored, snarky tone of someone who made his living dealing with rubes. Girls, he said, were a separate transaction. Fourth reluctantly handed over more money.

A girl arrived, took another eighty dollars, and began to dance for the five young men. For a few minutes, they were just some dudes in a strip club, haggling for lap dances in the back booths, whispering to the girl about blowjobs, trying to touch her. Other dancers came and went. The club was dead, and at least these guys had money. Still, the cocksure and defiant way in which they carried themselves gave club workers a certain foreboding. "Keep an eye on the girls," the floor manager's boss whispered to him.

One of Fourth's entourage, a tall guy in a red jacket, kept breaking club rules by slipping a baseball cap on his head. He dropped a dollar on the stage; when a girl leaned over for it he groped her crotch and wouldn't let go. The floor manager moved behind him, the girl twisting away.

"No slappin' ass and no grabbing titties," he told them.

Strike one. Another dancer took to the small VIP stage. When the same guy touched her, she took his hand and caressed it. Her eyes caught the floor manager's. He backed off. The girls had to make a living. Still, they wouldn't go with any of the five guys from Oakland to the booths in the back where private encounters occurred. Finally, just before midnight, Fourth complained the girls weren't putting out. The manager offered to refund some of the room fee. Fourth took the money back and then led his crew downstairs, where they took stage-side seats in the main show-room, bitching about how empty the club was and how none of the girls would get them off. What was the point if these bitches weren't going to give them any?

Then a dancer screamed. The guy in the red jacket had his hand between her legs and wouldn't let go. A bouncer ran across the floor and pulled him away, wrenching an arm behind his back and pushing him toward the door. Fourth and the three others threw their chairs aside and followed. The bouncer had made it about twenty feet, the guy in the red jacket flopping about, his feet stomping on the floor as he was driven forward, when they caught up.

An attack on one of them was an attack on all of them—that was the creed. And the code of leadership required Fourth to show no fear when it came to the welfare of his followers. His commitment mandated absolute loyalty. That was how his father had led. It was how he would lead. He drove his fist into the back of the bouncer's neck.

A maelstrom of blows followed. The bouncer let go of the guy he was pushing and tried to fight back. All five of them were on him; he couldn't block all the fists coming down; he was close to losing consciousness. He fell backward into a chair with wheels and used his legs to push himself away. Then three other club employees ran down the stairs and jumped in, pushing, shoving, yelling. They formed a scrum and drove Fourth's guys outside, then grabbed the doors, pulling them shut. The five Black Muslims began pounding the glass, yelling, ripping aluminum molding off the jambs, throwing it in the street. The guy in the red jacket had lost a designer sneaker and his cell phone in the melee. He screamed to be let back inside to retrieve them. His phone and footwear cost a lot of money. The bouncers held the doors tightly.

"We already called the cops," one yelled. "Just get the fuck out of here." But Fourth's guys wouldn't move.

If he had led his crew away at that moment, the next sixteen months of his life might have unfurled far differently. But to retreat, especially when someone had dared to lay hands on a soldier, was an act of weakness he could not commit.

After a minute or two, a bouncer walked outside. One of Fourth's guys held his hands out in front of his face, his fists clenched in a bizarre boxing stance. But he didn't throw a punch. The bouncer understood the code to strip-club fights: When they were over, they were over. Come back for the phone later, he said. We called the cops. Leave now.

A small crowd had gathered, strippers crowding the door, a man who

sometimes drove limousines for the club walking out of an adjoining ciga-
rette shop, a couple of street people slowing down, watching.

Fourth reached into his shirt pocket, pulled out a business card, and
handed it to the bouncer. That was a way to do it. Let him see the name. Let
this devil understand the gravity of his mistake.

The club exterior was well lit by neon and street lights and passing cars.
The bouncer had no trouble reading the card. He studied it for a second,
raised his eyes, and repeated to Fourth what was on it: "Your Black Muslim
Bakery. Yusuf Bey." He paused, chuckled, and said, "You're a baker?"

A baker? Is that who he thought Fourth was? *A fucking baker?* How
could he not know the name? Where was the respect, the fear? He had
laughed—*motherfucking laughed*—at a son of Dr. Yusuf Bey. This never
would have happened in Oakland. These San Francisco punks had to be
taught something.

Fourth drove his fist squarely into the man's face.

"You don't know my name?" he yelled, striking again and again. "You
don't know who my father was?"

His guys jumped on the bouncer, the other bouncers ran out from the
club and jumped in too.

But then, suddenly, Fourth was gone, running up Larkin, reaching for
his car keys. *Laughed? The bitch laughed?*

The BMW came fast down Larkin in reverse, weaving slightly, then skidding to a stop in front of the club. Fourth pulled the trunk release and ran
to the car's rear, frantically rummaging about.

"I got something for you. I got something for you," he yelled.

Everything stopped for a few seconds, a quick pall gripping the street
as people watched. A stripper ran back inside screaming. One of Fourth's
guys dropped his hands as if he were firing a machine gun in a sweeping motion. Another used his thumb and forefinger to fire imaginary
pistol shots. These motherfuckers were about to learn who they were dealing with.

Then Fourth slammed the BMW's trunk. His hands were empty, a perplexed look on his face. One of the bouncers laughed again.

Fourth climbed behind the wheel and stuck his head through the open sunroof.

"Let's go. Let's go," he yelled. "They fucked with the wrong people. We'll come back and deal with them. We know where they work."

But his men were still brawling with the bouncers and no one got in the car.

Down in the Tenderloin, San Francisco Police Sergeant Tim Flaherty was patrolling in a black-and-white SUV. A dispatcher radioed about a fight at a strip club on Larkin Street. *Great,* Flaherty thought, *nothing like dealing with a bunch of lead heads.* He hit his lights and sirens and began to speed up O'Farrell Street toward Polk Gulch.

Fourth sat down and closed the door, seething. He revved the engine. These devils had laughed at him. *Twice.*

One of the bouncers was directly in front of the car. Another saw what was about to happen and took a few sudden steps, dropping his shoulder, knocking his friend out of the way, but now he was right in Fourth's path.

Fourth pounded the accelerator.

The bouncer was six foot three and weighed 240 pounds. All he could do was jump. The bumper hit his leg, flipping him face first toward the windshield. He hit it flush, the momentum carrying him over the roof, his body cartwheeling. He landed between two parked cars.

Fourth cut his wheels left, toward the man who had been shoved out of the way. As the car sped past, he managed to extend his arms, his hands banging down on a quarter panel. The BMW clipped his leg and spun him to the pavement.

Across three lanes of Larkin Street, another bouncer had been fending off punches from two of Fourth's men. He saw the BMW's wheels turning toward him. He jumped. The front fender caught his right leg, and his torso bounced on the windshield and roof. As the car continued up Larkin, he lay in the street, slowly flexing his fingers and toes. Fourth hung a left on Geary, the wail of sirens rising in the distance.

The BMW gone, the cops coming, Fourth's men scattered. One ran after the car, the others ducked down an alley. Sergeant Flaherty had just arrived when the third bouncer who had been hit staggered toward him, an arm in the air, and reported which way Fourth went.

Flaherty looked around. There were about fifteen people milling about. *Shit. What a mess.* He saw the bouncer who had been hit first, his body wedged between two cars, and called for an ambulance. A patrol car raced up Larkin toward the club. Flaherty was about to get out and start questioning people when one of the bouncers said, pointing, "There's the BMW right there."

Flaherty saw it slowly moving along Geary as if the driver was waiting to be arrested.

Fourth had just picked up one of his guys and hung a right on Polk Street. Flaherty followed him, but when he made the turn the BMW was gone. He didn't have to look far, though. Fourth had turned into an alley. He and the guy he had picked up were slumped on the curb, gulping air. They had taken punches; their faces were swelling. But when they saw the cop walking toward them, they clambered to their feet and ran. Both had nearly made it to the end of the alley when Fourth stopped. The other guy kept going, but Fourth began to slowly walk back toward Flaherty.

"Why are you walking up on me?" Fourth said, and then Flaherty was spinning him into a wall, pulling an arm behind his back, a handcuff cinching hard on one wrist, then the other. The cop retrieved Fourth's wallet and looked to see who he was arresting. He had two driver's licenses and an ID card. Malik Zaid it said on one license, Yasir Akil Human on the other. The ID card said Yusuf Ali Bey IV. All three bore a photo of the same person.

Who was this kid?

The guys who had run off got word back to Oakland. The cops got Fourth. It was just a few hours later when the two young men in jeans and casual jackets, their hair shorn well above their ears, showed up at the scene. Cops were still there asking witnesses to write down what they had seen. The young men carried themselves in the same overly confident manner as those who had brawled with the bouncers. They skirted the edge of the crowd and spotted one of the victims. He had refused an ambulance, insisting that he stay and talk to the police. The young men seemed to know exactly who he was. The message they relayed in a hushed, grave tone was short and to the point: Give back the business card, the lost sneaker, and the cell phone, and then keep his mouth shut or he and others would die. They'd be back, they said, and disappeared.

Fourth was the only person at the brawl arrested. Police had three serious felonies against him. The third bouncer hit had been taken to the alley where Flaherty had found the BMW and made the arrest—he'd identified the car and Fourth as the driver. The BMW was splattered with blood. Well past dawn on April 27, 2006, Fourth landed in the San Francisco County Jail.

To a Black Muslim dedicated to spreading the teachings of W. D. Fard and Elijah Muhammad, jail is a sacred place, full of so-called Negroes in need of hearing the truth about themselves and their oppressors. Yusuf Bey had never turned away an ex-offender from his bakery, his son knew, and had often preached about his preference for "ex-murderers" and "ex-thieves," as they made the best converts. Submit to the glories of Allah and to him, Bey would tell those who came seeking work and shelter. If they did, they would, for the first time in their lives, walk as men and know who they truly were.

As he settled into his cell, Fourth reconciled with the idea that his jailing, however brief, was but God's will, an opportunity to both assert himself as a leader and expand his father's legacy. He knew that dozens of his followers would sit ramrod straight in suits and bow ties when he appeared in court and that his mother and spiritual wife would raise bail. Whatever time he had before that happened would be used to proselytize and recruit. Maybe he could find a good soldier or two while he was locked up.

Fourth soon met a short, well-built young man named Richard Lewis, who had been a football standout, playing the same position—tailback—for the same San Francisco high school where O. J. Simpson had first soared toward stardom.

Lewis was awaiting a murder trial. He assured his new friend he was going to win, and Fourth promised him a job if he did. During the nineteen days it took to arrange Fourth's $350,000 bail, he and Lewis bonded. Lewis promised that when he got out, he would join Fourth at the bakery.

When he was finally released, Fourth returned home a hero, the leader who didn't run from a fight and protected his men. Devils couldn't laugh at him without consequences. He was pleased. And he had recruited Lewis, who he sensed would make a leader of men. Just as he was leaving the jail, Fourth had given Lewis his first mission. Spread the word. Send some strong brothers to Oakland.

3

An Anguished Life

"Where justice is denied, where poverty is enforced, where ignorance prevails, and where any one class is made to feel that society is an organized conspiracy to oppress, rob, and degrade them, neither persons nor property will be safe."
—FREDERICK DOUGLASS

Him.

That kid. Over there. In the skullcap. With the iPod.

Him. That motherfucker. Hit *him,* someone at the other end of the crowded train car whispered, take *his* shit.

The kid had seen the pack of young guys, nearly howling, push their way on board a station back. He tried to divert his eyes, to ignore them. They looked loaded and out for trouble.

As the kid tried not to watch, Devaughndre Monique Broussard sliced through the crowd toward him, pushing, shoving, closing the distance. He ripped the white earbuds away; his other hand balled into a fist that slashed through the air and splattered the kid's face. The kid fell, the iPod now Broussard's. Broussard punched him again. But two mere blows and possession of a four-hundred-dollar music player were not enough to quell his anger and the years of nothingness that kindled it. Broussard kept punching, then started kicking, the kid's face becoming a lake of blood. Four of Broussard's friends joined him.

It was Halloween night 2005, a San Francisco tradition of tawdry revelry broken by punches and shouts. The little train, an outbound two-car on the K line, lurched into the Church Street Station, costumed bodies skidding. One of Broussard's friends grabbed the victim's wallet and left him curled in a ball and crying, his arms wrapped around his ribs, his face pressed into the dirty, rubberized matting on the floor. The car doors yawned open and Broussard and his cohorts poured onto the platform, but not before Broussard spotted a security camera in the train car. He had a red Magic Marker in his pocket and tried to color over the lens, looking right into it as he scribbled, as if his actions could somehow destroy recorded images.

The kid was really a young man, a twenty-year-old art student who somehow got to his feet and took a few staggering steps after them. A cop ran down nearby stairs and, not knowing what had happened—the randomness of it all—handcuffed the bloody young man and hustled him to a nearby bench, thinking him culpable in the violence.

The art student was the nephew of one of San Francisco's most prominent and savvy politicians. Former supervisor Tony Hall was an anomaly in city politics—a conservative voice in a left-leaning town. Hall opposed abortion and one of San Francisco's most sacred institutions: rent control. He had many friends on the police force who often fell short of embracing the city's liberal values. Hall wasn't going to just let his nephew take a beating from some hooligan.

Between his victim's uncle and the violence captured on the video camera, Broussard never stood a chance. Police scooped him up off a corner in the Fillmore District two weeks later and charged him with robbery, battery, and assault with a deadly weapon. Broussard pleaded guilty to assault. He could have gone to prison for three years; instead, the judge gave him a year in the county jail and probation. Two years later, when Broussard had been released after less than a year and committed a gruesome murder, Hall would climb on a soapbox and rail against the light sentence: "That punk should have never been out on the streets." Law-and-order types like Hall often seem quick to want to throw away a kid like Broussard with little examination of the circumstances. Broussard deserved time in jail for the beating; it should have been longer. No one, though, deserved a story like his.

Just weeks before Broussard attacked the art student, police had arrested his mother, Aundra Reniece Dixon, on drug charges. It was nothing new. Dixon had been in and out of prison for all of Broussard's eighteen years— starting when he was just ten months old in 1988. She struggled against drugs all her adult life, losing often. Broussard, born in San Francisco on October 11, 1987, was her second child. She would eventually have at least four children with four different men. Dixon lost custody of a daughter born in 1985 when she was arrested for drug possession just after her baby turned one. "She has had an anguished life," a lawyer wrote of her in February 1987. A judge modified Dixon's sentence so she might try to regain her daughter. Broussard was born eight months later, but Dixon returned to jail on more drug charges before his first birthday. Like his older half sister, Broussard ended up in a foster home until Dixon was released after eighteen months. By then, Broussard had begun to develop a stutter that would plague him into adulthood.

Dixon attended parenting and anger-management classes and met a man named Marcus Callaway. They moved in together in the Western Addition, a San Francisco ghetto just blocks from City Hall, its gilded dome modeled after the U.S. Capitol. Dixon soon became pregnant. But the relationship didn't last, and within a few years she was in prison again, first on more drug charges, then, in 1999, for shooting a woman. Social workers placed Broussard in a program for emotionally disturbed children at a campus of terra-cotta-roofed buildings near the ocean in southwest San Francisco. It was a long way from Richmond, the East Bay city where Marcus Callaway had moved when he and Dixon split. But Callaway was a good-hearted man; he loved Broussard as if he were his own son. Family was family and the child needed someone. So Callaway made the drive as often as he could, leaving his job as a mechanic and junk dealer unfinished and fighting traffic across the Bay Bridge. After a year of struggling with paperwork and other requirements to become a foster parent, Callaway took Broussard, then fourteen years old, home.

Richmond is one of the most hopeless and violent cities in America,

an oil-refinery town of 103,000 people, littered with shanties where shipyard workers lived during World War II. Callaway resided in a house on a
squalid corner lot behind a chain-link fence at the northern tip of an area
called the Iron Triangle, Richmond's killing zone. Two of his own sons lived
with him. So did one of Broussard's half sisters. And yet, in a neighborhood
where gunfire was more common than kids toting backpacks of school-
books, Broussard survived. Callaway gave him what he'd never had: slivers
of stability and what the youngster craved more than anything else, a person
who wasn't looking through him. Reality for a young African American
male in Richmond is measured by two things: If a day ends without his
either killing someone or lying naked himself on a slab in the Contra Costa
County coroner's office, it is a success.

But in this new home, Broussard succeeded and even showed that with
enough nurturing, he might thrive. Callaway taught him to play chess, and
he joined the high school team. The family called him Catfish because of
the stray, unruly whiskers that began to sprout from his chin. He pulled
a C-minus average at Richmond High School, nearly a miracle considering
where he had started. At the end of his sophomore year, one of Broussard's
teachers enrolled him in a summer camp at the University of California,
Berkeley's Haas School of Business. Broussard devised a mock investment
portfolio that won him a hundred-dollar savings bond. Those who knew
him spoke in hopeful ways. Catfish, they whispered, might make it.

Then Aundra Dixon got out of prison again in 2005 and wanted her
son back.

Three years later, Marcus Callaway stood one morning in the yard of
his tiny Richmond home. There were two battered Jet Skis on a trailer in
a driveway littered with car parts. Just beyond his chain-link fence, a four-
inch-long piece of what looked like raw meat sat on the sidewalk, attracting
flies. It was flesh and sinew ripped from the flank of a drug dealer's dog that
had encountered another mongrel. Callaway excused himself. He took a
rusty shovel, scooped up the carrion, and flung it high through the air and
into a stand of weeds across the street. He then went back to talking about
Broussard, soon bursting into tears. "He never was out in the streets, I never
let him," he said. "All my kids, I tried to send them to school because I

wanted them to be better than I was. I was trying to get him into a university, but then his mom came home and he went to her, and that's when he got into trouble."

Across the bay, the joy of a reunion with Dixon had lasted but a few weeks. Broussard and Dixon had moved in with her mother in a shotgun house in San Francisco's Bayview–Hunters Point neighborhood, a south-end slum not far from Candlestick Park. To finance the household, the two women peddled crack and heroin. Dixon became known around the neighborhood as "Lady D" and offered the house—for a fee—as a place where people could consume the drugs she sold. But the market was saturated. Dixon's mother suffered from AIDS and needed help. They weren't making enough money, and Dixon told her son to drop out of school and get a job. He took off instead. Dixon called police and reported Broussard a runaway. Within a week, police in San Mateo County, south of San Francisco, arrested him for robbery and he was placed in juvenile jail.

Around the same time, a social worker was sent to Dixon's house after someone anonymously reported child abuse. Dixon told the social worker she would follow him home and "fuck him up" if he didn't leave. He was scared enough that he obtained a restraining order and reported to police that Dixon was running a drug house. The anonymous caller about the child abuse was Broussard. It was his last attempt to save himself.

Police soon kicked down Dixon's door and found heroin and cocaine. She was released, but police were back again a few months later when a passing officer saw a man smoking crack on the front porch. This time, Dixon returned to prison. Broussard, released from jail, went to the streets, living on and off with a relative on Treasure Island, a former naval base. A few months later, on Halloween night, just after his eighteenth birthday, he saw a kid on a train with an iPod.

Broussard liked to tell people that Richard Lewis, the football star, was his cousin. But there was no blood between them, just two mothers who were tight as sisters, so close that their sons considered themselves kin. During Broussard's eight months in the San Francisco County Jail, Lewis was there also, but they were in different housing units and had no contact. Then, the day before Broussard's release in the summer of 2006, they finally ran into each other.

"What you gonna do?" Lewis asked him.

"Shit. Go back to the 'hood," Broussard said. He was tall and lean, a good four inches taller than the man he called his cousin. Lewis was wide and squat, his shoulders and chest pumped with muscle.

Lewis was enthused about a friendship he'd struck up that spring with a Black Muslim from Oakland who had celled with him for a few weeks. "You trying to work?" Lewis said. "I can get you a job. You gonna end up dead or back in jail fucking around out there."

"Like somebody hire me," Broussard replied.

"I know this dude, he got a bakery." Lewis said. "They Muslims. They for Black people. They don't be playing. They hiring Black people all the time. They tell you they gonna do something for you, they gonna do it. All you gotta do is cleanin' and bakin.'"

Before his arrest Broussard had drifted from one fast-food joint to another, filling out job applications. He never got calls back. The prospects for an eighteen-year-old African American with a record and no high school diploma were nonexistent.

But the Black Muslims? Broussard imagined a man in a bow tie on a street corner saying, "What's happening, my brother? You want to buy a bean pie?"

But Lewis insisted that the Black Muslim he knew from Oakland was different.

"Them Muslims, they're militant, man," he said. "They pushing a line. They don't take no shit from nobody."

They ran a place called Your Black Muslim Bakery, Lewis told him. The group was separate from the Nation of Islam, its own entity. "He needs soldiers," Lewis said of its leader. "He needs people who aren't scared."

Scared of what? Broussard asked.

"Enforcing their agenda," which Lewis described as helping other Blacks.

Broussard knew he needed help from anyone willing to provide it. He was about to be released on probation. It would be tough love, a probation officer telling him to get a job, not helping him find it. If the Muslims in Oakland could aid him, so be it.

"All right, I'll see what's up," he said.

A few days later, back at Callaway's house, Broussard had Yusuf Bey IV's phone number in front of him. He took a deep breath, hoping he could control his stutter and figure out what to say.

He dialed.

"Are y'all still hiring?" Broussard asked Fourth, not knowing that when it came to young men like him, fresh from jail with no education, the system having already badly failed them, the Beys were always hiring. Within a few hours, Broussard was in a black Mercedes-Benz C320, a guy in a suit driving him to Oakland.

It was the Wednesday-night meeting. Just as his father had done, Fourth gathered his men for drills and a lecture on determination and the will to wage battle against the devils with whom the righteous were at war.

Outside, the red, black, and white crescent sign hung above San Pablo Avenue, marking the only place in the world Fourth knew. As he prepared for the meeting, he had reason to think it would be a good night. A kid who had just gotten out of jail had called looking for work. Sometimes it was as if the recruits just fell from the sky. As long as California did so little for offenders, warehousing them in overcrowded conditions rather than rehabilitating them, sending them back to the streets bitter and destitute, prisons and county jails were a pipeline for the Beys, an employment service.

The bakery's back room was behind a pair of swinging wooden doors. The doors to salvation, someone once called them. Before Broussard could cross through, a stone-faced man told him to spread his arms. He ran his hands over his collar, then patted down his chest and back and sides and arms, then down each leg from hip to ankle. He told Broussard to lift each foot and tap his shoes on the floor, then made him empty his pockets. The man even flipped through Broussard's wallet.

They told him to sit. The exercising had already started. It was bizarre, lines of men with shaved heads doing close-order drills like soldiers, all of their motions in quarter turns as a man at the head of the line barked commands like a sergeant. Left, left, right, about face, right, left, as if they were new recruits in the army.

But the cadence being called out was like nothing Broussard had ever heard.

"Who is the original man?" the drill leader yelled.

"The original man is the Asiatic Black man, SIR!" the men in the line yelled back. "The maker, the owner, the cream of the planet earth, *God of the universe, SIR!*" They snapped salutes.

It was hot. Men sweated. Broussard didn't yet know that shorts were banned—no bare skin was allowed. There was so much else he didn't know.

"You want to see if you can do it?" said the man who had searched him, nodding toward the line.

Broussard could barely follow along, as if he didn't know his left from his right. It was like trying to learn to walk all over again, left, right, right, the others spinning perfectly on their heels. Then they were on the floor, pumping out push-ups. Broussard had worked out regularly in jail, veins roping his long, sinewy arms. The push-ups were no problem. But what was this? He'd shown up with the expectation of a job at a bakery and had walked into a boot camp. This place was another world.

Fourth knew immediately that Broussard would be easy. The new kid was naive as hell; he was so scared on the phone, stuttering badly, that he could barely finish a sentence. His malleability was transparent the moment he arrived. The kid, what had he said his name was, Dre? He was a joiner, no doubt about it. He wouldn't resist being trained; in fact, the ones like him were eager for it. Just give them a little something. A place to sleep, some food, the idea they belonged. Ones like this did whatever they were told.

Fourth's father had been a master recruiter. Hell, they'd do almost anything to be called a spiritual son of Yusuf Bey. How many had made the same call Broussard made, or walked in off the streets and asked for work and a place to live and been ushered through those swinging doors? Over the decades the number became countless. Some couldn't take the rigor, the endless kitchen work. Some couldn't give up dope or liquor, the poisons that weren't allowed. Drugs and alcohol were just bait of the devils— peddled in the ghetto to sedate the masses, keep them down. No, you must know the truth, Yusuf Bey would tell the recruits. We are the master race, the descendants of the ancient Moabites, those of the divine Asiatic nation. We are not colored. The Caucasians are the colored ones, the impure devils. We are the original inhabitants of the earth. Look at us, how beautiful we are, how strong, how perfect we are, Bey would bellow.

"You gotta know it's more than a job," Fourth said to Broussard after the push-up session. Broussard nodded. "More than a job," Fourth repeated. Broussard said the words meekly.

Fourth then ushered his new recruit upstairs to his living quarters for his first religious lesson about the truth of his race. Fourth also began seeding Broussard with hope and promises. If he did well enough, showed his strength, worked hard at being a good soldier, Bey IV would open the bakery's secrets to him. He could help him establish—through fraud—credit ratings that would allow him to borrow money, buy nice things, maybe even own a house. The Beys were masters of such deception. Stealing from the slave masters was justified; it was revenge. The devils were never going to waver in their oppression; they were never going to offer reparations for their terror. Blacks had to take what they wanted and deserved. Broussard's head swirled. Cars? Loans? A house?

There would come a time, after Broussard had committed heinous, cold-blooded acts, that he would look at a somber-faced prosecutor and say Fourth had him right there. It wasn't about religion for him; he wanted to laugh at Fourth about that, he would say. It was about what he believed he would never have any other way. Money.

"We from the 'hood," he would say. "We don't do what we do in the streets for the sake of righteousness. We do it cause we greedy. We do it cause we ain't got shit. People that never had nothing, show them something, just show them something and they gonna be ready for whatever."

The next day, at Marcus Callaway's little house in Richmond's Iron Triangle, Broussard gathered his things as a car idled outside.

"I'm with them Muslims now," Broussard told his foster father as he slipped out the door, clutching a knot of ragged clothes under his arm.

Callaway had attended a mosque for a while in the late 1970s, a time when the Nation of Islam, under the leadership of Wallace Muhammad, was moving toward mainstream Islam and rejecting rhetoric about hate and crazy stories of big-headed scientists and a man-god called Fard. No one still believed all that, did they? Even Malcolm got out of that at the end, and those crazy fools killed him for it.

Callaway hoped his foster son would be all right. Maybe he should go after him. But Devaughndre was a man now. He would have to make his own mistakes.

Back in Oakland, Broussard was taken to an empty space in a dirty second-floor room across from the bakery on San Pablo Avenue. It had no electricity and no bed for him, just an empty floor. The shower ran only cold water. Broussard put down his bundle of jeans and T-shirts and began the business of becoming a soldier in Fourth's Black Muslim army.

There would come a time when Callaway would reflect that he should have helped Broussard understand what he was getting into.

"You know what I'm so mad about? I encouraged him to go to the Muslims, 'cause I was a Muslim myself, but I didn't really look into [the Beys]," he said. By the time he did, it was too late.

"I found out they was a whole different type of Muslims."

part two

"Just why do you want to be like the people who have robbed, spoiled, and slain you and your fathers?"

This 1917 draft card reveals further information about the identity of the man the Nation of Islam and independent Black Muslims, such as Yusuf Bey, worshipped as God, W. D. Fard. Note the name in the upper left, Wallie Dodd Fard, and the following name, Ford, an apparent attempt to Americanize the last name. Fard listed his birthplace as Afghanistan, his race as Caucasian, and his birth date as February 26, the day Black Muslims celebrate Saviors Day. It is the same month and day (but not the same year) that W. D. Fard claimed to his followers in Detroit in the early 1930s. *Courtesy of the National Archives*

4

Love Ye One Another

"Africa is a Dark Continent not merely because its people are dark-skinned or by reason of its extreme impenetrability, but because its history is lost."
—PAUL ROBESON, "What I Want from Life," 1935

San Quentin State Prison is nestled on a spit of land that pokes into San Francisco Bay a few miles north of the Golden Gate, its sprawling vista magnificent. To the west, Mount Tamalpais slopes gently skyward, redwoods and oaks darkening its flanks. San Quentin houses California's death row for male inmates; it is the only place in the United States where those awaiting execution have a water view. For decades, developers have salivated at the thought of the state moving the inmates inland, visions of luxury waterfront condos swirling in their minds the way the condemned dream of absolution.

For those not facing death, the prison was, for most of the twentieth century, before it became overcrowded and populated with warring gangs, the best place in the state to do time. San Quentin, unlike Folsom Prison near Sacramento or Ironwood near the Mexican border, is temperate. The guards sometimes told stories about nights out in San Francisco. The library was well stocked. The water views gave men a distant place to fix their eyes as they schemed about the future.

From June 12, 1926, to May 27, 1929, a man named Wallace Dodd

Ford, assigned inmate number 42315, served a narcotics sentence in San Quentin without incident. He had been convicted in Los Angeles for sell- ing $375 worth of heroin to an undercover cop at a greasy spoon on South Flower Street. It was Ford's third documented arrest; he'd been charged with assault with a deadly weapon in 1918 and with selling bootlegged whiskey in early 1926.

Ford was five feet six inches tall, his weight about 130 pounds. He had olive skin, jet-black hair, and eyes listed in prison records as maroon. He could pass for Mexican, Asian Indian, or even Arab or mulatto. He was, simply, a chameleon, adept at inventing identities to match whatever eth- nicity served his present purpose.

Ford also possessed a confidence man's ability to obscure his trail by leaving behind varying documents and accounts of his life—an easy task in the age before Social Security numbers, photo IDs, and the Internet. When his son was born in Los Angeles on September 1, 1920, Ford claimed on the child's birth certificate that he, the father, was white and that he was born in 1894 in New Zealand.

Six years later, Ford told his San Quentin jailers that he was born on February 25, 1891, in Portland, Oregon. His parents, Zared and Beatrice Ford, he claimed, were from Hawaii, where they owned a bottling plant, no record of which exists. Ford told the parole board he lived in Portland until 1913, then moved to Los Angeles and met a woman named Hazel Burton, who bore his son.

But another document tells a different story about Ford's identity, one that is far more likely true.

On June 5, 1917, as World War I raged, Ford completed a draft card in Los Angeles, listing his name as Walli Dodd Fard. After the name "Fard," written in parentheses, is the name "Ford." The handwriting of "Ford" is different from the rest of the written information, as if the registrar decided to Anglicize the name "Fard." Ford identified his place of birth as the village of Shinka, Afghanistan, which was then in the eastern part of that country, approximately 150 kilometers from Peshawar in what is now Pakistan, a na- tion that did not exist in 1917. In response to the question "If not a citizen, of what country are you a citizen or subject?" he again wrote "Afghanistan" in a neat cursive. In response to the question "Race? (specifically which)," he wrote, "Caus."—obviously short for Caucasian.

Ford also listed his birthday as February 26, 1893, a date that would eventually prove quite revelatory about an identity he would one day claim. It would help show that blood spilled across America in decades ahead, in the name of a belief system that claimed the little, dark-eyed man as its God, was built on hucksterism. That belief system would exploit people who were already horribly exploited. Among the many victims of its pernicious teachings would be the famous—Malcolm X—and the obscure—the editor of a small weekly newspaper in Oakland, California, named Chauncey Bailey.

Like any good con man, though, Fard would not invent that belief system entirely on his own. He lifted much of it from another talented grifter who called himself Noble Drew Ali. Ali favored a maroon fez and a flowing white robe tied with a bright red sash over a suit and tie. Sometimes he donned a turban from which a single, curving ostrich feather rose skyward. Ali was dark-skinned handsome, his tightly trimmed mustache no wider than his nostrils. When posing for photographs, he sometimes placed his right hand across his stomach Napoleonically. Ali bore oratorical gifts, and when he took to the streets of Newark, New Jersey, and later Chicago, he could quickly draw a crowd, especially as America slipped toward, and then into, World War I and people were fearful of the unknown. Ali's sermons were reflective of the Gnostic writings of his time. He had also been a Freemason and a member of the Ancient Egyptian Arabic Order Nobles Mystic Shrine, commonly called the Black Shriners. He borrowed most of his regalia from the Shriners and his ability to speak in riddles and mysteries from the Masons. Like any good religious hustler, he came off with a sincerity that made people want to hear him again, even as his message troubled them.

God is angry, he would say. Black men were the world's kings but then forsook God for materialism. First slavery and now despair and impoverishment under the white man in America are our burden until we return to righteousness. If Africans had "not strayed after the strange Gods of

Europe," they would not have been taken into bondage. Ali told Black people that they did not know themselves or their collective identity. Their forebears were inhabitants of Morocco, he claimed. What's more, they were both members of what he called the great Asiatic Nation and descendants of the biblical Moabites. Their true religion was not Christianity; it was what Ali called Islam.

Jesus was not God's son; he was a prophet who traveled to Tibet and read the ancient tablets of Confucius. Ali himself, he claimed, had been to Egypt, where a cleric in the ancient cult of high magic led him blindfolded deep inside the pyramid of Cheops and left him alone to read the secret documents that enlightened him. That he had found his way to daylight again through warrens and vaults stood as proof that he was indeed the prophet of Allah. He then crossed northern Africa to Morocco, where the king granted his blessing for Ali to spread Islam in America.

When Ali was feeling it, when he sensed the crowd was anxious and his dogma was drawing affirmative shouts, he would tell how upon his return from Morocco he'd gone straight to the White House and won an audience with President Theodore Roosevelt, whom he informed that all the slave descendants in the United States were Islamists and would convert to their original faith. "Go ahead. Getting Negroes to convert to Islam will be about as easy as getting a horse to wear pants," he claimed Roosevelt had replied.

That Roosevelt had been out of office for nearly four years before Ali took up his proselytizing was lost on the crowd. So was the fact that Morocco was ruled by a shaky succession of feuding sultans unable to govern the divided country, which had become a French protectorate. Around the time Ali claimed to have sought the king's permission to spread Islam in America, the country's ruler, Sultan 'Abd al-Hafiz, was holed up in the city of Fez, begging for French rescue from attacking tribesmen.

Another Ali myth concerned the founding fathers: George Washington had hidden a Moorish flag in a safe at Independence Hall in 1776. Washington knew that in 1682 Virginia had exempted Moors from slavery, the myth went, and Congress had already decreed that only Negroes could be slaves. Since Moors weren't Negroes, they couldn't be held in bondage. But rather than upset the fledgling nation's dependency on slave labor, Washington, Ali's fictional tale went, said nothing and hid the flag so as not to remind the Moors of their true identity, which they had forgotten. In 1913, Ali wrote to President Woodrow Wilson, demanding the flag's return. Wilson obliged, the legend goes, and Ali claimed he used it to begin his new order.

Regardless of how history reflects on Ali's stories, they were convincing in real time. Across the industrial North, where Southern migrants were quickly losing the illusion that they had found the Promised Land, people listened.

Noble Drew Ali was born in North Carolina in 1886 as Timothy Drew. Some legends claim his mother was a full-blooded Cherokee. Others say the Carolina hills shook as Drew left his mother's womb, the earthquake announcing the birth of Allah's prophet. In another, he was raised by an evil aunt, who threw him in a furnace; his survival proved his divinity. Drew's family migrated to New Jersey, the Georgia of the North it was called then for its harsh treatment of Negroes. In Newark, Jersey City, and Elizabeth, Drew witnessed the influx of immigrant Muslims from the Middle East and Asia. Around 1912, Drew began to study under Mufti Muhammad Sadiq, an Indian missionary and member of the Ahmadiyya movement in Islam, also known as the Ahmadiyya Community. Its members believed that a cleric in Qadian, India, Hazrat Mirza Ghulam Ahmed, had returned to earth as the Messiah, as prophesized in the Holy Qu'ran and Bible. Orthodox Muslims systematically slaughtered Ghulam's followers for heresy, hastening the immigration of survivors. Those who came to the United States set up mosques in Northern cities and attracted a smattering of African Americans, who, like Drew, sought an alternative to Christianity.

Drew studied under Sadiq for about a year. Then, in 1913 in Newark, he formed what he called the Canaanite Temple. He undertook an intense study of the white spiritualist Levi Dowling's book *The Aquarian Gospel of Jesus the Christ*. Dowling claimed that during the eighteen years in which the Bible does not account for Christ's life, he traveled to Tibet and India, studying under Buddhists and Hindus and also in "Egyptian Mystery Schools." Christ's miracles were not the work of God; they were evidence of Christ's ability to tap his own divine essence—a potential within all souls. Christ survived the crucifixion, Dowling wrote, and lived for decades in India. Dowling's writing shaped much of American Gnosticism and New Thought in the early twentieth century.

Drew plagiarized Dowling, creating his own religious text, which he dubbed the *Holy Koran.** In it, he copied Dowling's word for word except that he changed all occurrences of the word "God" to "Allah." He also plagiarized another spiritual text, *Unto Thee I Grant,* which claimed to contain ancient Tibetan beliefs and the teachings of Confucius. A 1925 preface of that book claims it was written by Egyptian pharaoh Amenhotep IV, who, in the Masonic folklore in which Drew was well versed, is said to have founded the first great school of mysticism.

By stealing from both books, Drew laid the foundation of his teachings deep in spiritualism, which was gaining popularity in Negro churches in the urban North, especially Chicago. But he must have known that to complete his scheme he also needed to emphasize Negroes' lack of identity. Their forebears, his included, had been captured like animals, chained to the bottoms of ships, beaten, tortured, enslaved. Their survivors had no sense of heritage; it was as if they had undergone spiritual death. Drew understood the hollowness. If he could fabricate a believable historical identity for Negroes, he could build a following and make a lot of money.

He soon changed the name of the Canaanite Temple in Newark to the Moorish Science Temple of America. Drawing from Freemasonry, Drew shaped his rhetoric in layers and mystery. Slave descendants, he said, were Moroccan in ancestry and hence known as Moors. Moors, who were direct descendants of the original people on earth, were also members of what Drew called the Asiatic Nation, which he defined as people of color from all corners of the earth: Hindus, Asians, Persians, Arabs, Native Americans, Mexicans, South and Central Americans. All Asiatic people, he claimed, were Muslims.

Morocco, and not the sub-Saharan base of the slave trade, proved to be a provocative choice as his homeland for slave descendants. It carried a certain dignity, as if a North African ancestral land so close to Europe lessened the stereotype of Blacks as jungle savages. Shakespeare's Othello was a Moor. And it allowed Ali to craft an additional layer to his teach-

*Ali's Koran should not be at all confused with the Holy Qur'an of Orthodox Islam.

ings: Moors, he claimed, were descended from the ancient Moabites, who migrated to Morocco from the land of Canaan. There, they founded an empire that ruled most of Africa, America, and the "Atlantis Islands" before a massive earthquake cut off the Moors from their domain.

By casting his story around Canaan, Ali made a direct appeal to African American Christians that their true history had been stolen from them though God's anger, which led to their enslavement. In Genesis, God ordered Noah's sons to populate the world after the great deluge. Ham was the son sent to Africa, but not before Ham sinned against his father. God was angry and cursed Ham as punishment: Ham's fourth son, Canaan, and his descendants were to be slaves, "Hewers of wood, bearers of water," according to Genesis 9:22–27. Thus, inhabitants of the ancient land of Canaan—Africa—were slaves. Here, white Christians, especially antebellum Southerners, found biblical justification for enslaving Africans. Ham's sin against his father was interpreted as some sort of sexual misconduct, although its exact nature is not described in Genesis. It is written only that Noah got drunk and fell asleep in the nude; Ham and his brothers covered him. Interpretations vary from Ham's sodomizing his father to his raping his mother, and these were twisted into a rationale for enslaving Ham's descendants. Africans were "wicked and depraved," Presbyterian minister Robert Dabney of Virginia wrote in 1867 to excuse slavery. They were "degraded in morals," as shown by the "indecent and unnatural sin of Ham," which Dabney did not detail. Slavery, he wrote, had been God's "punishment of and remedy for the peculiar moral degradation of a part of the race."

African Americans had taken multiple meanings from the story of Ham and Canaan. It placed them as the rulers of ancient and important lands— Egypt and Ethiopia—and among the earth's original peoples. But they also rejected the idea that God's curse upon Ham justified slavery. There, Drew drove the wedge. How could they practice the same faith that whites used to justify enslavement? Ali claimed the dilemma proved Christianity a false religion for people of color.

Their true and original religion, he claimed, was Islam, although it was far from the Orthodox Islam of the Prophet Muhammad. In an interview with journalist E. Franklin Frazier, Drew admitted that "to Americanize the Oriental idea of Islam involves many changes that are more or less negative to the main purpose of the Islamic religion." Ali was winging it, grabbing bits and pieces of a story where he found them: the Bible, Dowling's book, the convoluted rituals of the Black Shriners.

To complete his idea of Moorish and Islamic identity, Drew changed his name to Drew Ali and called himself a prophet. He borrowed once more from the Shriners, giving himself the title "Noble." In his *Holy Koran*, Ali defined a prophet as "a thought of Allah manifested in flesh."

The Moorish Science Temple spread from Newark across Northern cities, where Southern migrants were finding that factory work came with the same palpable racism as Southern sharecropping. Discrimination wasn't simply an element of their lives; it was the embodiment of their existences. Drew built a following in Philadelphia, Buffalo, Pittsburgh, Cleveland, Detroit, Gary, and Chicago, where he moved his headquarters in about 1925. He began selling his flock identification cards, which became sources of great pride and empowerment:

> This is your nationality and identification card for the Moorish Science Temple of America and birthright for the Moorish Americans. We honor the divine prophets Jesus, Mohammad, Buddha and Confucius. May the blessings of God of our father Allah be upon you that carry this card. I do hereby declare that you are a Muslim under the Divine Law of the Holy Koran of Mecca—Love, Truth, Peace, Freedom and Justice. I am a citizen of the USA.

Ali ordered his followers to signify Moorish identity by adding the suffix "Bey," or "El," to their names. Men were required to wear a fez at all times and to grow long goatees. He told his followers that they were racially superior to "the pale faces" and that the white man was the devil—the embodiment of evil. Emboldened by their newfound religion, some male Moors began sneering at whites on the street, flashing their ID cards, calling them devils. The fezzes and goatees made the Moors extremely conspicuous, and after police visited his headquarters more than once, Ali took to his pulpit and ordered his men to leave Chicago's whites alone. Their time will come, he said; the earth will soon be cleansed of evil.

Noble Drew Ali's temples, associated businesses, and sales of products like "Moorish mineral and healing oil," "Moorish body builder and blood purifier," and "Moorish herbal tea" produced a profit of between fifteen thousand and eighteen thousand dollars monthly, roughly two hundred thousand in 2011 dollars. Ali preached self-sufficiency and formed what he called the "Moorish Industrial Group." His followers built flourishing small businesses—grocery stores, bakeries, restaurants. Ali published a newspaper and a magazine and became a South Side power broker, helping to elect the first Black member of Congress from a Northern state, Oscar De Priest, in 1928. Many who followed Ali were also admirers of Black Nationalist Marcus Garvey and also members of his Universal Negro Improvement Association. Ali did not push for a return to Africa, but his claim of Moorish identity put him on a plane with Garvey, whom he sometimes referred to as his cousin, drawing a parallel to the relationship between Jesus and John the Baptist. By 1928, there were as many as fifteen thousand practicing Moors in Northern cities, with Ali maintaining a thriving base on Chicago's South Side.

But Drew Ali had secrets. As prophet, he deemed it his right to take multiple wives from his flock and marry them in ceremonies that he alone sanctioned. (He was also quick to sanction divorces and to send women away in disgrace when he was finished with them.)

Ali also pursued young girls who attended his temple, seeking their mothers' permission to bed them as "Mohammad's representative here on earth." In 1929, a fourteen-year-old became pregnant. She knew of two other girls about her age who were "given over" to Ali for his pleasures, she eventually told Chicago police.

In addition to women and girls, money proved to be a scandal for Ali.

The temple's chief accountant, Sheik Claude Greene-Bey, had long been skeptical of the prophet; he knew that Ali spent the temple's money on a lavish lifestyle that included chauffeur-driven cars, a well-adorned apartment, frequent elaborate feasts, jewelry, and lots of women. But Greene-Bey was not completely virtuous himself; he went to Ali and demanded a higher salary in exchange for silence. Ali refused. In March 1929, Greene-Bey dumped Ali's financial records on the sidewalk outside the temple.

Three nights later, a trio of men found Greene-Bey at the temple at around 8:00 p.m. Greene-Bey led them to a small second-floor office. He apparently knew the men as fellow Moors and accepted them as emissaries of Ali. Minutes later, a janitor heard two shots. As he went to investigate, the three men rushed past him and ran out the door. The janitor found Greene-Bey's bloody body; in addition to the gunshots, he had been stabbed four times in the neck and torso. Police noted that it appeared Greene-Bey was on his knees when he was killed.

Police quickly began rounding up anyone wearing a fez. Within hours, fifty Moors were jailed. Several of them told police where Ali could be found; he was arrested with two of the men who had killed Greene-Bey. One of the jailed Moors said Ali had been actively recruiting him and others to "bump off" his adversary and that planning meetings had been held on the nights leading up to the killing. Ali, the informant said, was desperate to retain his profitable empire. Police charged Ali with ordering Greene-Bey's murder.

Ali issued a statement urging his followers to "hold on, keep the faith, and great shall be your reward. Remember my laws and love ye one another."

A grand jury indicted Ali for murder, but a judge granted bail, releasing him after two months in jail. The prophet returned to the South Side to find his once-lucrative empire collapsing, temple members fleeing in droves, suddenly fearful of a leader indicted for murder and being investigated for raping fourteen-year-old girls. Others, who knew just how much money the temple brought in with tithings and product sales, schemed how they could seize control.

Nine days after Ali made bail in Chicago, the gates of San Quentin State Prison in California swung open and Wallace Dodd Ford emerged, free. Ford told other inmates that he intended to leave California and begin life anew. Maybe he'd go to the Midwest, he said, to Chicago or Detroit, and become a salesman. It didn't take Ford long to get to Chicago. That he found the Moors just as the sect was collapsing would prove quite fortuitous. On the roiling streets of a South Side summer, the remaining Moors still wore fezzes, and most dressed like they were about to march in a Shriners parade. Newspapers—especially the *Chicago Defender*—were filled with stories about the disgraced prophet. In a matter of days, Ford joined the Moorish Science Temple. His entry was not questioned; he could have passed for a light-skinned Negro or a member of any number of the subcultures that Noble Drew Ali defined as Asiatic. The newcomer said his name was David Ford. He quickly amended his last name to "Ford-El" and offered to take on administrative duties. Ali, desperate for help, readily agreed. Ford-El was soon handling the temple's finances—Claude Greene-Bey's old job.

But within weeks, Noble Drew Ali was dead. The exact details were uncertain. The Moors claimed he was in poor health and died of tuberculosis he caught in jail. After his body was found in his home on July 20, 1929, rumors were rampant that other Moors, seeking vengeance for Greene-Bey's murder, had beaten him to death.

The temple fell deeper into chaos. Ford-El made a move to control the lucrative empire. He claimed that Ali had left him in charge; followers still loyal to Greene-Bey scoffed at the newcomer, who they said had not been a convert to Moorish Science and Islam long enough to be considered for leadership. They claimed that one of Greene-Bey's allies, Charles Kirkman-Bey, was now their prophet. Others backed another man, Ira Johnson-Bey. Ford-El tried to woo them by claiming he was Ali incarnate. Few Moors listened to him.

The feuding continued for weeks, culminating in the kidnapping of Kirkman-Bey by Johnson-Bey's followers on September 25. A gun battle followed in which several police officers and Moors were killed.

When it ended, sixty more men in fezzes and goatees were rounded up, and rumors spread that the police intended to eradicate the Moors, one bullet at a time. Terrified South Side Negroes saw the police response as an overwhelming abuse of force. Ford-El made another play for control of the temple, but the faithful remained doubtful. He still hadn't been among them long enough to prove himself. Who was this little man, really? Charles Kirkman-Bey had survived being kidnapped. Wasn't that proof enough that

Allah had chosen him to succeed Ali? The majority of Moors sided with the man they knew. Ford-El, mindful of the violence that had started with the killing of Greene-Bey, had every reason to think he was unsafe. He slipped out of Chicago and headed east, toward Detroit. The trip gave him time to think and to refine his schemes. Ali had proven that some Negroes embraced claims that they had emerged from a fictional heritage; their anger at whites was palpable and justified. It was also clearly exploitable. After all, weren't the storefront preachers all over the South Side really just peddling the same kind of hokum in the name of Jesus?

Ford had learned much by briefly observing the Moors. If a Southern transplant like Timothy Drew could build a fortune in the name of Allah, Wallace Ford could certainly do better. Ali's teachings were convoluted and difficult to understand. He had relied more on his charisma than on anything else. Ford would need a cleaner story. Morocco as an ancestral homeland of American slave descendants didn't make sense. The people Ford planned to manipulate were ignorant, not stupid. If they were to be told their roots were in Islam, then they should be told it emerged from Mecca, not Morocco, and that Islam was a religion of the whole of the African continent, from which their forefathers had been stolen. But there were Moors remaining in Detroit, and although the temple was in chaos, they would be easier to control if some Moorish terminology remained, such as "Asiatic" to describe people of color. Ford would keep it, but he would also teach a bit of Orthodox Islam, such as shunning the consumption of swine, to create authenticity. The best lies are, of course, based on half-truths.

Then there was his identity. If Ford was to perfect what he had learned in Chicago, he would need to reinvent himself again. Somewhere in his travels he must have decided that another simple tweaking of his last name would work. He was no longer Ford but was again Fard, the name written on his draft card thirteen years earlier. And he Americanized "Walli" to "Wallace." Wallace D. or W. D. Fard. That would work nicely.

Ahead of him lay Detroit and a group of people with an interminable history of victimization. They had only recently arrived there and were finding elusive the only thing they wanted: peace.

5

The Forces of Hell

*"There is a cause for everything in this world and there is no
way of removing the evil without removing the cause."*
—CLARENCE DARROW, speech to prisoners,
Chicago City Jail, 1902

When word reached Woodrow Wilson's White House about how French
military and civilians were interacting with American Negroes fighting in
World War I, the president's advisers became incensed. The damn French
were fawning all over them, treating them like human beings, like white
people. Anger flowed quickly through military channels. Within days it was
reduced to a written directive the French military issued on August 7, 1918,
to all officers in contact with Negro troops: "The increasing number of Negroes in the United States would create for the white race in the Republic a
menace of degeneracy were it not for the impassable gulf that has been made
between them. . . . [T]he French public has become accustomed to treating
the Negro with familiarity and indulgence. This indulgence and this familiarity is of grievous concern to the Americans. They consider this an affront
to their national policy. They are afraid that contact with the French will
inspire in black Americans aspirations which to them (the whites) appear
intolerable. . . . Although a citizen of the United States, the black man is
regarded by the white American as an inferior being with whom relations of
business or service only are possible. The black is constantly being censured

for his want of intelligence and discretion, his lack of civic and professional conscience and for his tendency toward undue familiarity. The voices of the Negro are a constant menace to the American who has to repress them sternly. We must not eat with them, must not shake hands with them, or meet or talk to them. . . . Make a point of keeping the native cantonment population from 'spoiling' the Negroes." When the French civilian authorities learned of the memo, they ordered all copies burned.

A few months later, Wilson sent Robert Russa Moton of the Tuskegee Institute to France to counsel Negro troops to remember their place when they returned home. Wilson expressed satisfaction that Moton had imparted sound advice "on how they should conduct themselves when they return to these shores."

More than a million Negroes served in France, but only about 5 percent saw combat. Relegation to the rear echelon presented just the type of contact with the French that Americans feared. To men used to being told of their inferiority, sudden treatment as human beings began to change everything.

A Black solider wrote to his mother in Baltimore: "America has to do a whole lot better in its treatment of our race in the future if it intends to come up to the standard of this country in pure democracy. The people over here do not draw the color line anywhere you go. A man is a man with these people regardless of race, creed or color."

His mother asked the *Baltimore Afro-American* to publish the letter. Across the country, similar writings were published, and Negro newspapers began to ponder in editorials why America, too, could not treat Negroes as human beings.

But in America, *Plessy v. Ferguson,* the Supreme Court case in which the justices decided 7–1 that strict segregation was constitutional, ruled the land. "If one race [is] inferior to the other socially, the constitution of the United States cannot put them upon the same plane," Justice Henry Brown wrote for the majority. The physical danger of having black skin existed for every relentless minute of millions of lifetimes. When that danger manifested in violence, nothing could save the victim—not the law, not powerful men, not anything. Even when the *Plessy* decision's lone dissenter, Justice John Marshall Harlan, who wrote that the constitution was color-blind, tried to stop the execution of a Negro sentenced to die for a rape he obviously didn't commit, he was powerless. A mob lynched the man in defiance, pinning a note to his corpse that read, "Justice Harlan: come get your Nigger now."

As Negro soldiers returned home, whetted by the tastes of humanity, they found a champion in W.E.B. DuBois, founder of the NAACP. DuBois printed the French military directive in his journal *The Crisis* and demanded an awakening. America, he wrote, "decrees that it shall not be possible in travel nor residence, work nor play, education nor instruction for a black man to exist without tacit or open acknowledgment of his inferiority to the dirtiest white dog. . . . By the God of Heaven, we are cowards and jackasses if now that that war is over, we do not marshal every ounce of our brain and brawn to fight a sterner, longer, more unbending battle against the forces of Hell in our own land."

To DuBois, born in Massachusetts, hell was hatred and condescension, a condition that existed without boundaries. But to Southern Negroes, hell was a matter of geography. They could escape it, just as runaway slaves had in the last century. Before the war, a trickle of Negroes had begun to move north. Soon after, factory owners looked to the South to both replace white workers-turned-doughboys and compensate for the decline in European immigrants as a result of the war. Recruiters and con men swept through the region, crowing about factory jobs up north. Some promised free transportation and help with housing. The Great Migration, as it is called, became nothing short of a biblical exodus.

Across the South, as Negro families packed, fears of labor shortages caused officials in some towns to ban recruiters or set astronomical fees for them to hand out flyers. But word spread regardless. So many Negroes left South Carolina that whites became the majority there for the first time in decades. In Georgia, forty thousand farms were soon fallow. In Alabama, a white farmer lamented to an agricultural surveyor, "There's been lots of darkies left here. Nearly all the good ones is gone."

The recruiters and hucksters, both Black and white, had seeded deep within those making the journey assurances that the North was their

Promised Land. For many, a chance to escape Jim Crow overwhelmed their natural skepticism. How could the North be worse? Did they wear sheets up there and swing our people by the neck from tree branches? Wouldn't Northerners welcome the Negroes and treat them the way the French had treated the soldiers? Wouldn't life in the North—the North that had fought for their freedom—simply be *better*?

The *Chicago Defender,* America's top Negro newspaper, promoted what it labeled the Great Northern Drive. It was so influential in lauding Chicago jobs that in Memphis, where its national edition had ten thousand mail subscribers, the mayor ordered police to arrest postal carriers to stop distribution. In some Southern cities, armed men patrolled train stations, refusing to allow Negroes aboard.

Southern Negroes wrote to the *Defender,* sometimes pleading for advice on how to escape. A New Orleans woman spoke for the countless: "Please do write at once and tell me of this excursion to leave the South. Nearly the whole South is ready for the drive. We are sick to get out of the South."

From Alexandria, Louisiana, a thirty-six-year-old meat packer wrote: "I have been here all my life and would like to go somewhere I could educate my children so they could be of service to themselves when they gets older and I can't do it here. . . . I will accept any job you can get."

When they could find notice of a train and whites didn't drive them away, parents herded their children together and cried through good-byes with their own parents and grandparents, some of whom had been slaves and were too old to leave. The families boarded with their hopes ascending, flowing skyward like the steam pouring from the churning locomotives.

For those on the northwestern migration, the muddy Ohio was more than the Mason-Dixon Line; it was their Jordan River, their mark of escape. As their trains crossed the rickety bridge from Covington, Kentucky, to Cincinnati, cries of "hallelujah" rose from the cars. They were in the South no more. The rail lines split in Ohio. One headed for Chicago and its stockyard jobs. The other, the Michigan Central Line, rolled slightly northeast toward Toledo and on up to Detroit. The Detroit Employers' Association stationed an agent in Cincinnati who prowled rail platforms, urging the migrants to choose Detroit's growing automobile plants and factories. Henry

Ford paid well for the right workers, the agent crowed. The Michigan Central was always jammed.

As a terminus of the Underground Railroad—freedom in Canada just a rowboat ride across the straits—Detroit had long held a place in Negro folklore. The city of Antoine Laumet de La Mothe Cadillac was believed to be a free one. In 1833, a Kentucky slave master learned his runaway, Thornton Blackburn, was in Detroit with his wife. The slave master sent a bondsman to secure their return; in advance of the bondsman's arrival, the Blackburns were jailed. A woman promptly helped the wife escape and ferried her to Canada. A band of whites and free Negroes attacked the bondsman, and Blackburn followed his wife to freedom. Four years later, a group of freedmen and whites formed the Detroit Anti-Slavery Society, which demonstrated frequently.

The geography that made Detroit the embarkation point for fugitive slaves gave it no great advantage in becoming the center of industrial America. It is nestled in the far North, facing the southwestern reaches of the province of Ontario. All ships moving between the upper and lower Great Lakes must traverse the Detroit River, making the city a natural fulcrum of marine commerce, but beyond that, automobile manufacturing could easily have taken root in Cleveland or Buffalo or Milwaukee. It was the dint of personality above all else that spurred Detroit's emergence as a manufacturing behemoth. That personality belonged to Henry Ford.

Ford's assembly-line revolutions hastened the end of the traditional agrarian society. As the Model T became a national craze, the company netted $13,500,000 after expenses in 1912. The next year profits doubled. But Ford took far greater interest in perfecting his industrial methods than in paying dividends. His insistence that profits go for expansion, for bigger and more efficient factories, angered stockholders like John and Horace Dodge, who eventually went into competition against him. By pushing growth above all else, Ford controlled access to what would become known as the American dream. Men flocked to Detroit for the jobs he was creating both in his own factories and in the ancillary businesses supporting them.

Those fortunate to secure Ford work found that the company attempted to control every aspect of their lives. To qualify for Ford's five-dollar-a-day wage, workers had to accept inspections from the company's Sociology Department. Visitors to their homes recorded the kinds of foods the family kept, what books were on its shelves, its debt, what church it attended, the level of cleanliness of people and their living quarters. Ford constantly saw depravity in America, which he blamed on the failure of people to adhere to what he termed "the White Man's Code." "A corrupt orientalism" had spread a "virus" among the white man that caused him to "pull back, remain sullen and stupid, and give as little as he can." Ford's code bore three main points: "Square dealing; Fear of God and absolute fearlessness of man; and unrelenting vigilance." Adherence to those points "would cleanse our country of every working foe."

Despite his "White Man's Code," Ford would employ men of nearly any race—Italians, Slavs, Poles. He would not, of course, as the county's leading anti-Semite, hire Jews. But others got chances at Ford jobs. Even Negroes.

Thanks mainly to Ford, the Negro population of Detroit grew 611 percent between 1910 and 1920. By 1930, more than 120,000 were living in the city, nearly all of them Southerners. At the height of the migration, one thousand Negroes a month arrived. No American city with a large Negro population saw a greater percentage increase. Trainload after trainload of uneducated itinerant farmers and their families arrived, dignified in their hopes the way the Italians and Poles and other ethnic groups were dignified in the hopes of their own migrations—that at journey's end they would find a better life for their children.

But equality quickly proved elusive. Ford gave them work, but a newspaper he controlled, the *Dearborn Independent,* told them in an editorial what he thought of them: "True friends of the Negro, and the intelligent and thoughtful among the Negroes themselves, must come to see that their lasting welfare lies in frank recognition of the racial differentiation which makes the assimilation involved in social 'equality' as impossible for the African as for the Asiatic elements of the population of this Republic."

Despite the organized recruiting of Southern labor, Detroit stood woefully unprepared for the influx, and most migrants, who had lived repressed country lives, were woefully unprepared for city life. The nonexistence of decent housing dominated all. Con men rolled through the streets accepting deposits for apartments that didn't exist, or they knocked on the doors of families that were lucky enough to have found a home, claiming to be the new landlord and demanding additional rent, threatening that to not pay it immediately meant instant eviction. Market rents quickly exceeded fifty dollars a month, easily more than half a worker's monthly pay, since many of the promises spread through the South about lucrative salaries were lies. Speculators threw up hundreds of rough-board houses. Roofs leaked at the first rain, and the thin walls might as well have been made of cheesecloth for all the good they did keeping out the north winds of a Michigan winter. More than two hundred freight cars of family belongings—Bibles, clothes, sacks of sweet potatoes—sat on rail sidings because migrants could find no place to take their things. Much was lost. Men sent their families back home and slept atop the tables in pool halls or in the backseats of cars. Or on the ground in alleys. Family after family accepted boarders into their packed quarters in order to make the exorbitant rents. In 1917, scarlet fever raced through Negro neighborhoods, its telltale red rash on the arms and faces of thousands. White leaders saw the burgeoning Negro population as a general health risk that had to be contained, and the epidemic provided a convenient excuse to ghettoize the migrants. Negroes were already densely packed, and forcing them into more crowded areas increased the risk of disease, but the leaders only cared about the health of the rest of the growing city. If the newcomers could be further compressed, the rest of Detroit might be spared their filthy plight. The *Detroit News* called a plan to restrict Negro housing to ten square blocks east of downtown "the final solution."

People soon called the ghetto Paradise Valley. An optimistic view of the name attributes it to a kind of tree that grew easily there. A more pragmatic and accurate thought is that the name was simply a cynical retort to the notion that the North would be different. Another nearby area, known as Black Bottom for its rich soil, was also ghettoized.

Tuberculosis, pneumonia, kidney diseases, and malnutrition were frequent causes of Negro deaths. Infant mortality rates were seven times higher in the ghettos than elsewhere in Detroit. Most ghetto homes were squalid shanties and hovels with no, or infrequent, electricity and heat provided by coal stoves that often caused fires. Inadequate water and sewer systems made sanitation difficult. Tenants who insisted on indoor toilets found them installed in living rooms or kitchens with no partitions. Rats were everywhere; infants sometimes bore scarred and disfigured faces from gnawing rodents drawn to their cribs by the sweet smell of mother's milk on their breath. By 1934, the average age of death in the Detroit slums was twenty-seven; elsewhere in the city it was fifty-four.

To police the ghettos, the city again turned to Dixie. By the late 1920s, nearly all of the police officers assigned to Paradise Valley and Black Bottom were white Southerners. More and more for the Negroes, the only difference between Detroit and the places they had left was the frigid winters. At least the hell down South was hot.

The jobs promised the Negroes were no better than the living conditions. Much of the supposedly high-paying work turned out to pay but a fraction of the promised wage. Inevitably, the jobs assigned to Negroes were the dirtiest, hottest, and most dangerous available. When demand for Negro labor was high, so was turnover, men quitting, moving on, searching for better work at the next factory, the jobs that those smoothies and sharpies back home had said were so abundant. Negroes found themselves in a factory's bowels, working at the blast furnaces as shakers, pulling red-hot engine parts from sand molds and transferring them to machines that shook loose the grit. So much dust and smoke filled their work spaces that they could barely see the next man a few feet away. Burns and injuries occurred daily. Lungs clogged with soot. Bosses—many of them white Southern migrants—harassed Negroes continuously. To react to the taunts and slurs—which is exactly what the overseers wanted—meant certain dismissal. Most laborers had children at home to feed and, in the winter, to keep warm. Mouths stayed shut, dignity—or the hope of finding dignity—washed away like sweat pouring down a shaker's back.

Henry Ford lorded it over his Negro employees like a plantation owner. In what would become the routine way powerful white men exercised control over the Industrial Belt's exploding migrant population, Ford cultivated relationships with the leading Negro preachers, making sure church coffers and ministers' pockets were flush. The ministers, in turn, crafted their sermons around themes of obedience and being good company men.

As the migrants struggled to adapt, the Detroit Urban League offered classes in city living and manners. It urged workers returning home not to crowd into streetcars while wearing dirty overalls, to wear shoes at all times, to not congregate on stoops and street corners and engage in loud talk, spit in public, or curse. A group of Negro professionals formed the Dress Well Club and handed out cards to the migrants urging them to buy better clothes. Urban League advisers also promoted self-respect, urging migrants to stop calling white supervisors "boss" as if they were still field hands.

Many established Negro residents treated the newcomers with resentment and scorn. "Those damn Southern niggers have spoiled jobs for all of us," Glen Carlson, who had lived in Detroit long before the migrants came, told an interviewer. "Some of us used to have good jobs here, but so many sub-skilled niggers from the South have come in that none of us have a chance now. They think we are all the same."

When World War I ended, some expected the migrants to return south, their sojourns just temporary to fill the labor shortage. White men came home from Europe wanting jobs. But the Negro soldiers were also returning, and they brought with them another kind of French directive—to seek freedom. The spread of stories about humane treatment caused murmurs of hope. And so the transplants in Detroit and other cities stayed put, while down south more boarded trains heading north.

But DuBois was right. Hell was a condition, not a place. The Ohio River was not a line above which the ugliest elements of race hatred didn't exist. As conflicts with whites began to rise, Negroes who had assumed that the Ku Klux Klan was a Southern plague on their beings learned they were wrong.

"The growth of the Ku Klux Klan has been greater in the North and East than it has been in the South," the Klan's imperial wizard, W. J. Simmons, a failed Methodist minister, told Congress in 1921. Simmons had revived the secret order in 1915 after seeing the film *Birth of a Nation.* The depiction of hooded night riders keeping the white race pure from Catholics, Jews, and Negroes after the Civil War inspired him. Simmons and two elderly Georgians who were original Klansmen climbed Stone Mountain outside Atlanta and lit a cross. In six years, the new Klan's hateful message of racial purity had drawn in tens of thousands. Supporters and Southern politicians surrounded Simmons as he testified to the House Rules Committee at a hearing called by Northern liberals because of mounting reports of Klan terror and killings.

"It has been charged that our primary aim was the intimidation of the Negro in the South," Simmons said, a charge he denied, standing as he spoke, his voice rising. The Klan was simply a Protestant organization committed to "love of country and pure Americanism." "Our robes are not worn for terrorizing people," Simmons yelled. "They are as innocent as the breath of an angel."

At least one small element of Simmons's testimony was true. The Klan was growing rapidly in the North. Membership in Michigan eventually exceeded 800,000, the largest of any state. At rallies in the hinterlands, Klansmen claimed Detroit should be the exclusive domain of Caucasians. Klan membership in Detroit grew from a few thousand in 1921 to 22,000 less than two years later. As ballot counters began tallying the results of the 1923 municipal elections, crosses burned outside city hall. On Christmas Eve, the Klan placed a giant, oil-soaked cross downtown. A man dressed as Santa Claus ignited it, and four thousand men encircling the conflagration bowed their heads, reciting the Lord's Prayer.

Any perceived advancement by migrants fell under the Klan's jackboot. Detroit's public schools hired several Negro teachers in 1920. Most of them soon received an unsigned letter: "Nigger! You are being watched very closely at present. You are too versatile [*sic*] with the White Students. If you value your hide, you will be more discrete [*sic*] and KNOW YOUR PLACE in the future. . . . Speak when spoken to and not OTHERWISE. You may be in the north but there are still tar and feathers up here."

Charles Bowles, a lawyer who did little to hide his Klan membership, ran for Detroit mayor as a write-in in 1924. He lost by about ten thousand votes—but about seventeen thousand write-in ballots were disqualified because of errors. More than one hundred ten variations of Bowles's name were identified. If all of the people who went to the polls intending to elect him had simply written Charles Bowles, he would have won.

Still the migration continued. As Detroit's ghettos became even more densely populated, more squalor filled, places where simply breathing could expose one to fatal infectious diseases, any Negro who tried to live elsewhere suffered the Klan's terror. They were repeatedly driven from other sections of the city even before they could rest their heads for a single night.

One such man was Dr. Ossian (pronounced "ocean") Sweet, a European-educated gynecologist who had worked his way upward from a poor, rural childhood in Florida to become a top physician. His attempt to move into a white neighborhood brought national attention—and the country's most prominent lawyer—to Detroit and its soaring race problem.

Sweet was married with an infant daughter. He bought a house in a neighborhood populated by Polish, Swedish, and German factory workers. It was the best advancement he could hope to make. Sweet was in his early thirties, a hardened, cynical man. As a child, he had seen another Negro youth burned alive by drunken whites. As a doctor, he had had white colleagues patronize and insult him; he had to accept it or risk losing his hospital privileges and the opportunity to treat Negro patients in sanitary conditions. When he had studied in Vienna and Paris, he had endured no such humiliation. Outside of the hospital, Sweet's intolerance of bigotry became demonstrative.

He and his family had just moved into the new neighborhood when crowds gathered outside. Several friends and other family members were also in the house. Knowing they would likely face a mob, Sweet stockpiled an arsenal: two rifles, a shotgun, seven pistols, and nearly four hundred rounds of ammunition. Rocks began to smash through the windows. Just then, Sweet's brother and another man arrived by taxi and ran for the house.

"Niggers! Niggers! Get the niggers," people in the crowd yelled. Bricks struck the men. Sweet threw open the front door. As the crowd closed in, Sweet and several of his friends grabbed rifles and fired. One man outside fell dead; another was wounded. Police, who had done nothing until the gunfire erupted, arrested everyone in the house.

"Doctor," the chief of police asked Sweet that night, "what business do you have moving into a white neighborhood where you aren't wanted?" Police charged each of the eleven people arrested in Sweet's house with conspiracy to commit murder.

Clarence Darrow didn't want the case. He was just back in Chicago from Dayton, Tennessee, and the "monkey trial." Sparring with William Jennings Bryan in a sweltering courtroom had left Darrow tired and irritable. His client, high-school teacher John Scopes, had readily admitted to breaking state law by teaching Charles Darwin's theory of evolution. Darrow argued theory—the absurdity of creationism compared to science—and he even put Bryan on the stand for a ridiculing examination of his literal biblical interpretations. As the trial ended, Darrow stunned observers by asking the jury to find his client guilty so the law banning the teaching of any science that conflicted with the Bible could be appealed to the state Supreme Court. Jurors obliged.

The monkey trial over, Darrow sought rest. But NAACP activists, desperate to aid the Sweets and to draw national attention to the plight of Detroit Negroes, pursued him. Darrow initially did what lawyers do to sidestep cases—he overpriced himself, demanding fifty thousand dollars. The NAACP's entire national budget was fifty thousand dollars in 1925.

Walter White, the NAACP's secretary, traveled to Chicago.

"Did the defendants shoot into the mob?" Darrow asked him. White hesitated. "Don't hedge," Darrow snapped. "I know you weren't there. But do you believe they fired?"

"Yes," White replied, "But . . ."

Darrow cut him off. "Then I'll take the case. If they hadn't the courage to shoot back I wouldn't have thought they were worth defending." His fee dropped to five thousand dollars.

To Darrow, the more than three hundred years of bondage and terror inflicted on Negroes in America explained the Sweet case perfectly: self-defense. The shots were fired to repel a violent mob bent on doing the people in the house grievous harm. It did not take a European-educated doctor to know what the stone throwers intended. The simplest field hand would have known, probably more instinctively than an urbane physician. Darrow's work, though, would be to convince an all-white jury in a city roiled by race that Negroes were entitled to protect themselves.

As the trial neared, Charles Bowles was again running for mayor. The Klan hung a large banner in the rotunda of city hall. The wife of a prominent protestant minister took to her husband's pulpit and said any woman not voting for Bowles should be tarred and feathered. Crosses burned nightly. Bowles lost, barely, but voters elected four Klansmen to the city council.

Darrow needed common humanity. What would any of them do if their home were attacked? Doesn't self-preservation know no racial line? Would the jury deny a Negro even that? Darrow knew that if the people in the house had been white and the mob outside black, police would have not have filed charges. But as the trial opened, several witnesses lied about the number of people present, the throwing of rocks, and the fervor building within the crowd. A few folks were milling about, that was all, the witnesses said. But they were no match for Darrow, who picked away until they had impeached themselves badly.

He would pace before the jury box as he cross-examined a witness, his eyes moving rapidly among those of each of the men seated before him, never bothering to look at the person on the stand. His voice, with a hint of a drawl, would become mountainous. Sometimes he would smile and chuckle at a witness telling an obvious lie. His coat would come off to show suspenders over a workingman's shirt, the tail of which he would quickly pull from his trousers. His style was the absence of style, hair unkempt, faced furrowed, his hawkish nose jutting like a prow.

At the end of the prosecution's case, the defense called Dr. Sweet. Darrow's co-counsel led Sweet through his life history—the burning of his childhood friend, the tales of his grandfather who had been a slave, how once in Washington he had seen a Negro pulled off a streetcar and beaten to death, how he knew a prominent Negro doctor in Oklahoma killed by whites.

The prosecutor objected. "Is everything this man saw as a child justification for a crime twenty-five years later?" he asked.

Darrow rose to answer.

"This is the question of the psychology of race," he said. "Of how everything known to a race affects its actions. What we learn as children we remember—it gets fastened to the mind. I would not claim that the people outside the Sweet house were bad. But they would do to Negroes something they would not do to whites. It's their race psychology."

The judge allowed Sweet to continue. Eventually, the doctor described the stones breaking the windows and said, "I realized I was facing the same mob that had hounded my people throughout their history."

Darrow's closing argument took hours.

"I am sick of this talk about an innocent man being killed. There were no innocent men in that bunch, not one," he said.

He pointed to the eleven defendants. "Do you think that these people, simply because their color is black, are to be forever kept as slaves of the white? Do you think that all the rights which you claim for yourselves are to be denied to them? Do you think they should be like beasts in the field who can do no better than obey the white man's demands? Who are we anyway? What is this white race that arrogates all of that authority to itself, what is that? Is it wisdom? Is it knowledge? Is it tolerance? Is it understanding? Or is it pure conceit and force? . . . You must imagine yourself in the position of these eleven over here, with their skins. With the hatred, with the infinite wrongs they have suffered on account of their skin, with the hazards they take every day they live, with insults heaped upon them."

The jury couldn't reach a verdict.

"I don't give a damn what the facts are. A nigger has killed a white man and I'll be burned in hell before I ever vote to acquit a nigger who killed a white man," one juror was heard yelling during deliberations.

For the retrial Darrow demanded all eleven defendants be tried separately. If they were to be convicted, it would take eleven juries. But the acquittal of one would likely force prosecutors to drop charges against the rest. If the first defendant—Sweet's bother, Henry—was convicted, the others would be compelled to take plea deals. Darrow knew that justice fell to him. He had to reach the jurors' hearts. His closing argument was perhaps the greatest discourse on race in America to that point.

"I do not believe in the law of hate. . . . I believe in the law of love, I believe you can do nothing with hatred. I would like to see a time when man loves his fellow man, and forgets his color or creed. We will never be civilized until that time comes.

"I believe the life of the Negro race has been a life of tragedy, of injustice, of oppression. The law has made him equal, but man has not. I know there is a long road ahead of him before he can take the place which I believe he should take. . . . I would advise patience. I would advise toleration; I would advise understanding. I would advise all of those things which are necessary for men who live together."

"Why are they here?" he said, more of migrants than of the Sweets. "They came here as you came here, under the laws of trade and business, under the instincts to live; both white and the colored, just the same; the instincts of all animals to propagate their kind. They came here to live. Your factories were open to them. Mr. Ford hired them. They were willing to give them work, weren't they? Every one of them. You and I were willing to give them work, too. We are willing to have them in our houses to take care of the children and do the rough work that we shun ourselves. They are not offensive, either. We invited them; pretty nearly all the colored population has come to Detroit in the last fifteen years. They have always had a corner on the meanest jobs. The city must grow, or you couldn't brag about it. The colored people must live somewhere. Everybody is willing to have them live somewhere else. Are you going to say they can work but they can't get a place to sleep? They can toil in the mill, but can't eat their dinner at home? We want them to build automobiles for us, don't we? We even let them become our chauffeurs. Oh, gentlemen, what is the use? You know it is wrong. Every one of you knows it is wrong. You know that no man in conscience could blame a Negro for almost anything."

The jury acquitted Henry Sweet; prosecutors dropped the charges against the others. Darrow had won, but even he couldn't quell the race war in

Detroit. Soon the jurors received anonymous letters: "Your part in the Sweet verdict has painted you as a nigger lover, you have no love or respect for the white race. If you have a wife, let some nigger keep her company. If you have a sister or a daughter, let some nigger marry them, your action is a disgrace. If you have spare rooms, rent them to niggers, you are not worthy of white people's company. [signed] WHITE MAN 100%."

Black Bottom and Paradise Valley continued to be filthy slums patrolled by violent white police. Negro factory workers would return home at night filthy and exhausted, lungs full of smoke and debris, living in constant fear of mistreatment because of skin color, worried about whether their children had enough to eat or would succumb to disease or freeze to death one night when there was no money for coal. As the stock market crashed in 1929, the Negroes were the first to lose Detroit's factory jobs as the Great Depression took hold.

What had Darrow's victory really changed? Klansmen laughed at him and burned crosses with impunity. Voters elected Charles Bowles mayor on his third try (though he would be recalled). Unemployment in the ghettos soared, and the city was slow to provide relief. Violence increased. Food became scarce. Fathers, as fathers do, feigned stomach ailments to explain to their children why they ate so little. Winter came and most families couldn't scrape together train fare to return south.

When the man now calling himself W. D. Fard arrived in Detroit after fleeing the Moors in Chicago, he took up residence near Paradise Valley. All the misery surrounding him was nothing but wide-open opportunity, the people ripe for exploitation. Not much time would pass before he would be telling those in the ghettos that he was their savior, their one and true path away from misery.

6

I Am the Supreme Ruler of the Universe

*"[T]he striking increase of cult groups in the large northern
centers is related in part to the psychological factors which
are implied first in a change from rural to urban life, and
second in the adjustment of mental attitudes to new mores,
especially with regards to the rights of different races, as these
vary greatly between the North and South."*
—ARTHUR HUFF FAUSET, *Black Gods of the Metropolis,* 1944

The blade deflected off breastbone, missing the heart. Rather than die willingly, as was the plan, James Smith began flailing and making guttural, desperate sounds, like a wounded animal. Robert Harris would claim he had waited 1,500 years for this moment, this crucifixion, he would call it, and now he had failed to kill cleanly. Harris's wife, Bertha, backed away, still clutching the clock that showed it was noon—the preordained time. Harris dropped the nine-inch dagger and pulled back a white sheet under which he'd hidden a piece of truck axle. He grabbed it and, as Smith continued to convulse, caved in his forehead. Several of the men who had come to witness the murder helped Harris lay Smith back down on the sacrificial altar built of packing crates. On it was a pamphlet open to underlined words: "The non-believer shall be stabbed through the heart."

"Aliker alump," Harris yelled, raising the dagger again. He thought the words were Arabic and added meaning to his task. This time his stabs found their mark. Blood burst from Smith's chest as Harris gouged his aorta.

Harris's children, Arsby, nine, and Ruby, twelve, couldn't stop screaming. "No, Daddy! No!" Their mother tossed the clock aside and rushed them away. Harris had threatened to kill her if she and the children didn't bear witness to the sacrifice. The other twelve witnesses followed, leaving the tiny white-shingled house on Dubois Street in Black Bottom through the porch door. Neighbors who heard the children's screams shatter the quiet of that early Sunday afternoon in November 1932 saw them go and called police. Harris gathered his family, blood still on his white shirt and dark suit, and rushed to his brother's nearby home. Smith's body remained upstairs, sprawled upon the altar of crates, the carpet below it matted with brown, coagulating blood, the knife still in his chest, buried to the hilt.

The man with dried blood all over his suit said his name was no longer Robert Harris. "My name is Karriem. King Karriem." He was forty-four years old, smallish, lean, and he had no problem—none, as long as they called him Karriem—admitting to detectives in clipped little sentences that he had stabbed James Smith through the heart: "I had to kill somebody. I could not forsake my gods. It was crucifixion time. He was an infidel. I am the king of Islam."

The arrest was easy—the killer had left the little house on Dubois Street, but neighbors told police he was probably nearby at his brother's. Once downtown, Karriem had surprised three homicide investigators—Detective Sergeants Oscar Berry and Charles Snyder and Lieutenant Paul Wencel—with his willingness to talk about how he had knocked Robert Smith unconscious, set him on a pile of packing crates, and stabbed him in the chest again and again as his wife held a clock aloft and a dozen men looked on.

"I told him I had been commanded to kill someone by the gods of Islam," Karriem said. He meant Smith, an unemployed laborer to whom he had rented a room. "He didn't want to be killed, but when I showed him he would be the savior of the world and he'd go to heaven right away, he said, 'All right.'"

The detectives formed a semicircle around him. Even though it was a Sunday afternoon, they wore jackets and ties. He wouldn't stop talking, and although the cops had no idea what he was talking about—gods, kings, Islam—they let him babble on.

Wencel, especially, was wary of the claim that Smith had been a willing victim in his own slaughter. Three years earlier, Wencel had investigated one of the most gruesome murders in Michigan history, the butchering of a faith healer named Benny Evangelista, his wife, and his four children, who ranged in age from fourteen months to seven years. It remained unsolved. Their killer had used an ax and a machete to decapitate them. Evangelista, too, had boasted that he was a deity. Now, here was this Negro claiming to be a king and babbling about gods after committing similar butchery. Could it all be a coincidence? How much did Berry and Snyder want to bet that Karriem had slaughtered the Evangelistas? Had those little kids been willing victims too?

Maybe if they could keep him talking about Smith long enough he'd slip up.

"How'd you do it?" Wencel snapped.

"Like this," Karriem said, grabbing a rolled-up newspaper and stabbing at Wencel's chest as if the dagger were in his hand again. "Smith was standing up against the altar. He groaned, so I picked up a rod of iron to quiet him."

Wencel kept circling back to what he really wanted to know. Why had Karriem killed the Evangelistas? Karriem said he had not killed a family; he insisted he had not been living in Detroit three years earlier. He had been in Tennessee, contemplating the northward migration like so many others.

The only real clue found at the scene of the Evangelista slaughter was a partial thumbprint. As Karriem talked, Wencel laid out his fingerprint kit. When he grabbed Karriem's hand to roll his fingers over the ink pad, Karriem went into a rage, screaming, swinging. The cops tackled him. With his arm pinned to a desktop, Wencel inked Karriem's fingers. But the prints didn't match. The Evangelista killings would remain unsolved. But before the fingerprints could be compared, a possible link between the murders would be prominently mentioned in the next morning's newspapers and the bizarre religious similarities would help sensationalize Smith's murder.

As soon as the ink was wiped off Karriem's hands, he calmed down and began talking again as if it was all just a cordial chat. He seemed willing to answer any question as long as no one touched him. The detectives still had to keep him talking. He could not have simply made it all up, this gibberish about gods and kings. Now that they had a confession, they had to figure out *why* he had killed Smith.

A pamphlet entitled "The Secret Rituals of the Lost-Found Nation of Islam" had been discovered near Smith, open to a page where, underlined in blue ink, were the words: "The nonbeliever must be stabbed through the heart." Another page stated: "Every man of Islam must gain a victory over the devil. Four victories and the son will gain his reward."

Several times Karriem had called the killing a victory; he'd also said he was due a reward. But if he was following what was written, he needed to commit three more murders. Or was Smith his fourth victim?

The cops asked Karriem who else he intended to kill.

The mayor, two judges, and a pair of welfare workers, Karriem replied, identifying each by name. The reference to Detroit mayor William Francis Murphy sent the detectives scurrying for phones. Murphy was fine. But their alarm was not without reason. A year earlier, a man who said his name was Abdullah had sent the mayor several ranting letters and tried to break into his apartment. Murphy, who would go on to hold key diplomatic posts in the Roosevelt administration and later serve on the U.S. Supreme Court, was unharmed. Abdullah had migrated from Mississippi to Detroit with the name James Manning. When police interrogated him, he ranted about grievances with the government of Haiti. They branded him a voodooist, believing that to be Haiti's native religion, and committed him to a psychiatric ward. Now here was another obviously demented Southern migrant who also wanted to kill Murphy. And, like Abdullah, he was claiming what Wencel labeled some sort of "Mohammadism" name. Maybe Karriem hadn't killed the Evangelistas, but a tie to Abdullah was obvious. Wencel told his colleagues that Karriem was also a voodooist. The label stuck.

Word of the sensational murder spread quickly; reporters from the city's three daily newspapers clamored for the story. They had free rein at police headquarters, watching Karriem's interrogation. Among them was young Sherman Miller from the *Free Press,* who had recently worked his way up from copyboy. Miller was clever and smart; he would go on to the *New York*

Times and later become a Fulbright scholar and a university professor. He was also all that daily journalism was to Negroes in 1932—paternalistic and blatantly racist. The cops let Miller close because he was easily malleable. He would print what they wanted known—and omit what they didn't—in exchange for unfettered access. He leaped when he heard them talking about voodoo as if they knew something about it. The next morning's Freep, as the *Free Press* was ubiquitously known, carried, in the style of the day, Miller's unbylined story in the top left corner of the front page.

> ## Leader of Cult Admits Slaying at Home "Altar"
>
> ### Police Trying to Link Voodoo Chieftain to Evangelista Case
>
> A self crowned king of a weird religious cult was being held Sunday night by police following his cool admission late in the afternoon that he had solicited and brutally murdered a sacrificial victim on an improvised altar in his home at 1429 Dubois St.
>
> Robert Harris, forty-four-year-old Negro, is "king" of the strange religious order which he claims boasts a membership of 100 Detroit Negros.

Miller described the possible link to the Evangelista killings and called Harris a "voodoo chieftain." Though the Evangelista link would dissolve when the fingerprints didn't match, the assumption that Harris practiced voodoo would continue for years and even become the position of social scientists. And the paternalistic idea that a Negro who believed something other than what he was told to believe was either insane, or someone who must be silenced, would remain as well. Police questioned Karriem's brother, who said that he, too, had been attending the "Temple of Islam." Karriem had obviously collapsed under the pressure of unemployment and the inhumanity of Detroit's assistance programs for migrants. But rational thought could not carry the day, especially when it could kill a good headline and story. No one seemed to ponder ghetto conditions as a factor in why a constantly degraded man might revolt from his beliefs.

In the days ahead, Miller's reportage on the murder would be a front-page fixture in the Freep as he parroted detectives and pushed out stories about how the cult had to be wiped out for the good of Detroit's white citizens and its burgeoning population of Negroes. Mixing stereotypes with his own ignorance, he would report that Negroes, as a race, were prone to fall for confidence scams and manipulation. When ministers, NAACP leaders, and city social workers called for the eradication of the "cult," Miller championed them and referred to the killer with a phrase he repeated often. Harris (none of the papers called him Karriem) was simply the "Negro lunatic."

Police kept Karriem in what was little more than a freestanding cage. Thirty-four years before the Supreme Court in *Miranda v. Arizona* affirmed criminal defendants' rights to remain silent and have legal counsel present before answering questions, cops and reporters constantly badgered and harassed him.

At city hall the next morning, Mayor Murphy was shown a booking photo of Harris. The mayor said he looked like the man who had tried to break into his home a year earlier, igniting a brief frenzy among the reporters. But Abdullah remained confined in the Eloise Insane Asylum in nearby Westland. He and Karriem were not the same man.

How Karriem had intended to get close enough to Murphy, or the two judges he had identified, to kill them was unclear. His race would have made him obviously conspicuous in their vicinity, just as Abdullah's presence in Murphy's apartment building had resulted in frantic calls to police. But the two other people Karriem said he intended to kill were social workers with whom he had frequent contact; one was his caseworker, the other a supervisor who had recently cut off his benefits.

As the winter of 1932 set in, welfare caseworkers were in the ghettos daily. Scores of unemployed people needed coal and blankets, not to mention food for their children. Workers were under constant pressure to trim the rolls. To receive aid, people had to prove they had lived in Detroit before 1930. Those who couldn't were told to leave. Hundreds of thousands of people were adrift in the country, seeking food and shelter. Detroit leaders didn't want word to get out that their city was a place where it was easy to find help. Those who received aid were constantly demeaned for it. Negro families were ordered to live together to reduce costs. Crowding and disease worsened. The city gave the destitute—and by 1932 most Negroes were destitute—two meals daily.

Gladys Smith was twenty-one years old and white. Her assignment was to provide just enough aid to keep families alive. Soon after Karriem said she was an intended victim, reporters were at her desk. Karriem, under the name Robert Harris, had first sought aid in 1930 when he was evicted for not paying rent, she said.

"We sent the family to live with another welfare client on Mullett Street, where they stayed all winter. The welfare department paid the rent. We gave them two meal tickets a day and later they received groceries, clothing and coal. Harris impressed me as being a carefree, stolid, humble and meek man who seemed to be satisfied with anything that was done for him and his family," Smith said.

She posed for photos in a short-sleeved sweater, her hair pulled back. The accompanying caption in the *Detroit News* did nothing to calm the hysteria sweeping the city:

MARKED FOR DEATH BY CULT
Fanatic Planned to Murder Woman Relief Worker

Reporters also quickly tracked down Karriem's other intended victim, Adele Ivey. The papers prominently identified her as a Negress. Her job was to inform families that they were being denied, or cut off from, assistance— news she had recently delivered to a Robert Harris. She had determined that he and his family hadn't been in Detroit long enough. Ivey wrote to their relatives in Memphis. In a return letter, a family member offered to take in Bertha and the children, but not Robert because he was "too much of a dude."

When Ivey went to Harris's home, she noticed small blue cards with a star and crescent on them. "'We are all Muslims now,'" she said Harris told her. "'This government is not going to last and those who are not members of Islam are all going to perish.'" Other welfare recipients had expressed similar beliefs. They, like the man she knew as Robert Harris, insisted that they now be called names like "Muhammad," "Abdullah," and "Bey." Members of the Moorish Science Temple had been in Detroit for several years, and Ivey had grown accustomed to encountering men wearing fezzes and long beards. But as the Depression worsened, she noticed a colder, more serious resolve among people claiming new beliefs. A man she knew as Joseph Sparks told her that he had forsaken his "slave name" for the name "Bey." "I can prove from records 1,500 years ago that my free name was Joseph Bey. A ship is coming from Asia to take away the faithful when the devils die in the Armageddon," he told her. Airplanes would drop leaflets to let them know when the ship arrived.

At police headquarters, reporters told Harris they had just interviewed Adele Ivey. "Mrs. Ivey!" he screamed, jumping about in his cell. "It's lucky for her, that infidel Christian. She pounds a typewriter too well."

When Karriem had calmed down, the detectives took another run at him. Whoever had written the pamphlet found near Smith's body was someone whom they might be able to charge with inciting murder. Karriem had muttered about his gods. *Just who is God?* Snyder and Berry asked.

Master Fard and Ugan Ali, Karriem replied.

These are men?

Yes, Karriem said. *They are men. Men who are gods.*

Where are they?

Karriem gave them the address of a meeting hall above a clothing store on Hastings Street in the heart of Paradise Valley. There, he said, detectives would find his gods.

Ugan Ali demanded to see a warrant.

Snyder scoffed. Since when did the Detroit Police Department need a warrant to roust a bunch of uppity niggers?

Ali was smallish; bloodshot eyes bulged from his head. He wore a fez and a dark suit. Sweat ran down his face. By the way he spoke he was obviously an educated man—not what the detectives had expected. None of it was. There were no shrunken heads; no witch doctors. This was a voodoo cult? It looked more like a business meeting.

A warrant, Ali insisted. *If you are going to come into our temple and disturb our services, you need a warrant.* About fifty men sat in chairs. They were orderly, nonemotional. Their pride in themselves—in their race—was evident. Little could have made the detectives more uncomfortable. Snyder and Berry were badly outnumbered. Plus, they'd let Sherm Miller tag along. The last thing they needed was to get a reporter killed. Miller looked around, jotting notes. An altar was draped with a bright red flag with a crescent and star, he wrote in the next morning's Freep. "The walls are covered with many weird designs, which apparently are symbols. A crude wooden canopy tops the platform on which the altar is located."

Miller noted that several times a man entered the room and was "greeted with some strange unintelligible password before he took his seat."

The men, speaking the little Arabic they knew, were saying, "As-Salāmu ʿAlaykum" ("Peace be upon you") to those joining them. Those so greeted replied, "Waleiykum assalam" ("And peace be upon you").

The detectives backed away, though they soon returned with a couple of dozen uniformed cops slapping wooden billy clubs on open palms. This time, Ugan Ali made no demands. That he and the others were assembled peaceably and freely practicing what the courts would eventually determine was their religion—supposedly indelible rights in the United States—mattered not at all.

As the uniformed cops stood watch over the seated men, who seemed unwilling to move without an order, the detectives pinned Ali in a corner and launched a fusillade of questions.

Yes, Ali said, a man named Karriem whose slave name had been Robert Harris was a temple member. Yes, Ali was his teacher; his title was "temple secretary." No, he had not instructed Karriem to kill Smith; there was no call for human sacrifice in the teachings of what Ali called the Order of Islam. The detectives held back the pamphlet that specifically ordered human sacrifice by stabbing the victim in the heart. They could use it against him later, after he had established a record of denying any instructions for bloodshed.

Ali's adversarial tone was not a trait to which either detective was accustomed in Negroes. In almost every answer, he used the word "tricknology." He was getting close to a beating. Then one of the detectives asked Ali why he was agitating "these colored people."

"We are not colored! No one colored us," Ali screamed. "We are Asiatics!"

The detectives handcuffed him and took him away. The crowd stirred but did nothing. The uniformed cops made the men line up and submit to pat-down searches. Then they ransacked the place, seizing written materials, including pamphlets like the one found next to Smith's body.

At police headquarters, Berry and Snyder pulled Karriem from his cell and walked him into a room where Ali sat with other detectives. When Karriem saw him, he screamed and tried to run. It took four cops to restrain him. The detectives asked him if Ali was his teacher. Karriem said yes; they dragged him away.

"He was just an ordinary member," Ali told Snyder and Berry. "But I guess he misinterpreted our teachings. Our order will not countenance any bloodshed until 1934."

Why 1934? they asked.

"That's when the Armageddon war will take place to determine whether the Asiatics or the Caucasians will have to get off this planet," Ali said.

The police ordered him thrown in a padded cell at Eloise, as the insane asylum was known.

The newspapers raced one another to sensationalize the story, regardless of how much it degraded Negroes. Inherent in the reportage was the stereotype that Negroes were, by nature, servile and docile and thus compliant to authority. Also inherent, then, was the stereotype that a Negro who was neither docile nor servile was insane.

The phrase "a hydra of jungle fanaticism" became a favorite of Miller's despite the order and discipline of the men he'd observed at the temple. The cult preyed on "certain ignorant elements of Detroit's Negro population" who practiced "a sinister worship [spread among the] gullible and highly emotional," he wrote, ignoring Ali's reasoned request to see a warrant.

The *Detroit Times* described an "Asiatic trend among Negro dole recipients" and referred to Karriem repeatedly as the "Voodoo King."

Only the *Detroit News* offered moderation, describing Ali's temple as a "religious society" and playing the story on inside pages as opposed to the bold headlines of the Freep and the *Times*.

The detectives fretted about what was obviously the next step of their investigation: finding the man whose name kept coming up—from Karriem and his brother, from Ali, and from a few other members of the order or nation or cult or whatever it was that was suddenly all across the front pages of Detroit and also on the pamphlet found next to James Smith's body: "The Secret Rituals of the Lost-Found Nation of Islam" by Wallace D. Fard Muhammad.

In two days of investigation, the name of the man who Robert Karriem had insisted was God had been mentioned constantly with varying descriptions. Fard was a fakir, a mendicant, a mystic. A Turk, a Moroccan, an Arabian. Rumors flew around the city that he had a financial interest in riling up the ignorant Negroes, requiring tithings at his temple and charging them the extraordinary fee of ten dollars for membership cards. He ordered members to wear suits and silks that only he could sell them. He ordered them to sign over their relief checks to him.

He was a huckster, a confidence man, a charlatan. He was the savior, the one who came to find his lost people and lead them from the wilderness.

He was also something that scared the detectives: powerful. Karriem had committed slaughter based on his writings. His underling, Ali, had at first stood up to the police. The men in the temple hadn't cowered. This Fard was suddenly the most wanted man in Detroit.

Police found him the next morning as he was leaving a hotel room. He was nothing like what they had expected.

"Are you W. D. Fard?" Snyder asked the little man as he was closing a door behind him. He wore an overcoat, and a scarf was wrapped tightly around his neck. The sight of the detectives didn't ruffle him. He must have learned that police had rousted the temple and prepared himself for arrest.

"I am Wallace Fard Muhammad," he replied sedately. The man had dark, wavy hair and prominent ears that curved outward. His eyes were dark, almost maroon. But it was his complexion that bewildered the cops. It was not quite that of a Caucasian, but it was also not quite ebony.

The detectives had never contemplated the possibility that the man behind the Temple of Islam, or whatever it was called, was anything other than a Negro. He had to be. Only another Negro could have controlled people as Fard had done, but this little guy didn't look like any Negro they'd ever seen.

Fard went along willingly. He had an accent none of them could place, but it was there, just the same. His English was excellent, but it seemed clear to Berry and Snyder that Fard was not American. There was something almost regal about him.

He didn't fluster under questioning, either. At least not initially.

The interrogation became a dance. One of the cops led with a question, and Fard followed along. There was no money, he said. He had to pass a hat just to pay the temple's electric bill. No, no, if Brother Karriem had stabbed someone in the heart, he misunderstood our teachings.

Again and again, he dodged and sidestepped and evaded.

Finally, one of the cops barked with anger: *Who are you?*

In the same serene tone that was driving his interrogators batty, Fard answered: "I am the supreme ruler of the universe."

7

Tricknology

"Since whiteness is a mark of degeneracy in many animals near the pole, the negro has as much right to term his savage robbers albinos, and white devils, degenerated through the weakness of nature, as we have to deem him the emblem of evil and descendant of Ham, branded by his father's curse. I, he might say, I, the black, am the original man."
—JOHANN GOTTFRIED VON HERDER, *Ideas for the Philosophy of History of Humanity,* 1794

Calling himself the supreme ruler of the universe ended the interrogation. The cops called for an ambulance to take Fard to Eloise. This guy, whoever he was, was certifiable. They'd just wrapped Karriem and Ugan Ali into straitjackets too. Fard made three.

They'd arrested a murderer, rousted the cult's temple, and put its leaders in the asylum. But with Sherman Miller and the Freep leading the way, Detroit's newspapers kept the story of the Smith killing alive for days. As reports about the "voodoo cult" sprawled across the front pages for the next week, what seemed to most shock Detroit was the notion that something was actually wrong in the ghettos. Aren't Negros naturally ignorant, docile creatures? At least most of them are, the good ones who know their place. They live in the slums because that's what they want. They certainly can bear no expectation that they are entitled to anything more. Well, a few uppity ones do. Troublemakers like that Dr. Sweet, trying to live in a white neighborhood.

———

The small man, lean and olive-skinned, his dark, straight hair parted to the side, is said to have arrived in Detroit on July 4, 1930. Black Muslim dogma is quite specific about the symbolic date. Black Muslims call it the birth of *the* Nation.

That Fard got to Detroit sometime during the winter of 1929–30 is far more likely. He took a room in a residential hotel near downtown and began selling raincoats and silks door to door in Black Bottom and Paradise Valley. Perhaps he had made or stolen enough money from the Moors in Chicago to stake himself to a supply of wares. He would not have stood out that much in appearance. Syrians and Persian immigrants were common in Detroit. The influx of people seeking factory work for two decades had made the city a gritty melting pot. The little man fit.

He was, by every account, charming to a fault, a natural salesman. He had just enough of an unusual accent to intrigue people, to keep doors from slamming in his face. He would introduce himself as W. D. Fard from the Holy City of Mecca.

His customers had little money, and had his intention been to merely hawk what they couldn't afford, he might have struggled. But once he gained entry to a home, he would often stay for hours, enthralling his hosts with exotic tales, sharing whatever food they offered. Quite often people did not want him to leave, and they would send children to bring neighbors to listen to him. They'd never met anyone like him. At the home of a factory worker named Lawrence Adams, Fard stayed for dinner and when it was finished told Adams's wife in the mildest of tones that she had served poison.

"After the meal he began to talk," Mrs. Adams said several years later, after she had changed her name to Sister Denke Majied. Fard said, "Now don't eat this food. It is poison for you. The people of your own country do not eat it." Fard extolled a healthy diet, free of pork and fried foods, salts, fats, lard. In her own country, he told Mrs. Adams, people understood nutrition and "enjoyed the greatest health of all time. If you would just live like the people in your home country you would never be sick anymore."

Her home country? Like so many slave descendants, Mrs. Adams had not thought much, or at all, about ancestry. She was just a Negro. Her home country? The one from where the slave traders had stolen her people, chained them to the bottoms of ships, and sailed them away? She had never even contemplated such thoughts. Mr. Fard certainly did not look like her; he could not have been from *her* native land, but he wasn't white, either. He spoke so well; he knew so much. "We all wanted him to tell us more about ourselves and our home country, and how we could be free of rheumatism and aches and pains," Mrs. Adams said.

The legend of the man who claimed to be from Mecca spread across Black Bottom and Paradise Valley, stirring souls. Their own country? Their own people? Very soon, the little man could not walk the neighborhoods without people asking him to tell them about themselves.

Fard, the old Los Angeles fry cook, stayed on the theme of nutrition early in his visits. He understood the Qur'an's prohibition against the consumption of swine: "Forbidden to you are: dead meat, blood, the flesh of swine, and that on which hath been invoked the name of other than Allah." The Bible carries similar instructions in Deuteronomy: "Swine, because it divideth the hoof, yet cheweth not the cud, it is unclean unto you. Ye shall not eat of their flesh."

Given that cheap, fatty pork was a ghetto staple, it must have challenged people to follow Fard's advice. He told them their diets caused "headaches, chills, grippe, hay fever, regular fever, rheumatism, also pains in all joints . . . foot ailments and toothaches."

But it would take more than nutritional advice to build the following Fard sought, one that would achieve the profits he had observed the Moors so successfully achieving—and shedding so much blood over—in Chicago.

"You were lost," he would tell people. "I came to find you."

After a few months of his walking door-to-door and talking at what were basically cottage prayer meetings, hats were passed and a hall rented. The room overflowed.

"My name is W. D. Fard and I come from the Holy City of Mecca," he said. He pronounced the last name "Fa-rad," saying it slowly, a bit of his breath catching under the vowel sounds, elevating them. The name sounded mysterious. Like his accent, no one could place it. "More about myself I will not tell you yet, for the time has not yet come. I am your brother. You have not yet seen me in my royal robes."

Fard immediately explained the obvious: "I know you think I am white. I am not. I am an Asiatic black man."

He mesmerized them with tales of Mecca. He had been born February 26, 1877, he claimed. (These were the day and month he'd written on the draft card in Los Angeles, though the year he'd written there was 1883.) He was from the Quraysh tribe, common ancestors of the Prophet Mohammad. He said he'd studied at Oxford University and as a graduate student at the University of Southern California. Neither claim was true. In California, he had encountered his "long-lost uncle," the American Negro, stolen into slavery four hundred years ago. Fard would often speak of the Negroes in avuncular terms, casting himself as their distant, kindly relative. He had, he lectured, taken some of the features of the white man in order to move freely about them and learn their evil ways. Now he was among family again.

At one meeting, Fard rattled off a litany of biblical errors about the basic facts of nature. In the audience was a lifelong Baptist, Charles Peoples, to whom the words were an epiphany.

"The Bible tells you that the sun rises and sets. That is not so. The sun stands still. All your life you have been thinking the earth never moved. Stand and look toward the sun and know that it is the earth you are standing on that is moving," Fard said.

Years later, as a devout Black Muslim renamed Challar Sharrief, Peoples spoke of what had awakened in him at the lecture. "After I heard that sermon from the prophet I was turned around completely. When I went home and heard dinner was ready, I said, 'I don't want to eat dinner. I just want to go back to the meetings. I wouldn't eat my meals, but I goes back that night and I goes back to every meeting after that. Just to think that the sun above me never moved at all and the earth we were on was doing all the moving. That changed everything for me."

Fard used different names that became interchangeable: Mr. Walli Farrad, Mr. Farrad Mohammad, F. Mohammad Ali, and even the anglicized name written in parentheses on his draft card, sometimes calling himself "Professor Ford."

He did not, at first, try to kindle hatred for whites in so many of the ghetto dwellers. But his cosmology evolved. Fard could not take to his makeshift pulpits and crow to his audiences about their natural righteousness without explaining their current condition. He had to answer the conundrum of his rhetoric: If the Lost-Founds, as he called Negroes, were indeed superior beings, the earth's original and righteous inhabitants, why, then, did they suffer so much and know so little? *Because the white man is more than your oppressor,* Fard said, *he is the devil. He is Satan.*

"Why does the devil keep our people illiterate?" Fard asked. "So he can use them for a tool and also for a slave. He keeps them blind to themselves so he can master them."

To make this claim work, Fard also needed to convince his followers that they had been tricked into worshipping the devil's God. And there, he knew, lay the question that his fledglings could not answer, the same question Nobel Drew Ali had asked those he called Moors: How could they worship the same God whose teachings the devils used to justify their enslavement and defilement?

The answer, Fard insisted, was that the devils worshipped a mystery God. The father, the son, the Holy Ghost. Who were they? Three gods or one? The true God of the Lost-Founds was not the father of Jesus. It was Allah. Christianity was just part of what he called the devils' "tricknology," designed to suppress the "so-called Negroes."

His followers memorized a crude renunciation of Christianity: "Me and my people who have been lost from home for 379 years have tried this so called mystery God for bread, clothing and a home. And we receive nothing but hard times, hunger, naked and out of doors. Also, beat and killed by the ones that advocated that kind of God."

Many rejected Fard's message. His lectures appalled middle-class and college-educated people. But they were not who he wanted. His early months in Detroit were spent honing his message, finding words to ignite the anger that welled in the poor. Studies later found that more than 90 percent of Fard's earliest converts had migrated from Virginia, South Carolina, Georgia, Alabama, and Mississippi, states where Negroes suffered tremendously, living in deep poverty and oppression. Fard gauged the reactions in faces, the tears, when he hit the right point about what the devils undertook in the name of their God. He allowed the call-and-response style of Southern churches. And the more he called out about the devils in his rented hall on Hastings Street, the louder the responses.

Look what believing in the white man's God has gotten you, he would say.

You were in chains cutting his cotton. Now you live here with rats and filth and cold. "The devil keeps our people illiterate so he can use them for a tool and a slave." He tapped the riffs that Drew Ali had lifted from Freemasonry. He also parroted the apocalyptic, the-end-times-are-here dogma of Judge Joseph Rutherford, of the Jehovah's Witnesses, even urging his followers to buy radios and listen to Rutherford themselves. But they should rely on Fard, and Fard alone, to interpret the meaning of what they heard, he warned. He also tapped a children's book, Hendrik Willem van Loon's *The Story of Mankind,* for the basic historical knowledge he imparted. Fard soon produced what he said was a copy of the Qur'an, knowing his followers couldn't read it and needed him to interpret.

There would be a war soon, good versus evil, and his followers knew who evil was. From the Bible Fard took the story of Ezekiel's wheel—the wheel within a wheel—and explained it was a "mother plane" orbiting the earth, preparing to launch bombers that would annihilate the United States and England. The attack would come in 1934, restoring the original people to their rightful place. Allah would soon make the devils pay mightily.

To explain the devils' origin, Fard created the story of Yakub, an evil, "big-headed scientist" who tried to destroy his own race. Yakub discovered his people had a "brown germ" and a "black germ," Fard's way of describing the genetics of skin color.

Yakub took 59,999 Asiatics to the Greek island of Patmos, where, over the course of six hundred years, he bred away the "black germ" by killing all dark-skinned babies and forcing those with "brown germs" to mate. Eventually, the white race emerged. Its people were grafted, like snakes, Fard said, and thus devils. Some were called Jews; others, who escaped Patmos and lived in the Caucasus Mountains between the Black and Caspian seas, were Caucasians. They caused trouble for the Original Man and were thus rounded up by a General Monk Monk and his army and force-marched 2,200 miles west to an area called Europe. Fard claimed the letters "Eu" meant "false" and combined them with the word "rope." The devils were false beings roped off from the original people. They wore animal skins, ate with their hands, walked on all fours, and lived in caves. But six thousand years ago, through their evil nature, the devils discovered tricknology and conquered the world.

Fard insisted there was nothing wrong with exacting revenge by killing them now, before Armageddon. "Slay four, stab them through the heart, and rewards will be yours," he wrote. And a devil need not be white. Black nonbelievers were tools and enablers of the devils: devils themselves.

Among the many migrants adrift in Detroit who eventually encountered Fard was a smallish, light-skinned Georgian named Elijah Poole, who spoke in awkward, often nearly broken sentences and who suffered from respiratory ailments exacerbated by dirty factory jobs.

Elijah also drank. Detroit had quickly proven to be no Promised Land, and liquor was easily found in the ghetto; Prohibition was something at which one merely snickered. Since he had come north in early 1923 and sent for his family in Georgia that fall, Elijah had worked at menial jobs in industrial plants—the American Nut Company, the American Wire and Brass Company, the Detroit Copper Company, the Chevrolet Axle Company. Conditions aggravated his chronic breathing problems; he searched in vain for work that spared him exposure to dust. Liquor became his salve.

Elijah was also a joiner. He tried the Black Masons, but that lasted only until he realized he was an outsider lacking in the social skills needed to advance. He tried Marcus Garvey's United Negro Improvement Association but didn't find what he was seeking—a spiritual answer to explain his suffering. For a while, he attended a Moorish Science Temple and wore a fez. But still he drank, and work became scarcer. As the Depression loomed, he wandered the ghetto's alleys, often stumbling drunk. More than once his wife Clara hauled him home. Clara, like many women, was the family's core. She and Elijah were on their way to having eight children, but Detroit gave them no greater hope for the future than Georgia. It was, in many ways, worse. It was Clara who searched desperately for an escape.

The legend holds that Elijah Poole heard Wallace Fard speak at a meeting and approached him afterward. Poole supposedly told Fard: "I know who you are. You are God himself." Fard is said to have whispered back, "That's right. Don't tell it now; it is not yet time for it to be known." Years later, when he was known around the world as Elijah Muhammad, leading what Fard had begun, Elijah said, "I recognized him. And right there I told him that he was the one the world had been waiting for to [*sic*] come."

Actually, Clara Poole first attended Fard's meetings while Elijah stayed home, drunk or sick. But Elijah's curiosity about the Bible was immense. As a child, he had witnessed his father's Sunday work as a traveling preacher in rural Baptist churches. But Elijah had never been able to reconcile Christianity with his people's reality; he couldn't ignore his doubts and sing hymns on Sundays. He was no sheep. In that sense, he *had* been waiting for Fard all his life. Clara knew that Fard could reach Elijah. She invited Fard for dinner; accustomed to building his following door-to-door, one forlorn soul at a time, he accepted.

Fard and Elijah talked for hours that night; they were soon inseparable. Elijah stopped drinking. He converted each member of his family, including his father, the Baptist minister. In Elijah, Fard found a deep, malleable vessel he could fill with what he passed off as the truth. Elijah yearned to be taught but lacked basic knowledge of the world on which he could gauge Fard's yarns. Years later, when *Reader's Digest* declared him "the most powerful Black man in America," when the FBI devoted untold resources to destroying him, when he had amassed great wealth, tithings pouring into his Chicago mansion from mosques around the country, Elijah reflected on his time spent huddled with Fard.

"He used to teach me day and night. We used to sit sometimes from the early part of the night until after sunrise . . . all night long for two years or more. All I have in my teachings is from him, this mighty one. He has given out his purpose and his aims. It is all from him. . . . I don't want you to look at me but as nothing but a messenger. That's all I am. Just a messenger to tell you what someone said to me."

Elijah also had from his past an incident scalded on his soul that helped him make sense of the claims that whites were devils. In January 1912, while he was living in Cordele, Crisp County, Georgia, he had witnessed the lynching of his eighteen-year-old friend, Albert Hamilton, for an alleged rape. Hamilton was beaten savagely, hanged from a tree, and blown apart with more than three hundred gunshots. A photo of his body was sold on postcards as a "memento" of the event, but Elijah needed no picture to remember the horror.

In August 1932, Fard declared Elijah ready to lead, naming him "Supreme Minister" of the "Lost-Found Nation of Islam in the Wilderness of North America."

The changing of a name, either adding an "X" to signify the unknown original name of a slave descendant or taking what Fard called a Muslim name, became a cornerstone of the movement. "The name 'Poole' was never my name," Elijah would later write, "nor was it my father's name. It was the name (of) the white slave-master of my grandfather."

But the names Fard doled out had nothing to do with African heritage. They were no more authentic than the "El" and "Bey" suffixes that Drew Ali had given his Moorish followers. Rather, Fard culled the names from his apparent Afghani heritage. They were revelatory of *his* hidden identity, not the African roots of the people like Elijah whom he was exploiting.

Fard gave Elijah's brother Jarmin Poole what he said was the Muslim name "Kallatt." It was likely a misspelling of the name of the Afghan village of Kalat near the Indian Ocean, not far from Karachi and due south of the village of Shinka listed on Fard's draft card. Another clue, first established in journalist Karl Evanzz's seminal biography of Elijah Muhammad, *The Messenger,* is the name Fard chose for what he called his lost tribe: Shabazz. It is the name of one of only three saints, or Qalanders, recognized by Orthodox Islamists: Shahbaz Qualandar, born Syed Usman Shah Marwandi in 1177 in Afghanistan. Millions visit his grave in Pakistan yearly. Another example of Fard relying on his own Afghani heritage to create a fictive African ancestry for his followers lies in another name he gave to Elijah briefly in 1932, Ghulam Ali. Ghulam was the name of the founder of the Ahmadiyya movement in India, Hazrat Mirza Ghulam Ahmed.

Yet another example of Fard's real identity came from Elijah's younger brother, Wali Muhammad, whom the FBI interviewed in 1942. Agents showed him a San Quentin mug shot of Wallace D. Ford and asked, "Who's that?" He answered that the person in the photo was Fard.

"My sweet savior," he exclaimed. "My all-powerful Allah!"

By the fall of 1932, Fard, with the help of Elijah and others, had converted thousands to the fabrication he called Islam. Like Noble Drew Ali in Chicago, he charged extraordinary prices for a membership card that claimed one was truly a Muslim. He ordered his male followers to wear suits, which he was quite happy to sell them. He passed collection plates and urged parishioners to give to his poor fund.

He insisted that Elijah and his other ministers teach judicially, to treat newcomers like curious children. "Give the little babies milk," he said of recent converts. To tell all would fluster the newly faithful. If Elijah's time trying to penetrate the Masons had taught him anything, it was how to lure people in without revealing all. It was America. People were free to worship how they wished, man-gods, spaceships, and big-headed scientists included. Did the cornerstones of Christianity, virgin birth and resurrection of the dead, seem any less nonsensical? In the American West, countless people believed that the prophet Joseph Smith had read gold plates on which God had revealed to him a new religion. Mormons seemed untroubled that Smith— and only Smith—had seen the words on which they wagered their souls.

It is true that much of what Fard and his ministers taught helped migrants improve their lives. Many ate better, became healthier, stopped drinking and gambling. Three services weekly made the temple the center of family life. But even as Fard urged solipsism, telling them repeatedly to know themselves, he read from what he said was the Holy Qur'an, insisting that only he could interpret its meaning. He continually preached hatred of the devils, searching for stories like that of Elijah's friend Albert Hamilton, and spoke constantly about the approaching Armageddon. The Lost-Founds, he said, had to prepare. He worked them as if he were driving them up a fog-cloaked mountain, assuring them the obscured summit was just a few handholds distant. Fard also began writing instructions and pamphlets to further manipulate his congregation.

"The nonbeliever must be stabbed through the heart," one of them said.

It was Robert Harris, W. D. Fard, and Ugan Ali who were sent to the asylum for James Smith's killing. Elijah, though, avoided the hounding reporters as Ugan Ali's wife organized marches demanding her husband's release.

Karriem appeared in court a few days after the murder, trying to walk free after admitting his guilt. When he referred to himself as king, the judge retorted with words that would make any jurist smile: "I am the king here," he said, and ordered Karriem returned to the asylum.

Detroit leaders tripped over themselves to call for the eradication of the voodoo cult, with the newspapers paternalistically playing along. "This whole business is an ominous menace to the social stability and welfare of Detroit's Negro population. It should be stamped out before it secures a grip on any more of a race that is first to suffer at a time of depression," Dr. David Clark, a psychiatrist at Receiving Hospital, told the *Free Press*. Miller wrote bluntly that Fard's followers were "confined to the ignorant and superstitious." Police were quick to blame unsolved ghetto killings on the voodoo cult, although no one was charged.

"Still digging out the deeply planted roots of the weird hybrid cult, detectives Thursday said they believed more than a score of recent Negro fatal stabbings had been perpetrated by deluded Negros incited by the exhortations of insane leaders," Miller breathlessly wrote.

But Fard was "apparently not driven to his sinister teaching through insanity," Miller quoted from a physiological report that he obtained. Doctors also found that Ali's "mental processes . . . [were] not those of [a] normal person" but that he was also not insane. Harris, though, was "mentally unbalanced" and never stood trial; he died in the asylum a few years later.

Fard and Ali were released. But even though he was not charged with a crime, Fard soon found living openly among his followers impossible. Negro preachers, urged on by white leaders, railed against him.

"This voodooism is an extremely dangerous cult and should not be tolerated by an organized society," the Reverend J. D. Howell of St. Stephens African Methodist Episcopal Church bellowed. "That its fanatical teachings and barbarous practices could have such a rank growth right here in the midst of our religious communities shows weakness on the part of our church life. It shows a deplorable lack of contact between the upper and lower strata of society." Yet he claimed Fard was "solely to blame. There must be quick and just punishment for those who come among us and for personal gain lead us astray. . . . The Nation of Islam must go."

Fard entrusted Elijah to run the organization and returned to Chicago, where another temple had opened. But Fard's bond to Elijah was too strong. He went back to Detroit in a few months, but police had hired Negroes to pose as new members of the Nation. Fard was arrested on unspecific charges, driven to the city line, and ordered to stay out of the city.

He returned again within a few weeks, and detectives' frustration became palpable. The Muslims would not denounce Fard no matter how they were belittled. In the months ahead, police would discover Fard's disciples, including Elijah, operating an unaccredited school for followers' children. Attempts to close it would lead to more front-page headlines, arrests, and riotous bloodshed. But for now, the cops just wanted to break the little man who spoke in riddles and wouldn't go away. They circled him. They were certainly not above beating a back-talker; Fard probably feared violence.

The cops were fed up with his claims that he was a religious teacher; they told him he was a con man, a charlatan, a huckster. *Admit it,* they threatened. Finally, Fard was rattled, if only for a moment.

"It was a racket," he blurted out. "I just wanted to get all the money out of it I could."

But claims that Fard never said such a thing, or that if he did he was only telling cops what they wanted to hear, would simply become part of the Nation's lore.

Just devils telling lies, they'd say.

Just more tricknology.

8

There Will Be Plenty of Bloodshed

*"Who will protect the public when
the police violate the law?"*
—RAMSEY CLARK, U.S. attorney general, 1967–69

By 1962, Elijah Muhammad had reached the height of his leadership of the
Lost-Found Nation of Islam in the Wilderness of North America. Time in
prison, battles within his hierarchy, and financial hardships had annealed
him; his faith never wavered. Nearly thirty years had passed since Fard had
left Detroit for the final time after admitting his hucksterism to police.
Now, mosques in nearly every major American city provided Elijah a constant stream of money. And it was his; Fard had long since vanished. The
Black Muslims continued to teach that he was God in the flesh, but Fard
never returned. Authorities would search fruitlessly for him for years.

The Nation had evolved into less of a religious organization than a
movement, an enterprise. It published a flourishing newspaper, *Muhammad
Speaks*. Elijah's lectures were pressed onto vinyl and sold. The Nation owned
apartments, office buildings, a construction company, a clothing factory, and,
eventually, a bank. A farm in Michigan supplied its grocery stores, restaurants, and bakeries. Elijah kept mansions in Chicago and Phoenix, where
he frequently retreated, believing the arid climate a balm for his damaged

lungs. Estimates of the worth of what Fard had begun by knocking on ghetto doors went as high as sixty million dollars.

Elijah's rise was phenomenal. When he had been imprisoned near the end of World War II for draft dodging, a psychiatric examination had diagnosed him with paranoid dementia and showed that he possessed the cognitive abilities of an eleven-year-old. He often struggled to speak in coherent sentences. Yet his followers saw his accumulation of power from such lowly beginnings as divine proof. Only Allah could have cast such events in motion.

As the sixties dawned, two things had pushed the Nation into the national consciousness. First, in 1959, Elijah gave an interview to WNTA television in New York for the show *Newsbeat* with Mike Wallace, who entitled his five-part series on the Muslims "The Hate That Hate Produced." Wallace, narrating between interview segments by reporter Louis Lomax, could barely contain his contempt for Elijah and other Black Nationalists. His paternalism reeked of endorsements of Negro docility and the civil-rights gradualism that Muslims despised. Elijah, Wallace said, "preach(es) a gospel of hate that would set off a federal investigation if it were preached by Southern whites." Ku Klux Klan membership was growing again across the South, thanks to the Supreme Court's school antisegregation ruling in *Brown v. the Board of Education* and the rise of Martin Luther King Jr., but Wallace didn't mention it. Nor did he explore any social conditions facing Negroes. Wallace showed a film clip of Elijah preaching to an arena-sized crowd: "The government of the United States has failed you. The Christian religion has failed you. You have no justice coming from anyone."

Then came an interview with Lomax. Elijah sat on a sofa across from him wearing a dark jacket, white bow tie, and kufi.

"Are there any good white people?" Lomax asked.

"Not one is good," Elijah replied.

"Will there be bloodshed in the years ahead?" Lomax asked.

"There will be plenty of bloodshed, plenty of it," Elijah answered.

"Are you preaching hate?"

"No."

"What are you preaching then?"

"Truth."

The program resulted in a surge of converts.

But the Nation's minister-at-large was a bigger reason for the increase in its profile. Malcolm X, the two-bit criminal turned true believer, gave ringing oratories in stunning contrast to Elijah's strained, staccato vernacular. Their differences made Elijah seem even more mysterious, furthering his divine image. Malcolm, with his fierce, signature statement that the Muslims would achieve deliverance "by any means necessary," became the movement's public face and voice. Often, Malcolm echoed DuBois of forty years earlier. Hell for a Black, he said, "isn't down in the ground. He will tell you that Hell is right where he has been catching it."

Malcolm didn't talk in riddles like Fard or Elijah. As race issues in America raged to a full boil, he offered a defiant, radicalized alternative to King. "Anybody can sit. An old woman can sit. A coward can sit. It takes a man to stand," he bellowed. "You might see these Negroes who believe in nonviolence and mistake us for one of them and put your hands on us thinking that we are going to turn the other cheek—and we'll put you to death just like that." Muslims vowed not to initiate violence but to return in vicious kind what they suffered. Men were required to join the Fruit of Islam, the Nation's mysterious paramilitary wing. It served as an internal enforcer, its notorious "pipe squads" delivering brutal beatings to members who broke rules or failed to turn over money. To the Muslims, pacifists like King were naive fools who believed the devil could make them whole. Elijah and Malcolm instead urged African Americans to accept no remnants of colonialism and slavery and rather to create a consciousness of self-determination, pride, and superiority. Integration was just more tricknology; the devil could never be trusted. In stark contrast to integrationists, Elijah demanded that the government grant the Nation several large states and enforce strict segregation there. Muslims didn't want to live with whites any more than Klansmen and Southern crackers wanted to live with Muslims.

Estimates of the Nation's membership were spotty. Some reached 250,000, which seemed unlikely. Others suggested it never exceeded 100,000 and may have been lower.

There were, to outsiders, few vestiges of a true religion within the Nation, and Elijah became reluctant to speak at length about his veneration of Fard, especially after he became a multimillionaire. That God took on human form was heresy to Orthodox Muslims, to whom nothing about the Nation resembled traditional Islam. Yet Elijah had made a pilgrimage to Mecca in 1959 during the non-Hajj season called the Umrah. The Saudis received him warmly despite his blasphemous claims that Fard was Allah.

Some Orthodox Islamists in the United States attempted to defrock Elijah. Black Muslims did not follow the five pillars of Islam: Shahada, the profession of faith; Salat, the ritual of praying five times daily; Zakat, the alms tax levied to aid the poor; Sawam, fasting during the month of Ramadan; and Hajj, the major pilgrimage to Mecca. One American Muslim leader, Talib Ahmad Dawud, maligned belief in Fard as Allah and claimed Nation members were heretics for not believing in a future "bodily resurrection" and failing "to adhere to proper prayer rituals." The Islamic Party of North America said Black Muslims "are not Muslims according to the Qur'an and Sunnah traditions."

Elijah also deflected occasional questions about Moorish Science and Noble Drew Ali's obvious influences on Fard. No, he said, Fard took nothing from Ali. No, Elijah lied; he himself had never joined the Moors. The groups were not related in any way.

The Nation became one of FBI Director J. Edgar Hoover's festering obsessions; he was soon bent on destroying it for sedition. Agents described it as a hate group in 1955: "The Muslim Cult of Islam is a fanatic . . . organization purporting to be motivated by religious principles of Islam, but actually dedicated to the propagation of hatred against the white race. The services conducted throughout the temples are bereft of any semblance to religious exercise."

Agents bugged Elijah's phones and built a network of informants within his ranks. Hoover believed that exposing Fard, the Nation's founder, as a fraud would destroy the organization. The FBI spent countless resources searching for him. The Los Angeles woman who had borne Fard's son in 1920 told agents in the early 1960s that the man she knew as Wallace Ford had returned unexpectedly to her doorstep in 1934. He drove a Model A coupe and possessed much unexplained money, she said. Flyers in his car proclaimed him some sort of prophet. He told her he was headed for New Zealand; she never saw him again.

The agents hit countless dead ends, and then made their last gasp, leaking documents calling Fard a fraud to a *Los Angeles Herald-Examiner* reporter who wrote an article entitled "Black Muslim Founder Exposed as a White." Elijah scoffed. It was all just more tricknology, he said, more lies, more deceit. What could one expect from snakes of the grafted type?

The spring of 1962 brought the Nation the largest and most violent crisis in its history. On the night of April 27, Los Angeles police shot up a mosque, killing one unarmed Muslim and wounding six, committing exactly the type of brutalities for which the Nation's dogma prescribed swift retribution.

It began when two white patrolmen, Frank Tomlinson and Stanley Kensic, saw two well-dressed Negroes standing next to a Buick with the trunk open on Broadway in South Central Los Angeles. The trunk was full of suits. The cops assumed the merchandise was stolen. It wasn't; Monroe X Jones worked for a dry cleaner and sometimes sold unclaimed items to other Muslims. His customer, Fred X Jingles, shined shoes for a living. When they replied "Yes sir" when asked if they were Muslims, the cops separated them. Jingles walked passively toward the front of the car but verbally objected when Kensic touched him. Kensic then wrenched one of Jingles's arms behind his back and threw him down on the car's hood. Jingles, following his training, fought back, breaking loose. Two other Muslims ran to Jingles's defense. Jones, meanwhile, grabbed Kensic's gun and shot Tomlinson in the arm, just as an armed nightclub bouncer who stopped to aid the officers shot Jones.

The fighting spilled over to the nearby mosque, where Friday-night services had just ended. Dozens of cops responded to calls for help and began beating Muslim men with nightsticks. A rookie officer, Donald Weese, drew his revolver. His first shot hit William X Rogers in the back, severing his spinal cord. Weese then saw another man, Ronald X Stokes, stop in front of him and raise his hands to surrender; Stokes, like the other Muslims, was unarmed. Weese killed him with a point-blank shot to the heart, leaving his body slumped against the back door of a paint store next to the mosque. Weese then reloaded and shot two more men. In all, six Muslims were wounded and Stokes killed. Police handcuffed the victims and beat them until ambulances arrived. Rogers would never walk again.

Inside the mosque, police lined other men up against a wall, slit their suits open with razors, and shoved nightsticks into their rectums—several victims vomited as they were violated—before dragging them outside in their underwear for arrest. "We shot your brothers," one cop taunted at the handcuffed Muslims. "Are you going to do something about it?"

Police charged fourteen men—including all the surviving shooting victims—with resisting arrest and assault. An all-white coroner's jury ruled Weese's killing of Stokes was justified. Even though Stokes's arms were raised, he'd moved one of his hands "menacingly," Weese testified, a motion that made him fear for his life, so he fired. It was, perhaps, the nadir of a police department with one of the worst histories of racial abuse and intolerance in the country, an urban Gestapo.

Stokes, who hailed from Boston, was thirty-two years old and the mosque's secretary. He had served in the Korean War and worked for the Los Angeles County government. For the Nation he was a rarity: Stokes possessed a college degree. Recently, he'd begun learning Arabic. His wife's father was close to Elijah. The couple had a three-month-old daughter, Saudia.

Malcolm flew out from New York bent on violence. It was a year before he would make his Hajj to Mecca and encounter blue-eyed, fair-skinned Muslims, the event that would spur him to summon the intellectual courage to reject Fard's teachings. In his brief, bright moment of enlightenment before his assassination, he would quote Hamlet and say, "I don't care what color you are as long as you want to change this miserable condition that exists on this earth." But in April 1962 he was still the Malcolm of hate and ridicule; he intended for the Fruit of Islam to engage the LAPD in war.

Elijah, though, blinked. "There's already been one bloodbath. Why do we need another? I told you we would lose some good soldiers in the war with the devils and we will lose more. Allah is the best knower. He will settle the score." Yet Elijah also told Malcolm that Stokes had died because he surrendered. "Every one of the Muslims should have died before they allowed the aggressor to come into the Mosque."

In Los Angeles, the Nation's soldiers awaited Elijah's order to attack but were confronted with a different command that shocked them: "We are not going out in the street now to begin the war with the devil. No, we are going to let the world know he is the devil; we are going to sell newspapers." The Muslims would use *Muhammad Speaks* to fight, not fists.

Elijah told reporters: "It would have been more safe for us on the 27th of April for our people in Los Angeles to be among wild lions than in civilized America." But he again did not call for the retaliation dictated in the Nation's doctrine. Malcolm seethed but heeded his leader. He told friends the stand-down order showed Elijah was "all talk and no action." King and other civil-rights leaders expressed solidarity. Elijah accepted it and again ordered Malcolm to bite his tongue.

Three weeks after the shooting, three thousand people attended a rally about police abuses at the Second Baptist Church in Los Angeles. Organizers first insisted that as a non-Christian, Malcolm couldn't speak. But when he entered the church accompanied by victim William X Rogers—a decorated Korean War veteran now confined to a wheelchair—the Christians relented.

Malcolm gave a brilliant, self-effacing lecture, aware he was speaking to non-Muslims. Stokes, he said, was not just a good Muslim but a good man who "practiced the highest forms of morals of any Black person on this earth." His blatant murder crossed all religious boundaries; it was not a Muslim problem but a Black one. (It was, of course, a human problem that crossed all racial and religious boundaries, but this was not yet the enlightened Malcolm.) All people of color needed to rise, he insisted. When he opened up on LAPD chief Robert Parker and Mayor Sam Yorty—who had run on a police-reform platform but who was now in lockstep with the race-baiting Parker—with blistering criticisms, Second Baptist's pastor, the Reverend J. Raymond Henderson, interceded. But Henderson's own congregants booed him down. Malcolm owned the night.

But Elijah's docility continued to frustrate Malcolm. The moment had come and Muslims sat. It was bad enough that they took no action when members of the civil-rights movement were routinely savaged. But Stokes was *a Muslim*. Tethered by Elijah, Malcolm appeared weak, his years of defiant rhetoric looking like nothing more than a bluff.

Back in Los Angeles in June, his frustration boiled, destroying the goodwill forged at Second Baptist when he reverted to the rhetoric that caused outsiders to fear the Nation so. When news came from France that more than 120 prominent white Georgians, returning from a month-long European art tour, had died in a jet crash near Paris, Malcolm claimed that God was responsible in retaliation for Stokes's murder.

"I got a wire from God today," Malcolm shouted. "Many people have been asking, 'What are you going to do?' And since the man is tracking us down every day to try and find out what we are going to do so he'll have some excuse to put us behind bars, we call on our God. He gets rid of one hundred twenty [whites] in one whop. And we hope that every day another plane falls out of the sky." In Chicago, Elijah backed Malcolm, saying the crash "was the work of Allah for what the white man has done for the so-called Negro."

The claims of divine retribution caused those who had stood with the Muslims after the Stokes killing to reel. King, for one, had canceled lunch counter sit-ins in Atlanta the day after the Paris crash as a show of sympathy. The Muslim leaders' words repulsed him.

The Stokes shooting and its aftermath in Los Angeles brought the Nation intense negative publicity. The *Los Angeles Times* and other papers accepted the LAPD's line that the Muslims were the aggressors, that officers fired in self-defense. Reporters who tried to give Malcolm voice were maligned by Mayor Yorty, Chief Parker, and everyday cops.

Muhammad Speaks gave an alternative, if slanted, view, as Elijah promised. It relentlessly reported on the mosque shooting as unjust and the criminal cases against the fourteen men as the "L.A. frame-up trial." It was far from objective or fair coverage, but the charges against the Muslims were little more than a cover-up of the blatant police attack on the mosque, and the Muslims had no other way to get their story out. John Shabazz, the mosque's minister and one of the defendants, wrote stories about the trial under his own name.

Malcolm was a fixture in court; he belittled the *Times* and the *Herald-Examiner* for failing to write about the cross-examination of prosecution witnesses by the defendants' prominent Black lawyers, Earl Broady and Loren Miller.

When the cop who had shot unarmed Muslim Robert X Rogers testified, Broady peppered him:

Q: "Couldn't you have apprehended Rogers without shooting him?"

A: "Maybe I could have but I was afraid and under attack."

Q: "What did Rogers do when you shot him?"

A: "He stood there."

Q: "Did you shoot him again?"

A: "Yes."

Q: "Did he make any untoward move at you then?"

A: "No."

Q: "He just stood there?"

A: "Yes."

Q: "And you shot him again."

A: "Yes."

The jury deliberated for eighteen days; it convicted eleven of the fourteen defendants. The August 30, 1963, edition of *Muhammad Speaks* bore an incredulous headline:

Why All-White Court Ruled
PRISON FOR THE INNOCENT!

The byline on the lead story was none other than that of Elijah himself. The poorly written article's strange diction and awkward rhythms clearly show that he did not use a ghostwriter: "As you may now know of the incident that took place on April 27, 1962, in Los Angeles, California, between the Los Angeles Policemen and my followers, one of my followers was killed outright while his hands raised and with nothing on him to do anyone harm. Every one of the Brothers was unarmed when nearly one hundred police officers swooped down upon them, well armed, out of the darkness of the night to kill the Believers of Allah and His religion Islam and stop the spread of Islam."

For more than a year, the shootings dominated the Muslims' newspaper; Elijah fulfilled his pledge to spread news about the devil. Perhaps he saw more opportunity to recruit new members through words than through violence. Despite its obvious agenda, much of *Muhammad Speaks's* reporting, save Elijah's screeds, was sharp and well written. The coverage, along with that of other Negro publications, incensed Mayor Yorty, a politician who believed that freedom of the press meant that he was free to control the press. In a speech at a race-relations conference in New York, he made a fool of himself when he called Negro newspapers, especially *Muhammad Speaks,* subversive and demanded they be screened by government censors before publication.

Every male member of every Nation of Islam mosque was required to sell copies of the paper. Street hawkers were motivated by a tightly held secret about the ruthless side of the Nation's business practices: Elijah demanded prepayment for each edition. The hawkers started work at a deficit and only made money by selling out. The aggressive circulation plan worked. Sellers blanketed urban areas, working relentlessly to break even. In Southern California, where press runs surged on the shooting coverage, Muslims trundled papers to anywhere with a Black neighborhood, even winding their way ninety miles north to Santa Barbara, where there was a small ghetto on the city's south end, abutting the 101 freeway. Among those who would later say they were just there waiting for Allah's message to arrive was a twenty-seven-year-old hairdresser named Joseph Hancil Stephens.

9

You Don't Hate People Enough

"Now I ask you, what good is Christianity to you
and to me if that religion will not defend us
against lynchings and rape?"
—ELIJAH MUHAMMAD, Washington, D.C., 1959

Joseph Stephens made magic with scissors and brushes; he was the coiffeur with panache. It was as if hair obeyed him. He and his brother owned a salon in downtown Santa Barbara called the Red Carpet. The carpet was red; so were the floors, the walls, the ceiling, the countertops, the mirror frames, the chairs, the sinks, the dryers, and the jackets of the proprietors. Joseph's younger brother Billy got his beautician's license in 1957. Joseph did the same three years later after a stint in the air force. The Red Carpet proved immediately successful. The brothers, who went by the names Mister Joseph and Mister Bill to their customers, were natural talkers, storytellers, gossipers, connivers. In laid-back Santa Barbara, with its University of California students, surfers, and beatniks, it became quite hip for whites to let Joseph style their hair—a chance to prove one was progressive on race by patronizing a minority-owned shop. "They did top work, all the Caucasians went to them," said a person then friendly with the brothers.

As the sixties dawned, Joseph and his friends were just looking for parties, often renting the local Elks Lodge and throwing boozy bashes on week-ends, the friend would say more than forty years later. Joseph had grown up in gritty, industrial Oakland, where his parents had migrated for work during World War II. Santa Barbara was a different world, a party town; there were beautiful women everywhere. Joseph was a player, a man obsessed with sex. He was married with a young son, but he chased women constantly, a quality that would one day, under a different name in a much different place, define him. He shared lovers with his brother Billy; they would each eventually father a child with the same woman.

Much had changed for his race during Joseph's life. When the LAPD killed Ronald Stokes in 1962, he was twenty-seven. Civil rights had gained momentum in the past years, beginning with the Supreme Court's anti-segregation ruling in *Brown v. the Board of Education.* Joseph had served in the desegregated air force. But anger seethed in him about racial oppression. Family members told horrible stories about picking East Texas cotton. Seventy years after slavery, his people had remained stooped under the scalding sun in the same fields where their forebears had been mere property. His parents had picked cotton, and Joseph had never quite understood how Blacks could worship the same God as the people who treated them as subhuman.

But as the sixties began, Joseph Stephens tried to stifle his anger and accepted money from white women to pile their beehives and trim their bangs. That would change. The Messenger would speak to him soon. Revelations waited.

Someone brought a copy of *Muhammad Speaks* into the shop. The Black Muslims had been in town hawking it again. Every issue another article appeared about how the white cops in Los Angeles had killed a brother named Ronald X Stokes, who had had his arms aloft in surrender. They'd wounded others too. Shot a man in the back, paralyzed him. It started over clothes in a car trunk. A brother couldn't even sell a used suit to a friend. Now the Muslims were on the march. Malcolm X was calling the mayor a devil. The man's *hands were in the air.* Not one Muslim had a gun; why were the cops shooting? Why did they tear up the mosque? Anybody could see the

cops had done wrong; now they were just sweeping it all away, charging the
Muslims with assault when the cops were the ones who had shot people.

Billy had married a woman with several sisters who sometimes hung
around the Red Carpet. So would Joseph and Billy's mother, Ruth Stephens, who had come south from Oakland too. Billy was discussing an
article in the newspaper when Ruth said, *Enough of this reading and talking;
it's time to go.*

Where? her sons asked.

Los Angeles, Ruth replied. *Go see what all this is about; see if these Muslims
are worth standing with.*

"My mother told me to close the shop and go. . . . We took 14 people with us," Abdul Rabb Muhammad—the former Billy Stephens—said
nearly fifty years later. At the Los Angeles mosque, they were searched before attending a lecture by Minister John Shabazz.

Shabazz was among the Nation's most gifted orators, a favorite of Elijah
Muhammad. He had backed the Messenger's use of *Muhammad Speaks,*
rather than violence, to retaliate for the Stokes shooting. The Stephens
brothers were enthralled. "We had never heard anything like it before,"
Abdul Rabb Muhammad would say. Joseph understood then, really for the
first time in his life, that it was impossible for him to reconcile with Christianity. It was there, in Los Angeles, that he took the first step toward becoming a Black Muslim.

The brothers left, intent on returning. They also soon began to frequent
a smaller mosque closer to Santa Barbara in Oxnard.

Elijah Muhammad avoided Los Angeles after the Stokes killing; Malcolm
was a better front man anyway, he reasoned, better with reporters. John
Shabazz was also immensely capable. But after the trial, Elijah decided his
Southern California faithful deserved to hear from him. They had been
through so much.

On August 9, 1964, a warm, breezy Sunday, Elijah assumed a lectern at
the Grand Olympic Auditorium in downtown Los Angeles, a venue generally reserved for professional wrestling. A banner reading THE ONLY GOD IS

ALLAH hung behind him. Although Elijah would forever deny that W. D. Fard was anything—or anyone—other than God, the auditorium stood less than a mile from the greasy spoon where police had arrested Wallace Ford for selling heroin thirty-eight years earlier.

"I declare to you that Allah has come in the person of Master Wallace Fard Muhammad," Elijah said. "The Messenger believes in what has been revealed to him by his Lord, as do the believers. They believe in Allah and His prophets and His books. We hear and we obey."

Men and woman sat separately, the men in suits, the women in flowing white dresses, scarves covering their heads. Searching all the attendees upon entering took hours. Members of the Fruit of Islam ringed the stage wearing red caps with little brims that looked as if they were borrowed from train conductors.

Muhammad gave his standard sermon that he had been seeding upon audiences for decades. But for those like Joseph Stephens, who had never before heard the wizened little minister's odd ramblings, the words were a sudden light.

"Just why do you want to be like the people who have robbed, spoiled, and slain you and your fathers? Is it not an act of intelligence and honor to desire to look and be like a member of your own Nation speaking the same language and seeking and building the same culture? You are trying to force yourself into white society rather than take the responsibility to build your own society. You are still disgracing yourself in trying to force yourself upon your slave masters' children so that they will continue to support you in the necessities of your existence. In those ways you are telling the world that you are too lazy to go for yourself. Allah and I want you to be freed of such childish thinking and begin thinking like men and accepting your responsibility."

This was what Joseph Stephens had waited his life to hear. The ministers in the mosque were good teachers, but the Messenger had received infallible instructions directly from Allah. Elijah's words removed any remaining doubt. Joseph accepted the impossibility of worshipping the white man's God and reconciling integration with their defilement of Blacks. Every day at the salon whites condescended to him. He went along like a little slave boy. His mother was right. The Muslims were worth standing with. Look at where the Stephens family had come from. How could they not accept the true solutions that the Messenger presented?

They raised the sign above Lee Street in the East Texas town of Greenville in 1920, the year Theron Stephens, Joseph's father, turned fifteen. It couldn't be missed. It was right there, in the downtown, just past the Greenville Hotel and Crawford's Grocery.

Greenville
Welcome
The Blackest Land
The Whitest People

The slogan quickly caught on, and postcards with photos of the sign became popular. A real-estate man, W. Walworth Harrison, dreamed it up to promote Greenville's farmland. Greenville was cotton country. So much cotton came in that tufts blew through the air like snow and formed drifts around the courthouse square. Rail lines stretched in six directions to haul cotton away.

Apologists claimed "the blackest land" was but a way of describing the soil. The rich, dark loam, when wet, was black as coal, perfect for cotton. And "white" simply meant pure, as in Greenville's populace was pure of heart, good, Christian people. It had nothing to do with race and certainly was not derogatory to the city's Negroes, the descendants of the slaves who'd turned the land arable, people who still labored in the fields and lived in a part of Greenville all those pure Christian white folks called "Coon Town."

Speculators formed Greenville in 1840; settlers who didn't come west with slaves soon imported them from Louisiana and Arkansas to harrow the grasslands. More arrived during the next fifteen years. In 1861, Texas joined the Confederacy; the cotton men wanted to keep their chattel. Some slave owners across the South, thinking Texas was beyond the reach of Union armies, sent their property there for safekeeping. Greenville's Negro population increased, as did cotton, rice, and sugar production. When President Lincoln signed the Emancipation Proclamation in 1863, Texas farmers hid the news from their slaves until the war ended.

East Texas is more in the South than in the West. Cotton and slaves assured that. Emancipation brought Negroes little change. They were free, but what did they possess other than hungry children? They needed work, and it was there in Greenville's cotton fields. Freedom, they quickly learned, was little more than a matter of semantics. It allowed them a shack and a tiny wage—from which the shack's owner withheld rent. They were now paid pennies for each one hundred pounds of cotton they picked. Joseph and Billy Stephens's father, Theron, was born in Greenville on March 1, 1905, to Fred Stephens and Stella Fuller. Stella, the fifth of six children of William and Nellie Fuller, was born in Greenville in 1884. Her parents were ex-slaves: William, born in Georgia in 1840, and Nellie, in Arkansas in 1849. A 1910 census form lists the birthplace of William Fuller's father as Ireland, suggesting that William was of mixed race.

Three years after Theron's birth, an incident occurred that defined Greenville for generations of its Negro residents. A fourteen-year-old white girl claimed a young Negro named Ted Smith had raped her. Her alleged attacker was quickly arrested, but a mob stormed the jail and dragged him away even as two county judges pleaded for restraint.

The mob dragged Smith to the city square, beating him as they went. Someone threw a noose over a tree branch. The crowd grew.

Then someone yelled, "Burn him."

The pure, good Christians of Greenville doused Smith with kerosene. He screamed and writhed and died. Barrels were smashed and added to the pyre. Someone climbed to a rooftop and took photos of the encircling mob, scores and scores of men in white shirts and hats keeping their distance from the flames. More photos were taken on the ground. Smith's charred leg, bent at the knee, protruded from a ball of flame on his torso. Among the onlookers were a woman in a long white dress and several children turning away. "Burning of the Negro Smith at Greenville TX, 7-28-08," someone wrote across the bottom of the picture.

No one was charged with Smith's killing. Years later, the county sheriff said he doubted that the girl had been raped at all.

In their ghetto, Greenville's Negroes reeled in horror. To men like William Fuller who had been born into slavery, the lynching was a terrible reminder of how little had changed. To younger men, like Fred Stephens, Smith's murder plunged existence in East Texas to a deeper hopelessness. Fall approached and there was cotton to pick, mouths to feed. They could, of course, do nothing. They also couldn't do anything a few years later when the infamous sign about pure people and black land appeared across Lee Street in the middle of town, belittling them.

Like most Greenville Negroes, Theron Stephens had learned to pick cotton with both hands, avoiding the dried bristles that cut like barbs, dumping the cotton in the sack, somehow tolerating the scalding sun. Each picker was expected to harvest a ton of cotton a day. Ten sacks, over and over and over. It was more than enough to make a man dream of being anywhere but there. But like everywhere else in the South, there were few options. While tens of thousands of other Negroes had fled to the North in the last decade, the Stephenses had stayed put. Now the word from cities like Chicago and Detroit was that conditions had deteriorated quickly, along with jobs and hope.

Theron Stephens married a woman named Ruth Vaughn. He was thirty when his first son, Joseph, was born in Greenville in December 1935. Billy arrived a year later. The Depression had gutted the cotton market. Greenville wasn't in the Dust Bowl, but droughts came just the same. Theron was a smallish man, and the field work took its toll on him. There had to be a better life somewhere, anywhere.

Their escape came shortly after Pearl Harbor, when President Franklin Roosevelt desegregated California's shipyards. The Stephenses and thousands of other Negro families headed west in another great migration.

Theron and Ruth passed on stories to their sons about Greenville's cotton fields, the sign, and the lynchings; and they stayed with Joseph. In the years he preached as Yusuf Bey, when he got loosened up, when he was feeling it, little Texas twangs would emerge in his voice. If someone believed all of the devil's tricknology, then he was "out of his cotton-pickin' mind." A favorite rhetorical tool about the devil was the story, supported by historians, that slaves—not Eli Whitney—had invented the cotton gin. (In doing so, they unwittingly caused an explosion in cotton production and thus a huge increase in the need for slaves.) Joseph Stephens, grandson of a Georgia slave, hated cotton until the day he died.

Once they got to California, Theron quickly found work in the Richmond shipyards and stayed employed there after the war. The family moved yearly from one North Oakland apartment to another. Theron had a temper, beating Ruth often. His sons were young and impressionable and often saw their father's violence against their mother. In 1951, Ruth filed for divorce but didn't leave the area. Oakland was now their home. Theron flitted in and out of their lives. He left the shipyards and went to work in a bakery. Joseph graduated from Oakland Technical High School and joined the air force. Billy, a year behind him, headed south to Santa Barbara. When Joseph earned his discharge, he joined him.

Shortly after Elijah Muhammad's Los Angeles speech, the Stephenses won approval to form a mosque in Santa Barbara. Billy Stephens would be minister, Joseph the secretary and second in command. They would choose a captain and lieutenant of the Fruit of Islam and appoint a head of the Muslim Girls Training School to teach women proper conduct and housekeeping.

Word spread quickly in Santa Barbara that the Black Muslims were active there. The local newspaper ran an unflattering story. Though the Stephens brothers found it impossible to reconcile the Nation's teachings with running a hair salon catering to whites, the newspaper story had scared away most of their clients anyway, and the salon closed. In the city's small Black community, the conversion of the brothers to a religion espousing thrift and abstinence encountered skepticism. The Stephens brothers were partiers. They liked money, women, a good time. They were Muslims now? Something didn't quite fit. *Wait and see,* it was said around the south end. *Only time will tell if it's genuine.*

With the Red Carpet closed, the Stephenses needed money. Elijah Muhammad's teachings about diet, which had their genesis in Fard's early conversations with Detroit's ghetto dwellers, interested Joseph. Muslims didn't eschew just pork; Elijah forbade corn bread and other starches, as well as peas and most fried and processed foods. He strongly urged his followers to eat only once daily or even once every other day, advocating the consumption of whole grains, fresh vegetables, and fish.

Elijah also ordered small businesses, and particularly bakeries, created to cater to fellow Muslims, with a percentage of their profits going to Chicago. Before he moved to Santa Barbara, Theron had worked for years as a baker in Oakland, and when he joined his sons he began experimenting with Elijah's recipes, working with egg substitutes and grains to perfect bean and fruit pies. While Billy sought converts, Joseph set up shop. Soon his little bakery was churning out enough products that he started making the ten-hour round-trip home to Oakland once a week with a vanloads of pies and muffins. Billy, meanwhile, began managing an apartment complex and urged his congregants to live there.

Among those he converted were his wife's sister, Birdie Mae Scott, and her husband, Wendell. They moved into a unit right above Billy's. Given the cheap construction of the place, Billy could hear just about everything that went on upstairs.

At first, the brothers appeared earnest in their conversion. But Joseph, especially, also seemed eager to use the Muslims' teachings to justify obtaining money any way he could and began ordering followers to help in committing fraud.

Twice, Cadillacs registered to his mother turned up forty miles away in Oxnard, the first on June 7, 1966, the second on December 12, 1967. Both times, the cars, parked on residential streets with their doors locked, inexplicably burst into flames, the windows blowing out, glass spewing in all directions. Each resulted in an insurance claim that paid off more than $10,000 in bank loans combined and netted $1,100 in cash. Police conducted only cursory investigations.

If Muslims were supposed to be so virtuous and superior, so moral and upright, why did Minister Billy and Brother Joseph keep committing fraud?

Once was bad enough. But twice? In the same city? In the same way? Someone was going to get caught, and that person was Wendell Scott, whom the bothers had ordered to torch each car. Wendell knew the secret: The Stephenses weren't upright Muslims; they weren't even close. But Wendell felt trapped. He and Billy were brothers-in-law. Birdie Mae and Billy's ex-wife, Mary, were sisters. Billy and Mary had divorced, but Wendell still felt the strain of family ties. Billy ordered him around a lot. When Billy didn't, Joseph did. Wendell had been in prison; he didn't want to return. He had also belonged to the Oxnard mosque, where ministers didn't order cars burned. The way the Stephenses did things had to stop.

Wendell prayed about an idea he'd been contemplating for weeks. He would write to the blessed Messenger, the Honorable Elijah Muhammad, and inform him of the wrongdoing and crimes. He would beg forgiveness. Surely Elijah the Messenger wouldn't tolerate the brothers' actions and would replace them. Wendell mailed his letter to Chicago, confident it would resolve things and allow his return to the ranks of the righteous.

But the reply was not what he expected. His naïveté about how the Muslims dealt with complaints and allegations is evident in the fact that he didn't take Birdie and the kids and flee immediately after opening the return letter from Chicago. It warned about making accusations that could not be proven. One who did "must reap the punishment for the charges you have [alleged]," the Chicago letter said. A copy of the answer, along with a copy of Wendell's complaint, was sent to the Stephens.

Joseph and Billy immediately suspended Wendell for six months and stripped Birdie Mae of a leadership position among the mosque's women. It was how Muslim leaders controlled followers—creating a closed group on which members became exceedingly dependent, then issuing threats of suspension or banishment. Wendell became an outcast, shunned by the other Muslims who lived all around him.

Birdie worked at an electronics factory assembling parts. One day shortly after Wendell's suspension, she told a coworker named Doris Smith, "You better know what you want before you wish for it."

Smith asked if she meant joining the Muslims.

"I shouldn't talk to you this way, you know I can't discuss our activities,"

Birdie replied. "You're a dead baby," she told Smith, a Muslim phrase for female nonbelievers.

Although she wasn't suspended like Wendell, Birdie told friends she still felt ostracized because of his ouster. Many of the women wouldn't speak to her. Joseph and Billy were ruthless. She told a friend that she believed she and Wendell were in danger.

Wendell tried to remain devout. He prayed to Allah and told friends he wanted to return to the mosque when the suspension ended. He wanted to be an upright man but harbored doubts that he could remain a Black Muslim.

At the aerospace plant where he worked, a friend named Cleveland Whitfield noticed Wendell seemed constantly on edge, and one day Wendell unburdened himself.

"I guess you know I'm a Muslim," Wendell said.

Whitfield didn't know but said it wouldn't affect their friendship.

"I guess you judge each man on his own," Wendell said.

Whitfield replied that he did. Then he said, "I don't think you're a very strong Muslim." He meant that Wendell lacked the anger and rancor the Muslims routinely displayed.

"You don't hate people enough," Whitfield said.

"I guess you're right," Wendell replied.

The gunman favored a lever-action 30-30 Marlin rifle. Its twenty-inch barrel made it perfect for shooting in tight spaces. It could be fired quickly, even in the dark.

It was never clear exactly how the killer got into Wendell and Birdie's home in the early-morning hours of August 17, 1968. The apartment door had been kicked and splintered, but there was a lot of speculation that that happened *after* the Scotts were shot in their queen-sized bed, that the killer had a key, snuck in, did the work, and *then* kicked the door on the way out to make it look as if it had been broken upon entry. The fact that at least one person told police they heard the loud cracks of rifle reports before hearing what sounded like the duller thud of a door being broken added to the intrigue.

But either way, the Scotts were dead, Birdie facedown in the bed, a bullet that blew through her brain buried in her pillow. Wendell, shirtless, lay sprawled on the floor as if he had tried to get up, a bullet in his chest, the carpet around him red with blood. Four spent rifle cartridges were scattered on the floor.

"All indications are this was a planned execution," detectives wrote in a national teletype. Money in the apartment hadn't been taken. The children were unharmed. Whoever had gotten into the apartment had done so only to kill.

Billy X Stephens called police and reported he'd heard a door being broken upstairs. Or maybe a gunshot. He wasn't sure. Three cops found him at the stairs that led to the Scotts' apartment.

"I wouldn't go up there," Billy said. One officer stayed with him; the others went to investigate. They found the hysterical children, then the bodies.

A cop asked Billy who might have a grudge against the Scotts. He said he couldn't think of anyone; told that the Scotts were dead, Billy cried. He said he had to go tell Birdie's sister, Mary, his ex-wife.

Already things didn't make sense to police. Why did Billy say "I wouldn't go up there" if he didn't know what happened? If he did know, then he feigned surprise and tears.*

Over a few hours, Billy repeated his story to different detectives. He'd been on the phone just before 2:30. Once he said it was a business call. He told a different cop he was talking to a nineteen-year-old member of the mosque whom he called his fiancée. Then, he said, as he entered what he called "twilight sleep," he heard a loud noise in the Scotts' apartment. Maybe it was a shot, or something breaking. He hadn't heard anyone walking above his bedroom, or on the stairs. Police pressed. Yes, he said, he could always hear the Scott family moving around above him. No, he

---

*In early 2008, questioned by journalist Bob Butler and the author, Abdul Rabb Muhammad, the former Billy X Stephens, vehemently denied involvement in the murders of Wendell and Birdie Mae Scott. "I didn't do it. I don't know who did it, nor did I know beforehand that it was going to happen," he said. "I don't have anything to hide." Santa Barbara police briefly reopened the investigation but made no arrests. Abdul Rabb Muhammad declined to be interviewed for this book.

only heard one loud noise; he rolled over and looked at his clock. It was 2:30 a.m. He said that he first phoned the Scotts and got no answer, then called police.

A dispatcher recorded the call as having come in at 2:35 a.m.

Other Muslims said it was extremely odd, if not downright hypocritical, for Billy to call the police. He railed against cops in his sermons. Police were devils; they could not be trusted; the minister ordered his followers not to contact them under any circumstances.

Why was tough-talking Billy so scared by a loud noise that he committed a hypocritical act? If something was wrong, why didn't he make a Fruit call, as rallying members of the Fruit of Islam in emergencies was known? That was the Muslim way. Even if Wendell was suspended, Birdie wasn't. Black Muslims' teachings were to protect their own, and Wendell and Birdie were still Black Muslims.

"We never call the police for any reason. We handle all of our problems ourselves," a Muslim told Santa Barbara cops.

It was also strange that Billy so tepidly described what he heard. Officers found people who lived seventy-five yards or more away who said they had heard the clear, loud ringing of rifle fire just after 2:00 a.m. How could Billy report that he heard a door slam but not rifle shots right above his bedroom? It made no sense.

But most important, others said they had heard the gunfire twenty minutes earlier.

A woman across the street told police she was watching a movie broadcast from Los Angeles. The lead character was a detective who went on a drinking binge because his son was kidnapped. At the end of the movie, son and father were reunited. It was just then, with that scene on the TV, the woman said, that she heard shots.

A Santa Barbara cop called the LAPD. A detective drove to the station's studio. Yes, such a movie was broadcast early on the morning of Saturday, August 17, he was informed. Yes, there was a reunion scene two minutes before the credits rolled. That was at 2:08 a.m. The detective phoned Santa Barbara. His report confirmed the woman's story, which, in turn, confirmed other witnesses' accounts: Shots were heard shortly past 2:00 a.m.

Billy became irate when confronted with the time discrepancy. Devils and their tricknology. He couldn't explain the twenty minutes' difference and refused to take a lie-detector test. Then detectives asked him about the Chicago letter, a copy of which they'd found in the Scotts' apartment. "Stephens was advised that we had learned that he had received copies of the letters and accusations and that these letters and answers might be of assistance to our investigation," Captain C. D. George wrote in a report. "He refused to confirm or deny that such letters were in existence and refused to produce them."

There is no documentation that police sought search warrants for Billy's copies of the letters or any other evidence. There is also no available documentation that Santa Barbara police attempted to get more information from the Nation's Chicago headquarters or asked Chicago police for assistance.

Still, detectives conducted a thorough investigation, interviewing more than one hundred fifty people, asking the FBI for help, and contacting urban police departments across the country about Muslim killings.

But it all kept coming back to Billy and Joseph and the letter Wendell wrote to Elijah Muhammad. Joseph was as belligerent as Billy. Members of the mosque grew deeply afraid.

The complaint letters were a strong motive; witnesses contradicted Billy's time reference; his claim not to have heard shots seemed implausible; he was the building manager and had keys to the Scotts' apartment. Was his delay in calling police designed to give the killer time to flee? Police tried to talk to Mary Stephens, Billy's former wife and Birdie's sister. But Mary refused. "Mrs. Stephens would not answer questions even to which officers already had answers. It is believed [she] knows a great deal about this case," a detective wrote. The investigators pressed on, but by the year's end their efforts were fruitless. Some Muslims had talked immediately after the murders, meeting detectives clandestinely. But as time passed with no arrests, self-preservation took over. Standing up to the Stephens brothers sure looked like it got people killed.

But while the investigation faltered, the fact that two members of the mosque had died because of what everyone seemed to know was an internal mess, made recruiting converts difficult. Some Muslims left. The bakery struggled; tithings fell. Newspaper sales dropped. The cops stayed around; if nothing else, an open double murder gave them plenty of reason to harass the Stephens. The devils put the mosque under a microscope.

Finally, the brothers received Chicago's permission to leave Santa Barbara. Get out, they were told. They had only one place to go.

Oakland.

part three

"I come from Oakland, shitbox of the West."

Yusuf Bey, wearing a kufi, surrounded by his men as he arrives for a court hearing in 2002 on charges he raped a thirteen-year-old girl. Bey would be dead in a year. His son, Antar, who would be killed in 2005, is to his immediate right. Several female followers in head scarves are behind Bey. *Photo by Nick Lammers/* Oakland Tribune, *courtesy of the Bay Area News Group*

Chauncey Bailey, pointing, is blocked by followers of Your Black Muslim Bakery leader Yusuf Bey as they clear a path for him to leave a court hearing in 2003 on charges of child rape. Bailey had covered the hearing and was attempting to interview Bey. *Photo by Nick Lammers/* Oakland Tribune, *courtesy of the Bay Area News Group*

10

Detroit of the West

"The victim of racism is in a much better position to tell you whether or not you're a racist than you are."
—COLEMAN YOUNG, Detroit mayor, 1974–93

When World War II ended, Oakland's whites saw themselves with a Negro problem. The city's Black population had increased nearly 300 percent thanks to the tens of thousands of migrants who flocked west for war-production jobs, mostly from Texas, Louisiana, and Oklahoma.

Business boosters called Oakland the "Detroit of the West," which was accurate in both intended and unintended ways. Wide swaths of flatlands ran for miles in three directions from downtown; sprawling rail yards sent lines north, east, and south; a deepwater port accommodated the world's largest freighters.

By 1946, plants that had fed the Pacific war effort had shifted to domestic production, turning out autos, steel, and the materials for vast civic infrastructure. It was California, the magnificent, golden West; the car would soon be king, great highways built, suburbs sprawling along them. California, perhaps more than anywhere else, would embody the American dream. Anything seemed possible, unless, of course, one wasn't white.

More than sixty thousand migrants lived in North and West Oakland and South Berkeley, clamoring for work. But no white veteran returning home after defeating the Axis wanted to lose a job to a Negro (or to a Mexican or an Asian, for that matter).

Institutional racism in California lacked Southern viciousness, but it existed nonetheless, often hidden behind a maddening disingenuousness.

Employers blamed their lack of Negro workers on Northern California's powerful labor unions, which were loath to admit them. Some found employment in Oakland's downtown department stores, like Kahn's and Hastings, and its restaurants, but only in low-paying, back-of-the-house jobs unseen by white patrons: washing dishes, hauling trash. Negroes could sit wherever they wanted on the region's trolley network, the Key System, but landing well-paying jobs driving a trolley proved impossible. Negroes could vote, but Oakland's whites outnumbered them better than four to one. Since city elections were at-large, with no representative district gerrymandered to their neighborhoods, Negroes could vote all they wanted but weren't going to elect their people. As suburbs began to sprawl across the state, restrictive covenants appeared in property deeds, limiting future sales to "members of the Caucasian race." Every suburban house sold to whites fleeing cities became bricks in a wall of exclusion.

Conditions in Oakland's ghettos deteriorated quickly. As in Detroit in the 1920s, city leaders recruited Southerners as police. Less than five years after the war, abuse was so blatant that the state assembly's Interim Committee on Crime and Corrections began investigating. A lawyer for the East Bay Civil Rights Congress summarized Negro life for the lawmakers in two sentences: "Oakland has the second largest Negro population west of the Mississippi. Yet the Negro citizens of Oakland live in daily and nightly terror of the Oakland Police Department." But he might as well have been talking to the wind.

The committee found "that there is reasonable cause to believe that acts of police brutality have and/or racial discrimination have occurred in Oakland. . . . The temptation for acts of angry force confronts a policeman continuously and it is a rare police force which does not suffer dereliction in this respect." So police could hardly be blamed for their actions in dealing with ghetto dwellers.

Men like George McDaniel learned quickly that, as in the South, their skin color made them targets for abuse. In May 1949, a man armed with a gun broke into McDaniel's West Oakland home. The gunman waved his weapon at McDaniel's wife, stealing fifty-one dollars and a pistol. Police quickly arrested the robber. McDaniel left work at a real-estate company, stopped home briefly to comfort his spouse, and went to city hall to get his money and his weapon returned. He was ushered inside, then arrested. The robbery investigator, an Inspector Charles Wood, informed McDaniel that police believed he was involved in robbing his own residence. Or perhaps Wood simply didn't like that a well-spoken Negro walked in and inquired about an investigation.

"Boy, you're lying," Wood said when McDaniel denied involvement in the robbery. He shoved McDaniel into a small room, shutting the door and ramming a nightstick into his stomach. As McDaniel cowered on the floor, Wood hit him across the shoulders and shins, then in his left eye socket, before drawing blood with two chopping blows to the face. Wood left, locking McDaniel inside. Thirty minutes later, he returned.

"I found out you're telling the truth," Wood said. "You can go home now."

From the floor, a hand on his swollen face, McDaniel replied, "Look at what you done to me for telling the truth."

"I didn't do that. You must have fallen over something and hurt yourself," Wood replied.

McDaniel limped away. Unlike some, he'd lived through his encounter with the Oakland cops. Among those who didn't was a man named Andrew Hines.

Sometime past midnight on April 17, 1949, Patrolman Spencer Amundsen noticed Hines near a rooming house on Thirty-seventh Street. Amundsen would later say Hines seemed suspicious; perhaps he was a Peeping Tom. Amundsen ordered Hines into the house, apparently to learn if he lived there. The officer instructed Hines to raise his hands, pointed his revolver at his chest, and attempted an interrogation. Three other people were present. At some point, Hines may have lowered his hands. One of the others said he heard Amundsen tell him to raise them again. Another said he heard nothing. The third person, a woman, told police she didn't remember anything because she fainted when Amundsen suddenly killed Hines, shooting him through the heart.

Police conducted a textbook investigation into the slaying of an un-armed Negro. Amundsen said that Hines had lowered his hands and ig-nored an order to raise them again. The Negro acted as if he might reach for a gun. Amundsen feared for his life and defended it with deadly force. If the others present offered anything contradictory, they were just lying Negroes. Amundsen, Oakland investigators concluded, acted properly.

Among the other institutions failing the ghettos' residents and adding deeply to their suffering was the city's daily newspaper, the *Oakland Tribune,* a broadsheet house organ of the ultraconservative oligarchy controlling the city. Its owner, Joseph Knowland, a former state legislator, had bought the paper in 1914 with great wealth his father amassed in timber and shipping.

As a young publisher, Knowland came to patronize a promising assistant city attorney named Earl Warren. Knowland eventually shepherded him to election, first as Alameda County district attorney, then as state attor-ney general, and eventually three terms as California governor. In his usual gruff way, Knowland said of Warren to other moneyed men: "That's the boy. You help him." Help they did, catapulting Warren through the politi-cal ranks. Warren owed the Knowlands much: In 1945 he repaid some of his debt when, as governor, he appointed Knowland's son—William Fife Knowland—to a vacant U.S. Senate seat, cementing the family's power.

The Knowlands controlled Oakland and its newspaper, which simply was an extension of their pro-business, pro–law enforcement, reactionary, and decidedly right-wing politics. It differed little from the Chandler fam-ily's *Los Angeles Times* of that era or the Hearst newspapers. The editorial-page slogan was "Home Owned, Controlled, Edited." The paper was so prim that Oaklanders called it "The Old Lady." And like most big-city publishers at midcentury, the Knowlands were inherent racists and far too busy making money—and supporting the moneymaking efforts of their friends—to insist their reporting staff cover Oakland's minorities and their struggles. They treated Negroes as a nuisance.

Yet the Knowlands' patronage of Warren eventually resulted in the un-doing of many of the right-wing principles they espoused.

As state attorney general, Warren made horrendously ignorant decisions advocating the internment of California's Japanese population during the war. Following his appointment as chief justice of the Supreme Court in 1953, however, he took part in cornerstone decisions that shaped social justice in the second half of the twentieth century: *Brown v. the Board of Education*; *Miranda v. Arizona,* requiring police to recite basic rights to arrestees; *Gideon v. Wainwright,* establishing the right of the indigent to court-appointed attorneys; and other significant cases. It can be argued that Warren and his liberal allies did more for minorities than any other national leaders, even presidents Kennedy and Johnson with their signatures on civil-rights legislation. The Knowlands cringed at each decision. Conservatives labeled Warren a traitor.

In the Senate, Bill Knowland, as he was known, rose quickly to become the Republican leader when Robert A. Taft of Ohio died in office. He was a socially awkward man who, thanks to Warren's gift of appointment, never had to earn his Senate seat. Knowland, miscast in the role as the head of his party's caucus, couldn't keep order in his ranks or push through much of President Eisenhower's legislative agenda. Eisenhower, often frustrated with Knowland's failures, confided to his diary, "There is no final answer to the question, 'how stupid can he get?' "

Knowland didn't involve himself much in civil rights until he decided to run for California governor in the 1958 election. In the years before meaningful civil-rights legislation, the political allegiances of Negroes remained an open question. Knowland's allegiance was of the party of Lincoln, while Negroes' biggest enemies were openly racist Southern Democrats. In the formative stages of his gubernatorial campaign, Knowland decided to court the Negro vote by warming to civil-rights legislation in 1957.

Passage of a civil-rights bill finally seemed possible that year, but only if a Southern filibuster could be defeated. Southerners had killed six similar efforts since 1936. Aspirations to higher office also motivated Knowland's Democratic counterpart in the Senate, majority leader Lyndon Johnson, who saw Northern Negroes as a constituency in his plans to win the White House in 1960.

Unlike Johnson, though, Knowland had no intention of seeing the legislation he publicly praised become law. By supporting a strong bill that Southerners would surely kill, Knowland could bluster all he wanted about Negro rights as he stumped for governor. But when he retreated behind closed doors with other powerful white men, he could assure them the status quo would hold. He couldn't afford to be labeled another Earl Warren among California's ultraconservatives. His strategy backfired, though, when liberal Republicans abandoned him to support a watered-down bill that passed, foreshadowing the passage of stronger legislation in the next decade. Knowland was slow to adapt, looking weak and inept to conservatives and uninterested in civil rights at all to Negroes, not that their support would have made a difference. Democrat Pat Brown ultimately destroyed him by twenty points in the 1958 gubernatorial election. Knowland didn't even carry Oakland.

His political career ruined, Knowland exercised his only option; he returned home, assuming editorship of the *Tribune,* which he turned even harder right, so best to pay back liberals. Oakland's Negroes would continue to find no solace—or justice—in the paper or elsewhere in the city Knowland controlled.

The worsening of ghetto conditions in Oakland became legend. In 1966, the writer Warren Hinckle described Oakland in *Ramparts* magazine as "a city planner's version of the seventh layer of hell: an ugly, squalid, depressing hodgepodge of commercial neighborhoods, smoke-deadened greenery and neglected residences of Victorian design and Edwardian vintage. The dominant color is gray." Oakland "is one of the worst examples of American society."

A full 47 percent of city residents lived in poverty. Unemployment was double the national average. The Alameda County Welfare Department was despised in the ghetto for doing all it could to limit benefits. At one point in the midsixties, state authorities investigated forty-nine complaints from Oakland Blacks claiming that welfare workers had illegally cut off or denied aid and substantiated *all forty-nine claims.* A handful of Protestant ministers and Catholic priests created their own antipoverty program. An Episcopalian clergyman traveled the country raising money to feed Oakland's poor, beginning his appeals by saying, "I come from Oakland, shitbox of the West."

Unlike in many other cities, Black Muslims lacked much of a foothold in Oakland. The Bay Area's only mosque was in San Francisco, near the edge of the Fillmore ghetto, where a hard-line follower of the Honorable Elijah Muhammad, Minister Henry X Majied, kept tight rein on a small congregation. His Muslim men at Mosque 26 wore suits, sold newspapers, sent tithings to Chicago, and followed orders. But while Minister Henry, as he was called, maintained the appearance of order, his was not an especially growing flock, in part because most of the region's Blacks lived across the bay in Oakland. And that's where the Stephens brothers headed when they fled Santa Barbara. Minister Henry didn't like Joseph and Billy Stephens from the day they showed up. While he didn't have a mosque in Oakland, he considered it his territory. Now, here came these loudmouths running away from Southern California, leaving dead people in their wake and thinking they were simply going to take over.

"They thought we were rooty-poots," said a man who came north with the Stephens, meaning rubes or bumpkins. "They didn't like us."

The Stephenses were no bumpkins, but there was immediate talk among the members of Mosque 26 that they didn't seem like good Muslims, either. They were obnoxious and certainly not pious. Joseph wore a little two-part mustache, a thin line of whiskers descending from each nostril that turned at ninety-degree angles across his upper lip, ending in tiny points. Elijah Muhammad was clean shaven, and the Nation frowned on style. No, Minister Henry didn't like these rooty-poots at all.

The Stephenses moved quickly. They wanted Oakland as their own and asked Chicago for permission to take it. Elijah said Billy and Joseph X could open an Oakland mosque, but it would be Mosque 26B, not an entirely new entity. Both Minister Henry and the Stephenses fumed, Henry because he was losing ground and Joseph and Billy because they appeared subservient to Henry. Nevertheless, the Stephenses rented a small building on Pine Street in West Oakland as Mosque 26B; thirteen miles away, on MacArthur Boulevard in East Oakland, they opened another bakery. Billy was again minister; but being second in command ate at Joseph. He was the older brother, albeit by only a year, and he harbored ambitions. He also chafed at sending a portion of his bakery's proceeds to Chicago. Elijah preached economic independence but demanded a piece of each enterprise. How truly self-reliant were those who had to cut him in?

And there were other problems.

Billy and Joseph both competed for the affections of the top female at the San Francisco mosque, Captain Sister Felicia X. She began openly spending time with each of them. Minster Henry forbade single females from even sitting in the front seats of cars with men. He ordered Felicia brought up on charges to strip her of her power; the proceeding would be taped and sent to Chicago so Elijah could personally render the verdict. Felicia showed up simply so she could storm out. She then announced she was defecting to 26B. She—and Joseph and Billy—had humiliated Henry.

Soon, open warfare erupted among Bay Area Black Muslims.

In the winter of 1971–72, at least nine people were killed and three seriously wounded in a series of Muslim-on-Muslim hits in Oakland, San Francisco, and Richmond. The war was over drugs and vengeance.

Some Muslims who lived in Oakland and attended the San Francisco mosque before the Stephenses arrived had been deeply involved in the narcotics trade despite the Nation's rhetoric against it. Whether Joseph Stephens intended to take over their territory to profit himself or drive them away has never been fully known. What is known is that a notorious Oakland hit man, "Friendly" Freddy Payne, joined Mosque 26B and was soon executing other Muslims. At 10:15 p.m. on November 14, 1971, Payne and two other men burst into the East Oakland house of Billy Mapp, a drug dealer who, like Payne, had recently become a Muslim but not abandoned his line of work. Mapp wasn't there, but his wife was, along with another Muslim named al-Rashid, who was visiting from Oregon. He drew a .38 pistol and began firing at Payne. The intruders shot back, killing him. They fled down a hall where Mapp's eight-year-old daughter, Kimberly, slept in an alcove. As she sat up in bed as the gunmen raced by, one of them shot her in the face, killing her instantly.

Just three nights earlier, a Muslim husband and wife living nearby had died in an attack that bore strong similarities to the murders of Wendell and

Birdie Mae Scott: Someone kicked in their door, shot them in their bed, took nothing, and fled, leaving a relative alive in a different bedroom.

All of the victims were members of either Mosque 26 or Mosque 26B—except for al-Rashid and another Muslim killed in San Francisco who was from Chicago, perhaps sent as a peacemaker.

Muslim rhetoric about obeying all laws, carrying not even a penknife, and never harming a fellow believer seemed like just so much talk, like big-headed scientists and mother planes. Elijah Muhammad might have really believed those things, but many of his followers, who were ingrained criminals, did not. Joseph Stephens certainly didn't. Though police were never able to trace the nine killings to him directly, his involvement seems indisputable.

Almost as soon as they got to Oakland, the Stephens brothers each read Mario Puzo's best-selling new book, *The Godfather.* White devil or not, Don Vito Corleone knew how to command power and respect, and the structure of the Mafia was worthy of emulation. The Stephenses passed the book around. *This is how we will do things,* they told the underlings.

The problem was, there could be only one boss.

Being number two became intolerable to Joseph. There was no reason why he, the eldest, should not hold the title of minister. He also wanted to acquire his own wealth. Memories of his family's poor beginnings in the Texas cotton fields remained indelible. Yet under the Nation of Islam, money from mosques and associated businesses flowed to Chicago, where Elijah and the royal family lived regally. Individual Muslims weren't allowed such accumulations of wealth.

But what if Joseph broke from the Nation and formed what, essentially, would be his own Black Muslim sect? Joseph could preach what the Nation preached, but he could be separate, his own man. The Nation, in fact, was an organization, not a religion. The religion was Fard's peculiar concoction of Islam. The Nation couldn't stop people outside its control from worshipping Fard and his teachings any more than national Baptist or Methodist organizations could keep a pastor and congregation from breaking away but still worshipping Christ.

In effect, that is what Joseph decided to do sometime in late 1971 or

1972. He would change none of Elijah's rhetoric; he would simply go preach it on his own and line his pockets with the proceeds. The Messenger would not be pleased, but Joseph couldn't help himself. He wanted to be rich.

Joseph spread the word among his loyalists and scouted business locations along North Oakland's San Pablo Avenue. The split was a palace coup. Billy was shocked and angry at his brother's dissension. How could Oakland, torn apart by years of violence, poverty, and strife, benefit from rival Muslim organizations? What's more, Joseph was taking some of the mosque's best men along, promising them jobs at what he said would be an industrial-sized bakery specializing in health foods. The city would be carved up. Joseph and his men had better stay off his turf, Billy warned. Joseph threatened violence, but neither brother would become Cain to the other's Abel. Billy stayed loyal to the Nation, but his time leading Mosque 26B was limited. Elijah and his lieutenants soon ordered Billy to leave Oakland and run a mosque in Las Vegas.

Another minister was assigned to Mosque 26B, which moved to East Oakland. That left North Oakland to Joseph, who soon found the storefront he sought. His father, Theron, who had helped set up the Santa Barbara bakery, agreed to aid him again; Joseph dubbed his new venture "Your Bakery." But even though Joseph was no longer a member of the Nation, Elijah reacted angrily when he learned of the name. The Nation's own grocery stores and bakeries were named "Your Grocery" and "Your Bakery." It was one thing to leave the Nation, it was another to take what was, in effect, one of its trademarks. Who did this Joseph X think he was?

Elijah made it clear that Joseph had committed an act of disrespect. Joseph had no choice but to ask for forgiveness; he understood the kind of vicious violence Elijah's enforcers could employ. He wanted to make money by emulating Elijah and parroting his teachings, not get his head bashed in with a lead pipe. He quickly changed the name to "Your *Black Muslim* Bakery."

Perhaps Elijah sensed that Stephens was not worth the bother of keeping and policing. Clearly, he had issues with the obedience to authority that was the Nation's cornerstone. In a sense, he could not be entirely broken and certainly not trusted. Elijah let him go.

The new name of his business confirmed for Joseph the identity he sought. He was an independent Black Muslim. But there was one other thing he needed to do. The use of an "X" was closely associated with the Nation. If Joseph were to truly become autonomous, he needed a new name. He picked "Bey," the name that the Moors in Chicago had taken forty-five years earlier from the Turks and Egyptians. He took "Yusuf" as a first name and "Ali" as a middle name. Joseph Stephens became Yusuf Ali Bey.

By May 1971, enough commercial customers were buying breads and pies from Your Black Muslim Bakery that Bey needed to employ three shifts of workers to meet demands. He soon developed a reputation for turning away no Black person who needed work and who agreed to adhere to his strict rules. They were to be observant Muslims, dress properly, behave piously. Women had to cover their heads at all times and learn to submit to both Allah and their man. No drinking or smoking. All had to attend Bey's frequent sermons. Bey could have asked them to worship anything as long as he issued paychecks, which, for a while, he did. A job in the early 1970s at a prospering business right there in the ghetto was almost too good to be true. Who else was doing anything for people in North Oakland? Not anyone in city hall or its shill of a newspaper, the *Tribune*. Not the police, not anyone at the churches people left to convert to the Islam that Bey parroted.

Bey broke a lot of rules to get ahead. He even went on TV to plug his products, giving an interview to a nightly news show, the kind of thing the Nation would never have allowed.

"We use natural products, pure honey, pure flavorings, pure vanilla," he said, standing in the bakery's doorway wearing a white shirt, a blue and brown necktie, and a camel-hair blazer of the style Elijah Muhammad favored. His interviewer didn't ask about his beliefs, and Bey, his brow furrowed and chin lowered, talked only about the food.

"We bake for vegetarians as well as health-conscious people," he said. "We have a honey prune cake that has no eggs or sugar. This is one of the first bakeries to go into this type of baking. Our food tastes good as well as being good for you. Most organic foods don't taste too good."

Across the bay in San Francisco, Muslims at Mosque 26 fumed. They saw Bey's interview as advertising to whites. Observing good nutrition was an order from the Messenger. It was meant only to uplift the health and lives of Black people.

But Bey was hungry for wealth, and if he got it by selling to the devil, so what? In that sense, the only color that mattered to him was that of money; Your Black Muslim Bakery did so well that Bey soon needed more space.

He found it a few blocks farther up San Pablo Avenue toward Berkeley in a two-story brick building built in 1908 as a hotel. The first floor, which had once housed a drugstore, was perfect for a bakery. Upstairs, there were enough small rooms for a contingent of men. Bey began offering the indigent, and those just released from prison, lodging in exchange for labor, making them dependent on him for more than just work. There was a back room large enough for holding Muslim services. An open yard behind the building abutted several houses on Fifty-ninth Street. Eventually, Bey would buy them, forming a compound. He was certain he had found the way to a truly independent and superior existence by shedding the Nation's tethers. Salvation and riches seemed at hand. For years, he was able to build a cult almost unnoticed. It was Oakland. The city, still in the wake of years of police abuse and the upheaval of the Black Power movement, had little collective desire to understand or assess the smooth-talking baker. Black Muslim identity had not yet captivated many Oaklanders; when it did, it would be the identity that Bey formed.

Just as Bey was settling into his new building in late 1972 and crowing that his form of self-reliance through hard work was true salvation, another, younger Black man, whose work habits and drive were just as intense, was looking for a chance to leave the region, at least for a while. His name was Chauncey Bailey, and he was obsessed with what he, too, saw as a way to help his people. Bailey's passion was journalism, and in the decades ahead, it would lead him to many intersections with the people in Oakland who called themselves Bey.

11

No Good Cause Shall Lack a Champion

*"I shall be a crusader and an advocate, a mirror
and a record, a herald and a spotlight, and I shall
not falter. So help me God."*
—P. BERNARD YOUNG JR., editor, *Norfolk Journal and Guide,*
"Credo for the Negro Press," 1942

"Yo-u-u-u sk-sk-sk ip-ip-ip-ed one," Chauncey Bailey would stutter, looking back at the house of a newspaper subscriber that his mother, Brigette, had just sped by. By the time he got the words out, Brigette would be halfway down the block. She'd stop and back up hurriedly, her left hand on the wheel, the right draped over the seat, her torso twisted. "Hurry up," she'd say sternly, and Chauncey would jump out and wing the *Hayward Daily Review* onto a porch. Brigette drove Chauncey on his route most afternoons. She was so busy rushing between her own jobs as a beautician and a practical nurse that she didn't have time to wait for him to do it by bicycle. Chauncey's younger half brother, Mark Cooley, was often in the backseat, folding the papers.

Chauncey dreaded missing a house or making any kind of mistake that could cause a subscriber to complain. Even as a youngster he seemed to know that some people—especially white people—would use any excuse to express dissatisfaction about a Black person. One customer had already called the paper and asked why some "little nigger" was making deliveries. The paper supported Chauncey, but he knew to keep it that way he had to do a better job than the white kids who delivered the paper in other neighborhoods.

His problem was that the station wagon always seemed to end up in reverse.

"Yo-u-u-u-u-u sk-sk-sk-sk-sk ip-ip-ip-ip-ip-ip-ed it," Chauncey would stammer at his mother again and again. It happened so often that Mark and other family members dubbed him Skippy. Other kids picked it up. Even in adulthood, people sometimes still referred to Bailey by the nickname.

Chauncey had the paper route because his mother demanded he have a job. Brigette believed that a solid work ethic was the key to everything in life. If people could just take care of themselves, things would be a lot better. A paper route required routine and discipline, and as Chauncey entered junior high school, it was time for him to learn those traits. A bundle of papers would be there for him every day when he got home. He would learn that a job was a responsibility, not some abstraction. He would have to learn to deliver papers when he didn't want to. Did he think his mother liked standing on her feet all day styling hair or staying up half the night caring for a patient, changing sheets, emptying bedpans? Work dominated Brigette's life so much that it seemed like she never slept. People would one day say the same of her eldest son.

Brigette Marie Duhe was born in Reserve, Louisiana, west of New Orleans, in 1908, a descendant of French Creoles and slaves. She attended nursing school and, just after World War II began, joined the Army Air Corps. She was eventually stationed in Portland, Oregon, where she met a soldier named Chauncey Wendell Bailey, who served in a segregated maintenance unit. Bailey was from Iowa, the son of a railroad cook named James A. Bailey, who was born in Mississippi in 1883, and Willie Tinsley Bailey, born in Tennessee in 1885. Both were the children of former slaves. Chauncey Bailey, the second-youngest of James and Willie's five children, was born in Des Moines in 1919.

Duhe and Bailey married in 1945 as the war ended and moved to Iowa, where he worked for the post office. Their first child, a daughter, arrived in November 1948, and Brigette became pregnant again in short order. Her parents had migrated from Louisiana to California during the war, and, needing the help of her mother, Brigette traveled west by train with her first baby to give birth to her second. Chauncey Wendell Bailey Jr. was born in Oakland on October 20, 1949, at 2:49 a.m. Brigette had a second son the next year in Iowa. But her marriage to Bailey soured and they divorced shortly after Chauncey's younger brother was born. Brigette took the children to California, where she ultimately remarried and had two more sons.

With five kids, Brigette and her second husband, John Cooley, needed more space than they could find in Oakland. They looked elsewhere, a courageous act for an African American family in early-1960s California. Blacks attempting to move into white neighborhoods had encountered endless racism. Even the baseball great Willie Mays was harassed and eventually driven out of an exclusive white neighborhood in San Francisco in the late 1950s. "Down in Alabama, where we come from, you know your place, and that's something, at least," Mays's wife, Marguerite, said at the time about racism in California. "But up here it's all a lot of camouflage. They grin in your face, and then deceive you."

Brigette found a house on a cul-de-sac in the southern Alameda County suburb of Hayward that lacked any deed restrictions on the race of a buyer. Her family was among that city's first African American residents. In 1963, California passed the Rumford Fair Housing Act, making racial discrimination in housing illegal and outlawing race-based deed covenants. The California Real Estate Association, whose membership found that guaranteeing subdivisions could be kept as all-white enclaves made a strong selling point, moved swiftly to overturn it. Proposition 14, which allowed a landowner to "decline to sell, lease or rent property to such person or persons as he, in his absolute discretion, chooses," went to voters in 1964 with the support of the John Birch Society and other right-wing groups. It passed with 65 percent of the vote. The next year, both the California and the U.S. Supreme Courts ruled Proposition 14 unconstitutional.

But that didn't make it any easier to be an African American in Hayward, where Bailey's family encountered not just the subtle kind of racism described by Marguerite Mays but sometimes hatred far more direct. Thirty years later, writing his mother's obituary, Bailey revealed that a cross had been burned on the front lawn shortly after his family moved in.

"Being young children we became friends with the neighbors and played with them, not putting emphasis on color," Bailey's sister, Lorelei Waqia, recalled. "For a while my mother and stepfather didn't let us go too far from the front of the house. We were not to play outside without one of them being home." But tensions eventually eased, and other African Americans moved into the neighborhood. Still, the situation made all of the children, including Chauncey, deeply aware of race.

Chauncey continued to stutter throughout early adolescence. People thought he was withdrawn and shy, but a blustery personality that few saw lurked inside him. Nonetheless, his embarrassment and frustration grew palpable as the stutter worsened. As expressing himself became more of an ordeal, he appeared more aloof. As both a creative and communicative outlet, Chauncey took to writing, spending long hours alone in the Hayward High School library.* Despite his speech problems, he had things to say and was in the midst of a growing awareness of the condition of African Americans, especially during the height of the civil-rights movement, when nightly television images showed Black people being beaten, bitten by police dogs, or assaulted with water cannons. He was trying to figure out what he could do to help. Seeing how much people depended on the newspaper, coupled with his love of the written word, had led Bailey to decide very early on that his future was in journalism. Much later in life, he would tell people close to him that when the racist subscriber to the *Daily Review* complained about the "little nigger" delivering newspapers, he had muttered to himself, "If you don't like this, wait until one's writing for it."

One day when Bailey was about seventeen years old, the stuttering stopped. "No medication, no therapy. He woke and never stuttered again," Mark Cooley recalled. Chauncey was free. Now no one could shut him up.

After graduation from Hayward High School in 1968, Bailey attended Oakland's Merritt College—where the Black Panthers began—then transferred to San Jose State to study journalism. The Black Power movement appealed to Bailey; when he graduated in 1972, he contemplated joining the Panthers and writing for their newspaper. Instead, a professor urged him to integrate a mainstream newsroom. He started at a San Jose television station as an on-air reporter, beginning a career-long flirtation with broadcast news. But Bailey also wanted to write and immerse himself in the

---

*The library would be dedicated to him in 2011.

culture of the traditional Black press. He soon left San Jose for San Francisco, where he took a job as a reporter for the *Sun Reporter,* the city's Black weekly, a newspaper that blurred the lines between activism, politics, and outrage. Bailey understood that Blacks needed their own voice. Newspaper owners like Oakland's Knowland family certainly didn't give it to them. Even the Nation of Islam had its own newspaper. Negro newspapers, in fact, predated emancipation, beginning with *Freedom's Journal,* which was formed in New York in 1827. "Too long have others spoken for us. . . . We wish to plead our own cause," the paper's editors wrote in the first edition. *Freedom's Journal*'s legacy became the *Chicago Defender,* the *Pittsburgh Courier,* the (New York) *Amsterdam News.*

In San Francisco, where a Black publication began shortly after the Gold Rush, the top such newspaper had eventually become the *Sun Reporter,* a feisty tabloid that exclaimed in its banner, "That no good cause shall lack a champion, evil shall not thrive unopposed."

The paper's publisher, Carlton Goodlett, who was also a medical doctor and sometime politician, liked Bailey's passion. The kid wanted to tell stories, he wanted to push, and he wanted, above all else, to do something for his people, to give them voice. Bailey wore a big Afro, or a natural, as the hairstyle was then called, and a mustache that drooped around his mouth. He easily fit into San Francisco of the early 1970s. Like his mother, Bailey had little tolerance for moderation when it came to work, and, like Goodlett especially, he wanted to pursue provocative stories, stories that would shake things up. "The black tail is never going to wag the white dog," Goodlett once said. "But if we live in the belly of the beast, we can cause quite a bellyache."

As he began work in San Francisco, excited to have joined a part of the traditional Black press that he admired, Bailey was headed for an unmanageable story, one with bloodshed and hatred that would immerse him in a topic on which he would report, on and off, for the next thirty years: Black Muslims.

12

Generate a Cause for Arrest

"The whites have always been an unjust, jealous, unmerciful, avaricious, and blood-thirsty set of beings, always seeking after power and authority."
—DAVID WALKER, Walker's Appeal, September 1829

The first victim was a young woman, mutilated beyond belief. Someone had taken a machete to her, hacking, slashing, severing her spinal column, her head hanging from her torso by just a few tendrils of flesh. Whoever had butchered her had done so with immeasurable anger, police would note. Somehow, her husband—snatched randomly off the street with her and thrown in a white van, a man knocking him unconscious with a tire iron—survived dozens of cuts from the same blade that killed her. It was October 20, 1973, a Saturday, fog and chill settling down on San Francisco with the night. The couple—Richard and Quita Hague—were dumped south of downtown alongside a rail spur. Their attackers sped away, exuberant.

"You should have seen all the blood gush out of her neck," Larry Green, the one who had killed Quita, told his companions, Jesse Lee Cooks and Anthony Harris.

Cooks and Harris had been in prison together at San Quentin. There, in the same cellblocks where nearly fifty years earlier Wallace Ford had begun to concoct the version of Islam that he would spread in Detroit, Cooks spoke incessantly about killing. He longed to "break necks, punch out eyes,

bust hearts" because whites "had castrated and killed and stomped our babies," words he lifted from Nation of Islam dogma. In early 1973, Cooks
had started boasting that when he got out he would join "the Death Angels," a secret sect of Black Muslims whose members killed random white
devils to achieve salvation. The fact that Cooks knew of the sect before his
release from prison showed it was already well established and perhaps recruiting new members.

By the middle of 1973, Cooks and Harris were paroled. Cooks immediately joined Mosque 26 in San Francisco. Harris first went to Oakland,
living in a halfway house and attending Mosque 26B, but moved across
the bay to join Cooks. There they met Larry Green, with whom Cooks
found he shared an unrelenting bloodlust. Within a few months they were
organized, disciplined, and bent on committing what they believed were
absolutely justifiable acts of heinous violence. For more than three hundred
years the devil had created chaos for Black people wherever they turned,
cruelty and torture their only reality. The time to reply in kind had finally
come.

The men knew that the unimaginable slaughter of the young couple
would likely confuse police, who might cast blame elsewhere. In the post-
sixties apocalypse that was California and America, almost any horror and
radicalization seemed possible. A killer dubbed the Zodiac for the symbols
he used to sign letters taunting authorities about their inability to catch
him remained at large after years of murders in the Bay Area. And there was
the Symbionese Liberation Army, revolutionaries using an ancient image
of a seven-headed cobra as their oriflamme, who had assassinated Oakland
school superintendent Marcus Foster and kidnapped newspaper heiress
Patty Hearst. Now the men in the van had added to the malaise that seemed
to hang over Northern California like an endless mist. Like the other zealots
of their time, they considered their acts deeply righteous, sanctioned, in
their hearts, by who they believed to be God.

A few minutes after the killings, the men arrived at Harris's apartment in Hunter's Point, a San Francisco ghetto. Harris's girlfriend, a heavy
woman in long, flowing robes, a scarf wrapped around her skull, heard his
approaching footfalls and met him at the door.

His pink shirt was blood soaked.

"Where have you been?" she asked as he pushed past her.

"Out killing devils," he replied.

A business called Black Self-Help Moving and Storage, which occupied a large storefront on San Francisco's upper Market Street, soon became the killers' base of operations. Its proprietor, Thomas 2X Manney, a member of Mosque 26, employed other Muslims, especially those fresh from prison who couldn't find work elsewhere. Manney had a fleet of orange and black moving trucks and also collected and sold furniture, his window displays full of dressers, lamps, knickknacks. Some of those who worked there lived upstairs in a loft.

Manney employed Green, Harris, and two other San Quentin parolees, J. C. Simon and Manuel Moore. Jesse Cooks hung around there a lot as well.

Forty-one years had passed since Robert Harris stabbed James Smith to death in Detroit, after following instructions in "The Secret Rituals of the Lost-Found Nation of Islam." The old teachings about killing nonbelievers and devils had not vanished. Neither, of course, had the vast atrocities committed against African Americans: dogs, water cannons, bombs, and guns used in attempts to deny some of them even the simple act of voting.

In San Francisco, a city where racial tolerance was still little more than illusionary, Green, Harris, Cooks, Moore, and Simon dedicated themselves to exacting revenge by killing whites, joining others as members of the secret sect of Black Muslim killers that Cooks had talked about in prison—the Death Angels.

Larry Green grew up in Berkeley. As a youngster, he'd dreamed of a sports career, but stints on two junior-college basketball teams exposed his middling athleticism. There would be no NBA stardom. The classroom didn't appeal to him, and Green, an articulate, well-mannered son of a University of California maintenance worker, drifted away, becoming increasingly radicalized and eventually joining the Black Muslims. Green kept a journal in which he wrote that his life's purpose was "to deliver the 17 million dead to the Lamb of God, the Honorable Elijah Muhammad." Elijah often put seventeen million as the number of Blacks the devils had enslaved, and Green apparently believed each should be avenged. Green wrote rhetorical questions in a style typical of Fard's teachings: "Why does Muhammad or any Muslim murder the devil? What is the duty of each Muslim in regard to four devils? What reward does a Muslim receive for presenting four devils at one time?" He answered in language nearly verbatim from Fard: "Because the devil is 100 percent wicked and will not keep and obey the laws of Islam. His ways and actions are like a snake of the grafted type. All Muslims will murder the devil because they know he is a snake and also if he be [*sic*] allowed to live he would sting someone else. Each Muslim is required to bring four devils, and by bringing and presenting four at one time his reward is a button to wear on the lapel of his coat. Also a [*sic*] free transportation to the Holy City, Mecca, to see Brother Mohammad."

Nation theologians would eventually try to explain that the rules were obvious metaphors. Murdering the devil means awakening the deaf and dumb so-called Negro. The duty of each Muslim is to drive the devil from the hearts of four nonbelievers, to revert them to their original religion. Black Muslims, like Baptists, fish for souls. Those who bring home converts earn rewards. The answers are not, Muslims say, literal commands to murder.

"Wallace D. (Fard) is making it very clear that when one speaks of the devil one is speaking of a state of mind, a behavior that is satanic. He had taught us that the divine mind of God can manifest itself in any people of any color," Nation minister Abdul Alim Shabazz claimed in 1975. But Green clung to the literal and had a particular penchant for slaughter. It was he who nearly decapitated Quita Hague.

Another of the San Francisco killers, J. C. Simon, carried Fard's writings with him wherever he went. Simon, who hailed from Louisiana, kept a binder of papers about bloodletting. "All Muslims will murder the devil because he is a snake," he wrote in what he would call "my symbolic literature which gives me support and moral strength in this world." He would eventually claim he was handed the papers directly by God.

Manuel Moore, another of the men, was one of fourteen children from a poor Southern California family, an illiterate ninth-grade dropout who proved susceptible to the same teachings.

By the end of 1973, Green, Harris, Simon, Moore, and Cook had killed six people in San Francisco and wounded several others, including a young political aide named Art Agnos, who would later serve as the city's mayor. The five men would become the best known of the Death Angels, their blood work in San Francisco dubbed the "Zebra murders." The name grew from the fact that police had set aside the last channel of their radio band, channel Z, or Zebra, for use by a task force investigating the killings. But the phrase almost immediately became known as a euphemism for Black-on-white slayings.

But there were other cells of Death Angels in California that were, and would remain, far less known, ones in Southern California, Sacramento, and Oakland, where its leaders included Yusuf Bey.

Bey, newly independent from the Nation of Islam, might not have committed any killings himself, but he was an enabler and protector of those who did. Your Black Muslim Bakery—like the moving company headquarters where the San Francisco killers were based—was a perfect place to plot slayings. Its autonomy allowed those involved to scheme without fear of being discovered by other Muslims and reported to Nation of Islam leaders in Chicago, who, in the early 1970s, would have quashed by any means plots that might have interfered with their sole concern of accumulating wealth. Yusuf Bey wanted to be rich too. But he also held tightly to Fard's teachings. If God said to kill, there was no other way.

A run of seemingly random murders in Oakland and Berkeley and other East Bay cities had begun in August 1970, starting with the shooting of a Berkeley motorcycle cop on a busy street. By the end of the year, six people were dead, shot with no explanation, wallets left on them, car keys and money in their pockets, showing that robbery wasn't a motive. Nine more people died the following year and one in 1972, a man hacked to death with a machete in Oakland. In 1973, thirteen attacks occurred in the East Bay, all but two of them in the fall and early winter, the same time the killings in San Francisco began. Most of the victims were shot in the back of the head with handguns late at night when they were alone on the streets. One man was shot through his living room window, another knifed to death.

The body of a woman with gruesome hack wounds very similar to Quita Hague's was found dumped in an industrial area not far from the Oakland Athletics' baseball stadium.

None of the East Bay killings—thirty in all—would ever be solved.

But as the murders and attacks in San Francisco surged in late 1973, those across the bay seemed unconnected, at least to the public. The gunmen there were careful and calculating, taking few risks. In San Francisco, there were witnesses, people describing clean-cut Black men, dispassionate as they fired at close range, then walking calmly away, sometimes getting into a dark car. In Oakland and Berkeley, the shooters picked quieter, lonelier spots; the police were far less likely to leak the few details they did obtain to reporters; and the *Tribune,* in its long-standing mold of reportage under the Knowlands, underplayed crime and was unprobing about it, printing only what the police wanted printed.

One hundred miles to the northeast of the Bay Area, in Sacramento, members of a Nation of Islam mosque also found literal meaning in Fard's teachings. Three of its members committed several shotgun attacks before being caught. One of their victims died, a man who had been recently discharged from the army after serving in Vietnam, shot though the window of his parents' home.

The Black Muslim triggerman, nineteen-year-old Russell Lang, was eventually arrested, convicted of murder, and sent to prison for more than thirty-five years. He told a panel of parole commissioners in 2006 that the overwhelming "need for acceptance" within the Nation of Islam drove him to kill. "I didn't have any personal animosity against whites as a race of people or as a group of people or anything. I was raised to accept people at face value until they showed themselves otherwise." His family had moved from New York City to Sacramento when he was a teenager; the transition was hard on him; he drifted to the streets, vulnerable, looking for something, what he didn't know. He thought he had found it in the Nation; the bond the Muslims offered overwhelmed him.

It "was that strong in me at that time. It was an incredibly stupid thing to do. I can't make any excuses for myself." He had "an incredibly gullible state of mind. I was a Black Muslim, believed white people were the devil,

incarnation of evil on earth. . . . I have sincere remorse for what I did." Lang
was eventually paroled. Another of the Sacramento killers, Larry Pratt, also
eventually expressed deep remorse to parole commissioners, telling them
that killings around the state were coordinated by Muslim elders. "It definitely was a racial crime. It was predicated on our racial beliefs. [Under] the
Nation of Islam, whites were considered our enemies. As a matter of fact the
word used was *devil.* This was constantly taught at the time. We had books
on it, little pamphlets. This is what I see now as part of the brainwashing
effect."

As 1973 ended, police had few leads about any of the killings in San Francisco, Oakland, and the other East Bay cities. They began to slowly form a hy-
pothesis that the slayings might be an initiation rite for some sort of cult, but
there was little evidence pointing directly at Black Muslims, including Yusuf
Bey and his followers, or the men at the San Francisco moving company. As
a new year dawned, though, much would be learned about the bloodshed.

On Friday, January 25, 1974, a van carrying four Black Muslims who
had been selling fish door-to-door crossed from South Berkeley into North
Oakland on Baker Street. NATION OF ISLAM was inscribed on the van's rear,
along with the words IMPORTED FISH. The four men inside had nearly sold
out for the day; the smocks they'd worn over their suits were piled in the
back now, little left in the crates but melting ice and a few loose scales. It
was a good enterprise, taking healthy food to the people in the name of
Elijah Muhammad. It was also a chance to work the neighborhoods, to cast
about for converts.

Just over the city line, lights flashed in the side mirrors. A Berkeley cop
had trailed them into Oakland. Herbert Tucker, the van driver, pulled over,
but the officer didn't move at first. Then two more police cars pulled up,
and then three officers fanned out from the vehicles and approached the
van. They were under secret orders from their department to "generate a
cause for arrest" when encountering Black Muslims. In other words, the officers were to provoke clean-cut, unarmed Black men who were acting lawfully into actions that would cause them to end up in custody. Police would
claim the order was issued because door-to-door peddlers had recently at-

tacked and robbed two elderly women. The cops had had few investigative leads and no other ideas except to use brute force against any Muslims they encountered, knowing that the Muslims were trained to fight back if physically provoked. The cops hoped that after being arrested one of them might admit to attacking the women.

One of the cops who approached the van, David Byron, had once been fired for beating and kicking a Black man. Though he got his job back through appeals, the facts were never in dispute. Motivation to "generate a cause" to arrest Black Muslims wasn't a problem.

Officer William Cooper walked to the van driver's window as Byron and the third cop, Jerry Bounds, covered him. Cooper ordered Tucker to show identification. Tucker balked, and the Muslims spilled from the van, demanding to know why they had been stopped. They didn't need much provocation before they resisted: three cops, loudly demanding they submit to searches, shoving them, telling them to get spread-eagle.

Cooper began wrestling with one of the Muslims, Larry 3X Crosby, who grabbed for Cooper's revolver and would later plead to a judge that he was defending his life. As they brawled, the cylinder of Cooper's revolver opened and the bullets spilled to the ground. When Crosby twisted the weapon away and tried to shoot Cooper, it dry fired. Crosby flipped the pistol around and beat Cooper with its butt, the blows sounding like someone hitting a watermelon with a hammer, Cooper's jaw shattering. Cooper collapsed; Crosby, still not realizing the gun lacked bullets, tried again to shoot Cooper. As he did, Officer Bounds broke free of the Muslim he was fighting and shot Crosby three times. Crosby would never walk again.

Civilian investigators would later cite too many "gaps and inconsistencies" in police accounts of the brawl to determine exactly what had happened as the police attempted to keep hidden their orders to antagonize the Muslims into a physical confrontation. The shooting bore strong similarities to events in Los Angeles twelve years earlier when police had killed Ronald X Stokes. The fish peddlers had been acting lawfully until police confronted and demeaned them. Like the Los Angeles Muslims, Crosby and the other men in the van were arrested for assaulting police officers, while no cops were charged with wrongdoing.

In San Francisco, Minister John Muhammad, who had replaced Minister Henry at Mosque 26, expressed outrage at Crosby's shooting, calling a mass meeting for the following Sunday. The fish peddlers had worked out of Mosque 26B in Oakland, but the Muslims—and all Black people—needed unity in the wake of the assault, Muhammad said. His call drew several thousand people. Anyone of color "should be tired of having their Black brothers shot down in the street," Muhammad bellowed. "They weren't carrying weapons. None of the members of the Nation of Islam even carry a penknife."

But there were Muslims who did carry and use weapons and for whom speeches meant little. After Muhammad's meeting, Larry Green, Anthony Harris, J. C. Simon, and Manuel Moore gathered to plan retribution for the shooting by the Berkeley cops. First they debated blowing up school buses. But what if there were Black kids aboard? What if Blacks were walking past? The discussion shifted. Could they use a high-powered rifle to shoot down a jet at San Francisco's airport? But the same arguments arose; Blacks could be on the plane. They finally decided that the best vengeance would be to simply to continue what they had been doing—killing devils wherever they were found.

The next day, Monday, January, 28, 1974, Simon and Moore drove to Oakland, where they met with other Muslims, presumably including Yusuf Bey. Bey was shrewder and smarter than the men across the bay, more cunning and stealthy. He knew how, as others exacted revenge for what the police had done to Crosby, to keep the blood off his own hands.

He likely convinced the group that the retribution murders should occur in San Francisco to lessen the appearance that they were directly related to what had happened in Oakland three days earlier. Simon and Moore drove back to San Francisco at dusk, getting a traffic ticket on the Bay Bridge on the way.

Over the next six hours, they, along with Green, shot six people, four of them fatally.

The first person killed was a woman awaiting a bus. A Black man ran from his car to help her, folding his jacket under her head as she bled out. "I didn't do anything. I didn't do anything," she cried.

Next was an old man walking home. Police radios blazed with reports of the second shooting. Television and radio stations broke into their programming with the news. Just as the city descended into chaos came the third killing—another man on the street.

Reports of more gunfire occurred every thirty minutes or so, blurring together. Detectives scurried from crime scene to crime scene, unable to keep up. The next person murdered was a mother washing her family's clothes at a Laundromat; then a woman was shot as she carried boxes into her new apartment. She survived. Witnesses described each shooter as a clean-cut Black male, who, without provocation, approached the victims, firing multiple times from a few feet away with an automatic pistol, then retreating to a waiting car.

The sixth victim was a hitchhiker who stood alongside a highway on-ramp extending his thumb at passing cars. It was after midnight, more than two hours since the last shooting. A dark-colored Cadillac, just like the one Simon and Moore had been driving earlier when they got the ticket on the bridge, roared up, then slowed. The hitchhiker thought it was a ride. Then a man reached out the passenger window, firing three times, little muzzle flashes licking at the night. The Cadillac sped off. The young man staggered away but somehow survived. Each bullet had passed through him and wasn't recovered. Neither were any shell casings. But an emergency room doctor said the wounds were consistent with a .32-caliber round. What made that shooting different from those committed earlier was its location—the East Bay, just blocks from Your Black Muslim Bakery's San Pablo Avenue compound. The on-ramp was on the most direct route between there and San Francisco. The kind of car, its direction, the time of shooting, and the apparent caliber of the weapon all strongly suggest that at least two of the men who had committed the five San Francisco shootings earlier that night had been in North Oakland, where two of them had also been earlier that afternoon. There was only one place where they could have been safe in that neighborhood: Yusuf Bey's headquarters.

The headline in the *San Francisco Chronicle* on January 29, 1974, blared, "Four More Street Killings—Toll Is 10 in Four Months." In Oakland, that afternoon's *Tribune,* its reporters uncharacteristically aggressive, furthered the story, reporting that police had admitted that five recent killings there were similar to those in San Francisco. The next day, newspapers reported that the FBI and police from across California had huddled secretly in Oakland three months earlier to compare similarities between unsolved murders and attacks around the state. Alameda County District Attorney Lowell Jensen confirmed that he had called that meeting but said little for attribution, other than that leads were being followed, detectives were working relentlessly, the typical police blather when evidence and leads are scant. Nothing was said publicly about the racial aspects of the East Bay killings other than that they seemed somwhow related to those in San Francisco. Privately, though, police leaked to reporters that as many as sixty-five unsolved murders all over California fit the same scenario and that they now believed that some sort of Black cult was responsible.

"The chilling account, pieced together by police from numerous interviews, indicated that the killing of a white was required for initiation into the inner-most circles of the Black sect," the *Chronicle* reported. "Police said the victims of the ritual slayings are always white, usually male and customarily attacked when they are alone on the street at night."

It seemed unmanageable, killers sweeping the region, panic becoming palpable. Police advised people to stay home at night or, if they had to go out, to travel in groups. Some who had ignored Black coworkers for years were suddenly smiling and asking them to walk them to their cars. San Francisco neighborhoods with vibrant nightlife, like North Beach and the Mission District, were deserted. Only Japanese tourists seemed oblivious to the terror.

Despite the panicked pace of the investigation, the Black cult theory developed slowly. In faraway Detroit, police reports and newspaper clippings about Robert Harris and Fard's pamphlet entitled "Secret Rituals," all shoved away in file drawers, might have provided direction. Reams of documents the FBI had compiled on Fard, Elijah Muhammad, Malcolm X, and others, and Black Muslim writings about devils and how they should be slain, could have helped. But detectives had no time to delve into history.

African Americans in the Bay Area reacted angrily when the theory of a Black cult was reported. It seemed, many of them said, like just one more racial slight. The *San Francisco Examiner,* the city's afternoon paper, sent a reporter and photographer to the Fillmore District to garner person-on-the-street reactions. Among the men they stopped was a tall, hurried twenty-four-year-old with a big Afro and a thick mustache. They asked his name: Chauncey Bailey, he answered.

The sidewalk interview took place not far from the *Sun Reporter*'s office, where he was a rising star, in love with the city and his role as a journalist. Bailey identified himself as a "writer for the *Sun Reporter*" and, when asked about the killings a few days earlier, expressed an opinion that would prove to be incredibly prescient: "In light of recent events in the East Bay, I would say they were sequential." He meant the shooting of Larry 3X Crosby in Oakland the previous week. Bailey not only suspected the San Francisco killings were in retribution for Crosby, he'd made an obvious link to Black Muslims as the San Francisco gunmen.

But when Bailey wrote an article for that week's *Sun Reporter* about Crosby with the headline "Charges of Police Harassment in Muslim Shooting Incident," he made no mention of a link to the January 28 killings. It was one thing to express his theory as opinion to the *Examiner.* It was another thing to print it under his name as fact. Still, Bailey was one of the few Black reporters covering the murder sprees, and his race gave him obvious advantages. He'd attended the Sunday rally at Mosque 26 after Crosby's shooting. Bailey was doing what he intended to do with his journalistic career—he was writing about the lives of urban Blacks, and the slayings had given him his first big story. They also put him in direct contact with Muslims, whose outward message of economic self-sufficiency and hard work appealed strongly to Bailey. He was his mother's son.

But there was much Bailey could not have known, such as Yusuf Bey's involvement in the East Bay killings and the visits of the San Francisco gunmen to Oakland that framed the January 28 murders. He would, though, remain well ahead of other reporters as the story unfolded.

———

The San Francisco killers didn't strike again until April 1, when they gunned down two Salvation Army cadets walking to a store, killing one. Then two teenagers were wounded and the eighteen-year-old heir of a wealthy Delaware family died from three bullets to his back.

The next morning, April 2, Mayor Joseph Alioto—a balding, boisterous Sicilian with long-rumored ties to La Cosa Nostra—frantically endorsed what police dubbed "Operation Zebra," a plan to interrogate without other cause anyone who fit the killers' general descriptions. Police would stop "a large number" of young Black men, Chief Donald Scott said. "We're not going to stop very young Blacks or big fat Blacks. We're not going to stop seven-foot Blacks or four-foot Blacks."

A federal judge ruled the profiling blatantly unconstitutional, but not before police had questioned 567 men, gotten no leads, and incurred the wrath of Black leaders. Bailey wrote the *Sun Reporter*'s lead story. It began:

By Chauncey Bailey

What many members of the Black Community called an ugly animal bred by homicide investigators and fueled by racial tension – Operation Zebra – reared its ugly head this week in the wake of assaults on whites.

It was last January 28 when four persons were murdered and a fifth wounded in the streets when the city found itself gripped with fear as police formed a cadre of 100 officers to work around the clock in its manhunt for "black, crazed killers."

In another story a week later, Bailey made an astonishing revelation about the attacks in the East Bay, reporting that a white man had been robbed and wounded by a well-attired Black man in Berkeley, also on April 1, the same night the killings resumed in San Francisco. Also that same night, a white liquor store owner in San Leandro, just south of Oakland, had also been robbed and wounded by a Black man in a suit, raising speculation of a relationship to the Zebra killings, Bailey wrote. He had also gained enough confidence in his facts to finally write that the Larry 3X Crosby shooting was a possible motive for the San Francisco killings in late January. It was provocative, news-breaking reportage, keeping Bailey ahead of other reporters. Then a few weeks later, the *Sun Reporter* carried an unbylined story about the shooting of an Oakland cabdriver by a Black Muslim named George Foreman, who was immediately arrested. A getaway car he had parked nearby was found to contain Black Muslim literature and notebooks like the ones the San Francisco killers carried.

Foreman was also charged with the Berkeley and San Leandro shootings about which Bailey had previously reported. With Foreman in custody, the Zebra-like attacks in the Oakland area stopped.

Foreman was not charged for any of the East Bay killings. If he was investigated for a connection to them, it was not made public. But a prosecutor wrote of him: "George Foreman is an extremely dangerous individual who should remain in prison for the rest of his life."* He shot the victims with a .32 revolver "only after they had handed him money, the robbery complete, his only purpose to kill. The victims said Foreman 'never said a word' during the robberies." Foreman was "cold, calculating and emotionless. Only Foreman knows how many other people he terrorized." Did he "shoot the victims because of religious-political beliefs as a Black Muslim?" the prosecutor asked rhetorically. The answer may have been in "a black suitcase containing [Foreman's] considerable Black Muslim literature, Nation of Islam books . . . and several notes and notebooks [about] Black Muslim" doctrines that were found in his car. It is unclear if authorities examined those papers with a critical eye for clues about unsolved East Bay murders.

If they had, might those papers have led them to Yusuf Bey and others involved?

Although he did not report it in detail, Bailey obviously knew that the phenomenon of the Zebra killings was not limited to the gunmen working out of Black Self-Help Moving in San Francisco. It was a larger, organized

---

* Foreman did not serve a life term for shooting the cabdriver. He was released several years later and knifed a woman to death and then stabbed himself with the same blade in a failed suicide attempt. He returned to prison.

effort that had begun years earlier. How else could Jesse Cooks have said in prison in early 1973 that he intended to join the Black Muslims' "Death Angels" when he got out?

Bailey had proven himself to be eerily prescient in his reportage about what would become of his own life more than three decades later. The story of a Black Muslim killer of devils in Oakland who was arrested only when he began robbing people—the apparent story of George Foreman—would one day be told by a son of Yusuf Bey. That son would become intent on replicating the bloodshed of the early 1970s and, like his father, would dispatch gunmen into the streets to do his bidding. Thirty-three years before he would be blown to pieces on a city sidewalk, it was as if Bailey had written the prologue to his own murder.

Bailey had built sources within the Muslims, and he understood that not all Blacks in suits were killers. Had he stayed in the Bay Area, he likely would have provided insightful coverage of both the Zebra trial and the region's Black Muslim movement, including the continuing rise of Yusuf Bey.

But Bailey planned to accomplish things in journalism. Shortly after the Zebra arrests broke, and despite how much he loved the *Sun Reporter,* he left it to attend a summer program for minority journalists at Columbia University. From there, he landed a job at the *Hartford Courant* in Connecticut, a stepping-stone to large metro papers. But his desire to write about Black Muslims would stay with him for decades, right up to the last morning of his life.

San Francisco Police finally made arrests for the Zebra killings in their city on May 1, 1974, after Anthony Harris—who insisted he had never personally murdered anyone but had witnessed the others kill—phoned detectives to claim a thirty-thousand-dollar reward. Mayor Alioto insisted on questioning Harris personally and arranged a grant of immunity in exchange for his testimony. Eventually, Green, Cooks, Simon, and Moore were convicted and sent to prison, where each remained more than thirty-five years later.

The day after the San Francisco arrests, the *Oakland Tribune* reported, without citing sources directly, more details about the thirty unsolved slayings in the East Bay dating back four years. A breathless front-page story reported that "the attacks . . . all seemed to come on their victims suddenly, wantonly, viciously and only because the victims happened to be in the right place to be attacked."

Yusuf Bey and the others responsible for those killings would never be held responsible for them, and the "Death Angels" would fade into history— for a while.

Yusuf Bey, well before he became widely known in Oakland, was already a monster, one very adept at keeping secrets.

13

A Boy in Seaside

*"When he told me that I was made for his use, made to obey
his command in every thing; that I was nothing but a slave,
whose will must and should surrender to his, never before
had my puny arm felt half so strong."*
—HARRIET JACOBS, *Incidents in the Life of a Slave Girl*

The little girl cut her pinky slicing carrots.

She dropped her paring knife. It was a baking day; she was making muffin batter, the ovens already hot, the kitchen a whirl of men and women. On a wall behind her was a photograph of the Honorable Elijah Muhammad smiling innocently in a bow tie and camel-hair blazer. Written in red on the wall next to the photo was a quote from Marcus Garvey: "Up you mighty nation, accomplish what you will!"

Jane was ten and would have been a fifth grader if Yusuf Bey, who controlled every aspect of her life, had let her go to school. But instead of school, instead of childhood, she labored in Bey's kitchen six or seven days a week, often from dawn until late into the night. She was a tiny thing, barely five feet tall, not yet weighing ninety pounds. Jane's sister, Nancy, a year younger, was also Yusuf Bey's chattel.

Like all his followers, Jane looked at Bey with awestruck fear and perceived divinity within him. He preached self-determination and independence, bellowing in sermons that African Americans needed to wake up and think for themselves. Yet inside his compound he controlled every bit of his followers' lives. It was as if he meted out the air they breathed.

Bey looked at Jane too. He'd been waiting; he just needed to get her alone.

She held her bloody pinky in her other hand and weaved through the maze of work tables and fifty-pound sacks of flour until she found him. He had a mustache as thin as a pen line and wore a dark baseball cap, a red apron wrapped over kitchen whites.

"Brother Bey, Brother Bey, my finger's bleeding," she said.

He pressed a napkin into her hand and told her to squeeze it. He could be so kind, so gentle. "Come with me, sister," he said softly. "The Band-Aids are upstairs." Bey kept a bedroom on the second floor. Jane knew she shouldn't be alone with him. Even at ten, she'd heard the rumors. They all had.

He shut the door and got behind her to affix the Band-Aid, his arms reaching over her shoulders, pulling her closer. Jane tensed. So the stories about him were true. He did things to girls. Bey began grinding against her. "It's OK, it's OK," he whispered. "I'm not going to hurt you." It went on and on, Bey rubbing himself against her clothed body. When he'd finished, he said: "This is our secret, yours and mine. Don't mention this to anyone." He promised to buy her new sneakers for being good and sent her back downstairs to make his muffins, her finger neatly bandaged, her life never to be the same.

What Jane didn't know when Bey molested her that day is that he had already begun the same kind of abuse with her sister, Nancy. The girls' father, Vincent, had tried for years to shake a drug habit and had turned to Bey for employment and spiritual guidance. But by doing so he had unwittingly exposed his daughters to a demon. When Nancy was eight, she and her father attended one of Bey's Sunday sermons, the minister resplendent in a tailor-made suit and matching kufi as his screed about devils exceeded an hour, an image of W. D. Fard, his head bowed solemnly, directly behind him. Afterward, Bey approached Nancy. One of the bakery women had recently had a baby girl. Would she like to stay and see the infant?

Later, Bey went to the apartment where the baby's mother and two other women lived. All three considered themselves his wives simply because he told them they were. Bey took Nancy to the laundry in the apartment's rear, picked her up, and rubbed against her for a long time. When it ended, he said, "You better not tell anyone. No one will believe you."

Despite Bey's rhetoric and the rigor of the work life he provided, Vincent continued to use drugs and struggled to support his children. Their mother wasn't around, and Vincent finally asked Bey to take his daughters in while he tried to straighten out his life, saying he wanted them to be molded into proper Black Muslims and receive "a good moral upbringing." Bey agreed, provided that Vincent would surrender his parental rights so Bey could receive government assistance for the girls' care. Bey certainly wasn't going to pay out of his own pocket to feed and clothe Vincent's kids, even as he propped up the myth that the bakery's main purpose was to help the downtrodden.

Bey ordered a woman named Alice to go to court and seek appointment as the children's legal guardian. She was twenty-three years old and also called herself his wife. A few years earlier, she had borne his daughter. He had taken the baby away from her and given it to another woman who had recently miscarried twins. Bey wanted that other woman as a plural wife and thought the gift of a baby would make her submit to him. The pain this caused Alice was unbearable. She tried to block out the memory of giving birth. He told her she could have other children, that giving up one was a simple sacrifice for him.

A family court judge approved Alice's application for guardianship of Nancy, Jane, and their younger brother, Timothy, without objection on February 22, 1979. Alameda County issued her about $1,500 a month for the children's care. She dutifully gave the money over to Bey, just as all the other women in the compound did with their government assistance, asking no questions about where it went. Legal guardianship was a well-calculated move. It gave Alice and, thus, Bey, far more control than if she had merely become the children's foster parent. And it paid more per child. For all legal intents and purposes, Alice was their mother. That limited social workers' power to only verifying aid eligibility, not evaluating Alice as a caregiver. It also made Yusuf Bey their de facto father.

———

Yusuf Bey's desire for money and power had driven his separation from the Nation—he wanted wealth and to control his own followers. But it could be argued that he admired Elijah Muhammad so much that he wanted to emulate him in every way, including absolute authority over his domain. Bey didn't want to worship the Messenger as much as he wanted to build his own small version of the Nation, in Muhammad's image, within Oakland. But Bey also had other reasons for wanting his own Black Muslim sect.

Like Elijah Muhammad, Bey couldn't control his lust for young women and girls.

For years, beginning as early as the mid-1950s, Elijah had been ordering teenage secretaries at the Nation's Chicago headquarters to submit to him, telling them it was the will of Allah that they accept his holy seed. Just as the Moorish leader Noble Drew Ali had used his claims of divinity to bed young girls, Elijah claimed his status as the Messenger of Allah entitled him to the virginity of his teenage followers. It was rank hypocrisy—a Black Muslim's harshest sin—for a man who preached fidelity and family. In all, six girls bore Elijah nine out-of-wedlock children by the mid-1960s. Several of the girls were subjected to secret Muslim trials on charges of promiscuousness and ostracized from the Nation. Some of them demanded money for child support, threatening to publicly expose Elijah's paternity. As his inner circle dealt with the crisis, Elijah even suggested that a particularly demanding and aggressive young woman might have to be "put down," as if she were a bothersome dog.

The lesson for Bey in Elijah's scandal was not that he couldn't satisfy the similar desires he kept hidden within him but that to do so he would have to insulate himself deeply, build literal walls around him and his people, and become ruthless and violent in his control over them, especially females. Bey had also seen some Muslims in the sixties attempt to engage in plural marriage, drawing conveniently from aspects of traditional Islam practiced in other parts of the world. Even Elijah kept a woman—in addition to the young secretaries—so close to him that she was considered his "second wife" by his holy decree. When the scandal with the teenagers finally broke, Elijah tried to soften its impact by claiming he was spiritually married to them.

Bey loved and imitated Elijah, and he never hid his desire to emulate the Messenger in all ways, including by practicing plural marriage. Bey also intended to copy another of the Nation's secrets: its reliance, late in Elijah's life, on criminal enterprises to add to the royal family's wealth. The FBI suspected the Nation of involvement in credit card fraud, auto theft, and other scams in the early and mid-1970s. The Nation financed, among other things, the private jet that whisked Elijah between Chicago and his desert retreat in Phoenix. Bey had no aversion to such crimes, beginning with his insurance fraud with the torched Cadillacs in Santa Barbara.

Still, even as a Black Muslim separatist, Bey had to remain careful not to embarrass Elijah. But then Elijah was gone and everything changed. The Messenger of Allah died on February 25, 1975, at seventy-seven. Elijah's son, Wallace Muhammad, took control of the Nation and quickly began to move it away from his father's dogma, dismissing the teachings that Fard was God and that whites were devils and the creationist myths about Big-Headed Yakub. Wallace's immediate moderations moved the Nation quickly toward unification with Orthodox Muslims.

As this happened, Bey fully seized his autonomy. He was a hard-line adherent to the very tenets that Wallace Muhammad now dismissed. With the Nation spinning away from those teachings, Bey had to answer to no one. With Elijah dead, he was free.

Bey began to tell more female followers that, by his decree, they were his wives and must learn to submit themselves completely to him. He also began openly molesting—and was soon raping—girls such as Jane and Nancy.

But there was one other related secret to which Bey continued to cling. His father, Theron Stephens, who had taken a Muslim name and become a revered figure among his son's followers, was also a child rapist. Theron had been charged when he was sixty years old in 1963 with statutory rape when it was revealed he'd had sex hundreds of times with fourteen-year-old twin sisters, sometimes in Oakland parks in the middle of the day. He received a light sentence, with no jail time. Theron's history raises provocative questions about the roots of Bey's own sexual abuses. Was he a victim of his own father? A man who rapes, beats, and humiliates children is very likely to have suffered severe abuses himself. When that man's father is a known abuser of children, the likelihood becomes even higher.

All of Bey's tender pretenses quickly vanished after Jane and Nancy's father agreed that he could raise them. Bey told Jane she was old enough to learn how to submit and please a man. He started raping her before her first period. He would leave her face bruised and swollen from his fists. Her whole body shook from the threats that he would kill her and her family and dump their bodies in the bay if she told anyone. He threatened that if she didn't submit, he'd take her to San Francisco and pimp her; that the johns there would do worse things to her than he did, if that was somehow possible. He broke her will through heinous, subhuman acts—forcing her to swallow his feces, urinating in her mouth and then smothering her with his hands, forcing her to swallow as she gagged and thrashed. He would sodomize her and then force her to perform oral sex on him.

Jane and Nancy, whom Bey also continuously abused, got no protection from Alice—though she was their legal guardian, charged with keeping them safe. Rather, Alice was Bey's enabler, even prepping the girls for him, bathing them, powdering them, fixing their hair. He would take them into a bedroom as she stood there, watching the door close.

Once, Nancy courageously confronted Alice. How she could allow this man in his forties—this supposedly pious minister who went on cable television every week preaching upright behavior—to rape and violate her, telling her to submit, slapping her face, peeing on her.

"He doesn't do anything to you he doesn't do to the rest of us," Alice replied, telling Nancy that all of Bey's so-called wives feared he would kill anyone who failed to submit to him.

Like any predator, Bey hunted the most vulnerable prey, not that it was hard for him to find those he wanted. His regal bearing, the money from his bakery and other small businesses he owned, the appearance of order and discipline in his ranks, and his strength were deeply appealing, especially to women. Here was a Black man who talked proudly about being Black. He had money and fancy cars, and he dressed well, didn't drink, didn't smoke, didn't take drugs, didn't hang out on the corner. He gave folks jobs when no one else would. The Black Panthers might have been cooler, hipper, but Bobby Seale and Huey Newton had faded. Salvation was Bey's guise and, when that failed, avarice. He would rub his diamond rings and flick lint from his two-thousand-dollar lapels and order his Mercedes waxed daily. His expression and tone both seemed fixed in permanent smugness, his face never letting completely loose of his smirk, just as his words never seemed to completely lack sarcastic tinges. But all those years of coiffeur gossip in the Red Carpet salon had gilded his slickness. He honed his ability to seduce, becoming a champion raconteur. Proselytizing Fard's dogma, he cast all his charms into the allure of his mysterious Allah and claimed he and he alone was the cure for all misery.

He hid well his pedophilia and sadomasochism.

Though Bey didn't parrot much of Elijah's segregationist rhetoric, which demanded the government designate part of the country for Blacks only, he was an isolationist and a supremacist. The buildings around the bakery connected through a maze of hallways and common areas into a tight compound. He trained men to be his guardians, telling them that whites were physically and intellectually inferior. They drilled like soldiers and studied martial arts. The Nation of Islam called its paramilitary the Fruit of Islam, the best men the tree of life had to offer, and Bey built himself a similar army. A "Fruit call" resulted in soldiers showing up anywhere, at any time, ready for anything. There seemed to be little question they would die for him, and their unwavering loyalty further allowed him to do whatever he wanted with his female followers.

The jobs he offered women came with living quarters and food but with little or no money. He waited to strike until they were dependent upon him for nearly everything, until he'd cast a shroud tightly around their lives and they believed his spiels about devils and spaceships, until they ached for his kindness and feared his cruelness. They must know how to submit and please a man, he would say. "The woman is to obey," he bellowed in his sermons. "The woman is the floor that we walk on." The women, sometimes dozens of them in floor-length, shapeless white dresses, white scarves wrapping their heads, sat in folding chairs, segregated from the men, nodding affirmatively, their eyes not moving from him. When the cameras recording his sermons occasionally panned the crowd in the bakery's back room, some of the women looked, at times, as if they adored Bey. But mostly they lived with the deepest of fears. They knew what might happen to them if they muttered anything about what he did to them or the children.

His name was Brother Usman. He was six foot two, gangly, good-natured, friendly. Like all the other bakery men, he wore his hair close cropped like a marine. He had a small mustache and sometimes let the whiskers on his chin grow. He was an Oaklander, born to unwed parents, whose mother had sent him to live with relatives in Louisiana. She believed that there was something wrong with him, that he was, as she said, "slow." When he returned to Oakland as a young man, she sent him to the bakery for work and housing.

It wasn't so much that Usman suffered intellectual disabilities as that his mind seemed uncluttered. He liked work and did well enough. Whether or not he understood or believed them, he showed up for Bey's sermons regardless. Bey couldn't rely on him to be much of a soldier, but he could point him toward a pile of dirty pans and say, "Scrub," and he scrubbed until the pans shined. For seven years, Usman obeyed orders and lived around the corner in what everyone called "the brothers' house."

By the mid-1980s, Bey's followers tiptoed in terror around his open, horrible secret: He was a monster who would fuck anyone, often by brute force. Women, men, children, he seemed not to care. He obsessed about anal and oral sex. His conquests occurred daily. He was usually careful, but in June 1986 he forced a boy into a bathroom and didn't lock the door. Bey was in the midst of raping him when in walked Usman.

"Brother Bey! What are you doing?" Usman yelled, then ran. He lacked the sense not to talk about what he'd seen. Or, for that matter, to leave the bakery altogether, to run away; he knew nowhere else. He told people repeatedly about having seen Brother Bey in the bathroom with a boy. "I couldn't believe it. I couldn't believe what I seen with my own eyes," he blurted to the women.

Two nights later, an officer patrolling North Oakland found Usman sprawling from the passenger door of a Ford van on Marshall Street a few blocks from the bakery. He'd been shot in the head and chest at close range and died later that night on an operating table.

The van belonged to another bakery worker. Police publicly labeled the killer's motive as robbery but wouldn't say much else, even whether anyone else was in the van. No one at the bakery who had heard Usman babble about what he saw in the bathroom said a word. Rumors swirled that Bey had ordered his favorite son, fourteen-year-old Akbar, to achieve manhood by killing Usman to silence what Bey said were but vicious lies. Detectives knew where Usman lived and worked but found the bakery culture impenetrable. The murder remained unsolved, but everyone in the compound understood what it meant. To talk about Bey meant death.

Jane and Nancy's father sometimes drifted back into their lives as he struggled with his addictions. Separation didn't quell his love for his children. There was even brief talk that they might return to live with him—a sign, perhaps, that he was ignorant of the ramifications of his release of parental rights. During those occasional visits, he noticed the girls were withdrawn, angry, difficult to reach.

Vincent called a social worker and said he thought something was wrong with his daughters. He'd been around the bakery enough to have heard the rumors too. He reported nothing specific, just paternal instincts. The social worker called police, but a father's gut wasn't enough to base an investigation on, an officer told her. Get something solid. The social worker went to the compound and asked the children, in front of Alice, if they were being abused. *No,* they said. Did they wish to leave? *No,* they said.

Twenty-five years later, in court documents, the social worker declared: "The children appeared to be healthy and comfortable in the Bey home and appeared to have a loving relationship with [Alice] Bey. I could not determine and did not determine that the children were being molested." She did note that the children told her they were being made to work long shifts in the bakery. She wrote: "My supervisor responded that the county had no jurisdiction over the issue because the court appointed [Alice] as the children's guardian and [Alice] therefore had the right to determine how to raise the children." That Jane and Nancy and were too young to legally work in a commercial kitchen didn't arise. Neither did the fact that the children weren't attending school. When social workers visited to check on aid eligibility, Alice always had some papers to show off. The children said quietly that school was fine. But the school of which they spoke was Bey's school, a back room he dubbed the "Proper Learning Center," where students studied the teachings of Elijah and Fard. There is no record that social workers checked with the public schools to determine whether the children were enrolled. Bey's abuses continued unabated.

Nancy became pregnant first. She was thirteen. It was 1981, four years after her father left the children in Bey's care and two years after Alice became their legal guardian.

The news sent the bakery women into frenzy. What would they tell the social workers or doctors when they asked who the father was? What would Bey do to protect himself?

Then one of the women said, *A boy did it.*

Yes, a boy, another said.

The children's grandmother lived in Seaside, down the coast in Monterey County, and the women used that fact to concoct a cover story: Nancy had been allowed to visit her grandmother and had sex with a boy while there.

You better say a boy in Seaside did it, Alice told her. Say he was sixteen. *Bey will kill you otherwise. You and your baby.*

Nancy knew she had to lie to protect herself, to survive.

Since she wasn't in school, the pregnancy was relatively easy to hide from the outside world. Nancy gave birth ten days before her fourteenth birthday. No paternity was identified on the birth certificate. The secret, though, almost got out.

A woman who had been briefly involved with Bey in the early 1970s and had had a child by him knew the young sisters. She had been a Black Panther. Unlike many of the other women Bey pursued, she was tough, self-reliant. Once, when Bey punched her, she called the police. No charges were filed, but the fact that she'd stood up to Bey rattled him. She slipped away from the compound but remained in touch with some of the other women. When she learned that Nancy had delivered a baby, she knew damn well the father wasn't some boy in Seaside and called the child welfare department.

Nancy had never gotten along with Alice, and when she came home from the hospital she took her baby, moving across the compound to live with a woman named Tammy, who had been at the bakery since she was fourteen and eventually bore Bey eight children, including his favorite sons, Antar and Yusuf IV. One morning the phone rang, followed by pounding on Tammy's door. *The county's coming,* Alice yelled. Either the investigating social worker had called in advance or someone else—Tammy had sisters who worked in the welfare department—had called with an alert. Nancy grabbed her baby, and she and Alice rushed to Alice's apartment, which they quickly staged to appear as if Nancy still lived there.

"They are coming to question you," Alice said. "Brother Bey told me to let you know that if you say that's his baby, he's going to take very good care of you." Nancy knew exactly what that meant.

The social worker came in but had no intention of doing a thorough search for facts. He noted the omission of paternity on the baby's birth certificate and asked Nancy, as Alice sat near her, who the baby's father was. *A boy in Seaside,* Nancy replied, her eyes fixed on Alice's. She didn't know his name.

His inquiry complete, the man left.

He could have questioned Nancy alone. He could have questioned her sister, whom Bey was also raping regularly. But he didn't.

With the county's minimal investigation over, Alice soon became the legal guardian of Nancy's baby, a process that met with no objections. The amount of public assistance money she received monthly increased; Bey continued to take it from her.

When Nancy moved in with Tammy, it didn't stop Bey from raping her. But Tammy sometimes mustered the courage to confront Bey and try to protect the girls. One night, Bey had both Jane and Nancy alone. He forced one girl to stand in a closet while he raped the other, then made them trade places. Tammy pounded on his bedroom door, yelling at him to let them go.

Bey threw open the door. As the girls ran out, he pulled Tammy inside and beat her bloody. Jane and Nancy huddled in the hall, terrified, the sound of Bey's fists reverberating though them as if they were absorbing the blows themselves. "None of your fucking business," Bey yelled again and again. "None of your fucking business."

Another time, Tammy objected to something Bey said to children at the Proper Learning Center. His punch sent her to the floor. As she tried to get up, he pulled his belt from his pants and, as a dozen children watched, whipped Tammy viciously as she cowered at his feet.

Nancy had her second baby by Bey less than two years later. She was fifteen. Her third came at eighteen. Jane bore her first child by Bey at sixteen, then another at twenty-one.

All around the compound during the 1980s, women were bearing Bey's children at an astonishing rate: Tammy, eight; Alice, four; a sister of Alice's, three; another woman, six; yet another, three. The best estimate on the number of Bey's offspring is forty-two, although the actual number is likely higher. Some in the family, though, have insisted Bey fathered fewer children, although they still didn't deny his prodigious paternity. "Daddy didn't do half of what they said he did. . . . Maybe there was twenty or twenty-five," Yusuf Bey IV said years after his father's death.

In his sermons Bey often demanded slavery reparations, an issue on which he wasn't alone but one he took up well before the topic gained moderate momentum in the 2000s. Yet he was nothing more than a modern-day slave master. Jane and Nancy stood for so many hours on the concrete baking floor that they developed varicose veins before they turned twenty.

"Slaves, we were just slaves," Nancy said in 2005 when asked to describe her childhood.

But there was Bey on television every week railing about slavery. "Ninety-nine percent of black folks would forgive Caucasians for slavery and don't want reparations. The Negro don't want no repay because he thinks he was supposed to be a slave," he said one week, parroting a standard Nation of Islam line from the 1960s. "Why is it Israel, the Jews, got a country? Some of the people getting reparations in Israel never been in the ovens of Germany." When he sarcastically imitated Christian ministers who suggested their congregations reject the reparations movement, Bey would rise up and lean over his rostrum, tilting his head back and grinning like Stepin Fetchit, the actor who portrayed African Americans as simple, smiling fools. "You can't put no price on slavery," Bey mocked the ministers as saying.

Yusuf Bey, though, put a price on everything, slavery included. He wouldn't wait for government reparations; he would take money by bleeding the public beast for as much as he could get. He continued to order his women to omit his paternity on their children's birth certificates. Since he wasn't legally married to any of them, they were, to the state, unwed mothers eligible for aid. They made up identities of fathers for social-worker visits and sometimes joked they couldn't keep the names straight. "Mr. Bey gave me instructions," Alice later testified. "All the women, the wives . . . didn't put his name on the birth certificates."

"Did these women receive aid?" a lawyer asked.

"Every last one of them," Alice replied.

"Did their checks go to Mr. Bey?"

"Yes, they did."

Jane and Nancy proved especially lucrative. Not only did the county pay money for their care as minor children, it paid for their children's care. Bey soon cooked up another way to siphon more money: Several women applied for Section 8 housing aid to live with children Bey fathered in apartments that he owned. At the height of his schemes in the 1980s and 1990s, he raked in tens of thousands of dollars in monthly government money.

After more than a decade of abuse, Jane and Nancy struggled to find ways out of the horrors. Nancy, especially, asked for help from other women within the cult. She went to Farieda Bey—Yusuf Bey's legal wife—and asked her how she could stand to have a husband who bedded so many other women. "It is the will of Allah," Farieda replied.

Nancy turned to Bey's mother, a feeble though revered woman who treated her son as if he were God. One day Nancy broke down, pouring out stories of the abuses—rape, sodomy, worse things. The old woman called her a liar. That night Bey beat Nancy brutally. She stayed shut in her room with her children for days until the bruises and swelling subsided.

Shaken but undaunted, she continued trying to find someone to make the abuses stop, going to other bakery women asking for help. Finally, one of the older women screamed at her, revealing her and Jane's deepest secret, one that immediately ostracized them among the Black Muslims: Their mother was white. "You're half devil. You're a liar." From then on, whenever Nancy tried to talk about the abuses, the women said they didn't believe her because she was a half-breed, a retard, a freak whose parents had given her away because she was no good.

Once a year the county sent someone to check that the girls and Alice remained eligible for benefits. Nancy, despite the beatings she received for seeking help, had slowly grown more emboldened as she approached sixteen. She mentioned in front of a social worker that she was thinking about calling police and reporting that she was forced to work in the bakery without pay. Alice—there as Nancy's guardian—reeled. But the social worker seemed unconcerned. She looked through Nancy to Alice and said, "I have foster kids. If they called the police on me I'd beat their asses."

More than fifteen years later, Nancy was asked why she didn't run away.

"People who was there, grown people, was letting all this stuff happen. All of them that lived there was letting him molest their kids. He messed with his grandson. He molested his daughter. I am not going to put my life in jeopardy and my family's life in jeopardy over something that the authorities couldn't even do something about. Put yourself in my shoes. All you know is this is a man who had people killed," she answered.

It had been two decades since that "man who had people killed" had returned to Oakland from Santa Barbara. Yusuf Bey had achieved the power and wealth of which he'd dreamed. His involvement with the Death Angels years earlier remained a buried secret. His bakery had made him millions, much of it thanks to ruthlessness and illegality. He'd committed systemic public-assistance fraud. He commanded an army of loyalists ready to commit violence at his command; he went on television every week in an endless screed about the devils and slave masters. He had dozens of young children who bore his name, sons in assent. He beat and abused women with impunity. But from the outside, his separatist Black Muslim ministry appeared to be a thriving success. Even Christian ministers joined local politicians in paying Bey a grudging respect for getting people off the streets and seeming to turn their lives around. And unlike Elijah Muhammad, Bey had managed, thus far, to conceal his true nature from the outside world. As he reached middle age, it seemed as if there was little he couldn't accomplish.

14

Totally Ludicrous

*"Have you forgotten that once we were brought here, we were
robbed of our name, robbed of our language? We lost our
religion, our culture, our god . . . and many of us, by the way
we act, we even lost our minds."*
—KHALID ABDUL MUHAMMAD, former Nation of Islam spokesman

In the years that he had entrenched his Black Muslim splinter sect and built
his Oakland empire, Bey had avoided politics. Even at the height of the
civil-rights movement, Elijah had always turned his followers inward, away
from the inevitable inclusion that would come with political involvement.
But Elijah's death freed Bey from any of the constraints that, even from afar,
the Nation could impose on him. What's more, Bey remained motivated by
both his bottomless ego and greed, and he sought to enhance the outward
image that masked him deeply. There was no better way to publicly insist
that he was simply a tough, pious leader than to officially enter the city's
leadership.

On February 15, 1994, Yusuf Ali Bey declared himself a candidate for
mayor of Oakland.

He would challenge the one-term incumbent, a former state assembly-
man and wily lawyer, Elihu Harris. Harris was Oakland's second consecutive African American mayor, following the 1982 election of Lionel Wilson,
a superior court judge, in what was, finally, a radical departure from the
Knowland oligarchy. While Bey called both men out as "house niggers"

because they were creations of Oakland's new political establishment, he grudgingly held respect for each, if for no other reason than that they were African American men who had won election.

At first, Bey treated his candidacy, at least outwardly, as a chance to garner more attention for his businesses. "If people want change it is obviously they will vote for me. If whites fear my candidacy, it is only because I am going to make a difference," he said. "Even if I lose, the winner is going to have to use a lot of points of my program. So how can I lose?" In the well-honored tradition of first-time candidates, Bey insisted he wasn't a politician but a businessman with the acumen to change a long-suffering city. His constituency was "the bottom rung," people on the street living through the crack epidemic, committing crimes, the forgotten, he said. A white candidate who declared her candidacy the same day spoke of Oakland's need for "a reasonable and clear open space policy . . . a holistic view of the city." The fissures between the hills and the flatlands were never more apparent.

Inwardly, Bey wanted badly to win. He had to imagine that if he was elected, city government would lie before him like piles of war spoils. But it was a crowded field, and achieving victory would be a challenge; he was one of eight people in the June open primary trying to force Harris into a fall runoff.

As his followers handed out flyers across the ghettos, Bey sought to distinguish himself. The mere presence of a Black Muslim in the race drew media attention, although few reporters seemed to understand exactly who Bey was or what he believed. He was often misidentified in newspaper articles—including in the *Oakland Tribune,* whose local staff should have known better given it covered Oakland—as a Nation of Islam leader, even though his direct affiliation with the Nation had long ceased.

There was no doubt that Bey forced his opponents to pay more attention to the city's poorest neighborhoods than they would have liked. He proved to be an able campaigner on his chief issues, economic self-sufficiency and police abuses. "We don't even have one Black-owned supermarket in Oakland. That's a crime," he said. "Blacks working for white-owned businesses are modern day slaves. A slave was brought here for one thing. To get a job, go to work, pick that cotton."

Police were a favorite target. He criticized officers for not living in the city where they worked—a legitimate complaint of many urban mayors—and for acting like an occupying army. "They have no concern for us," he said, as if their job was to "go down to the zoo and work eight hours. They are out of touch. They are not serving us any longer. They're slave masters and overseers."

Even though Bey was rich, he ran—unlike the other candidates—as if he weren't, speaking to ghetto dwellers like he was as poor as they were. It resonated. "If you're not in the soup you don't know what it tastes like," one supporter said.

As the campaign spotlight brightened, Bey was confident his secrets were secure. That was never more apparent than when he said that while Oakland was rife with teenage pregnancy, there was no such problem among his followers, that he was the candidate best able to institute social programs to confront the issue.

At one point during the campaign, a reporter asked him how many children he had.

"Quite a few," Bey replied. Pressed, he wouldn't give a number and hurried on to another question.

But although he tried, Bey could not hide the basic thuggery at his core or in those closest to him. Shortly after he announced his candidacy, two men he considered his spiritually adopted sons and members of his inner circle, Nadar Bey and Abaz Bey, asked for a meeting with a Nigerian immigrant they thought had cheated a friend in a real-estate deal. The Nigerian arrived at an apartment, where Nadar, Abaz, and three other Bey soldiers trapped him. They beat and kicked the man, he later testified. Nadar hit him repeatedly with a flashlight. Abaz Bey heated a butter knife on the stove until it glowed red and branded the man's arms and hands. When he screamed, they shoved a towel into his mouth and demanded that he pay them thirty thousand dollars, which he didn't have. They forced a pistol past his lips and threatened to fire; they pushed his head into a toilet. They dragged him outside and threw him in the trunk of his car. When they let him out, he saw a police car and ran. As more officers arrived, so did about thirty heavily armed men from the bakery. One Muslim yelled he would gladly martyr himself if it meant killing police. Eventually, though, the outnumbered Beys backed down and cautious police let them disperse.

Nadar and Abaz were charged with several felonies that they eventually plea-bargained down to misdemeanors. A judge sentenced each to home detention. At the time they tortured the Nigerian, both men were Bey's representatives on Oakland's anticrime commission, spots he had been asked to fill as acknowledgment of his civic activism. Yet the obvious hypocrisy drifted away and didn't become a campaign issue, and Bey scoffed when asked if the charges would hurt his candidacy. But he did complain about posting bail. "This is money that could be used in the community. Instead, it's going to a court system. That's totally ludicrous."

Bey needed a way to garner more attention for his campaign than what he got from his underlings' arrests. He found it in an old friend, Khalid Abdul Muhammad, whom Louis Farrakhan had recently relieved as the Nation of Islam's national spokesman following an infamous speech railing against Jews at New Jersey's Kean College in late 1993.

For a sulfurous Black Muslim to attack Jews and devils was certainly not new. Elijah had done it. Malcolm had done it as the Nation's public face. But times had changed, memories grown hazy. In 1975, Elijah's son Wallace had become W. Deen Mohammed and changed the name Nation of Islam to the World Community of Al-Islam in the West, a movement in which tens of thousands of African Americans had become Sunni Muslims, practicing in multicultural traditions. Mohammed even destroyed the Nation's historical archives out of embarrassment about his father's belief that Fard was God.

Although Louis Farrakhan had in 1980 rekindled the fable-based Islam that Bey had never abandoned, reconstituting the name "The Nation of Islam" under his control, the organization had done little to promote itself.

But in November 1993, students at Kean, a liberal-arts school in Union County, paid Khalid Muhammad to speak on "The Secret Relationship Between Blacks and Jews." He was asked to discuss their histories as oppressed people and Jewish support of the civil-rights movement. But Muhammad had other things to say.

Jews "went in there to Germany, the way they do everywhere they go, and they supplanted, they usurped, they turned around, and a German in his own country would almost have to go to a Jew to get money," Muhammad said. He pointed east, toward what he called "Jew York City" and "Columbia Jew-niversity." The names "Rubenstein," "Goldstein," and "Silverstein" derived from the fact that generations of Jews had been "stealing rubies and gold and silver all over the earth. We can't even· wear a ring or a bracelet or a necklace without calling it Jew-elry," he said.

Muhammad soon changed the subject to what he hoped Blacks in South Africa would do to whites: "Kill the women . . . kill the children . . . kill the babies . . . kill the blind . . . kill the crippled . . . kill the faggot . . . kill the lesbian . . . kill them all. When you get through killing them all, go to the goddamn graveyard and dig up the grave and kill them a-goddamn-gain because they didn't die hard enough." He also called Pope John Paul II a "no good motherfucking cracker. Somebody need [*sic*] to raise that dress up and see what's really under there."

In the uproar that followed, Farrakhan at first refused to reprimand Muhammad, claiming Jews were plotting against them both. Under enormous pressure, though, Farrakhan soon removed Muhammad as spokesman, saying he took issue with "the form, not the truth" of Muhammad's remarks, whatever that meant. When both the U.S. House and the U.S. Senate formally condemned him, Muhammad accepted the votes as if they were gold medals.

Although he was relatively unknown prior to the Kean speech, afterward Muhammad claimed that he was overwhelmed with invitations to speak around the country, mostly on college campuses and at Black Muslim gatherings.

"The white man is a no-good bastard. He's not *a* devil, the white man is *the* devil. . . . If you say you're white, god-damn-it, I'm against you. If you're a Jew, I'm against you. Whatever the hell you want to call yourself, I'm against you," he said in one such speech.

The tumult was slow to fade, and as Yusuf Bey sought to increase the profile of his mayoral campaign, he booked Muhammad for a rally on Friday, May 13, 1994. In doing so, Bey demonstrated an overarching lack of political skill. Could he possibly have thought that Muhammad might so ignite Oakland's Blacks that they would propel him to victory? Or did Bey know he had no chance and cynically brought in Muhammad to spread hate and increase his exposure to people prone to his manipulations?

Bey's limited worldview certainly makes both scenarios possible. Any sound political counsel he could have received would have insisted he avoid Muhammad, but he surrounded himself only with like-minded subordinates. By the mid-1990s, Oakland was becoming one of America's most diverse cities, one with little collective tolerance for extremism of any stripe. While Bey thrived behind his brick walls, his flock never exceeded a few hundred people. He either simply had no idea how people beyond his ignorant minions would react to Muhammad or just didn't care.

Given Muhammad's New Jersey speech, his appearance in the midst of the election was certainly newsworthy, and among those journalists assigned to it was the *Oakland Tribune*'s new African American affairs reporter, Chauncey Bailey. Bailey had been back in the Bay Area for a year after a long stint at the *Detroit News,* where he eventually ended up after leaving the *San Francisco Sun Reporter* for Columbia and then Hartford. When he first returned, he had worked as the news director of a radio station owned by two African American politicians: state assembly speaker Willie Brown of San Francisco and the very man Yusuf Bey was trying to unseat, Oakland mayor Elihu Harris. Bailey also went back to work for the *Sun Reporter,* writing freelance pieces. Within a year he was hired by the *Tribune,* returning to full-time newspaper work in the city of his birth. Bey's campaign also put Bailey back where he had been twenty years earlier for the *Sun Reporter:* writing about Bay Area Black Muslims. Bailey apparently saw no conflict of interest in covering a race involving his former employer, Harris, or if he did, he and his *Tribune* editors chose to ignore it.

On May 13, as Bailey joined other journalists crowding into an Oakland theater with 1,750 people to hear Muhammad speak, he couldn't have known, of course, that writing about Bey and his legacy would be a consistent part of his work for the next thirteen years.

Attendees contributed ten dollars each to Bey's campaign to attend

Muhammad's speech, applauding as he took the stage. He began by mocking the movie *Schindler's List* as "Swindler's List."* "Our babies are used to seeing people get shot in the street every day. . . . Let's kill some white folks in a movie for a change. We got to see some white folks die somewhere. . . . There is a little bit of Hitler in all white folks. . . . You Jews make me sick, always talking about the Holocaust. . . . You say you lost six million? We lost over six hundred million. Our holocaust was 100 times worse. The Jews want a special corner for catching hell." He went on like that for more than two hours.

"You don't need a mayor who will sell you out, cut a deal under the table. There is no sugar in Bey. . . . Vote for one of Elijah Muhammad's men," he bellowed at the end.

Bey then tried to match Muhammad's rhetoric. He knew a group of rabbis and ministers were holding a prayer service nearby in protest and spoke as if he were addressing them directly.

"Mr. Rabbi, when you challenge us, you're the oppressor," he said. "Those rich guys are really something—picking on a poor ex-slave. The white rabbi says I teach hate. Nelson Mandela has forgiven whites in South Africa, but Jews haven't forgiven Germany. Why are they still looking for war criminals? . . . The Jews paid for the ships that came to get us in Africa, Jews were in the Confederate army to preserve slavery. I don't hate them. They aren't worthy of being hated."

Bey then went after gays or, in his word, "faggots." "In the Middle East, when you get a man jumping on another man's back, they take their heads off," he said. His campaign promises included ridding public schools of gay teachers and banning same-sex couples from adopting.

Other candidates and civic and religious leaders immediately condemned both speeches. Bey defended Muhammad's words, somehow describing them as "positive and very informative." But unequivocally, his campaign was over.

---

*A few weeks earlier, a group of African American high school students in Oakland had been kicked out of a theater when some of them laughed at a scene in *Schindler's List* where a Nazi shot a woman in the head.

The damage went beyond a failed political bid. Droves of retailers dropped his baked goods from their shelves. Even several churches that bought his discounted, day-old leftovers for distribution to the poor shunned him. In San Francisco, gay activists led a largely successful campaign to rid the city of Bey's wares.

Bailey and the other journalists covering the race were swamped with follow-up stories, but the most troubling facts went largely unanalyzed. The large crowd at the rally had often cheered loudly as hundreds of others milled about outside. Conditions in Oakland's ghetto still made the destitute ripe for exploitation by demagogues.

That he finished the election with less than 5 percent of the vote seemed not to bother Bey, at least outwardly.* "They live in glass houses," he said of his critics. "They think they're holier than thou. They're religious hypocrites and just as much part of the problem as gang bangers and dope dealers."

Both publicly and privately Bey did all he could to recover from his mayoral drubbing. He had businesses to run: the bakery, several stores that sold his food, a restaurant, a dry cleaner, and his latest endeavor: security companies. With the loss of customers in the backlash to Muhammad's speech, Bey needed ways to make up for lost revenue. For nice fees, he rented out his menacing henchmen. His muscle for hire became popular among apartment building and business owners looking to quiet rowdy tenants, scatter drug hawkers, or simply intimidate people. Bey's men delivered beatings to make a Pinkerton proud.

Bey wanted to involve his sons more in his businesses, even the young ones like Antar and Yusuf IV, whom he was raising to be strong men, ministers of the faith, just like him. He also had high hopes for Akbar, who was older and perhaps ready to join his father in business. But shortly after the campaign ended, Akbar was gone. On September 1, 1994, twenty-one-year-old Akbar Bey was gunned down at three thirty in the afternoon outside a theater in North Oakland. He had gotten into an argument "over nothing important," his father told a reporter that night, his voice a sad whisper. He

*Elihu Harris won a second term as Oakland mayor in November 1994.

was in tears. "It just brings a social problem home. This is what's happening to someone every day."

But the truth about the killing remained unspoken. Akbar used and sold drugs, trying to escape the horrors of his father. He was high on cocaine, morphine, and codeine when he got in an argument with a twenty-four-year-old man named Lavell Marce Stewart concerning $1,200 worth of marijuana that Stewart said was missing from his car. "One of you mother-fuckers knows what happened to my weed. We've been out here enjoying ourselves all day, and my shit didn't just come up missing like this," Stewart said. He accused Akbar of thievery, which Akbar denied. Stewart then pulled a .357 Bulldog revolver from his waistband and shot Akbar in the jaw, in the skull, and twice in the chest. He was arrested within an hour, convicted of murder, and sentenced to sixty years in prison.

A week later, a thousand mourners filled a borrowed Baptist church. Bey led a close-order drill team in tribute to his son but did not speak. A person who did eulogized Akbar as "a loving warrior. Our community is flooded by guns. This has to stop." Akbar's mother, who had managed to escape Bey and marry another man, said her son "loved the brothers in the street. In too many ways he was like his father."

Funeral rhetoric aside, Akbar was "a little street thug," a police lieutenant told the *East Bay Express,* the kind of criminal his father had publicly railed against on the campaign stump but privately nurtured at Your Black Muslim Bakery. Akbar's tattoos included "Night Stalker" on his left upper arm above a figure holding a sickle, "Gangsta" just below images of two Uzi subma-chine guns crossed at the barrel on his chest, and "Blackman" and "Break Yoself" surrounding a hooded figure on his left forearm. He also had "Akbar" inked on his chest, a pistol on his right upper arm, and several images of the Black Muslim crescent moon and star in various locations.

A few months earlier, Akbar had been charged with evading police and carrying a concealed weapon. He'd led cops on a high-speed chase through North Oakland in his green Chevy Nova, pitching a 9 mm handgun out his window as he raced along residential streets.

Police had also once encountered Akbar carrying multiple weapons and donning a bulletproof vest. He was far from an adherent to the codes of conduct his father promoted: no guns, no drugs, no street corners.

Yusuf Bey retreated from public view after Akbar's murder—but not for long. He had made connections in his campaign and he intended to use them. Despite his reprehensible comments as a candidate, Bey won government approvals to sell food at Oakland's airport and baseball stadium. Among those who helped him apply pressure to win those deals was a state senator named Don Perata, who would go on to become one of the most powerful people in California as senate president, a cigar-chomping buddy of Governor Arnold Schwarzenegger. Despite his disastrous campaign, some now saw Bey as a ghetto power broker. The few thousand people who voted for him for mayor were a small but vocal constituency that he controlled. He had become a player. And since he needed to do more than peddle tofu burgers to travelers and sports fans to make up for the loss of wholesale customers after the campaign, being a player helped him achieve a major score. After years of haggling, Bey and his followers browbeat a one-million-dollar loan out of the Oakland city council to fund a nonprofit home-health-care business dubbed Elijah Muhammad Health, or EM Health for short. Bey's point man was Nadar Bey, the nasty business of torturing the Nigerian behind him. Bey's business plan claimed EM Health would train welfare recipients (this was the era of Newt Gingrich and welfare reform) as home-health-care aides for the elderly. Medicare would pay for the service, seniors could live in their homes longer before going to nursing homes, and poor folks would get jobs.

That there were enough questions about the Beys for city officials to reject the plan on its face cannot be disputed. Any close examination would have revealed the thousands of dollars in public aid that poured into his compound monthly and where the money went. Nadar Bey had beaten and tortured a man. Yusuf Bey had brought Khalid Muhammad to Oakland and applauded his every word. The bakery even owed the city sixty thousand dollars in back taxes. But the Beys were thugs and people were scared. So scared they couldn't say no. Mayor Elihu Harris's administration gave Bey the money shortly after the council vote.

Not surprisingly, the borrowed money and the business vanished within a year. The Beys—particularly Nadar Bey, who carried the title of EM

Health's CEO—blamed the failure on the city, claiming it hadn't provided *enough* financing to successfully start the business. That Nadar had paid himself and his wife nearly six-figure salaries, given high pay and fees to other family members and ancillary Bey businesses for advertising, security, and consulting, paid himself consultant fees, and given the business short-term loans from his salary at double-digit interest rates was beside the point, Nadar insisted. The business had failed because the city shorted the start-up capital. EM Health folded. The loan was never repaid.

Although he had lost his mayoral bid, Yusuf Bey's entry into politics had paid him obvious dividends. He probably wouldn't have received public contracts and loans without trading on political stock. Bey remained unapologetic about the campaign. His detractors were just devils anyway. The negative publicity would have made lesser men wilt, but to Bey it symbolized his defiant, radical nature. They could write what they wanted about him in the newspapers. He had become a public figure. By running for office he had opened himself to scrutiny and, even after he embraced Khalid Muhammad, the worst about him wasn't even yet known.

15

An Instrument of Community Understanding

"Detroit turned out to be heaven,
but it also turned out to be hell."
—MARVIN GAYE

Chauncey Bailey must have had no idea how often his new assignment at the *Tribune* would have him writing about the Beys, or what those stories would entail. Even after the campaign, he liked going by the bakery, hanging out. It's what reporters did when they were still new on a beat. It was a place in North Oakland to make contacts. Sure, there were questions about Bey. Bailey would have seen—as others saw—the women in their head coverings, some pregnant, others bruised. He would have seen—as others saw—the children working, baking. But who else was asking probing questions? Your Black Muslim Bakery had existed on San Pablo Avenue for more than twenty years; it was institutionalized, accepted; its owner had run for mayor. Yes, Bey was a racist, an anti-Semite; he went on television every week and said some crazy things. But Bailey was of a generation of African Americans who were cautious about judging one another. Bey was a kook. But who wasn't?

Of course, Bailey didn't know that Bey was far more sinister than he even seemed. Bey had raped one of his own daughters and then cast her out. Years later, when she had married and had children of her own and sought some kind of reconciliation with her father, he had raped one of her daughters, his own grandchild.

Bailey didn't know because no one on the outside truly knew. There were a few women who had gotten out and left the compound, yes, but they remained fearful. They all knew what Bey was capable of, and they kept their mouths shut.

If Bailey did suspect anything, he wasn't going to spend weeks and months digging it up. There were birth certificates for children with the Bey surname that did not identify a father. There were welfare records, police reports, court documents. Together, they could have been used to assemble the puzzle that was Yusuf Bey.* But Bailey had no time to probe. As he worked his new assignment at the *Trib* in the late 1990s, he had long come to define himself as a journalistic dray horse, pulling his publication along by producing stories every day. He was the kind of reporter that a daily paper can't live without, the kind that fills pages. He enjoyed action, the fast turnarounds of working on deadline. There was really little about newspapering that he didn't love.

The bus ran all the way downtown, where Bailey would get off at West Lafayette Boulevard across from the hulking offices of the *Detroit News,* its once-open street-level arches bricked off after rioters in 1967 nearly forced their way inside. It was a building suited for a big urban newspaper, unadorned, solid, but fading, like the city itself. Bailey had joined the *News* in 1982 after his time at the *Hartford Courant* and then brief stints in Chicago at United Press International and in Washington as a congressional press secretary. But newspapers, not wire services or politics, were his calling, and his passion for the work impressed his editors. Bailey could provide copy. He saw stories everywhere. The *News* was a major daily in one of America's biggest cities. Detroit was also, for all intents and purposes, fifty years after the great migration, the American city most associated with African American culture, surpassing even Chicago. Bailey had made it. He got it down

---

*These were the very documents Chris Thompson would use a few years later to paint a devastating picture of Bey.

and got it in. When they needed a story quickly, editors knew who to assign. It increased the paper's credibility to have an educated and capable African American reporter out in the streets. Bailey always seemed to return from assignments brimming with ideas for more stories, including some in the tradition of the Black press. One of the first appeared under the headline "Few Black Detroiters Shop Black."

Bailey believed newspapers could change people's lives for the better. As he took the bus to work one morning, he noticed other passengers just staring out of windows, biding—not using—their time. The next day, he went to one of the *News*'s red street boxes, grabbing a handful of papers. He began at the front of the bus, handing the metro pages to one rider, the sports section to the next, the business pages to someone else. "Read the newspaper," he said. "Have a newspaper. Read the newspaper." It became a ritual—every day he handed out papers to bus riders like he was tossing copies of the *Hayward Daily Review* onto a porch while his mother waited impatiently in the family station wagon, as he had done nearly a quarter century earlier.

Bailey was thirty-two when he joined the *Detroit News,* his fiery personality long cast. There was at least one newsroom fight, with Bailey going over the top of another reporter's desk, fists flying as a result. "Dynamite" is how an editor who hired Bailey would one day describe him. He occasionally went off.

Bailey could muster charm when needed, but he was brusque by default. He could put people off with the quickest of looks. They learned to give him the short version of whatever it was that he wanted.

"I don't think 'abrasive' is a bad word," his half brother, Mark Cooley, would say. Bailey "was abrasive because there wasn't enough time. People could get caught up in his style. He wanted it in thirty words." Bailey "asked questions that would go down in you," Cooley said. "Some people didn't like it." One was Detroit mayor Coleman Young, legendary for his own bluntness.

"I don't like black reporters who come out to do a hatchet job on me," Young once snapped at Bailey.

"You don't like black reporters who ask tough questions," Bailey retorted. The stinging comeback won him the mayor's respect.

In the mideighties in Detroit, Bailey met and eventually married a broadcast journalist named Robin Hardin. "We didn't listen to music. We didn't go to movies. We just did news and we were both fine with that," Hardin said of the marriage. "We were so boring. People would come over and say, 'Do you have any music? Is there a glass of wine in this house?' There was no wine . . . no beer. There were newspapers, magazines, books, news radio, talk radio and us. It was great." It was a few years into the marriage that the couple began to care for Hardin's nieces, ages five and seven. Even in becoming an instant parent, Bailey found a way to promote journalism.

At a parent-teacher meeting, he volunteered to create a weekly newspaper for the girls' elementary school. The principal balked, looking at Bailey as if he were insane, but Bailey won her over. The kids wrote the stories and Bailey did the rest, enforcing strict deadlines, laying out the pages, making copies of each tiny edition. He told Hardin that he believed children who didn't like reading would at least read the work of their classmates. He also believed that if he hooked youngsters on reading a newspaper, it could become an enriching lifelong habit. He believed in living an informed life and that the people of battered Detroit—even children—needed as much meaningful information about the city as they could find. Detroit was a tough town, but newspapers could provide a sense of community.

Bailey covered Detroit during the years when the crack epidemic turned the city into a wasteland. More than fifty years after W. D. Fard had gone door-to-door in Black Bottom and Paradise Valley carrying with him claims of the approaching end of days, Detroit had finally become postapocalyptic. The mother plane hadn't bombed it into oblivion, crack had, its siege relentless.

As industry fled Detroit and hope mocked it, Bailey covered city hall and African American affairs for more than a decade. But after thirteen years in the city, he had had enough. The cold got to him. He couldn't stand walking the winter streets, people bundled in parkas, their heads down, faces hidden behind ski masks. He wanted to go home. In 1993, Bailey and Hardin amicably split, and Bailey headed back to Oakland.

Oakland—Detroit of the West, as its postwar boosters called it—had endured its own crack apocalypse. Industry fled, and the gigantic port mechanized, slashing jobs. The West Oakland ghetto's biggest employer was the U.S. Postal Service, with jobs paying at a subsistence level. Gertrude Stein had famously said of Oakland, where she was born, "There is no there there." There wasn't. A few years earlier, in 1986, the city's—and one of the country's—biggest drug lords, Felix "the Cat" Mitchell, had been killed in federal prison. His coffin was laid on a caisson and pulled through the streets of Oakland by a team of draft horses trailed by fourteen Rolls-Royces. Crowds cheered. "It was like Martin Luther King had died," a local radio announcer said.

The *Oakland Tribune* had changed greatly in the previous twenty years. William Knowland had committed suicide in 1974, a man broken by increasing debt and a collapsing personal life. Three years later, his heirs had discarded the paper to an Arizona billboard company. The *Trib* had recently been labeled "arguably the second-worst newspaper in the United States." (The first wasn't listed.) But then the growing media company Gannett, quickly becoming known for its cookie-cutter, graphics-heavy approach to news and its soon-to-be launched national daily, *USA Today,* acquired it.

Then, to the shock of Oakland, Gannett appointed an African American editor.

Robert Clyve Maynard was already a legend in journalism. The son of parents who had emigrated from Barbados to Brooklyn, he dropped out of high school at sixteen to write for a Black weekly, the *New York Age.* He went to live in Greenwich Village, sometimes hanging out with James Baldwin. Maynard eventually integrated the editorial staff of a Pennsylvania newspaper, the York *Gazette and Daily*, then in 1965 received a Nieman Fellowship at Harvard University, where he studied economics, art, and music. He joined the *Washington Post* in 1967 as a national correspondent, quickly producing a highly praised series on the state of urban Blacks that probably should have won a Pulitzer Prize. In 1976, when millions of Americans watched the final debate between Gerald Ford and Jimmy Carter, they saw, for the first time, an African American journalist questioning presidential candidates. Maynard would not fade from the national scene—he became a regular on *This Week with David Brinkley* and *The MacNeil/Lehrer Report* and wrote a widely syndicated column.

Introducing himself and his vision to Oakland in the *Tribune,* he defined a newspaper as "an instrument of community understanding."

He turned the *Trib* around quickly, diversifying the newsroom and pushing—for the first time in the paper's history—substantive coverage of Oakland's minorities. Circulation rose, and awards covered the newsroom walls.* In 1983 he bought the *Tribune* from Gannett for $22 million, making him the first African American owner of a major metropolitan newspaper in America. Awards and acclaim, though, are not what turn profits. For all its good journalism, national advertisers scoffed at Oakland's demographics. Many who now found voice in the *Trib* didn't shop at Macy's or Bloomingdale's. Why should big chains advertise in a city where they didn't have stores? Maynard kept the paper afloat as long as he could, staying steps ahead of creditors. He was nearly forced to shutter the newspaper in the late 1980s but was saved by an eleventh-hour loan. Then, in 1988, he was diagnosed with prostate cancer. He beat it into submission twice, but when it reappeared in 1992, he sold the *Tribune* to a notoriously tightfisted and colorful Texan, W. Dean Singleton. Maynard died the next year, his legacy of both journalistic achievement and newsroom diversifications in place.

"This country cannot be the country we want it to be if its story is told by only one group of citizens. Our goal is to give all Americans front door access to the truth," Maynard said in a speech shortly before his death.

For the first time in its history, the *Tribune* had embraced Oakland's diversity, covering those struggling at its gritty core. At the same time, African Americans, beginning with Lionel Wilson's mayoralty, had taken over city government. The *Tribune*'s new owner needed to maintain Maynard's diversified staff and focus, and as a result, Bailey was assigned to cover African American affairs.

Bailey rented an apartment in East Oakland, telling friends that since he covered the ghetto he ought to live there. A hurried figure, his personality as blunt as his clipped, rapid-fire style of questioning and declarative writing, he was soon seen all over the city, at government offices, churches, schools, any place, really, where people gathered—including Your Black Muslim Bakery.

---

*Maynard's legacy includes a Pulitzer Prize for the paper's coverage of the 1989 Loma Prieta earthquake.

Forever his mother's son, Bailey soon took a second job at a shoestring cable television channel called Soul Beat that catered to Oakland's African Americans. Bailey became its news director, putting himself on television every night, furthering his seeming ubiquitousness. Soul Beat also gave him talk and call-in shows in addition to his nightly newscast. In a sense, Bailey had become Mr. Oakland.

The more well known he became, though, the more editors and colleagues began to notice problems. Many of his *Tribune* stories were glowing features on local businesses and their owners written almost by formula—an African American entrepreneur struggling to make a go of it—and often boosterish to a fault. Bailey, who had always struggled financially, also began to lean on people for the types of perks and freebies with which the news business had long been associated—meals, drinks, gifts—but that many journalists with newfound senses of ethics had come to solemnly avoid. At one point, a public-relations executive for the Golden State Warriors NBA franchise complained to *Tribune* editors that Bailey frequently asked for free tickets, often saying he was writing a feature on fans. But such stories never appeared in the paper. Editors told Bailey to improve his ethics.

In addition to the *Tribune* and Soul Beat jobs, Bailey took as much freelance work as he could land, writing features for the *Sun Reporter* and other Bay Area African American publications. In 1996 he authored a four-part series for the *Sun Reporter* on life in Iran after spending a week there. He did lots of side work for his old paper, including a ten-part series on the history of the Black press that won an award for in-depth reporting.

But his primary focus remained Oakland, where Bailey churned out copy for the *Tribune* and filled broadcast hours for Soul Beat.

It was at the television station that he would sometimes run into Yusuf Bey, who paid Soul Beat to broadcast his weekly television show, *True Solutions*. It usually began with one of his underlings talking about pies and cakes, an infomercial that gave way to Bey's Sunday-afternoon sermon. At the height of the show—when Bey had retail stores in San Francisco and around the Bay Area—he paid other cable companies to run it too. Bailey maintained a distant respect for Bey despite his frequent rancor, but Bey seemed to keep a skeptical attitude toward Bailey. He'd written about the mayoral campaign, about those whiny Jews and Christians complaining about Brother Muhammad's speech. Bailey also worked for a newspaper owned by a white man, and so he had, to Bey, a slave mentality like too many others in Oakland whom Bey still referred to as "so-called Negroes." But at least Bailey came by the bakery sometimes and spent a little money, maintaining a casual acquaintance. That would soon change.

16

The Evil Old Man Is Dead

"By not coming forward, you make yourself a victim forever."
—KELLY McGILLIS, actress, rape victim

Nancy knew there was something wrong with her daughter. There had to be, the way she was acting so withdrawn, so damaged. There could only be one reason. Nancy had lived through it. So had her sister, Jane. They'd seen the other women and girls at the bakery too. They knew. Nancy's daughter didn't appear to have been beaten. She didn't have bruises on her face or neck like the others he'd choked and stomped in his uncontrolled rages. But Nancy knew. Yusuf Bey was still raping.

Nancy and Jane had managed to leave the bakery in the late 1990s, struggling to somehow find their equilibrium in a world they were unprepared to face. But none of his victims ever truly left Yusuf Bey. They all had children who called him "Daddy." They were all bound to his cult even as they hated and feared it and its patriarch. Nancy hadn't wanted her children anywhere near the monster, but the sense of power and superiority of being a Bey was difficult to resist. Her daughter, the middle of her three children whom she had borne at fifteen, wanted to know her father.

Extracting the details took time, and Nancy knew she needed the specifics if she was ever going to take down Yusuf Bey. When it had been happening to her, she had no one older in whom she could confide. Neither had Jane. Now, at least, Nancy could see her daughter's symptoms, and unlike all those women at the bakery, she wouldn't turn away. Finally, when her daughter was eighteen, she admitted what Bey, her father, had done to her. The anger that coursed through Nancy was uncontainable; it extinguished the last of her fears. On June 20, 2002, she walked into the Oakland Police Department and said she wanted to talk to a detective.

It was as if the building shook. No one wanted the case. Yusuf Bey? Child rape? He'd run for mayor; he had deep political connections. Senator Perata had gotten him contracts. The city loaned him money. The cops' unofficial rules of nonengagement with the Beys were well in place. The few times they did throw one of the Beys in the back of a patrol car, other bakery soldiers would chase the cruiser all the way downtown. More than one cop had had to radio ahead to have the department's sally-port doors opened because the Muslims were right on his bumper. Who wanted to mess with them, especially on something like this, some woman claiming Bey was a demon?

Well, there was one cop in the sex crimes unit, Jim Saleda. He took the case and bore down on Yusuf Bey from the moment Nancy showed him birth certificates showing she'd conceived at ages thirteen, fifteen, and seventeen.

The boxes where the father's name was supposed to be were blank. She didn't tell him any made-up story about a boy in Seaside. She wasn't a scared little girl anymore. If DNA showed Saleda that Bey was the father of those children, then he'd raped her. She was ready to confront him. Over the course of several interviews, Nancy told Saleda of how she and other victims of Bey suffered, the things he did to break them. It was enough to get search warrants for DNA from Nancy's and Jane's children and from Bey.

Saleda moved cautiously, calling Bey to suggest that he come to the police station, give a DNA sample, and go on his way. There was no sense making a big deal about it, Saleda said. The woman could be lying, but he had to check out her story and use the available science to eliminate Bey as a suspect. They could keep it quiet, out of the news, for now, anyway. One of Bey's sons, a lawyer, phoned back.

Bey had fallen ill and was undergoing medical treatments. Yusuf Bey, it would soon be publicly revealed, had colon cancer. But Bey also had AIDS, a secret he desperately wanted kept hidden. All those years of sexual conquests—the women who passed through the bakery, some of them serious junkies, the prostitutes he sometimes had his soldiers procure for him, the men with whom he had secret liaisons—had caught up with him. With the advent of AIDS in the mid-1980s, bakery women began to fear that Bey would acquire HIV. Some begged him to use condoms when he assaulted them. He refused. Now, everything about his perverse secrets—AIDS, rape, the other things he did to humiliate his victims—was crashing down on him. Bey dodged giving the DNA sample, missing appointments, claiming fatigue from medical treatments, retreating to the safety of his compound. Saleda sought the counsel of lawyers in the district attorney's office. What if they had to take a sample from him against his will? What if Bey remained defiant and police had to raid the compound just to obtain a cotton swab of an old man's spit? It struck no one as inconceivable that Bey might even remain defiant to the point of forcing gunfire and bloodshed. Police put the bakery under surveillance and noted what seemed like both increased activity and countersurveillance of the cops.

Inside his cult, Bey justified both his polygamy and his sex with young girls as perfectly permissible under his fictive version of Islam. Didn't Muslims in the Middle East have multiple wives? Didn't some of them take wives as young as thirteen? Hadn't the honorable Elijah Muhammad engaged in his own form of such things? Wasn't it clear under both Black Muslim and Islamic laws that women were to submit?

Finally the tension eased when Bey showed up at police headquarters looking tired and defeated, allowing a saliva swab to be taken. At the bakery, the allegations could not be kept quiet. Bey's soldiers talked openly about what ought to be done to whoever was betraying their leader, how she should suffer for spreading such vicious falsehoods.

But the DNA didn't lie. On September 20, 2002, Yusuf Bey surrendered peacefully to police on a single count of rape, bearing a cashier's check for bail. He was too sick to put up much of a fight. More charges would follow. The news broke and Saleda started getting phone calls. Most of them came either from a pay phone or with the caller ID blocked, making them anonymous. "You only scratched the surface," one woman said. Another said she knew of several victims who were in counseling. A third said one of Bey's sons had tried to commit suicide after others at the bakery learned his father raped him. More women called and said they had been raped and had firsthand knowledge that Bey raped his own children. Another left a message saying that Bey had fathered more than the forty-two children attributed to him. The real number was higher, the caller said, because Bey refused to acknowledge those born to white mothers, another four or five kids at least.

As Saleda probed, Bey mustered defiance, and his ego soared when, a few days after he was charged, he attended a meeting of African American leaders who called themselves Black Men First. Their goal was to lower soaring homicide rates. Ministers and businesspeople dominated the gathering. It was Bey's style to make grand entrances, encircled by as many as a dozen young men in suits and bow ties. Even though he often mimicked Elijah Muhammad by calling Christianity a "spook" religion, he relished being in the company of ministers, who had supported his successful candidacy for vice president of the group. But now, as Bey arrived at the meeting late with his retinue, a man accused of committing heinous acts with girls who had barely reached puberty, he must have wondered how people would react. Then the crowd began to applaud. One by one, men stood. As Bey made his way forward, a smug smile creased his face. He took the stage and sat next to Oakland's police chief. His smile remained as the organization's president, nationally known Baptist preacher J. Alfred Smith Sr., pointed at him, proclaiming loudly, "Yusuf Bey is my brother!"

The bewildering ovation and Smith's pronouncement may have come from long-held frustration and anger many of the men carried about the city's infamous police department and its decades-old history of abuses. They simply distrusted police so much that they refused to believe in the validity of any action cops took—even charging a monster like Bey with rape based on scientific evidence.

From a seat near the room's center, Chauncey Bailey noted the details. His story in the next day's *Tribune* caused women's groups to aggressively rebuke the men who had applauded; in short order, Bey resigned from Black Men First, his smug smile gone.

———

Within a few weeks, Nancy helped police convince her sister Jane and two others to cooperate. The number of counts of rape Bey faced swelled to twenty-seven. He was in court, dressed in a gray suit and matching kufi, when a judge ordered his bail increased from fifty thousand dollars to one million and Bey jailed until it was posted. As his men, their faces suddenly a sea of bewilderment, glanced about and then surged forward, a bailiff quickly pulled Bey's hands behind his back, cuffing him and then moving him away, plucking the kufi from his head just as he passed from view though a door and into a holding cell.

Once he made bail, Bey mustered all his remaining physical strength, ignored the advice of his attorney, and filmed an edition of *True Solutions,* rambling about the charges.

"I didn't do it. They're out to get me," he said. "I enjoy a war, you know. I'm not going in with my head down. I'll be scratching and fighting and putting anything in my hand for a weapon to defend myself." His son Antar stood at attention to his right, urging his father on. Images of Elijah Muhammad and W. D. Fard appeared behind him. "I want you to understand that you ain't playing with no Uncle Tom, no house Negro. I don't turn no damn cheek. I got young men behind me. If I say something, they will do it."

He looked harshly into the camera and said to the brave women who'd come forward: "How can you go to a lyncher, to a rapist, to a murderer, and turn in your brother? How can you do that?"

During another sermon a few days later, Bey called forward a son whose mother he'd raped.

"At one time, I was able to call my mother a mother," the younger man said as Bey watched, smiling. "We have devils. We have a black devil and a white devil. It's a mentality. A black devil could be a woman with a scarf on with a dark-complexioned face. I know who you are. You reform the devil. And if you're not reformed . . . then I must take your head off."

The young man embraced Bey, sobbing, "I love you, Daddy. I appreciate what you done."

Bey leaned into his rostrum.

"The brother tells the truth. I did not ask him to come. I don't ask him to lie. . . . He wouldn't do it anyway. He's a strong Black man. He's just like his father. He's got his seed."

A few weeks after the rape charges were filed, the deputy district attorney prosecuting Bey received an envelope in the mail with no return address. There was a lump in it, something odd. She tore open a corner. A bullet fell out. Undeterred, she pressed on with her case.

Chauncey Bailey, now entrenched at the *Tribune,* wrote numerous stories about the charges against Bey, as did his colleagues. The arrest was a huge story in Oakland, especially as details emerged about the abuses his victims suffered and they granted interviews, their anonymity assured.

But in Bailey's other job as news director of the Soul Beat television channel, he was muted. The station's owner, a man named Chuck Johnson, yielded to Bey's demands as a paying advertiser that Soul Beat not report on the charges. It put Bailey in a horrible predicament that deeply undermined his credibility. Johnson's self-serving decision was based on either his bottom line, physical threats from the Beys, or both. It tied Bailey's tongue on a major story and made it look to viewers as if he was exercising his own judgment to simply ignore the case. Some journalists, fearful of the impact on their integrity, might have resigned in protest. But Bailey was stuck; he needed the money to supplement his *Tribune* salary, and he relished the exposure.

Even with the TV blackout, Bey's followers remained unhappy with Bailey for his *Tribune* coverage. They seemed to expect him to somehow report the facts differently because he was Black. But the story had a life of its own that Bailey couldn't ignore. The man had been charged. There was nothing to do but report it, no matter what the Beys said. Bailey confided to the *East Bay Express*'s Chris Thompson that the Beys had "threatened to kill [him] on multiple occasions" because of what he'd written about the sex case. There were also more subtle threats. In one episode of Bey's show, a young man read an awkward poem filled with veiled promises of violence against his leader's detractors that included the line "Mr. media man . . . you seem to have lost your soul."

There was only one "media man" the would-be poet could have meant.

That Bey would defeat neither the criminal charges nor the diseases ravaging his body became readily apparent in 2003. His lawyers called in doctors who testified that Bey was too weak to endure a trial. At one hearing, his attorney argued for an hour that Bey couldn't sit comfortably in court but for minutes at a time as Bey watched stoically from the defense table in little apparent discomfort.

But his endgame eventually slipped into focus. Bey wanted to stall long enough that the charges against him would not be proven in court. His children could say forever that they were mere allegations against Daddy and that a jury never found him guilty of a goddamn thing. Daddy had, in fact, beaten the devil in death, laughed at the devil. And those devil prosecutors and cops, they hated Daddy so much they forced him to suffer through all those days of going to court when he should have been allowed his dignity.

As the deathwatch unwound over the late summer and into the early fall, Bailey had plenty of time to prepare Bey's obit for the *Tribune*. A lot of reporters would have had it in the can, in newspaper speak, then thrown a few fresh paragraphs on top and been done with it. But that wasn't Bailey. Bey died on September 30, 2003, too late at night to get his obit in the next day's paper, so Bailey swept into the newsroom in the morning, working the phones, waiting for the family to release a list of Bey's "accomplishments." Bailey filed eight hundred words at deadline. His story began:

> By Chauncey Bailey
> Staff writer
>
> OAKLAND – Yusuf Bey, the controversial and charismatic Black Muslim leader who infuriated some while inspiring others, died late Tuesday. Bey died at 10:07 p.m. at Alta Bates Summit Medical Center in Berkeley, according to family members. He was 67.
>
> The cause of death was not immediately known, but Bey was suffering from cancer, according to his attorney who had sought to

delay court proceedings on his behalf earlier this
year. Bey had been facing charges that he raped
a girl under age 14 in 1994 and 1995.

It wasn't sharp. Bey certainly did more than "infuriate some and inspire
others." An overwhelming record was emerging that he was a master criminal who had killed, raped, and stolen in Oakland for thirty years. But the
obit read as if Bailey had intentionally gone soft. Was he scared of the Beys,
or did he think Bey deserved some deference in death? He even erred, identifying Bey's birth name as "Samuels," not Stephens, and failed to report,
in what was, essentially, a historical record of Bey's life, that he had run for
mayor of Oakland. While he didn't completely bury what was obviously
the most newsworthy about Bey—the monstrous acts that cut to his very
core—Bailey didn't write strongly about them either, and he didn't mention
that Jane, Nancy, and others had sued him, the bakery corporation, and the
county, seeking millions in civil damages. The reality of the man Yusuf Bey
really was had been lost in the obituary Bailey authored.

At the *Express,* where Thompson had free license and a different set of
journalistic values, he captured Bey and his passing in six simple words:
"The evil old man is dead."

Bey's cult, though, remained alive. The evil old man, everyone knew,
had sons.

part four

"Kill no one that Allah has not ordered to be killed."

After the murder of journalist Chauncey Bailey, Your Black Muslim Bakery leader Yusuf Bey IV denied involvement in the killing and told detectives that "guns aren't allowed on our premises, period." This photo of Bey IV, holding a pistol and an assault rifle at a building in the bakery compound, was part of the evidence that disproved that claim at his murder trial. The photo was seized in his bedroom when police raided the bakery on August 3, 2007. *Photo courtesy of the Alameda County District Attorney's Office*

17

We Have Enemies

"O the bleeding drops of red,
Where on the deck my Captain lies,
Fallen cold and dead."
—WALT WHITMAN, "O Captain! My Captain!"

As death neared, Yusuf Bey had faced the decision of naming a successor. Even with the sex charges pending against him, Your Black Muslim Bakery remained a legacy he sought to protect. Of his array of offspring, he seemed to especially care for the seven Tammy had borne. They had been raised in his compound; Tammy, despite frequent beatings and abuse, had stayed loyal to Bey. If Bey had sons who would one day assume his role, they were Tammy's sons—Antar and Yusuf IV. But Antar was just twenty-one and Fourth only seventeen. Bey knew his sons needed time. He ordered a man who managed the bakery's day-to-day affairs, Waajid Aljawwaad, to succeed him. Waajid was a smallish man with a shrewdness that Bey admired. He wanted Waajid to prepare his scions to one day run the business.

For the religious face of the organization, though, Bey chose Antar, whom he had groomed to lecture in the Black Muslim tradition. It was Antar, his shaved head so shiny it looked buffed, who often "stood post" next to Bey as he preached, his rather blank eyes fixed straight ahead. Everyone called Antar "the Captain" because of his ability to drill the soldiers.

"We have enemies. We know it's not going to be easy. But we've got an army. . . . We will continue to stick together. We will continue to hire brothers off the street," Antar bellowed at his father's funeral after he and a dozen others in white tuxedos and red bow ties had performed a close-order drill in tribute. Six of them, including Antar and Fourth, then carried their father's coffin from the same Baptist church borrowed years earlier for their half-brother Akbar's funeral.

Afterward, a line of cars snaked to a cemetery north of Richmond, and Bey was interred next to Akbar and his own father, Theron Stephens, who'd died in 1988.

It finally began to sink in for cult members: Yusuf Bey was gone. How could they go on without their patriarch? He was everything to them, especially the men, their commander in chief, their champion who befuddled the devils at every turn, even in death. Daddy had died an innocent man, a lion.

Antar wanted to be a lion too. Daddy had raised him as the crown prince, the next in line. He had to keep the flock in order, the Fruit ready and strong. Antar's priority was perfecting his rhetorical skills and Islamic lessons. Daddy had groomed him to lead men. He could learn to count coins later. Fourth might have made a leader too, despite his bumptious immaturity. But it was Antar, not Fourth, who was the oldest son in the chosen line, and he was determined to live a long and prosperous life on the foundation his father had built.

Waajid was only a placeholder; a little mathematician, Yusuf Bey once called him. The money man.

Waajid was raised a Pentecostal in Tyler, Texas, where he was born with the name Carl Hambrick, the oldest of eight children. He excelled at football, but an injury ended his career. He left home at twenty-one and ended up in San Francisco, where he took jobs in hotel kitchens, working his way up to headwaiter. Unlike many of Yusuf Bey's followers, he had no criminal record, no sordid past. In fact, he had an accounting degree. Despite his education, he was drawn to Bey's fictive Islam because it answered questions for him about Black identity that Christianity did not. He relished an enterprise that allowed African Americans to help themselves.

"I get the opportunity to work with Black people, in a Black environment from the top to the bottom. . . . We represent all Black people," he said in 2001.

Anyone as close to Bey as Waajid was had to know the secrets—the abuse of the girls and women, the rapes, the beatings, the isolation forced upon them, the children kept as slaves. As Bey's money man, it is impossible to believe that Waajid didn't know where the government checks intended for indigent women and children ended up. Anyone that close to Bey knew he sometimes skipped taxes and played games with the pay of workers who believed him their savior. Everyone who surrounded Yusuf Bey enabled him. Few, though, seemed better positioned than Waajid to carry on after his death. But he wouldn't get long, not the hawkish way he watched over the money.

At about 5:00 p.m. on February 28, 2004, five months after Bey's death, Waajid dropped off a friend in East Oakland and went home to his neatly kempt apartment. He was tired, he'd told his friend, and intended to nap briefly before taking a shift at a hotel where bakery men served as security guards. Even the company president was expected to work there. He turned on the television. Then someone knocked on the door.

The next day, bakery members reported Waajid missing to the police when he didn't show up for work. Going to the authorities was odd, given the Beys' long-standing resistance to law-enforcement intrusions in their affairs. Detectives took a report; it became clear that something was amiss. Rumors had swirled since Yusuf Bey's death that his organization would not long keep its order, not with all that money at stake. Now the patriarch's handpicked successor was missing and his young, ambitious son stood to control a lucrative business. Antar played it cool and concerned. Flyers with Waajid's photo were distributed around Oakland. To those outside his inner circle, Antar spoke of the need for his soldiers to conduct their own investigation. How could they trust the police? With those closest to him, Antar expressed relief that the man who clutched the purse strings like they were his was gone.

While police poked around a missing-persons case that they suspected involved more than a stray accountant, Antar quickly seized power.

Just two days after Waajid disappeared, Antar summoned the bakery's directors and suggested that they appoint him, their number two, acting

CEO until Waajid returned. In the months ahead, Antar would produce a document that stated the directors resolved "that Antar Bey will serve as president and CEO of the said corporation." But some bakery directors would call that document a fake, claiming no such vote occurred. It was a pivotal moment, a coup. Yusuf Bey's favorite son couldn't wait for what was his; he simply took it. Hadn't that been how Daddy defined success? In the years ahead, several bakery members would continue to dispute the claim on the business, saying that Antar and his line of Beys had no rightful claim to it. In a few years, one of them would talk to a reporter and try to instigate a newspaper story.

But in March 2004, when Antar Bey announced that he was now president and CEO of Your Black Muslim Bakery, it was left unsaid—but nevertheless understood—what would happen to anyone who challenged him. And Antar pointed out that Waajid was only missing. He might have run off with a woman or just disappeared with a stash of money. But the truth was known even though the facts remained buried. Anyone who thought Waajid remained alive was a fool.

The feuding in the organization worsened when Farieda Bey, Yusuf Bey's legal wife, claimed a chunk of the business as hers. She owned several houses that she had transferred to the bakery corporation to help her husband raise bail in the rape case. Waajid had assured her that they would be given back to her, she claimed. But now, with Waajid gone, Antar told her the properties would not be returned. Seeing no other alternative, Farieda sued him. She still came to the bakery daily; Antar got a restraining order to keep her out of the business.

Antar had assumed his father's televised sermons on the weekly cable television show *True Solutions*. Each episode began with a member praising the nutritional value of honey-prune cake or pies made with white navy beans, and then Antar would lecture in front of the photographs of Elijah Muhammad and W. D. Fard that had always flanked his father, whose image had been added to the backdrop.

But Antar lacked Bey's fire, and the orations were thin in Fard's historical rhetoric. His screeds typically dealt with empowerment and were sprinkled with occasional references to devils and oppression. He mostly ignored the mother plane, its bombers, Armageddon, and Big-Headed Yakub. Often,

Fourth volunteered to stand post during the sermons, knowing just when to encourage Antar with a robust outburst of "Teach!" or "That's right!" Fourth seemed intolerant of his older brother's plodding. Antar often remained as dull eyed and languid as when he had stood post for Daddy. Fourth, though, was animated, his eyes alive, as if he wanted to push Antar aside. But he was just a kid, only eighteen during Antar's first year in charge. He stood close to his brother's shadow, so near and constant that Antar couldn't have been blamed if he took Fourth's loyalty for granted.

Despite his shortcomings, Antar, the Captain, did what he could to position himself as a spiritual leader. He even commissioned an artist who painted his likeness seated at a table with his late father, along with Elijah and Fard. Water glasses sat before the men, as if they were all on a panel at a conclave. Yusuf Bey's left arm was draped gently around his son's shoulder. Muhammad, in sunglasses and fez, had his head raised, looking away. Fard's face was bowed toward a book in his hands, his skin pale, his short, slick hair distinctly parted. The men wore dark jackets with red pocket squares. The painting made clear whose company Antar imagined he kept and how he wanted his followers to think of him. He aspired to be his father, and although the Beys remained separatist Black Muslim renegades, the painting showed renewed reverence to the founders of the faith.

Soon after Waajid disappeared, Antar borrowed $700,000 from a finance company, using the bakery as collateral. It seems unlikely that Waajid would have allowed such a move, especially putting the money in the hands of someone so lacking in business experience. But Waajid was gone, and Antar talked about expansion and improvements—even opening a bakery in Los Angeles—as a way of ensuring Daddy's legacy. But some of the money was for him. Antar used loan proceeds to buy a $75,000 BMW that he adorned with $5,000 rims. He took his Daddy's old custom license plates—DR BEY—and slapped them on the car. A twenty-one-year-old CEO needed to travel in style.

King Estates Park is a wind-shorn nub of a hill in East Oakland. From its crest, jets taking off from Oakland's airport five miles to the west appear to be at eye level after about ten seconds of flight. An elementary school abuts it to the south, a service road to I-580 to the east, residential neighborhoods to the north and west. The park isn't much of park, a lone crumbling asphalt path crossing it, its soil eroding, most of the hillside brown, grassless. Still, the area is alive with dogs from the nearby neighborhoods from dawn to dark, many allowed by their owners to roam the sandy expanses untethered despite local leash laws, noses to ground, as free as the wind.

There may be more moronic places in Oakland to ditch a body in a shallow grave, but not many. All one needs to do is look up at the real hills to the east and know that woods, canyons, and backcountry are behind them. Up there, in the isolated night, one could dig deep and dispose of a corpse for eternity. But whoever killed Waajid Aljawwaad instead chose King Park Estates to bury him. The only surprise is that it took five months for a dog to finally wander off a trail and then bark until its owner came over and saw a decomposing human hand protruding from the earth.

Given the body's decay, it was impossible to determine exactly how Waajid had died. Police couldn't even tell at first whether it was him. Then a gloved hand dug into the pocket of the moldy pants hanging limply on the skeletal remains and pulled out a set of keys. A detective drove to the police impound yard where Waajid's car was stored and slipped one into a locked door. It worked.

The cause of death was speculated to be some sort of blunt-force trauma. There was what appeared to be a cut just above where his right eye had been and a corresponding dent in the skull. Maybe he'd opened his door and his attackers had beaten him down. Or they stuck a gun in his face and Waajid went along quietly. However it happened, he was gone. Detectives knew Antar had the most to gain from Waajid's death but possessed no evidence with which to charge him. As always, the Beys remained impenetrable.

A few men within the bakery's establishment fumed at Antar's takeover and mourned their friend's murder. But what was the sense of more bloodshed? Antar and his young henchmen played by their own rules. His soldiers were loyal to their captain. The bakery was still open, putting people to work and producing healthy food as an alternative to the devil's poisons. But Antar sensed that he would not have complete control if the men loyal to Waajid remained. Among those who worried him was John Bey, a follower whom Yusuf Bey had deemed worthy of the esteemed surname. John Bey ran the security operation at the downtown hotel where Waajid had dutifully taken shifts. He worked at the bakery too, though he remained distant from Antar, often avoiding him. The tension was high enough that John Bey moved his family out of the bakery compound to a relative's house in an isolated part of Oakland called Montclair far up in the hills.

On a spring morning eleven months after Waajid's body was found, John Bey left his Montclair home before dawn to go to work at the bakery. As he walked toward his car, something stirred behind him and shots erupted from pistols and a shotgun, booms and flashes shattering the calm. John Bey ran, bullets hitting his legs. Somehow—perhaps because it was still dark or perhaps because his attackers were simply unskilled marksmen—he survived. But he got the message; as soon as he recovered, he and his family fled Oakland.

Farieda's lawsuit was still winding its way through the courts. And there was another Waajid loyalist still around, Ali Saleem Bey, who was married to one of Yusuf Bey's daughters. Then there was yet a further complication— Jane and Nancy had sued Yusuf Bey's estate, the bakery corporation, and the county, seeking damages for their years of rape and servitude. But Antar apparently thought none of those people posed too serious a threat. He was confident the lawsuits would resolve themselves. The media was no longer interested in anything related to the bakery. It appeared to Antar that his troubles had passed.

What Antar didn't suspect was that Fourth had grown frustrated with being his older sibling's subordinate, with being told to mop floors, wash dishes, make sandwiches. A lifetime of being number two at Your Black Muslim Bakery in no way appealed to Fourth. He was different from laid-back Antar, impetuous, moody, violent. Within the bakery's culture of incessant gossipmongers and amateur psychologists, Fourth was always viewed as "having mental problems," a relative would one day say. He had inherited his father's immense ego and within the first few months of Antar's reign had decided that he would make a much better leader and caretaker of the family legacy.

Antar and the mother of his children were living around the corner from the bakery on Fifty-ninth Street in one of the duplexes that formed the back of the compound. As summer faded into autumn, shots were fired on two occasions at Antar's residence. True to his code, this time, Antar didn't report the shootings to police. Whatever was going on, he would deal with it himself. One night, at the end of the summer of 2005, Antar's wife answered the phone and heard a voice whisper that Antar would soon be dead or in jail. It sounded to her like it was Fourth on the line, but she dismissed it. Why would he threaten his own brother?

On the night of October 25, 2005, at about 7:30 p.m., Antar wheeled into a gas station at Martin Luther King Jr. Way and Fifty-fourth Street, pulled under the red and white canopy, and began to fill up at pump number two. The gas station was in the heart of North Oakland. Elevated BART tracks loomed over MLK, trains on the Richmond line screeching past. Single-family homes lined the side streets, little stucco-sided boxes interspersed with occasional shoebox-shaped apartment buildings. The neighborhood was primarily African American and spilled over into South Berkeley. Unlike his father, Antar didn't travel with bodyguards. He liked to drive his new BMW himself, to be alone and play music.

Antar probably would not have been the least bit concerned if he had seen a young guy in a peacoat and skullcap walking across Fifty-fourth Street toward him. The gas tank was on the passenger side, and Antar was letting it fill while he talked on his cell phone. He shifted his weight from one foot to the other, swaying slightly. It was dark; all the cars on MLK had their lights on. Above the door to the station's office, a pair of white security cameras rose a few inches on poles, silently doing their work.

Alfonza Phillips was a small man who favored a big gun—a chrome-plated .44 Magnum. It packed a wallop; it was the kind of weapon with a huge maw that nearly caused people to faint when it was pointed at them. The gun made Phillips, a nineteen-year-old street kid who hustled a living selling whatever drugs were in demand, feel large. He kept it tucked in his pants wherever he went.

Antar pressed his phone to his ear as the gas-pump numbers flitted up-ward. He wore only a white T-shirt and blue jeans. Phillips came across Fifty-fourth Street behind him and then onto the faded concrete of the station. His pace quickened. He drew the gun early enough that people stopped at a traffic light on MLK would tell police they saw it in his hand as he strode. At point-blank range, Phillips extended his arm and shot Antar once in the middle of his lower back; motorists were startled by the muzzle flash and the loud report.

Antar fell, the phone dropping. He had $214 in his pocket, but Phillips didn't linger over the body. He darted around the car, leaned into the open passenger door briefly, then pulled back and took off toward Fifty-fifth Street, slipping into the night. One witness would say he entered a waiting car; others disputed it.

Antar crawled toward MLK, pulling himself with his arms for a few feet, his T-shirt soaked in blood, gobs of red splattered on the concrete deck near the pump. After a few seconds, the man known as the Captain didn't move again.

We have enemies, he had said at his father's funeral two years earlier. Per-haps in those final, fleeting moments he finally realized who his enemy was.

18

A Swarm of Muslims

"He who has no brother is like one going into battle
without a weapon."
—Charter of Hamas

Who killed Antar Bey?

As people from the bakery swarmed the gas station and then the lobby of Highland Hospital, Oakland's trauma center, women crying, men yelling for vengeance, it seemed as if everyone suspected that Antar's killing was, finally, retaliation for Waajid's murder nineteen months earlier. Police immediately joined that speculation, theorizing that the slaying was another part of a war for control of the bakery. They were right; it was. But Antar's murder wasn't retaliation for Waajid. It wasn't what they thought at all.

Obviously, the cops needed to find the smallish man in the peacoat who had walked up to Antar and shot him in the back. In that sense, the killing was a whodunit. Who was he? Was he from a different faction of the Beys? Was he a hit man? It was already a frantic—but not atypical—night for Oakland police: Antar was one of five men felled by bullets within a few hours of one another that evening. But in a city where only about one out of four murder cases ended with a conviction, investigations were hardly thorough or efficient and were sometimes thin to the point of anorexia. The homicide unit was grossly understaffed. The police department, under a federal judge's order to end decades of abuses, had thirty detectives assigned to investigate itself in internal affairs and only ten assigned to investigate Oakland's killings. There just weren't enough investigators to do painstaking casework. Some homicide detectives put in so much overtime just to keep up that their gross salaries topped a quarter million dollars a year.

The 25 percent or so of cases that resulted in arrests and convictions typically involved reliable witnesses, domestic disputes, or other situations where the facts were obvious. When police found suspects, it helped greatly if those suspects waived Miranda rights and talked. Like most police, Oakland cops never asked, "Do you want a lawyer?" The standard admonishment—upheld by courts—involved telling a suspect he or she had the right to remain silent and have a lawyer present but finished with the words "Having these rights in mind, do you wish to speak with us?" Detectives spent lots of time convincing suspects it was in their best interest to talk, to help themselves. Or, since the law allows police to intentionally deceive whomever they wish, they often lied, telling suspects that witnesses had seen them do it or that someone else involved was cutting a deal, selling them out. The bottom line with Oakland's harried, understaffed homicide squad was that if detectives didn't get people to talk, murders didn't get solved.

One of the two detectives assigned to Antar's murder favored fashionable dark suits, well-shined shoes, and a shaved and buffed head. Sometimes, when he wore a sharp bow tie, he looked as if he, too, were a Black Muslim. He wasn't, but it was an observation he would eventually find himself vociferously refuting.

Derwin Longmire had been an Oakland cop for twenty years and had come to know Yusuf Bey, building one of the department's few cordial, or at least unantagonistic, relationships with the bakery leader and his top lieutenants. Longmire began going to the bakery in the mid-1990s when he was training for a bodybuilding contest and thought Bey's health food might give him an advantage. Once, Bey invited him up to his office, wanting to discuss how he might better position himself to win government contracts. Longmire had only stopped in for a cookie, but he followed Bey upstairs, a little nervous, thinking "shit" to himself when Bey used a keypad to open the locks on his private office. But Longmire was confident in his

ability to handle himself should he have to. Like a lot of cops, he'd made his
share of undercover drug buys as a young officer, walking into dark places
with little more than his wits and a hidden gun. At least now, as Bey asked
him to sit and talk, his sidearm was right there under his jacket. But talk
was all Bey wanted that day—at least on the surface. But did Bey really
think a detective could help him with contracts?

To a cop like Longmire, one constantly building a network of sources,
a conversation with Bey was part of the job. If Yusuf Bey wanted to talk,
then Longmire would talk. His strengths were creating an image of effective
communication and empathy. He would one day describe his philosophy
by saying, "Where [Oakland Police] have fallen so often is just dealing with
people in a dignified way."

Detectives, of course, never knew when they would need street intelligence to break cases, and if Longmire left Bey with the impression that
he was fair, honest, and nonjudgmental—that he had some credibility—he
might be able to call on him in a time of need. So their conversation ended
amicably enough.

Despite his strong interpersonal skills, which made talking even with
a man like Bey effortless, Longmire possessed few other techniques to aid
in the solving of murders. Like many cops, Longmire was not a person of
immense intellectual curiosity or imagination. A senior police commander
would eventually describe Longmire to special agents of the state justice
department as "not the sharpest tool in the shack. His thoroughness left a
lot to be desired." He spent his spare time cashing overtime checks, playing softball, lifting weights, and coaching kids' sports. Keeping detailed
case files, delving into forensic evidence, even employing basic probative
techniques like tracing cell-phone records, were not his forte. But in the
overworked, understaffed homicide unit, which relied too heavily on interrogations to solve what killings it could, he was among the best interrogators. To put it simply, Longmire mostly fit the old cliché of being a "people
person." He was a humanist, one capable of reaching even those who might
barely meet the definition of being human themselves.

———

At nineteen years old, Yusuf Ali Bey IV possessed not even the average worldview of someone that age; he certainly wasn't in any way prepared to run a business. But Daddy had designated a line: After Antar, Fourth was next.

Like his father's, Fourth's face—pimples aside—seemed forever fixed in a cocksure smirk. He was taller and skinnier than Antar and a better orator. Fourth had paid studious attention to his father's style. He'd seen the cars, the money, the followers' subservience each day of his young life. He'd seen Daddy beat his mother, Tammy, and so many other women when they refused to submit. Fourth was hotheaded, power hungry, his ego immense after all those years of absorbing his father's dogma. He was obsessed with guns, posing for photos with assault rifles and pistols. He had his father's arrogance, his ruthlessness. There seemed to be little question that, more than any of his brothers, Fourth was indeed his father's son.

As the family grieved Antar—Tammy was hysterical—Fourth calmly accepted the mantles of power and responsibility the very night his brother died. He seemed, somehow, prepared. This time, there would be no power sharing, no accountant guarding the money. Fourth answered to no one and would react violently to even minor instances of what he perceived as disrespect. Not long after he assumed control, Tammy took cash from the bakery till for kitchen supplies without asking him. Fourth beat her to the floor, dragged her by her hair to the door, and kicked her into the street.

Antar's funeral was conducted in the same Baptist church the family had first borrowed for Akbar Bey's eleven years earlier and then Daddy's. Antar's was an anguish-filled service. At least Daddy had lived his life. Antar had been taken before he achieved greatness. At the bakery compound on San Pablo Avenue, a five-foot-square photo of Antar in a dark overcoat and trilby was hung above the "Taste of . . . the Hereafter" sign. But Black Muslims didn't believe in eternal souls. Dead was dead. Gone was gone. What mattered was the here and now.

The here and now for the Oakland cops was solving Antar's killing before it resulted in what they fully expected would be more retaliatory bloodletting.

Though Fourth was a bit of an unknown quantity to police, he was a Bey. What else did they need to know?

The fact that the killing involved a member of that clan made everything different, increasing pressure on police, forcing the case under a political microscope; news organizations were reporting on the murder of one of Yusuf Bey's sons. It was one thing for the cops to not engage the Beys in day-to-day policing. But they obviously couldn't ignore one of them being shot dead. Then there was the question, though, that if the small man captured on the gas station's grainy security footage camera was a Bey himself, how would they ever break through the cult that had proven so often impossible to penetrate? As with a lot of Oakland murders, without someone to interrogate, the investigation was going nowhere.

Then a cop got a phone call from one of his street sources, a junkie named Dwayne. His stepdaughter, Althea, had been fooling around with a kid named Alfonza Phillips. Phillips, Dwayne said, had confided to him, "I shot the Muslim." But Phillips had just ripped off Dwayne in a minor drug deal, so the call was pure revenge—and a chance at a thousand dollars cash from the cops if the tip turned out to be correct. It was the only break they'd gotten, though, and the cops rushed to Dwayne. They'd kept some details of the shooting out of the media for just such a moment. Did Dwayne know Phillips to carry a gun? Yeah, Dwayne replied, a big chrome-plated .44 Magnum. He got his grand.

Police finally found Phillips, along with Althea, two weeks later. Phillips was unarmed, which seemed odd because if a North Oakland street kid like him knew anything, it was that if the Beys got to him first, he'd need firepower. Lots of it. That's assuming, of course, as the cops did, that he had probably made a horrible mistake and shot Antar randomly, without knowing he was a Bey until it was too late. That was the alternative theory the cops had been mulling over—what if Antar's killing wasn't an assassination? What if it was just a carjacking gone bad? Antar's BMW, with its expensive rims, certainly was a prize. What if Phillips hadn't seen its DR BEY license plates and just thought Antar was some random man, then panicked and run? The carjacking theory caught a bit of traction as days passed and Fourth made no retaliatory strikes against other Bey factions.

When police arrested Phillips, they also took Althea downtown and left her alone in an interview room to wait, sweating her, as cops often did in interrogations. Eventually, Longmire and his partner entered. The partner was the primary investigator and took the lead, but when Althea became difficult and said she didn't know anything about her boyfriend killing anyone, it was Longmire, she would later claim, who began shouting. The result was a glimpse of what routinely went on during interrogations in Oakland—and one that would prove revelatory about how they were really done, especially when police, in the future, shifted from investigating Antar Bey's murder to investigating how the Beys, themselves, murdered.

"I haven't slapped a young Black bitch in a long time," Althea claimed Longmire yelled. Althea was lucky she still had her teeth, he told her. She had better start talking. Did she know who Phillips had shot dead? Did she know what the Beys would do to her if the cops let it out that she was protecting Antar's killer? Did she want "a swarm of Muslims" set loose on her family? Did she know what "an eye for an eye" meant? *He told you it was just a carjacking gone bad, didn't he?*

The thought of Bey soldiers attacking her family was too much, Althea would later testify, so she told the detectives what they wanted to hear, reciting back the carjacking theory, saying that Phillips had told her he just wanted the BMW's rims.

Only then did the cops produce an audio recorder, calm Althea down, change their tone, and take a formal statement. It was a standard policy in Oakland—and one long abandoned by more progressive urban police departments—to record not actual interrogations but only the final statements given by tired, frightened suspects and witnesses after they were interrogated. Althea would testify that she had simply parroted what the detectives had told her before they began recording.

Longmire would simply say she was lying about his threatening her. Althea was just some "Black bitch." Who would believe her?

Police charged Phillips with Antar's murder, calling it a failed robbery. There was no war going on between the Beys, they said. Antar was simply at the wrong place at the wrong time; it was just a carjacking gone bad.

In actuality, Antar's murder *was* an assassination, part of a power struggle for control of the Bey cult. But it wasn't the other factions that challenged Antar's seizure of the business following Waajid's murder who were responsible. It was Fourth. He had paid Phillips to kill Antar so he could get control of the bakery and its money. To protect himself if his assassin got caught, Fourth had told Phillips he was on his own. If Phillips talked, then his father, who lived near the bakery, would be killed in retaliation. That threat was Fourth's insurance, and Phillips took it gravely, staying silent when he was arrested. He stupidly told Dwayne, "I killed the Muslim," but he never told him why, and he couldn't dare risk his father's life to cut a deal with authorities by giving up Fourth. If Fourth would have his own brother killed, he would certainly kill again to protect himself. How Fourth would have the father killed and who would do it seemed murky, though, especially if Phillips made a secret deal with prosecutors and police suddenly scooped up Fourth. But even if Phillips did talk, would he be believed? What could confirm his story to make him look like more than a desperate liar? He'd pulled the trigger. That was all police cared about anyway. It was, after all, Oakland.

All that must have given Fourth confidence that Phillips wouldn't snitch.

However, Fourth would also prove himself to be a leader vulnerable to worry and stress, even panic. But Antar was out of the way and the cops weren't probing beyond the surface details of the carjacking theory, and Fourth needed to assert himself as the bakery's new leader. Plus, there was still a big chunk of the money that Antar had borrowed that Fourth now controlled.

Now it was time to make his presence felt.

A month after Antar died, Fourth rallied a dozen followers in the bakery's back room. It was Thanksgiving Eve, 2005. Most of them were about his age, embittered young men, some of whom were amassing thick criminal files. One, though, was older: Donald Cunningham. The seventy-six-year-old was a jazz clarinetist who had long admired the Black Muslims' message of self-sufficiency but dodged much of the religious dogma. Like many African American Oaklanders, Cunningham found the Beys' positions palatable because he lived the realities of daily ghetto life: the lives lost to alcohol and drugs, the lack of economic opportunity, the police abuses.

It was time to do *something*. Now that he was in charge, finally, Fourth wanted to announce himself to the community loudly and boldly, something Antar hadn't done. He foisted his plan for the evening on Cunningham and the others as he disassembled the microphone stand where his father had once given sermons. As the pieces came apart, he was left with a heavy, four-foot metal rod. There was another stand nearby; he broke that one down too. *Let's go,* he said. The soldiers donned coats over their suits and bow ties and followed along.

A short while later, they marched into a corner store called San Pablo Liquors, fanning out around the little bodega. Each man stood at attention, awaiting orders. All wore gloves.

"No money. No money," one of the two Yemeni clerks behind the counter shouted, thinking it was a robbery.

Cunningham wore a dark fedora; the collar of his blue dress shirt was open. He stood at the counter and leaned in, his right hand moving up and down as he spoke. Fourth was next to him, nodding gravely, his hands in his pockets. The old man brought the mission credibility. "Why do you poison our people with liquor?" Cunningham asked. "What kind of Muslims are you?"

The others waited. One of them turned and lifted his eyes toward a security camera.

Then two soldiers raced around the counter and pushed the clerks aside, raining punches down on their faces. Another man came in behind the counter, sweeping liquor bottles off the back shelf, fifths of whiskey and vodka smashing on the floor. The others swatted at anything near them, knocking over potato chip racks, raking bottles of cheap wine off shelves. The men with the sections of microphone stand used them like batons to shatter the beer cooler's glass doors. Another grabbed cans of beer and hurled them about, his feet slipping as he sought traction in the mix of alcohol washing over the floor. Fourth paced back and forth, barking orders, telling his men to tear up everything they could find. As he did, one of them waved a black handgun at the clerks.

After a minute and a half, the store's stock smashed and strewn about, the clerks cowering in a corner, the men calmly walked outside. It was 11:33 p.m. They headed north on San Pablo Avenue, gloved hands wiping glass splinters and drops of booze from their coats. Black Muslims were as stoic and solemn as, say, Pentecostals were demonstrative and hysterical. To call the men excited about what they had just done wouldn't be accurate. But some of them were now resolved to follow Fourth further, pleased he had found a new way of making a statement and allowing them to take the issue of the devils' poisons into their own hands.*

But Fourth may have had a different agenda, or at least an additional one. Surely the men were risking arrest, and if police responded quickly, there was a good chance they would go to jail that night. Once there, they might have encountered Alfonza Phillips. Fourth knew they'd kill Phillips in retaliation for Antar's death without any urging. He didn't even need to bring it up. Phillips had killed their captain—that much was true—and any of the men would have slain him in an instant. What better time to try it than over the long Thanksgiving weekend, when the minds of the devils would be elsewhere? Phillips's death would remove a grave worry for Fourth, sealing the secret of Antar's assassination. It also would have made the Beys appear omnipresent, even invincible.

Fourth's men left San Pablo Liquors, but there were no wailing police sirens, no cop cars skidding to stops, no arrests. A few blocks away, the men hit another store, New York Market. As they let loose again, a clerk reached under the counter and wrapped his hand around a pistol-grip 12-gauge shotgun, a pump-action Mossberg. But when he raised it, two men pounced on him, fists flailing. They took the shotgun and ransacked the store. When they left, the police still weren't around; there would be no Muslims arrested that night. Maybe the police thought it was just a simple vandalism, a few broken bottles, and didn't respond immediately.

---

*But busting up liquor stores wasn't even a new idea for the Beys. Yusuf Bey himself had done it in Richmond in 1993 when he tried to establish a business in a drug-ravaged neighborhood there, ordering his men on a rampage inside a store owned by an Orthodox Muslim.

There would be no opportunity to get Phillips. But Fourth was pleased about one thing: The little shotgun, "the shotty," as it would come to be known, was designed for point-blank urban terror. It would prove quite handy.

Although they tried, the Oakland police couldn't suppress the onslaught of media interest in the store attacks. The problem was the videotape from surveillance cameras at San Pablo Liquors. Detectives were using it to try to identify the guys in the suits and bow ties. But somehow the tape was leaked to a television station, and it was on the news all over Northern California: grainy, dramatic footage of young men smashing beer coolers with pipes and hurling bottles of liquor to the ground. Now that the public had seen what had happened, the cops would have to do something.

News organizations, wanting to keep the story alive, began to examine just how many liquor stores there were in the ghettos. It was soon reported that in North Oakland, where three such establishments often stood on a single block, there was one for every 290 residents. But up in the affluent hills, the ratio fell to one store per three thousand people. The story became about the social issue of liquor in the ghetto and not solely about the attacks themselves. Whatever Fourth meant, his actions had raised a provocative issue.

As shocking as the video was to the public, it was nearly terrifying for Fourth's mother, Tammy. She'd just lost Antar, and now Fourth was on the news committing felonies. His arrest seemed imminent. The only good that had come from her years as a concubine was her children, and the thought of Fourth being jailed seemed to nearly paralyze her. She had to do something.

Sergeant Longmire had made a strong impact on her while working Antar's murder, giving her empathy and respect. Few, if any, other members of the department would have bothered, but it was an example of Longmire's strongest skills, and his efforts had impressed Tammy greatly. She'd lived within a culture of deep contempt for police and she also knew little about being treated with basic human dignity. Now, as she worried about Fourth, Tammy began calling Longmire, inquiring about an investigation that wasn't his, asking him to help.

Longmire didn't deny her. And he would say several years later that at the same time she was calling him, Deputy Police Chief Howard Jordan and Investigations Captain Jeffrey Loman secretly ordered him to get involved in the liquor-store investigation. They were afraid of both the negative publicity and the Beys and knew Longmire had built a relationship with them that was now strong given the arrest of Antar's killer. Longmire understood how to follow orders, even fishy ones from superiors he would one day come to despise and who would eventually deny giving them. But in a department where some cops secretly harbored the belief that Longmire's cordialness toward the Beys meant he was a sympathizer—if not a closeted Black Muslim believer—his actions would only cause more rumors and insinuation.

The investigator assigned to the liquor-store attacks was a well-liked sergeant named Dominique Arotzarena. The brass apparently didn't tell him Longmire was looking over his shoulder, and he was working on the case when Longmire phoned saying Fourth's mother had called him, asking questions. What could Arotzarena tell him that he could pass along?

Nothing, Arotzarena snapped. He told Longmire not even to say that Fourth was a suspect and got off the phone.

What the hell was going on? Why was Longmire poking around? Of course he couldn't pass anything along. What was he thinking? Arotzarena wanted a square case, no bullshit. People were watching and the damn thing was all over the TV. He opened his file and noted that at 2:00 p.m. on November 27, 2005, "I received a call from Sgt. D. Longmire. He advised me the mother of Yusuf Bey IV had called him. She wanted Longmire to call him about the case. Longmire wanted to know what he could tell Bey about this case. I advised him not to reveal any details . . . including the possibility of Bey (IV) being a suspect."

Ninety minutes later, Longmire called again. Tammy had phoned a second time, asking if he would speak to Fourth. Again, Arotzarena noted that Longmire had called, but he didn't write down how he had responded.

Arotzarena was a good, methodical detective, his thorough notes showing step-by-step how he built his investigation. But this case involved the Beys, and that meant it wouldn't be trouble free. The day after Longmire called him, Arotzarena was summoned upstairs to a meeting with the deputy police chief and investigations captain that seemed disproportional to the vandalism of two liquor stores. Jordan and Loman told him Fourth had phoned and demanded a meeting. It seemed almost surreal, a nineteen-year-old criminal suspect dictating when and where he would talk to cops.

Arotzarena noted: "I met with DC Jordan [and] Captain Loman. . . . Captain Loman advised me that Bey [IV] was coming to the police department. . . . Bey [IV] wanted to talk to police about the vandalism." The two commanders "advised me that if Bey [IV] was completely forthcoming with information, we were to release him pending review of the case by the district attorney's office."

How could this kid be both so damn egotistical and powerful that he could demand and receive such treatment? But all Arotzarena could do was keep working his case. He caught a break when two men who had worked at the bakery with Antar called and said they'd seen the video and knew the names of everyone in it. They were scared, they said; Fourth was crazy; he might even kill them if he knew they'd called the police. But the men said their hatred of Fourth exceeded their fear. Their information sealed the investigation. Arotzarena pounded out an affidavit for arrest warrants, and a judge signed them the next morning. Arotzarena wasn't going to give the kid a pass. He was going to make an arrest.

Then, at 11:25 a.m., the new leader of Your Black Muslim Bakery strutted into police headquarters and met with Longmire. That the judge had signed warrants was a tightly held secret—at least Arotzarena thought it was: "Yusuf Bey IV came down to the Oakland Police Department. He [met] with Sgt. D. Longmire. Bey advised he was going to call his lawyers. I never asked Bey to come down . . . during this investigation. Additionally the [arrest] warrants weren't obtained until this morning. Their involvement was not made public by this department nor me. . . . Longmire organized his visit. . . . At this point I never spoke with Bey or told him he was under arrest."

———

Fourth was charged and booked, and he eventually posted bail.

But what about the stolen shotgun? Why hadn't police done their duty to recover it? Surely a judge would have signed a search warrant for the Beys' compound if police had sought one. Here was their chance to finally take the bakery down, to recover what they knew was an arsenal in there and stop Fourth from committing future crimes. Arotzarena wanted to hit the place and send this little punk who thought he was so big a message. But it went nowhere. No search warrant, no raid. All the brass wanted was to make it all go away. It was Oakland. Fourth could get firearms anywhere; let him have his little shotgun. Who cared?

After he was freed on bail, and despite still being a criminal defendant, Fourth gave interviews. Keeping his mouth shut had always been a problem—one that would get worse in the years ahead. When several Christian ministers played into his hands by calling a meeting to discuss liquor sales, Fourth couldn't help himself. He toned down his usual blood-red bow tie with a soft gray one and slipped a V-neck sweater over a white shirt. He spoke softly as television cameras crowded him: "In the Black community they are all over the place," he said of liquor stores. "I am not sure if it is a plan to keep Black people in the condition they are in or not. But to me that sounds like that's a problem. And maybe by the incident that went on, however it came about, people are concerned about it now."

Fourth was emboldened. He'd seized the bakery. Senior cops were afraid of him. Police wouldn't try to recover a stolen weapon they knew he possessed. Although he probably didn't know it, police had even threatened to sic a "swarm of Muslims" like dogs on a reluctant witness. He was on his way to power. The time had come to recruit more soldiers and stride toward his destiny.

19

I Got Hella Flaws

*"We cannot think of being acceptable to others until
we have first proven acceptable to ourselves."*
—MALCOLM X

One of Fourth's new recruits was a tall, lanky kid from San Francisco. He told the others to call him Dre, short for Devaughndre, and said he was the cousin of some dude Fourth had met in jail after he ran down those strip-club bouncers with the BMW. Dre had a bad stutter; when he got nervous, he barely formed words. And he had this little quirk of tilting his head as he spoke, drawing his face up as if he was about to laugh but then didn't. Fourth had him washing pans and hauling supplies. Sometimes he sent him out in a cheap suit with the other guys to stand around and look menacing. People at the bakery assumed that Dre was the type who showed up when he had nowhere else to go. He wouldn't commit and wouldn't stay long, they figured. He wouldn't even take a Muslim name. But Fourth was trying to bring him along anyway, giving him a document called "The General Orders of the Bakery," which listed the rules of conduct and identified Fourth as commander in chief. Fourth also made sure Dre had a copy of another document that all the soldiers were ordered to memorize. It was entitled "The Twenty-four Rules of Islam" and ended with the words: "Kill no one that Allah has not ordered to be killed."

Devaughndre Broussard's arrival in Oakland in the summer of 2006 came nine months after Fourth's ascent to leadership. Working there was "more than a job," Fourth had told him that night he came down from Richmond; it was a cause, a chance to help Black people, a chance to help himself.

Fourth was building a cadre of absolutely loyal soldiers to do his bidding without question, like the men he'd brawled with at the New Century Theatre, and Broussard was one more. He was foot-soldier material, big, strong, his native intelligence deeply concealed behind his stutter and street jive, but foot soldiers were needed. The ranks had to be filled. Fourth must have sensed something he liked in Broussard. The savage beating he'd given that kid on the train showed violence wasn't a problem for him. Fourth wanted men like that.

But he needed lieutenants too, and he kept thinking of Richard Lewis, the guy he'd celled with in San Francisco, who was still awaiting trial for murder, the one who called Broussard his cousin and had sent him to Oakland. Lewis had pledged to join the bakery when he was acquitted, which he claimed repeatedly would happen. Given Fourth's rising bloodlust, he badly wanted Lewis at his side. Lewis was strong, determined, ready to do whatever was needed. The murder case against him proved that. Lewis had helped rob a drug dealer; his friend had badly wounded the dealer and killed his girlfriend. Someone unafraid of killing was exactly what Fourth wanted.

Lewis had already demonstrated his worth by sending his eager and desperate friend Broussard to the bakery. The kid had immediately lunged at one of the biggest pieces of bait Fourth dangled in front of him—the chance to learn the secrets of crimes committed not with weapons but with a pen. Broussard would come to call Fourth's schemes "the credit hookup." The financial scams that threaded through the bakery had deep roots: Yusuf Bey's health-care company that defaulted on government loans, the public-assistance fraud that made him rich and his businesses appear legitimate, even the burning of the Cadillacs in Southern California for the insurance money all those years ago. The belief system that W. D. Fard had created after observing the wealth of the Moorish Science Temple in Chicago justi-fied the schemes Bey employed to enrich himself by any means necessary. "Fuck the white man before he fucks you" is how he once described his philosophy to someone he knew. The white man, of course, was not the only target. When Bey first joined the Nation of Islam in the early 1960s, it was rife with internal corruption as Elijah Muhammad and his family built riches upon the tithings and work, like newspaper sales, they forced on members, thousands of whom lived in or close to poverty. Given the number of his own followers he exploited during his decades in Oakland, Bey's schemes were color-blind.

History, of course, was lost on Devaughndre Broussard. He thought of Muslims as the guys hawking newspapers and bean pies. He'd never given much thought to what Islam was or whether what the Beys practiced was anything close to it. In exchange for work, a place to live, and a chance to be a part of something, anything, he probably would have agreed to worship a rag doll or a dog. So he told Fourth that, yeah, he could follow orders and thought Black people deserved the help of their own. In exchange for that, Broussard got his little flat across San Pablo Avenue from the bakery without heat, electricity, or hot water. "It's a cause," Fourth had said; the movement created by his father was bigger than any one individual. Broussard had to learn how to sacrifice, to give up material desires for now. But Broussard would soon learn that everything at the bakery centered on the one, not the many. Fourth had learned well from his Daddy how to make it his kingdom.

Broussard would eventually stammer that he had no place else to go, that he stumbled into legal adulthood with an arrest record, little education, and deep antisocial problems.

"I got hella flaws," he would say one day.

Broussard's life inside the system—group homes, foster care, juvenile hall, jail—had left him with few options and, worse, no idea how to access what options might have remained: remediating his education or, most important, finding the mental health care he so obviously needed. Broussard considered his San Francisco probation officer, in his phrase, "a dick head" for sternly ordering him to find work, always threatening a return to jail if he didn't. The system wasn't designed to provide severely damaged nineteen-year-olds with help no matter how much their penchant for violence. To Broussard, the world outside of street culture and institutions was indecipherable and abstract, and all probation did was shove him toward the unknown. What made the bakery so appealing was that it was within the realm of what he understood, a thuggish, violent culture. When Bey IV talked about scams and crime, Broussard knew he was home.

To achieve the powerful machine of which he dreamed, Fourth needed more cogs than just Broussard. And he didn't want to look solely to outsiders. He needed Bey blood too, and to get it he recruited two of his half brothers, Yusuf Bey V and Joshua Bey.

They were sons of Yusuf Bey by different women and so were each other's half brother too. But Fifth and Joshua were also first cousins. They represented a deep legacy of horrors within the cult: Fifth's mother was Nancy; Joshua's was Jane. Fifth hadn't spent much of his youth in Oakland. He was the third child Nancy had borne Yusuf Bey. When she left and tried to form some semblance of a life, she spared Fifth much. As an adolescent he lived with relatives in Palo Alto, forty miles away, but he still knew his father and half siblings. Fifth faced a fateful choice in life when he was about eighteen: stay out or go to his blood and his faith. The pull of being a Bey proved irresistible. He chose blood and faith. His time away had not convinced him there were other things in the world for a son of Yusuf Bey. Fifth held Fourth, older by a year, in great fealty and slid easily into the role of his consigliere and second in command.

The best Fourth could hope for from Joshua was that he would make a good soldier. Like Fifth, Joshua had spent his childhood elsewhere. His mother, Jane, hadn't stopped running from the Beys until she'd reached the East Coast. But even there, Joshua felt the bakery's pull. Against her better judgment, his mother let Joshua make summer visits. He worked in the bakery, where he became close with several half brothers he hadn't known well when he was younger. Finally, just before his senior year of high school, Joshua called his mother and said he wasn't coming back.

Joshua struggled with complexities. His brothers called him slow, or retarded, riding him constantly. He wore gold caps and grills on his teeth and always seemed to be snapping photos of himself with his cell phone. But he gave Fourth and Fifth absolute loyalty. Joshua became a good soldier, or at

least he tried, but what he needed most was for his brothers to take care of
him, to protect him. It was as if he were a naive, gangly puppy. He would
follow them anywhere, do anything they asked, always seeking the acceptance they withheld.

Building his army with men like Broussard, Joshua, and Fifth was one thing
for Fourth. Running a business was quite another. Even the simplest tasks
were often beyond him. Fifth noticed immediately that Fourth seemed incapable of managing the bakery—the bread wasn't even wrapped right. Sales
were dismal and a sense of dread was rising among the followers. Receipts
were stuffed in paper bags, file drawers, shoe boxes. Bills and invoices were
strewn about. Cash was often not accounted for; most of it went in Fourth's
pocket. Soon, registered letters from the IRS about unpaid taxes started arriving. And there were calls about unpaid bills too. Suppliers wanted their
money. Despite the problems, Fourth always had cash, ate in fancy restaurants, bought three-thousand-dollar Armani suits and cars for people. He
was paying lawyers to defend him in his felony cases, the assault of the strip-
club bouncers and the attacks on the liquor stores. At one court appearance, he strutted past television cameras in a cream-colored suit, gold braids
covering his shoulders as if he were a general or perhaps an emperor. As he
walked, his men formed an oval around him, moving when he moved, stopping when he stopped, turning when he turned, like a school of fish.

Yusuf Bey had instilled in Fourth a sense of absolute entitlement to acquire what he wanted however he wanted. Within weeks of taking over the
bakery, Fourth had begun committing identity theft and fraud and using
the proceeds to entice Broussard and others. The spoils included a used
2002 Mercedes-Benz CL500 that was selling for $55,000. Fourth drove it
away from a dealership after presenting a fake driver's license and filling out
a credit application with false information. A couple of months after stealing the Mercedes, he used another forged driver's license, this one with the
name "Yasir Human," to help convince a car salesman at another luxury
dealership to let him drive off with a Jaguar before his credit application
cleared. Two of his soldiers drove off in luxury cars too. But their bigger
scores involved real estate.

Throughout 2006, Fourth used three false identities to acquire property loans, starting with $550,000 in mortgages on an East Oakland house. It was the easiest scam yet: No-income-verification loans seemed surreal, a gift from Allah. Using stolen notary stamps, his forged driver's licenses, and, in one case, the forged signature of a Superior Court judge on a bogus name-change document, Fourth and seven others secured more than six million dollars in loans from ten different lenders in a little more than a year. They bought twelve houses spread across the East Bay, pulling flips, stealing equity.

In the midst of listening to Fourth's incessant bragging about those scams and seeing his luxury cars and tailored suits, Devaughndre Broussard asked Fourth to pay him for scrubbing baking pans. Fourth had told him that most of his money would be off the books, cash here, cash there. But when Broussard asked for it, Fourth would rant about Broussard's need to invest in the bakery's survival and stop thinking about himself. Finally, Broussard got in his face.

"Now brother, just calm down," Fourth told him. They walked to a corner.

"I'm working for free. Fuck that," Broussard snapped.

He was taller than Fourth, ganglier, veins still roping his arms. One punch and Fourth would curl to the floor. But beating down the leader would get Broussard killed. His hands unclenched. Fourth told him not to discuss money in front of others. If they all knew Broussard got paid in cash, they'd want cash too, he said.

"Take me to the side if you need to talk, brother. Don't tell nobody," Fourth said, falling into the spiel that had helped the cult exploit people for years. "It's a cause. You gotta stay strong. We need soldiers like you that's willin' to sacrifice for the bakery."

Fourth eventually gave Broussard three hundred dollars for several weeks of work, which appeased him a little. Broussard began to "feel the brotherly love," he would say, and paid more attention to Fourth's lessons and rants about racial history. Fourth hyped sacrifice, and for a while Broussard kept listening. The bakery did put a roof over his head and give him food, after all, and Fourth often reminded him he should consider that part of his pay too.

When Fourth turned twenty-one in January 2007, he wanted a party worthy of a young king. There might not have been money for bills or paychecks, but there was enough to rent a Lake Tahoe villa and transport dozens of people there for a multi-day celebration. That sent Broussard back to the overwhelming sense that he was getting played. Broussard saw that others, like Fifth and Joshua, were getting paid more consistently than he was too. The three hundred dollars Broussard had received was treated like a big deal, like it had to be scraped together, but now Fourth could afford to rent a villa? Who did he think he was fooling?

Broussard was not invited to Fourth's bash—he was one of the soldiers assigned to stay behind at the bakery. There was also security work at a strip mall in a rough East Oakland neighborhood; he took shifts there, standing around all day, unsure if he would ever get compensated for his time. When on the weekend of Fourth's birthday Broussard's relief didn't arrive, he called the bakery and was told there wouldn't be any. He was ordered to work another eight hours. Broussard hung up and called Marcus Callaway, who came to get him. Fourth returned from the mountains to learn a soldier had quit. Callaway and others counseled Broussard not to go back, but Fourth was persistent, calling and calling, and Broussard relented. Besides, if he told his probation officer he'd left the bakery, he'd have to find another job or end up back at jail.

But as he returned to San Pablo Avenue, Broussard began to curse his fate. If Fourth hadn't gotten arrested in San Francisco and met Lewis in jail, Broussard would have been someplace else. Maybe that place would have been better; it was hard for him to imagine anywhere worse, except back in a cell. All he could do now was work and hope something changed.

Among the other security jobs Fourth arranged was for his men to serve as bouncers at underground clubs. They were mostly all-cash businesses, and who better to keep the peace than the Bey soldiers with their intimidating dark suits and vacant stares?

At one assignment, Broussard and another Muslim, an older man whose name Broussard didn't even know, got into a tiff. The older guy didn't like Broussard telling him where to stand. They exchanged hard looks, hostilities rising. One of them suggested they go in the bathroom and slug it out, but before punches were thrown, Fifth intervened, the dispute ending peacefully. Later, though, when word trickled back to Fourth about what happened, he confronted Broussard. "Anybody who fucks up . . . loses us money, loses their life," he said.

Broussard reeled, asking himself, *Did he just threaten to kill me?*

Here was this motherfucker, always talking about sacrifice and brotherhood, loyalty, making people sit in meetings and listen to his bullshit, making them memorize his rules and read the gibberish in Elijah Muhammad's books. For what? So he could tell people they'd die if they made a mistake?

Is that what brotherhood was really about?

Broussard quit again, and this time he resolved not to go back.

20

The Gang That Couldn't Shoot Straight

*"As he lay there in the silence he listened carefully for
the sound of dogs. But there was nothing but stillness
all around him. Was it possible? Was he really going to
make it this time?"*

—ALEX HALEY, *Roots*

The inevitable occurred on October 24, 2006, a day shy of the first anniversary of Antar's murder. Your Black Muslim Bakery filed for Chapter 11 bankruptcy reorganization, citing a combined $900,000 debt to the IRS and to the finance company that had lent money to Antar. Fourth identified assets totaling $1,850,000. That asset claim was, of course, false. There would be no legitimate attempt to deal with the unpaid loans. Bankruptcy was just one more scam, a chance to buy time to figure a way out without having to repay the money. With the creditors' collection attempts on hold, Fourth quickly transferred several properties the business owned—worth a total of $2,228,000—to his mother in an attempt to conceal them. He eventually agreed to a reorganization plan requiring seven-thousand-dollar monthly payments on the loan at 10 percent interest. Even if he had intended to make those payments, Fourth would have struggled, given that he had no idea how to create a legitimate cash flow. He managed to sell a few fish sandwiches and bean pies, but that was about it. He seemed not to understand the situation's gravity, thinking that his scams would work or that Oakland's politicians would step in and somehow keep the bakery from going under.

Rather than work on a legitimate business plan, Fourth undertook other endeavors—like building an arsenal.

Weapons were all around the compound: automatic pistols, AK-47s, assault rifles, shotguns—including the little shotty stolen from the liquor store, the one police hadn't tried try to recover; at night he and others would go up to the roof and fire into the air, terrorizing people living nearby, Lucifer at it again. Ammunition was scattered everywhere, boxes of shotgun shells—mostly heavy loads of slugs and buckshot—clips of assault-rifle rounds, loose pistol bullets. Fourth even started wearing a holstered sidearm, a big .45 automatic. He was playing with it in a crowded room one night when it went off, a bullet piercing the leg of one of his half sisters, though she refused to tell police anything.

Besides guns, Fourth also bought a decommissioned police car, a big Crown Victoria with flashing lights on the grill and a spotlight on the driver's door. It looked just like a real cop car. It was ostensibly to give his security business more credibility, but Fourth liked to play around in it, rushing up behind cars while hitting the lights and laughing as he swerved out of the way. Everything was a joke to him. At least it seemed that way.

In early May 2007, Fourth got unbelievable news. Richard Lewis had beaten his murder rap; a jury had found him not guilty, just as he'd predicted.* He was ready to join the bakery.

Lewis had gone to Sacramento to visit relatives, and Fourth readied an entourage and a motorcade to go and get him, attaching the red-crescent flags he liked so much above the doors of the cars. Fourth's men raced across the Central Valley, the little flags snapping as if the cars were carrying diplomats. They brought home a soldier whom Fourth immediately elevated high into the organization.

Lewis's arrival coincided with a plan Fourth had to keep his creditors

---

*Lewis was acquitted after a judge threw out on legal technicalities a statement Lewis made to police in which he admitted involvement in the murder.

at bay. He seemed to resolve that he would have to pay them something to string them along. To do so, Fourth decided, he would go for a big score by robbing not street-level drug hawkers but a big wholesaler.

The Beys' public persona was that they hated narcotics, but Fourth was friendly with a midlevel Oakland cocaine dealer named Johnny, mostly because he was interested in one of Johnny's daughters as a possible third or fourth plural wife. Around the time Lewis joined the bakery, Fourth asked Johnny for a loan, an idea Johnny had the good sense to reject. But Fourth was insistent, and Johnny had other problems. He had recently suffered a home-invasion robbery in which he lost a lot of jewelry and cash. He had a pretty good idea who had set him up—a rival drug dealer and a woman to whom he had once sold small amounts of cocaine for redistribution. Johnny wanted retribution, and who better to use to achieve it than a violent fool like Fourth? They cut a deal. If Fourth robbed the rival drug dealer—according to Johnny, a guy named Tim who dressed all flashy in white and drove a white Mercedes like he was a cocaine merchant sent from central casting—then Fourth could keep whatever money he scored. Johnny would take the drugs. It seemed clean enough.

Fourth ordered Fifth and Joshua to begin surveilling Tim, which, despite his conspicuous style, proved challenging. Eventually, Tim would tell police he had been wondering who the guys were who kept trying to follow him, the ones he found it easy to give the slip. Johnny, though, was nothing if not persistent, telling Fourth that there was a big score ahead of them. Fifth would eventually testify that Fourth thought the "operation," as he called it, would result in his obtaining $500,000, an absurd figure. Johnny would say he told Fourth maybe it would net him $30,000. But Fourth had a way of making everything seem far bigger than it was.

Johnny grew frustrated when Fourth's guys couldn't find Tim, so he decided to speed things up. On the night of May 17, 2007, he called Fourth and reported that the woman who bought cocaine from Tim was at a bingo hall in East Oakland. Fourth ought to get some guys out there, Johnny said.

Fourth seized on the idea, yelling to Joshua to get to the bingo hall. But Joshua didn't know his way around Oakland. Another soldier named Tamon Halfin was ordered to drive him. Fourth then found Fifth and Lewis and told them to get guns and masks and dress in black. Fourth dressed the same way. He was going with them. Sure, commanders let soldiers do the work, but there was a lot of money at stake, or so he thought. He needed to be there this time.

A short while later, the Crown Victoria roared away from the bakery, headed east.

Shit. Cops.

All sorts of police lights flashed behind her from a big car that had just pulled up on her bumper. *Was I speeding?* JoAnne thought. She pulled over to the shoulder of I-580. JoAnne had reason to worry about the police. She had cocaine in her purse. Not a lot, but enough to get busted. Her mother was with her, and since it was late, just past 10:30 p.m., her mother's dementia had really kicked in, as it did every night. Maybe if she told the police that, they'd give her a break. Regardless, she reminded herself as she pulled over, just stay cool. It was a ticket. Nothing major. Suddenly a scalding light shot into her rearview and side mirrors, the reflections blinding her.

Men in masks with guns were on her in a second, yelling for her to get the fuck out. A tall one had a pistol; a smaller guy, a rifle. She climbed out of her gold Pontiac and, in a panic, tried to bolt across the highway. The tall one yanked her back. Then there was another one, his face masked too. He grabbed her and threw her in the back of the police car. The other door opened and the tall guy had JoAnne's mother. *Oh God, not her too.* But he pushed her in. One of them pulled a garbage bag over JoAnne's head; another handcuffed her. First she couldn't see because of the blinding light. Now she had a bag over her head. Through all that, she had never seen anyone's face. There were five of them in total, but she hadn't gotten a clean look at any of them. She had no idea who they were—but they were certainly not cops.

There was yelling and doors slamming, and then she felt the car accelerating hard onto the highway. She started crying. The garbage bag muffled her; she couldn't breathe. She composed herself enough to ask for a breathing hole. Someone tore a slit in the bag. The car pulled to the right and down an exit ramp. JoAnne didn't know that her gold Pontiac was right behind them. Just in back of the Pontiac, another young man trailed in a third car as they stayed in a tight formation across the East Oakland flats. Then they stopped and the men pulled JoAnne out. They scurried about, one of them barking orders. JoAnne still couldn't see, but it seemed like they were leaving her mother in the car. She sensed she was being taken inside a building, maybe a house. There was a gate, some steps, a door. They forced her into a wooden chair, the garbage bag clinging to her face. She couldn't think. Then someone asked, "Where the fuck's Tim keep his money, Bitch?" and the first wave of pain roiled across her body.

"I don't know nothing about Tim's money," JoAnne cried, her words trembling. One of the men took a knife—it had a long, curved blade and a handle shaped like brass knuckles—and slowly opened slits on her arms, blood dripping onto the chair. They pulled her skirt down. Then one of them hit her again; they barraged her with questions. Yeah, she knew Tim, but nothing about his stash. One of them went outside and got her purse from the Pontiac. There was only one dollar in it—she'd lost fifty bucks playing bingo—and a few small bags of cocaine. This bitch didn't just know where a dealer stashed his money; she was a dealer herself. That changed things. The one with her purse smashed JoAnne's face with a .357 Magnum pistol. The blow nearly knocked her out. They kept screaming about the money. Where was the money? But she couldn't tell them what she didn't know. They kept hitting and cutting her.

If she didn't start giving them answers, one of the men said, then he was going to shove a hot curling iron into her vagina. Another took deep breaths and asked her if she smelled gasoline—were they going to immolate her? Someone said they would take her up in the hills where no one would find her body. She was going to die, she told herself. Maybe at least they'd make it quick.

Each time she said she didn't know where Tim hid his money, they hit her harder. She had to know. Then the questions shifted. Did she have money? She sold drugs—look at the cocaine in her purse—so where was her money? She didn't have any. Where did she live? She told them. One of them hit her on the kneecap with something metallic—the butt of a gun or the knife hilt.

She nearly vomited from the pain. They said there'd better be money at her house.

Then someone came in from outside and JoAnne was left alone for a moment as they huddled in the empty living room under a little golden chandelier. Behind them, vacant bookshelves surrounded a small fireplace. It wasn't working, one of them said; either she really didn't know where Tim the drug dealer kept his money or her life wasn't worth very much to her. Maybe there would be drugs at her house. JoAnne could hear their whispers. She knew they would find nothing of value at her home and come back and kill her and her mother.

Back out in the street, a lone police officer searching for a stolen car was driving toward the house. It was pure luck. Of all the streets in East Oakland, he just happened to be on the one where the Crown Vic was parked. He saw it and, thinking it was a police car, made a U-turn to see what was going on. When he did, his headlights shined through the front window of the little house where JoAnne was being held prisoner, illuminating her attackers.

Shit. *Real* cops. *Run,* Fourth yelled.

They took off toward the back of the house. Glass broke loudly, and Fourth, Lewis, and Joshua scurried through a busted window. Fifth simply opened a door and stepped outside. The four of them hopped a fence and kept going across backyards, running wildly into the darkness, Fourth's scheme destroyed.

JoAnne heard them fleeing and began screaming. She tore at the garbage bag with her cuffed hands—it was nearly all that covered her bloody body—and ran to the front window. Now she could see it: "a real police car," she would call it. In her panic she elbowed the window, shattering it. The cop slammed his car into park and jumped out his door, running toward the chain-link gate, throwing it open, oblivious to anything other than a woman yelling frantically. She opened the door and, still screaming, pushed past him onto the porch, the tattered bag flapping, her hands still cuffed. Then he got her and helped her away, his arms around her, as she sobbed uncontrollably.

Behind them, Tamon Halfin, the man in the Crown Vic, picked up his gun. What should he do? Take them out? He was certain the cop had seen his face. A day would come when Fourth would admonish Halfin for not killing the police officer right there. But instead of shooting, Halfin opened the door and slipped away, leaving Joanne's mother in the backseat under a blanket.

Between JoAnne's sobs, the officer could hear fences rattling in the night as they all got away, but her cuffed hands clutched him now—her guardian angel, she would call the cop who saved her life—and she wouldn't let go.

Little that Fourth would ever do could eclipse how the botched kidnapping illustrated his combination of hubris and brazen idiocy. As he and his fleeing soldiers hid under cars and ducked behind bushes, trying to escape, their crime rapidly unraveled. They'd left two cars at the scene—the Crown Vic and a Chrysler that Joshua and Halfin had driven to the bingo parlor. Within minutes, cops had traced their license plates. They also soon discovered that the little house where JoAnne was tortured had until recently belonged to one of Fourth's many brothers-in-law, who had sold it to a man involved in Fourth's real-estate scam ring. Joshua, in his panicked flight, had dropped his bright yellow Nokia cell phone behind the house, full of photos of himself and numbers of more than a dozen people close to Fourth. And the knife used to slice slits in JoAnne's arms and torso had Lewis's DNA on it. As they ran, Fourth used his own cell phone to call the bakery for help, creating electronic evidence of his location.

It was enough bumbling that one day a judge would give them the title of an old Jimmy Breslin novel about an inept Mafia crew, *The Gang That Couldn't Shoot Straight.*

But it would take the Oakland police months to put the pieces together, and as Fourth sought other ways to extricate himself from the bankruptcy and assert his power as the spring of 2007 turned to summer, shooting straight would prove to be about the only thing that his men could do right.

21

Crazy-Ass Hitters

"If a man puts out the eye of a patrician,
his eye shall be put out."
—Code of Hammurabi

Devaughndre Broussard was probably in San Francisco the night that JoAnne was tortured. He had been gone from the Beys for two months, drifting around the Fillmore, occasionally going over to Marcus Callaway's in Richmond. He was essentially homeless. Broussard had enrolled in a general equivalency diploma program, but he was still looking for work to appease his probation officer, who was riding him about making restitution payments to the art student. On May 11, 2007, a San Francisco cop spotted Broussard on lower Haight Street, an area known for drug sales, and, recognizing him as being on probation, stopped and searched him. Broussard had $120 in small bills in his pants pocket. He denied selling dope and wasn't arrested. But he was clearly headed back to jail if something didn't change.

A few weeks later, he was walking along Page Street in the Fillmore one day when he saw a black Charger crawling toward him. He looked more closely. Was that Fourth's car? Then a door swung open and Richard Lewis emerged. . . . Richard was out! The men embraced. Lewis, just days into his new life at the bakery, was driving around San Francisco looking for his little cousin Dre. Lewis told Broussard he wanted him to come back to Oakland. But Broussard resisted, saying he'd tried that not once but twice and didn't want to return to Fourth's constant carping about sacrifice.

"Don't trip," Lewis replied. "I'm here now, your big cousin. It's gonna be better. Come fuck with us." Lewis went on, telling Broussard that he would protect him, that his presence around Fourth ensured regular paychecks for them both.

Broussard knew he couldn't say no to Lewis because Lewis knew the truth, that Broussard had nothing else. Broussard's only other option was joining some of his cousins in the Page Street Mob, a bloody San Francisco gang, slinging dope with them. Even that seemed better than the bakery. Although he had started the GED program, the first step he needed to take to get anyplace, Broussard believed there was little hope—or help—for someone like him. In a long-held Black Muslim tenet, Elijah Muhammad would have said Broussard had a "slave mentality," the self-defeating attitude that his circumstances and race destined him to failure. But where the Muslims went wrong was in teaching that hate and segregation were the cures for such thinking. And the Beys, especially Fourth, had twisted the tenet further, to the point of complete exploitation of people like Broussard. As Lewis continued to push, telling him that hanging around San Francisco meant nothing but a return to jail, the renewed promises of protection and steady pay intrigued Broussard. He finally agreed to go talk to Fourth.

That night, back at the compound, Fourth told Broussard that the doors to salvation always remained open to strong young men. And Lewis, his lifelong friend, looked right at him and said it would all be fine now. After being in jail for two years and somehow dodging a murder charge, Lewis would never do anything stupid enough to go back, he insisted. But little did Broussard know that less than two weeks after Lewis heard the words "not guilty" in his murder trial, he had shoved a rifle in a woman's face as he helped kidnap her and left his own DNA on the knife he had used to torture her. The one Broussard trusted the most was more committed to being Fourth's chief henchman than he was to helping anyone else.

But Lewis's pressure was too much; Broussard relented. He would try the bakery for a third time since getting out of jail less than a year earlier.

The Black Muslims' history with the incarcerated had always been mixed. Elijah Muhammad had steeled his resolve in Fard's teachings while in federal prison for draft dodging during World War II; Malcolm X had converted while serving time in a Massachusetts penitentiary; Wallace Muhammad had returned to his father's good graces and put himself on a path to succeed Elijah as head of the Nation in 1975 when he served a federal term without complaint after not registering for the draft in the early sixties. But by filling their ranks with people possessing criminal records, the Black Muslims invited in those who found conversion to a pious lifestyle difficult. "You can put a bowtie on a pig, but he is still a pig," a Muslim minister named Aksia Muhammad told a San Francisco newspaper shortly after Elijah Muhammad's death in 1975. "Some of these people have been hoodlums for twenty years and members of the Nation for two years. When they want something they revert to what they know best."

What the people Fourth now brought in knew best was violence. Just as Broussard returned, Lewis also offered refuge in the compound to another San Franciscan with an incredibly unpeaceful past, Antoine Arlus Mackey.

Mackey was twenty-one that summer of 2007. His big, sleepy eyes concealed a killer's soul. San Francisco police suspected Mackey had several gang slayings to his credit, but they lacked the evidence to charge him. Mackey had racked up several gun violations and been charged as a juvenile in a hideous sex case, pleading guilty to forcing a girl to perform oral sex. He became a registered sex offender at just thirteen years old.

As he built his criminal life, Mackey also became a ghetto legend for having survived three shootings and a stabbing, attacks in which he nearly died. His wounds left him with chronic headaches, and the left side of his body alternated between sensations of numbness and coldness; he could never get warm. His right hand suffered lingering paralysis from a bullet. Doctors had told him he'd just have to accept a life of pain and limitations.

"I just feel crazy," he once said about the pain, of his inability to play sports as he once had. He'd dreamed of a football career, but now, he said, he couldn't do a single push-up. He'd lost weight he couldn't gain back. He could not, he said, accept his plight. He would be angry forever. Mackey also had a long fascination with weaponry. When he was a kid, a relative had let him see a Tec-9, an unreliable but deadly machine pistol. Mackey adored that gun, once imitating the sound of bullets spraying from it, saying how he loved the thought of blowing someone away.

In May 2007, after Mackey was shot for the third time, Lewis, who knew him from the Fillmore and from attending the same high school, urged him to get out of San Francisco and hide at the bakery before he got killed. Mackey agreed.

Mackey was tall and handsome with a raspy, rattling voice. Women were drawn to him, especially when he acted stoically about his brushes with death. He was immediately popular at the bakery, and Fourth quickly decided that his new soldier with the sleepy eyes had suffered so much at the devil's hands that he should take a Muslim name immediately, dubbing him Ali. Broussard and Mackey formed an instant bond, becoming as "thick as thieves," Broussard would say. Along with Lewis, Fourth called them his "San Francisco muscle," the bakery's "crazy-ass hitters."

With Lewis and Mackey around, there was a new efficiency at the bakery; they were, for a while that summer, drawn to the idea of a Black-only enterprise. Mackey took over the front counter, charming customers with his wit. Lewis replaced Fifth, who had been jailed on a gun charge a few months earlier, as Fourth's second in command, which benefited Broussard further. He was finally getting paid regularly and had resolved to become a good soldier. Fourth still dangled the "credit hookup" scam in front of him as incentive. Lewis already had a forged driver's license. Broussard wanted one too, and he was ready to earn it.

But even though he was now at the edge of the bakery's inner circle, Broussard remained somewhat leery of Fourth. His rhetoric of superiority and blood vengeance mostly failed to match his actions. Fourth often claimed he hadn't asked for so many stressful problems. He had simply done his duty when his brother was killed. The leadership had been thrust upon him.

But why, Broussard wondered, in the nearly two years since Antar's death, had Fourth not exacted retribution, especially given all his tough talk?

Over time, the random carjacking theory had stuck. Everyone thought that Antar had simply stopped at the wrong gas station in the wrong car. Alfonza Phillips had kept his mouth shut about being Fourth's hit man, and no one from the bakery had gotten to him in jail. But, Broussard wondered, what good was a faith of blood vengeance if none was ever carried out? If everyone really thought Phillips had just acted impulsively, then didn't they wonder why Fourth had not struck back for his beloved older brother? Was Fourth weak?

Did he do anything other than break bottles, beat women, sign bogus loans? When Phillips appeared in court, Broussard would don his suit and join the other soldiers in shows of strength. At one session, Fourth pointed out Phillips's father—and suggested Broussard begin surveillance on him. The father didn't live far from the bakery. Broussard took early-morning jogs around his block, trying to get a fix on the man's comings and goings. But he never saw him. The plans drifted away, and Fourth never seemed that interested. Was it simply to be ready in case Phillips revealed his secret to police?

Now Fourth had his "crazy-ass hitters," and still he did nothing. But Fourth may have thought that killing his father would push Phillips to talking. It was a chip he couldn't play.

Then, one day in late June, Fourth and Broussard were sitting at a sidewalk table outside the bakery. A man who hung around the neighborhood, sometimes hustling a few dollars to buy drugs, walked past. Long dreadlocks curved around his thin face, a mustache and goatee framing his mouth. His name was Odell Roberson; he often asked for handouts. Broussard was among those who sometimes passed him a fish sandwich. Yusuf Bey had told his followers that the devils aspired to addict all Blacks to poisons to render them unable to do anything for themselves. Mercy should be extended and chances given for such oppressed people to find Allah's salvation.

"How you doing, my brothers?" Roberson said as he passed.

Fourth and Broussard returned the greeting. As Roberson shuffled off, Fourth leaned in and whispered to Broussard, "Do you know who he's related to?"

Before Broussard could answer, Fourth said, "Dude who killed my brother."

Broussard stiffened.

"And he's just like walkin' around?" he asked.

Fourth's eyes narrowed. Yeah. Roberson was Alfonza Phillips's uncle, and he was just walking around.

Broussard didn't say what he was thinking: *You knew this and did nothing? All your preaching, all your eye-for-an-eye shit and a relative of the man who killed your brother is just walking around begging for handouts?*

Then Fourth said, "That's why we need brothers like you."

Broussard nodded. Here, finally, might be a chance to get closer to a real payday.

Fourth seemed to take the question about Roberson as a slight, but it was likely more from insecurity than anything else. If Broussard perceived Fourth as weak and hypocritical for not enacting revenge for Antar, did others think that too? Fourth hated doubts. As long as Phillips stayed silent, his father stayed alive. But there was no deal about an uncle. Killing Roberson would send a message to anyone else in the cult who thought like Broussard. It would say that blood vengeance was more than rhetoric. Fourth gave the order: "Take him out when you get the chance."

At midnight on July 6, Broussard and Mackey said they would take a security patrol outside the compound. Fourth was always on them to roust drug dealers and prostitutes whom he didn't want on the surrounding blocks. When Broussard had first arrived the previous year, he had watched Fourth spray fire from an assault rifle out of a window at a gaggle of streetwalkers, making them scatter for their lives.

Now Broussard watched as Mackey took one of Fourth's favorite weapons—an SKS assault rifle loaded with 7.62 mm rounds—and put it down the leg of his baggy pants. He walked stiff-legged to conceal the gun. They slipped out of the side of the compound, and Broussard pulled the hood of a black sweatshirt over his head. They turned right on Fifty-ninth Street, then left on Herzog Street. There, a block away, unexpectedly, stood Odell Roberson.

Might as well get this done, Broussard thought, pulling the hood of his sweatshirt over his head.

"Y'all got some work?" Roberson asked when Broussard and Mackey got closer. He meant crack.

"Yeah," Broussard said, and walked toward a tree on the far corner. Its branches offered additional cover. Roberson followed him. With the hoodie concealing much of Broussard's face, Roberson must have mistaken him for a street dealer and fished around in his pocket, pulling out wrinkled bills.

Broussard turned to Mackey, his back to Roberson as if he were reaching for a satchel of drugs in his own pants.

"Guess what? I got this one," Broussard whispered.

Mackey looked at him blankly. Broussard hadn't told him he'd made a deal with Fourth to kill Roberson. Mackey might have done it himself to earn points. Fuck that. This was about Broussard accomplishing something, getting somewhere

"You want this one?" Mackey asked in his gravelly voice.

"Yeah. I'm on this. Pass it to me," Broussard said as Roberson stood a few feet behind him. Now Mackey understood and pulled the SKS, stock first, from his pants.

Roberson must have glimpsed the rifle as Mackey handed it to Broussard, because he broke for the far side of the street.

Broussard whipped around, clicking off the safety as he jammed the stock into his shoulder, his eye lining up with the sight.

"Freeze!" he yelled.

Roberson turned, his hands rising in surrender.

Broussard was perhaps fifteen feet away when he fired.

Roberson dropped his money and tried to shield himself from the barrage. A bullet passed through his hand, another through his wrist. Others hit his face and yet more his torso, blowing out his back. He collapsed, Broussard following him down, the final shots making Roberson jerk on the sidewalk. Broussard fired until his magazine was empty, the muzzle flashes a nearly continuous flame. Roberson sprawled on the ground, his money— ten dollars and five cents—lying in a heap under him, empty rifle casings scattered on the street, the smell of cordite sudden and strong in the summer night.

22

We Should Not Become the Evil That We Deplore

"Stupidity combined with arrogance and a huge ego will get you a long way."

—CHRIS LOWE, musician

Roberson's murder may have given Broussard confidence and provided Fourth a surge of satisfaction and power—and affirmed his rhetoric to his followers—but it was worthless when it came to both of their real problems: the bankruptcy for Fourth and Broussard's want of monetary rewards. Seven weeks had passed since the failed attempt to rob the drug dealer, and Fourth still needed to find a way to pay off his debts. Both the creditors that had loaned Antar money and the IRS remained unappeased and unrelenting: They began to push to convert the bankruptcy of Your Black Muslim Bakery from Chapter 11 reorganization to Chapter 7 liquidation. By July 2007, the judge in the case had no tolerance as Fourth begged for more time. Broussard, meanwhile, received nothing for killing Roberson. But Fourth kept baiting him. The kid had killed once, and with a little more incentive, he would probably kill again. Fourth could get more blood work out of him before he finally had to produce his long-promised payoff.

But Fourth had other, more immediate concerns. To some people who had been at the bakery under Yusuf Bey, the organization had ceased to exist after the disappearance of Waajid Aljawwaad more than three years earlier. Antar had been an illegitimate CEO, and so was Fourth by succession. The man who still pushed this point the hardest was Saleem Bey, who claimed the bakery had been a legitimate enterprise under Yusuf Bey. But all of Yusuf Bey's followers had enabled his horrors, giving his conduct tacit approval. Few were blameless.

Saleem Bey had been born Darren Wright, which he considered a slave name. Unlike many drawn to the Beys, he had no criminal record, simply a scorching hatred of how his people had suffered throughout history. Saleem Bey remained a law-abiding citizen. After his close friend John Bey was nearly killed, Saleem, rather than simply arm himself for protection, applied for a concealed-weapon permit. The application was rejected, but by seeking the permit rather than just buying a gun on the street, Saleem showed that, unlike most of his brethren—and especially Fourth—he was a person who played by society's rules.

As the bankruptcy situation worsened, Saleem convinced Fourth to meet with him. Perhaps they could reconstitute a board of directors for the business. Saleem suggested that Fourth could remain in charge, but with several members of the old guard who had business experience in oversight and advisory roles. There still might be time to put together a business plan and save the bakery from foreclosure. But Fourth rejected the proposal out of hand. He and he alone, a blood son of Yusuf Bey, would remain in charge. He was, as he liked to boast, *Yusuf Ali Bey the Fourth.* He would listen to no one.

After that disastrous meeting, Saleem took his claims that Antar had used forged documents to seize the company to police; they told him it seemed like a civil matter and declined to investigate. He went to IRS agents; all they cared about was collecting back taxes. He tried to formally enter the bankruptcy case but was rebuffed; he lacked standing, he was told.

Saleem's next option was to try to convince local politicians to intervene. Perhaps political pressure could be applied to the bankruptcy. The longer that liquidation could be stalled, the longer Saleem would have to figure out a way to get Fourth out of the bakery. It was obvious the kid was on a course of self-destruction, facing felony charges over the liquor stores and the strip-club assault in San Francisco. Sooner or later he was going to prison. But if the bakery compound had been sold off to pay debts by the time that happened, it would be too late for all of them.

Putting pressure on politicians was also very much on Fourth's agenda. It is exactly what his father would have done, crow about how the bakery was the one institution in Oakland trying to get people off the streets, offering work and shelter. It was exactly how Yusuf Bey had bled the city for loans for his failed health-care business and obtained contracts to sell his food in public venues. Fourth, of course, lacked Saleem's contacts and credibility, but he did have his father's name to trade on, and he was the one with the keys to the bakery.

As Fourth and Saleem separately began to make the political rounds seeking help, they each paid a visit to Oakland's mayor, Ronald Vernie Dellums.

Dellums was seventy-two years old in 2007 and less than a year into what would be a miserable tenure as Oakland's leader, one filled with violence, indecision, and inaction. Beginning in 1970, Dellums had served thirteen terms in Congress representing Oakland and Berkeley as a self-described socialist, earning a place on Richard Nixon's infamous enemies list, and becoming a darling of the liberal elite. He rose to chairman of the House Armed Services Committee, and his greatest political achievement was a bill known as the Comprehensive Anti-Apartheid Act of 1986, which became law after Congress overrode Ronald Reagan's veto of it, forcing U.S. businesses to divest South African holdings. It was the first time in the twentieth century that Congress had overcome a presidential veto of foreign-policy legislation. Dellums was a hero to African Americans. In Oakland, his family name was legend. His uncle was the labor leader C. L. Dellums, who, along with civil-rights giant A. Philip Randolph, had founded the first Black trade union in the country, the Brotherhood of Sleeping Car Porters. Black Oaklanders revered C. L. Dellums and for decades extended those affections to his tall, handsome nephew. That is, until they elected him mayor.

Running a city, especially a deeply dysfunctional city, is very different from running a congressional staff or a committee. Dellums, the socialist, lived in a Georgetown mansion after he retired from Congress and lobbied

for health-care companies, Rolls-Royce, the government of Haiti. Before
his election to the House, he'd been on the Berkeley City Council, his only
other elective office. Yet in 2005, a committee formed to draft him to run
for mayor the next year. Dellums would eventually claim that he hadn't
wanted the job and that his intention had been to decline to reenter public
life. But as he made his way to a podium at Oakland's Laney College to
formally tell his supporters no, they began chanting, "Run Ron, run . . .
Run Ron, run." Dellums's emotions got the better of him, and he declared
his candidacy off-the-cuff. Dellums then won the city's open primary in
June 2006, avoiding a fall runoff by less than one quarter of 1 percent of
the vote. He spent the next six months sitting around waiting to be sworn
in, regretting his impulse, lamenting the looming job he didn't desire. By
the time he assumed office in early 2007, his enthusiasm had vanished. But
people still had great expectations for Oakland's third African American
mayor.

To Fourth, the mayor's ethnicity meant everything; there was no question in his mind Dellums would help him save the bakery. As a congressman, Dellums had lavished praise on Yusuf Bey, even as Bey's outward
business conservatism and calls for self-determination stood at odds with
Dellums's avowed leftist philosophies. Dellums had also once tried to inter-
fere in the murder trial of two Black Muslims in Oakland, urging that they
receive better lawyers, receiving a sharp rebuke from a Superior Court judge
for an improper intrusion. During his meeting with the mayor, Fourth insisted that Your Black Muslim Bakery existed only to help Black people and
strengthen the Oakland community. His request for help convincing the
bankruptcy judge to give him more time to reorganize the business met no
opposition. Saleem asked Dellums for essentially the same thing, since liquidation wouldn't help him, either. After Fourth and Saleem saw the mayor
in separate meetings, Dellums ordered his staff to draft a letter of support in
an effort to appease them.

Dellums didn't bother to ask the opinion of police or prosecutors, even
though both the liquor-store attacks and Fourth's assault case for running
down the strip-club bouncers in San Francisco had received substantial news
coverage. If he had, Dellums might have been told confidentially that police

were more than a month into an investigation of Fourth for the highway kidnapping of JoAnne and her mother and the torture that followed it. The Alameda County District Attorney's Office was also piecing together real-estate fraud charges against him and several of his cohorts that included, among other details, the forging of a judge's signature. Dellums also obviously knew about Yusuf Bey's abuses of his followers and that he had also orchestrated the fleecing of the city for more than one million dollars.

But regardless of facts, Oakland politicians still didn't say no to the Beys.

"I am writing . . . in support of Your Black Muslim Bakery," began the correspondence to the bankruptcy judge above Dellums's signature. "The bakery has established itself as an integral part of the community and its loss would be distressing to untold numbers of Oakland citizens. Not only has it been a source of nutritional, additive-free baked goods, but it has also provided stability by way of employment to many of our residents. I am sure the owners will avail themselves of every direction and opportunity you can extend to them that will ensure their business remains opened [*sic*]."

While Dellums's support helped, Fourth needed more than one letter. He pursued Black leaders all over Oakland and then went after the support of the person he thought could help him the most—the woman who had succeeded Dellums as Oakland and Berkeley's representative in Congress, Barbara Jean Lee.

Six years earlier, Lee had thrust herself from the House's back bench into a glaring world spotlight when she became the only member of Congress to vote against granting President George W. Bush authorization to retaliate for the September 11 attacks. Giving Bush and his minions war powers would "spiral out of control," Lee predicted. A right-wing hack writing for the Unification Church's *Washington Times* said Lee sprang from Northern California's "leftist fever swamps" and had longtime communist ties. Her decision to vote against war in Afghanistan came after she attended a prayer service at the National Cathedral. "One of the clergy members said that as we act, we should not become the evil that we deplore," Lee noted. Following Lee's decision, a Southern California state lawmaker who had

served with her when she was in the state legislature before her election to
Congress dismissed her as "always advocating on behalf of poor people." In
Oakland, where poverty sprawled unabated across the flatlands, Lee rou-
tinely won reelection to the House with more than 80 percent of the vote.

The Beys for years had foisted a public image that they, too, were advo-
cates for the poor. But it was a delicate dance for Yusuf Bey to endorse Barbara
Lee. To Bey, Lee and other African Americans in national leadership were just
"house niggers." He deplored Jesse Jackson and the Congressional Black Caucus, which Lee would eventually lead, seeing them as servants of the white
establishment, used only to placate the masses. Unless, of course, he wanted
something from them. Then mainstream African American leaders became
tolerable. By the time Lee succeeded Dellums in 1998, Bey had said much
publicly about the role of women—they should stay home, they were to submit, they were not meant for leadership. She didn't denounce him.

Like his father, Fourth saw women as inferior beings designed by God for
submission, but he needed Lee's help and had an inflated sense of how
much of it she could provide. Both he and Saleem thought Lee had the
power to sway the bankruptcy judge. Fourth wanted her to call for a halt
to the liquidation; Saleem believed that if he could convince Lee that the
bankruptcy was, in his word, illegal, she might endorse his claim to take
over the business.

On July 11, 2007, Fourth and his entourage—Mackey, Lewis, and
Broussard included—stormed into Lee's district office. Fourth must have
thought his name demanded so much respect that he could barge in, un-
announced, and win an immediate audience with her. Apparently, Fourth
thought members of Congress simply sat around their district offices waiting for walk-ins. But Lee wasn't there; the House was in session three thousand miles away.

As his soldiers stood at attention, Fourth demanded to see Lee, then
members of her staff. Fourth had an in with the office. He had known Lee's
director of constituent services, Saundra Andrews, for years. She wasn't a
member of the bakery or the Bey family, but she was very much a supporter

and a friend. She would eventually tell prosecutors that Fourth was like a son to her. In the same interview, she would also claim that authorities were using "tricknology" to make her say incriminating things about the Beys.

Andrews ushered Fourth into an inner office to talk with her and Lee's district director, a woman named Leslie Littleton. Fourth demanded, not asked, that the congresswoman help him. Littleton reeled. Who were this kid and his collection of goons? He had no idea of what a member of Congress could do for him. Lee certainly couldn't—as Fourth wanted—order a federal judge to halt a bankruptcy liquidation.

But Andrews was on his side, and she pressured Littleton to let her draft a letter for Lee's signature lobbying the bankruptcy judge to give Fourth more time to reorganize and settle with creditors. Littleton was cautious. She realized Fourth was a bully. But she grudgingly yielded to Andrews's demands that they help. A letter would go to the IRS only, asking its Taxpayer Advocate Service to give him another chance before liquidation. Andrews wrote the letter, which was stamped with Lee's signature.

"I am well acquainted with Your Black Muslim Bakery, Inc, and the important position it holds in our community," it stated. "I have been a supporter since its inception 45 years ago and personally witnessed its commitment to our youth and individuals in need. . . . Mr. Bey IV is making every attempt to save this business and maintain the most needed services it provides to our community. Given its importance to my district . . . Mr. Bey deserves every opportunity available to rescue his business."

Forty-five years earlier, in 1962, Lee had been a sixteen-year-old army brat living all over the country. Fourth's father and uncle had just been beginning their conversion to the Black Muslim religion. They wouldn't even open a bakery in Santa Barbara for several more years. Clearly, Andrews was, at best, greatly exaggerating in a letter that would carry Lee's automated signature.

That correspondence, though, was supposed to be little more than a form letter, Leslie Littleton would eventually testify. "It's a pretty standard letter," she would say. "You fill in the issues."

But instead of sending the letter to the IRS, Andrews attended a bankruptcy court hearing with Fourth the next afternoon and personally handed it to the judge. It bore no real importance, though, and the IRS was out of patience and wanted its money. Fourth had even stopped sending in payroll taxes. He wasn't getting a break.

But the letter was not meaningless to Fourth, not in the least. It showed the power of his name, his ability to maneuver in high political circles, to demand respect, action, and deference. He could march his entourage into the office of a member of Congress and get what he wanted.

Look at him. He was *Yusuf Ali Bey IV.*

23

Convenient but Not True

"It's torture coming here, reliving the crimes, and being face-to-face
with those who have murdered or maimed our loved ones."
—ROXANNE McMILLIAN, survivor of a January 1974 Zebra shooting,
speaking at a parole hearing for Larry Green, September 2009

Bursts of rifle fire rang in the distance, three shots followed quickly by three shots again and then three more. Broussard knew the difference between the sound of a pistol and the firecracker-like report of a Russian or Chinese assault weapon. He didn't think anything of random gunfire at night. It was Oakland. But then Fourth called Broussard's cell phone, yelling, "Open the back gate. Open the back gate." It was 3:12 a.m. on July 12—four days after Broussard had killed Odell Roberson and about fifteen hours after Fourth had shown up at Barbara Lee's office trying to get her to intervene in the bankruptcy proceeding.

Broussard ran outside and threw open the gate. The Charger roared down Fifty-ninth Street and made a sharp left into the compound. Broussard watched as Mackey and Fourth raced from the car in different directions: Mackey, carrying the SKS assault rifle, toward the back duplex, Fourth toward his apartment above the bakery.

What the hell had those motherfuckers done?

Broussard went after Mackey, finding him in his bedroom wiping down the rifle.

"I knocked one down," Mackey said. He smiled, his eyes no longer seeming so sad. Then he burst into laughter.

"Who was it?" Broussard asked.

Then Fourth walked in and embraced Mackey. Broussard asked again, "Who got shot?"

"Go see for yourself," Fourth said.

The shooting had happened just a few blocks up San Pablo. Broussard threw on jogging clothes. If the cops stopped him, he could claim he was just out for a late-night run. He made it four blocks north and there were red and blue lights slicing at the darkness, crime-scene tape already strung from light pole to light pole, cops all over the place.

"What happened?" Broussard asked a lady who stood watching.

"They shot that boy," she said, nodding toward a body across the street sprawled on its right side in front of Golden Gate Elementary School, blood pooling around it on the concrete.

Michael Wills was a thirty-six-year-old sous-chef who put in long hours at a restaurant near Lake Merritt. He played in rock bands, painted his toenails black, and dabbled in recreational drugs. Wills lived near the elementary school and knew some of the guys from the bakery who did security at the school's playground. He had worked up a casual acquaintance with some of them as he came and went. That night he'd come home, slipped on a pair of soft, brown shoes without laces, and headed out for something—cigarettes, a snack—at a gas station across San Pablo Avenue. The natural way for him to get there from his apartment on Sixty-third Street was to cut through an asphalt walkway that separated two softball fields from the school's playground.

That pathway was nearly one hundred yards long, with high chain-link fences on either side, forming a gauntlet.

Fourth and Mackey had been driving around with the SKS in the car when they spotted Wills entering the path from San Pablo on his way home.

Fourth had apparently been giving Mackey lessons in Black Muslim lore—talks that focused on slaying devils and the legend of the Zebra killings and Death Angels of more than thirty years earlier—that had been passed down to him by his father and bakery elders.

It was their topic of conversation just as they saw Wills walk into the path.

One of them must have said, *There goes a devil right there,* and they decided impulsively to kill him.

They turned on Sixty-third Street and raced behind the school to the other end of the path, beating Wills there, cutting him off. He must have seen Mackey waiting for him with the rifle and turned, sprinting for his life. But the distance back to San Pablo Avenue was too great; Mackey, skilled with guns and aided by several glaring overhead lights, had time to line him up. As Wills neared the street end of the path, passing a grove of towering eucalyptus trees that would have given him refuge if not for the fence, bullets tore into his upper back and exited his chest. He staggered and then fell dead on the sidewalk just five feet from the street, the soft blue lights of Alaska Gas glowing across the street, nine 7.62 mm shell casings scattered about nearby.

As Broussard arrived and stood watching the police evidence technicians scouring for clues, camera flashes going off as others photographed Wills's body, he was perplexed as to why Mackey and Fourth had killed the guy. Odell's murder had a reason—revenge for Antar, or so Broussard believed. But why this man?

When he ran back to the compound, he found Mackey and Fourth still chopping it up, their phrase for talking. Mackey went on about how he'd dropped into a low crouch with the rifle. It made Broussard think of the cartoon character Elmer Fudd hunting rabbits. The impact of the bullets to Wills's back as he sprinted must have twisted and contorted him, because Mackey said one of his victim's legs flew into the air as if he were kicking a football. As Broussard watched, Mackey and Fourth pranced around the duplex, kicking their legs in the air to imitate Wills, then throwing their arms in the air like a referee signaling a field goal and shouting, "It's good!" They took turns saying it, laughing like children, their arms shooting skyward again and again. "It's good!"

Neither of them, though, would tell Broussard why they had killed Wills, at least not yet.

Sometimes cops look at a crime scene and know in an instant what happened. That was certainly true when they saw Wills's body. Roberson's murder had been just four nights earlier. It didn't take much to figure it out. Two men shredded by high-caliber rifle fire, both just blocks from Your Black Muslim Bakery, in the part of Oakland where police had long since ceded the streets to the Beys. They had to be responsible for the killings. The pieces fit into a terrifying scenario. It had been nearly eight weeks since two cars registered to the cult members had been found outside the East Oakland house where JoAnne was tortured. Before someone had thrown a bag over her head, she had seen a masked man carrying what she described as a big gun. Could it have been the same kind of assault rifle used to kill Roberson and Wills?

Police certainly had the evidence to get some answers. Both murder scenes were littered with shell casings. (But because both men suffered through-and-through wounds, no bullets were recovered.) Whoever shot them had been incredibly sloppy. They had left the casings right next to their victims as if they arrogantly believed they couldn't be caught—perhaps another sign the Beys were involved. Within a few hours, police were rushing ballistics tests to determine whether the same gun had been used in both killings.

They also had evidence from another shooting, one where no one died but that they knew was linked to the Beys. Months earlier, Fourth had ordered the retaliatory destruction of a car belonging to a man who had argued with his brother Fifth and fired shots into the air outside the bakery. The only reason Fourth didn't have the man killed was because he happened to be the father of two children of a woman at the bakery whom Fourth was pursuing as a plural wife. She begged Fourth to let him live. So Fourth ordered a group of soldiers, including Broussard, to riddle the man's car with bullets instead. When police arrived, the man was edgy and evasive, but he told them that he knew "the guys from the bakery" were responsible. The police gathered up dozens of spent rifle casings, bullets, and shotgun cartridges. But the man was too scared to cooperate further, and the investigation faltered. In the priorities of the Oakland police, the shooting of a car ranked pretty low; it was just a property crime.

But they did have all those shell casings filed away, and detectives working the Roberson and Wills killings asked for a comparison between the casings found at the killing scenes and the ones recovered months earlier at the car shooting. A match quickly came back—the same assault rifle that had fired the bullets that killed both men had been used to shoot the car. If the car owner's statement was correct—that bakery members did that shooting—then there was now a very strong likelihood that people from the bakery had also killed Roberson and Wills.

And they weren't typical Oakland murders, if there were such things, a few pistol shots exchanged over drug turf. These involved innocent men blown to pieces with automatic weapons, killings that were deeply psychopathic. Every instinct investigators possessed told them they needed to look no further than the brick citadel of Your Black Muslim Bakery rising just blocks away. But now what? How did they crack the cult that Oakland had enabled for more than three decades, whose leader had deep political ties? Had they blown a chance when they hadn't gone after the shotgun stolen in the liquor store attacks two years earlier? There were strings of other incidents—from loose pit bulls terrorizing the neighborhood to constant reports of gunfire in the compound. But when cops did show up, they seemed taken aback at shows of force by the Beys' soldiers, retreating, appeasing. Fourth kept racking up arrests—the liquor stores, the San Francisco brawl, the luxury cars stolen by fraud—but none of them had kept him in jail for long.

Now police needed to hit the bakery with search warrants and find the assault rifle used in the two murders. But judges don't sign search warrants based on intuition, which is what police were mostly left with after all those years of tepidness.

However, they also had the kidnapping and torture investigation, in which detectives—thanks largely to Joshua's dropped cell phone and Fourth's panic-stricken decision to report the two cars abandoned at the scene as stolen—were making slow but steady progress.

The stories of the stolen cars were, to investigators, total bullshit from the moment the calls came in. The reports were, in fact, a glaring sign of Fourth's guilt. Fourth had to be desperate; he made Joshua, the kid whom he often called a retard, make one of the reports. Joshua's story fell apart in minutes.

But just because police knew the Beys were involved didn't mean they knew exactly *which* Beys were involved. They obviously needed specifics— a quest hindered by JoAnne's inability to identify her assailants. And, like most other units in the Oakland Police Department, Felony Assaults was swamped with work. The eight detectives assigned there when JoAnne was kidnapped in late May 2007 were investigating more than 1,200 cases between them. By the time Roberson and Wills were killed in early July, it had even taken the detectives ten days to get a warrant to search the house again after the night of the crime. It was then that they found Joshua's phone and the numbers in it of other bakery members. It took yet more time to subpoena those calling records. Then they had to subpoena other records and use them to trace what cell towers Fourth's calls had gone through around the time of the kidnapping to triangulate where he was. It was thorough, methodical police work, above the way Oakland police generally did things, but nevertheless it was obvious when the ballistics tests came back linking the Roberson and Wills slayings to the Beys that it was not happening fast enough.

Two days after Broussard saw Wills's body on the San Pablo Avenue sidewalk, Fourth revealed more about what had happened. A bunch of them were upstairs—Mackey, Fourth, Broussard, Lewis, a couple of others—watching the movie adaptation of one of Mario Puzo's final novels, *The Last Don*. Like his father and uncle decades earlier, Fourth drew inspiration from depictions of La Cosa Nostra, mimicking much of what he saw. "We watched hella Mafia movies," Broussard would say of his time at the compound. Fourth often insisted that his men speak to him as if he were a don himself, especially about killings: I got one. I knocked one down. I knocked one off. I whacked one, I smacked one. Clap. Knock down. Play it out. Air it out. They were all euphemisms for murder.

But Fourth never accepted one aspect of the Mafia's basic codes. He couldn't keep his mouth shut. Midway through the movie he began talking about Michael Wills.

"We got a devil," he said.

He went on to describe how he and Mackey had been driving through the neighborhood, talking about how the Zebra Killers had given whites "a dose of their own medicine" in the name of justice and how "white devils had no value."

Fourth, Broussard would eventually testify, claimed to know much about the days of terror in the early seventies. They were subjects of high lore and admiration within the cult. Fourth went on a spiel about vengeance for "Blacks getting lynched, and stuff like that, from way back," defining the Zebra Killers as "Muslim brothers" who got fed up and wanted revenge.

He also gave a clue that he knew the story of George Foreman—the Black Muslim gunman who had shot people in the Oakland area and been arrested in the spring of 1974 with literature and notebooks after robbing and shooting a cabdriver.

Fourth told Broussard and the others that none of the Zebra Killers were arrested "until they got greedy and started robbing people."

That's not what happened in the most well-known spate of murders, the ones that occurred in San Francisco. Fourth's story matched up far better with the lesser-known East Bay killings—the ones in which his father was involved and that ended when Foreman was arrested for shooting people after he'd robbed them. In that sense, Wills was yet another of Yusuf Bey's victims.

Fourth had lived his life only, one of the people closest to him would tell police, "in that little box" of a compound where Yusuf Bey was God, with all his polygamous wives and his sons who were told they were superior beings. "He didn't know the real world," the person would say. His world was one where men were motivated by elements of Black Muslim dogma that stretched as far back as Robert Harris's 1932 knife murder of James Smith in Detroit.

Given his personal limits, Fourth would not have been aware that the best known of the San Francisco Zebra Killers had long since rejected the Fardian rhetoric they had used to justify the murders between 1973 and 1974. Larry Green, Manuel Moore, J. C. Simon, and Jesse Lee Cooks all continued to deny killing anyone,* but Green and Moore had converted in prison from Black Muslims to Orthodox, or Sunni, Muslims.

"The doctrine of the Nation of Islam was that the black man was God and the white man was the devil, which was convenient but not true," Green

---

*All four convicted Zebra Killers have been denied parole multiple times by the State of California.

told parole commissioners in 2009, adding that he had come to think of "the white race as I think of the black race, the yellow race, the brown race, or any other race; that they are part of the human race."

At a parole hearing in 2010, Moore described for commissioners how he now did all he could to observe the five pillars of Orthodox Islam and hoped to one day make the Hajj to Mecca.

But in the summer of 2007, Fourth wasn't exceptionally well versed in Black Muslim history or philosophy, let alone Orthodox Islam. Although he read from Elijah Muhammad's *Message to the Blackman in America* and *The Theology of Time* in his sermons and ordered his followers to read those books themselves, he had yet to take up an intense study of the texts. That would come. In a letter he would later write to one of his followers, Fourth would say that he understood his duty to kill four devils as commanded by Fard and Elijah Muhammad. Salvation indeed lay in such bloodshed. But he admitted being bothered by some of it—the reward part, anyway. He had no interest in achieving the promised trip to Mecca for bloodletting. He preferred, instead, to receive passage to Rio de Janeiro. Brazil, he wrote, was sure to have better-looking women than Saudi Arabia.

But as they sat around talking about the Wills killing in July 2007, he did have at least an understanding of the basics. For instance, Fourth talked about how devils did not necessarily have to be white. A Black man, Fourth said, could be a devil if he was judged to be working against his own people.

24

Highly Questionable Circumstances

"A newspaper can't love you back."
—DAVID SIMON, *Esquire*, February 2008

Chauncey Bailey's career had been in descent for several years by June 2007, when it finally bottomed out. There was really no other way to describe his long decline from what had once been an unsensational but nevertheless productive work-life in daily newspapers to his appointment as editor of the *Oakland Post*. Bailey was back, in a very real sense, where he began: working for a tiny African American tabloid quite akin to the *San Francisco Sun Reporter* of thirty-three years earlier.

The blurring of reportage and advocacy in the traditional Black press had been what drew Bailey to journalism in the first place, and it remained ingrained in him. He'd been proficient at writing straight, foursquare news stories, but his calling had always been to explore the African American condition. In those pieces he did little to mask his championing of causes, his cant obvious. But more and more frequently, the causes he had taken up were his own.

Newspapers can be maddening places to work. Reporters are among the most habitually underpaid professionals in the country, yet ones who carry tremendous public responsibility. Bailey believed his work, in essence, was community service. Otherwise there was no point. But an adult has to sometimes accept living like a relative pauper to stay in journalism, especially at the midlevel newspapers like the *Oakland Tribune*. The very things about a person that might call him or her to reporting in the first place— a rejection of a life of shallow materialism and superficiality—can become grating when one passes their fiftieth birthday, as Bailey did, never having purchased a home or even a new car. Buying thrift-store suits was one thing, but a lifetime of hand-to-mouth existence was another. Bailey, juggling his jobs at the *Tribune* and the Soul Beat television station, wanted financial stability in his life.

In 2003, with Soul Beat losing money and in debt to the IRS for unpaid taxes, its owner, Chuck Johnson, had filed for bankruptcy. Johnson, the man who had barred Bailey from mentioning Yusuf Bey's sex case on the air, ran a threadbare, nearly unsustainable operation. He once hired a talented young reporter and paid him for his first month of work; when the reporter asked to be paid for his second month, Johnson suggested that if he needed money he could sell advertising on the side and take a commission. The reporter quit.

Bailey was an integral part of Soul Beat's operation, with full knowledge of how Johnson did things and the perilous state of the business, yet he somehow agreed to try to buy the station for $2.5 million. He gave Johnson a $15,000 nonrefundable deposit—a small fortune for Bailey—for a sixty-day window to arrange financing for the purchase. Bailey approached nearly everyone he knew—including people he covered as a *Tribune* reporter, creating obvious conflicts—but failed to find investors. When he asked Johnson for his $15,000 back, Johnson, citing their contract, said no. Bailey then began his evening newscast but soon turned it into a tirade against the station's owner, announced his resignation, and stormed off the set.

But Bailey wasn't finished. He coauthored an unbylined story about Johnson in a minority paper, the *California Voice,* suggesting that a rival station aimed at Oakland's African American population might soon be competing with Soul Beat—a station featuring none other than Mr. Oakland, Chauncey Bailey. That story contained detailed information about Soul Beat's advertising rates—rates Johnson claimed were proprietary and that he had given Bailey only to aid him in his search for investors. What

Bailey did "wasn't ethical or professional," Johnson said. When a reporter writing about the dispute asked Bailey where he'd gotten the information, Bailey said he'd gleaned it from Soul Beat's bankruptcy file—an interesting response from a reporter who didn't dig.

With his television job gone, Bailey turned to more freelance work to make up the lost income. Writing features for the *Sun Reporter* and the *California Voice,* in turn, distracted him from his duties at the *Tribune.* He needed more money, though, and that became his priority, even on the *Tribune*'s time. But the extra work, for which he was paid as a contractor, also put Bailey in habitual arrears to the IRS, creating additional strains on him.

Bailey's career spanned the period when newsroom ethics became open for public debate and ridicule, pushed by the fabrication scandals involving reporters like Stephen Glass of *The New Republic* and Jayson Blair of the *New York Times.* A *Cincinnati Enquirer* reporter hacked into the voice-mail system of the Chiquita Banana company to help gather information for stories that alleged a host of corruptions ranging from cocaine smuggling to bribery. Journalism suffered greatly as a result of these substantial lapses. And while the big disgraces were well known, many others weren't. As Bailey's career began spiraling downward, his ethical dilemmas were of smaller and of more personal magnitude. He couldn't separate other aspects of his life from journalism; his inability to even basically compartmentalize cost him his career in daily newspapers.

In the spring of 2004, Bailey had sold his 1974 Mercedes-Benz for one thousand dollars on an installment plan of fifty dollars a month. But he committed a seller's error: He signed the pink slip right away, leaving nothing to secure the deal. The buyer registered the car free and clear, then skipped the payments. Bailey should have been mad at himself, but he was a reporter, not a car salesman. He'd made a mistake, one where his redress was small-claims court. Instead, he reported to police that the car was stolen— the buyer, Bailey claimed, had forged his signature on the pink slip, which Bailey said he had inadvertently left in the vehicle. Police took an incident report—not the stolen-car report Bailey demanded, and advised him to sue the buyer. Instead, he took out his frustration on the California Department of Motor Vehicles, writing several ranting letters—on *Oakland*

Tribune letterhead—claiming that the DMV had screwed him by allowing the buyer to register the car. Putting such letters on a newspaper's stationery alone breached ethics, clearly implying that he deserved special consideration because he was a journalist. Bailey's complaints grew so loud that the DMV assigned an investigator to the matter, who asked the state Justice Department to compare the signature on the pink slip that Bailey claimed was forged to his signatures elsewhere. A handwriting expert determined that they were the same. Bailey had signed the car's title away himself, an act he'd repeatedly denied. When confronted, he claimed he'd forgotten signing the pink slip. The DMV investigator went to the district attorney and pushed for perjury charges—Bailey had signed a formal report alleging the buyer had committed forgery, an accusation he now admitted was false. The district attorney declined to prosecute.

Bailey grew even more indignant when he learned the buyer had sold the Benz for $450. He called a DMV media-relations officer, threatening to write a story painting the department as negatively as possible if no one got him his car back immediately.

A letter to three *Tribune* editors arrived in January 2005 detailing an "extraordinary and disturbing interaction" between Bailey and the DMV that had dragged on for eight months. "This sort of misuse of a newspaper's power and good name for the personal, off-duty benefit of an employee . . . involves intimidation by threatening bad publicity under highly questionable circumstances," state officials wrote. The editors rightfully fired Bailey. But his union, the Newspaper Guild, struck a deal to save his job. He could stay on, but there would be no further tolerance of such behavior; another ethical lapse would mean immediate termination. After such deplorable conduct, it was a last chance he was lucky to receive.

But within a few months, Bailey wrote a glowing feature story about a small business owned by the woman he was dating. He had sought no guidance about the obvious conflict nor informed editors of it before publication. The editors who had wanted to dismiss Bailey for the DMV dispute refused to tolerate his latest transgression. He'd broken the deal. This time the union didn't intervene; Bailey's firing stuck.

With the *Tribune* and Soul Beat both gone, Bailey tried to make a living with his freelance work, but he was rudderless. He briefly moved to the

Caribbean nation of Saint Kitts and Nevis before returning to Oakland. Desperate for work, he went to the *Oakland Post,* where he wrote unbylined stories and was sometimes listed as the tiny paper's travel editor.

At first glance, with its biblical quote in the banner and the predominance of posed photographs on its front page, the *Post* could be easily dismissed. It was simply devoid of serious journalism, yet it remained an institution within African American Oakland. The *Post* was a breezy read, often filled with little more than fluff, but people still read it; it was free, and its circulation and penetration kept it profitable. The *Tribune,* especially since Bailey's firing, never equaled it in the number of positive stories people craved: the teenager who made it out of the ghetto to the Ivy League, the deacon honored for good works, the beaming church lady celebrating her centennial birthday. The *Post* had its community niche. If it seemed reminiscent of the traditional Black press Bailey had always admired, it was because the need for such a publication remained.

In June 2007, Bailey was named the paper's editor. "He's a known journalist throughout the Bay Area community," its publisher, Paul Cobb, told the *Tribune.* "Because of familiarity, he will bring confidence. Chauncey is full of energy and ideas. Even though he's 57, he . . . moves and maneuvers like he was 27." Bailey's firing over his poor ethics two years earlier wasn't mentioned.

Cobb, like Bailey, had blurred all sorts of lines between being an activist and sometime journalist, although one of generally thin abilities. As a young man, he had traveled to the South and sent the *Post* dispatches about the civil-rights movement. He loved showing off a photo of him with Martin Luther King Jr. in Selma while claiming he was there as a reporter *and* served as a King bodyguard on the march to Montgomery. Later, he wrote a religion column for the *Tribune* that carried little more than church gossip, and he won appointment to the city school board after backing Jerry Brown for mayor. He bought the *Post* in 2005. Cobb was a caustic, bitter man who immediately became embroiled in a lawsuit with the paper's former owner. The litigation, he claimed, cost him hundreds of thousands of dollars in legal fees and lost advertising revenue, ruining his chances of improving the

Post. Given Cobb's personality, the *Post*'s meagerness in both circulation and format, and the extent of his own troubles, it is difficult to imagine Bailey landing any lower.

But Bailey quietly told friends he was happy with the new job. It might only be the *Oakland Post,* but for the first time in his career, his title was "editor." With Cobb's two-fisted clutch on the paper's finances, Bailey wouldn't have much of a staff. He would still have to write stories, which is what he wanted anyway. He still wanted to keep his name as public as possible, to be Black Oakland's griot. And he still had a wide network of sources from all his years at the *Tribune* and Soul Beat. One of them was Saleem Bey.

Saleem was not among those Beys who hated Bailey for his coverage of Yusuf Bey's sex case. That was the territory of the younger, biological sons and perhaps a few of the dimmer spiritually adopted ones. The two men had, in fact, enjoyed a cordial relationship for years. Since Waajid's disappearance in 2004, Saleem had mentioned to Bailey the possibility of sourcing him for a story about the bakery's inner workings and Antar's coup. Despite the talk, though, Saleem remained hesitant. The Beys were insular; they solved their own problems. While Saleem respected Bailey as a reporter, he wasn't sure he wanted to be involved in a story. He insisted that Bailey agree that whatever they discussed be deeply off the record. The best Bailey could obtain was Saleem's word that if and when he ever did want to talk to a journalist about the Beys' problems, Bailey would be first.

As the summer of 2007 dawned, though, the possibility of giving Bailey information for a story began to weigh more heavily on Saleem. Fourth was destroying what was left of the business. Saleem was finding no forum to air his theory that the bankruptcy itself was illegal because Fourth was the bakery's illegitimate owner. As he continued to compete with Fourth for the help of politicians like Ron Dellums and Barbara Lee, Saleem could see his brother-in-law held the upper hand. Saleem's claims, although factually accurate—the corporate papers placing Antar in charge had been forgeries—were difficult to prove and seemed like so many sour grapes. At best, it looked to outsiders like an internal struggle within a family that many people were simply too afraid to get involved in. Saleem talked to Bailey about it all in early July, and Bailey insisted that a story would help. It would be harder for politicians to endorse Fourth if Saleem's claims were on the public record, even if that record was just the *Oakland Post*. And Bailey wanted stronger stories in his newspaper. People would read what he wrote about the bakery. It would help him prove he was still a relevant journalist.

Saleem decided that he would take one more run at the politicians, especially Barbara Lee, whom he had known for years. But after that, if she didn't agree to help him stop the bankruptcy, then he was going to exercise his last option. He would go to Chauncey Bailey.

25

Are These Dangerous People?

"There is a slowness in affairs which ripens them, and a slowness which rots them."

—JOSEPH ROUX, French clergyman

In the tradition of his father and Antar, Fourth recorded his sermons on video and they were played on a local cable channel. He would always have money for that, no matter how he had to fight away the devils to spread his word. On a Sunday in July, he gathered his people in the bakery's back room, put Lewis on point next to the rostrum, and looked straight into the video camera.

"Anybody out to get Your Black Muslim Bakery or sabotage Your Black Muslim Bakery, God has plans to go right back against you," Fourth said. "This is the reason that, after 45 years, we're still in business. As long as you are doing what God wants you to do, and God is in your favor—excuse my language—the hell with everybody else."

His jaw set firm, his scowl unflinching, Fourth's words were unrelenting. He stood at the lectern where Daddy and Antar had preached. Large images of the Honorable Elijah Muhammad and W. D. Fard hung behind him, as did images of Yusuf Bey. But this was not the bakery of Fourth's daddy.

To Fourth's left, Lewis wore sunglasses to hide bloodshot eyes. He'd broken the rules and gotten drunk the night before. On camera Fourth acted as if the room were filled with people clinging to his every syllable. But it was nearly empty, and the few that were there, like Joshua, barely paid attention.

But Devaughndre Broussard was in attendance. Ever since Lewis had brought him back to the bakery, he had been paying more attention to the Muslim teachings. Things were better, just as Lewis had promised. There was pay, and while Fourth still harped about sacrifice, he still promised Broussard the so-called credit hookup if he did well.

So Broussard listened as Fourth ranted desperately for the camera as if he were addressing Oakland as a whole, as if people outside the bakery's back room somehow cared about what he said.

"There should be no reason in the world that they can harass an organization like this and our preachers don't come out and give us a hand or our Muslim brothers don't come out and assist us," he said. "It's OK. Anything that is weak is wicked, and anything that is wicked, we can't use in this organization. But it's good to know that we have strong brothers here. You give us a little more time, and I guarantee you, you are going to see what we have to offer."

He seemed obsessed with why Oakland didn't rally to him as the devils tried to close the bakery.

"How in the hell can you pass up Your Black Muslim Bakery when we sell all-natural food for the human body? But you'll pass this bakery up to go buy bread from Pak-N-Save, or go buy bread from Safeway, all because you don't like Your Black Muslim Bakery, or you don't like what we say in here, you don't like what we do here. You go to the white man's establishment. We have a Black mayor and City Council members, we have Black people in city government; we have Black police sergeants and police chiefs." But those people, he claimed, failed to use their jobs to help other Blacks.

"We fight the government, we fight the police, we fight our own families, we fight our own people, and we fight Caucasian people daily—just to do right. They use our own people to go against us—people like you or I—to go against a strong organization like Your Black Muslim Bakery. It's going to take strong men to stand up, it's going to take strong soldiers to stand up and do something for ourselves. I don't care how bad it might look, if you really believe in God, have faith in God and less faith in the damn white man, you'll be a lot better off."

But despite his fiery rhetoric and cocksure posture, Fourth seemed to know the bankruptcy was closing in on him. His plan to stall until he could rally enough political support and community outcry to force a halt to the proceeding wasn't working. Even though Saleem didn't seem to be gaining any traction with his arguments, he wasn't going away. And Farieda Bey, his father's legal wife, had formally entered the bankruptcy to try to reclaim the property she said was hers before it was liquidated. Fourth was beginning to feel like he had no room to breathe.

He also kept thinking that Barbara Lee was somehow his way out of the whole thing.

But Leslie Littleton, Lee's district director, remained deeply leery of dealing with anyone from the bakery. A big part of her job was to keep Lee from being embarrassed. And something wasn't right about this whole thing. Even after Fourth got his letter to the IRS, he and his posse kept trying to barge into the office and make demands, this twenty-one-year-old kid so self-aggrandized he surrounded himself with bodyguards. She thought seriously about telling the Federal Protective Service not to let anyone with a bow tie near the tenth floor.

Saleem Bey kept coming around too, and e-mailing her, and calling. He was much nicer and more professional, but rather relentless. He insisted that Lee was going to be badly chagrined about the letter her staff had written to the IRS supporting Fourth, the one that Saundra Andrews had made a show of giving the bankruptcy judge.

Back and forth the sides went, the intensity of their demands increasing as a decision on whether the bakery would be liquidated grew closer. It had to end. Littleton called both Fourth and Saleem and told them to come in and meet with her together. It didn't take long. Her mind was made up. Obviously, whatever was going on was a family dispute, and Littleton told both Fourth and Saleem that Lee could not and would not involve herself in family disputes. The congresswoman's support was for the bakery as an institution, not for either side of a feud. She told Saleem again to get a lawyer and sue. She had already told Fourth that no more letters of support would be forthcoming concerning the bankruptcy. He'd gotten a letter to the IRS, just like any constituent with a valid request. There would be nothing more.

Even though Fourth was instructed to stop seeking Lee's help, he left the meeting believing he still had a considerable advantage over Saleem, who had gotten no help at all. Maybe Fourth's scalding denunciations of his detractors and enemies were working. He strutted though the rotunda-like lobby of Oakland's federal building surrounded by his men as if he were protected by the Secret Service. He'd left Devaughndre Broussard standing at attention near the doors in a dark suit, white shirt, and bow tie, a sign for all who entered that Yusuf Ali Bey IV was in the building.

Saleem knew he was nearly out of options. Lee and other politicians weren't listening. He needed to get his version of the facts in front of people in a forum that could not be ignored. There was only one way to do that. He had no choice. Saleem called Chauncey Bailey at the *Oakland Post* and told him he was finally ready to give him his long-promised story about the bakery.

When they met, the first thing Saleem told Bailey was that he couldn't use his name. Saleem would be his source of information for a story, he would tell Bailey all he knew, but he would not allow it to be attributed to him directly. Fourth, Saleem said, was out of control, and Saleem was not going to take the risk. They even discussed whether Bailey should put *his* name on the story as its author or run it with no byline, given Fourth's fanaticism and violent tendencies.

What Saleem obviously hoped was that a news story would spur authorities to finally investigate his claims or motivate a litigator to take the case. It didn't matter to him whether Bailey's name was on it or not or whether it was a well-written, balanced article. Saleem just wanted the story out there in the community; he was confident it would validate him. Bailey was eager to write it because, like others in Oakland, he still held the long-standing assumption that the bakery had at one time been legitimate. If it could be restored, it might help people again, he seemed to think. While he probably didn't know that Yusuf Bey had propped it up with thousands of dollars a month in public-assistance fraud, he knew that Bey had raped children and lived in open polygamy. Bailey had covered Bey's campaign rally featuring the hate-filled screed of Khalid Abdul Muhammad. He knew that the Beys frequently used violence to get their way. He knew about the one-million-dollar loan they had received from Oakland and never paid back.

Bailey certainly knew enough about the Nation of Islam's original apocalyptic dogma about spaceships, devils, and an evil scientist—dogma that remained current for Fourth and other cult members—to be dismissive of the entire notion of legitimacy. But Bailey also believed deeply in the self-determination and Black empowerment inherent in the Beys' message, despite how twisted their beliefs were. His mother had taught him that work and self-respect were the answers to everything. He had been willing not to look too deeply at the Beys prior to Yusuf Bey's rape and abuse case. On the surface, what was wrong with Black pride?

When he and Saleem sat to talk, Bailey understood the basics. Fourth, Saleem claimed, was not the bakery's legitimate owner. Saleem had documents. When Farieda Bey, Yusuf Bey's widow, entered the bankruptcy case, she produced statements from members of the board of directors saying that their signatures had been forged on minutes of a supposed meeting where the board placed Antar in charge.

To a person other than a newspaper reporter pursuing a story, Saleem's claims of fraudulence and forged papers might have seemed like so much drivel. But in good reporting, documents often mean everything. Skilled investigative reporters often say they possess an ingrained "document state of mind." To them, a paper trail tells a story better than a person can. But Bailey wasn't that kind of reporter. His default position on all his work was to talk to people in his clipped and hurried tone, often grabbing just enough information from them to just write something quickly and move on. His career had been about the art of the deadline story, the fast turn, the get-it-down, get-it-in realities of being a reporter who fed the insatiable beast that is a daily newspaper. He'd been that way in Hartford and Detroit. He'd been that way at the *Oakland Tribune,* and he remained that kind of reporter at the *Oakland Post.*

In the months ahead, there would be those who would call Bailey an investigative reporter, who would say that he had undertaken an extensive probe of the bakery and its out-of-control leader. But such statements, though often meant with respect and deference, were inaccurate. They were also unfair to Bailey and the kind of reporter he was, as if those who covered communities and churned out copy should somehow be considered beneath those who did in-depth investigative reporting. Journalism is often history in a hurry, and Bailey, with all his personal and professional flaws, was a hurried, sometimes frantic, historian.

What he intended to do was take what Saleem was telling him, pound out a hard and fast story, and get it in the paper. He believed that it was important that the story contain the fact that in addition to the bankruptcy, Fourth had racked up a slew of criminal charges against him all over the Bay Area. Since he'd succeeded Antar, he'd been charged with crimes in five counties. Assault, car theft, forgery. All of what Saleem was telling Bailey was available in public documents. But Bailey pursued no other records. His story would be largely free of attribution, and he had no intention of calling Fourth to get his side of things. Bailey jotted down a few things; that was it.

As Saleem Bey was preparing to leave Bailey's office, the two men stopped to shake hands. Just as they did, in walked a woman named Nisayah Yahudah. Among the other names she had been known by throughout the years were "Nisa Bey," "Nisa Islam," and "Sister Felicia X"—the same Sister Felicia X who had met Yusuf Bey when he was still known as Joseph X Stephens in the early 1970s. Later she had become one of Bey's wives for several years. Now she worked as a salesperson in the *Post*'s advertising department, and while she had been gone from the San Pablo Avenue compound for more than two decades, she still maintained deep and complicated ties to the Beys. Seeing her scared Saleem; it could easily blow his cover as the anonymous source in Bailey's article. He quickly concocted a cover story, telling Yahuda that he had met with Bailey to discuss a computer business he owned. Given the frequency with which Bailey wrote features on African American–owned small businesses, the explanation was plausible. But Saleem was certain that people at the bakery would soon learn that he was talking to Bailey, and they wouldn't believe it had anything to do with computers.

He was right. After Saleem left, Bailey told Yahuda what he was working on. By the time Saleem got home from the interview, word had already reached his wife from her own sources in the compound that he had fed information to Bailey. Saleem panicked and phoned Bailey, yelling, "What kind of news organization are you running?"

Bailey told him that he had spoken to Yahudah and asked her about the bakery; his only intention was to write a stronger story. Saleem Bey told Bailey that he failed to grasp the grave nature of the matter, saying of Fourth and his minions, "These dudes are killers."

Soon after he was told that people at the compound knew he had talked to Bailey, Saleem's cell phone rang. He answered and heard the unmistakable voice of Fourth snap at him, "Keep my name out of your mouth."

He called Bailey and told him that Fourth knew. Bailey decided he had to write the story and get it in the paper now.

Not far from the aging, pale brown Financial Services Building at Fourteenth and Franklin streets, where the *Post* occupied a cramped office suite, Oakland police were attempting to do their own writing about the bakery and Fourth. It was in the form of affidavits they would take to a Superior Court judge to ask for search warrants.

The investigation of the kidnapping and torture of JoAnne and the killings of Odell Roberson and Michael Wills had effectively merged. Plans were slowly coming together that police, finally, would raid the bakery compound to search for evidence in all three crimes.

The kidnapping case was a little ahead. The cell-phone records that detectives had pieced together clearly showed Fourth's involvement, and the cars left at the scene were strong evidence. Overcoming the fact that JoAnne hadn't seen the men who took her to the torture house was a challenge, but the analytical work detectives had performed was strong. Joshua Bey's cell phone was a huge clue, and Fourth's stolen-car stories were just plain stupid.

Unlike in the episode with the liquor stores and the stolen shotgun, police had finally become interested in everything that Fourth was doing. The ballistic tests on the assault-rifle casings confirmed for them the frightening truth. Fourth wasn't just giving fiery speeches. People were dying and being tortured. But gathering enough evidence to do something about it was proving to be cumbersome. They just didn't have enough yet to convince a judge to let them storm the Beys' compound.

The cops still needed a mole, someone who could provide human intelligence about what went on inside the bakery. But who would talk?

It had been nearly eight months since Fourth had sent his men to shoot up the car of a man he perceived had disrespected him. That man had been terrified that night. Who wouldn't be? He'd seen those big brass rifle casings. He knew the kinds of guns that fired those shells. Everyone in the Oakland ghettos knew what those kinds of bullets could do. He'd probably said too much as it was; he was more worried about body bags and life insurance than anything else that night. Now, though, people were dead. The commander of the homicide unit, Lieutenant Ersie Joyner, a talented street cop whom department higher-ups had miscast as an administrator, called the man who owned the bullet-riddled car and made a personal appeal for his help. The cops were desperate to make arrests before someone else got killed.

The man was a twenty-five-year-old single father of two sons who knew the risks of informing on the Beys. But the shooting months earlier nagged at him. Now he could do something about it. On July 17, five days after the Wills killing, he accepted Joyner's plea and agreed to tell detectives what he knew.

The mother of his two sons was no longer involved with Fourth, and she had told him everything about the car shooting, he said.

Slowly, Sergeant Louis Cruz and his partner, Caesar Basa Jr., extracted the information they needed for a judge to sign a warrant.

The man had worked at the bakery briefly. He'd even delivered a dryer upstairs and carried it into Fourth's apartment. He drew Cruz and Basa sketches of the floor plan.

He'd seen Fourth with a gun, a holstered .45. All of Fourth's bodyguards carried guns too. He'd seen assault rifles, pistols, shotguns in the compound.

Cruz had a theory. Roberson was a crackhead. Wills was white. Were the Beys trying to purge their neighborhood of those they deemed undesirables? Were they cleansing?

The man didn't know.

Well, would they kill people they didn't like?

They'd kill anybody, he said.

"They smart and they stupid," the man said of the Beys. They could create sophisticated criminal plans and then post MySpace photos of themselves posing with guns. "If something gonna happen it is in their inner circle. The women know a lot but you'll never get them to talk because they fear for their lives."

He knew a lot, he said, because the mother of his children was still living with him when she started working there. Women were pretty much locked into the compound, he said. "They don't want them out walking around."

Cruz had assembled a stack of photos of people who were associated with Fourth.

He settled into a routine in the tiny interview room. He would show the man a photo. Did he know the person?

"Yes."

From where?

"The bakery."

"Did you ever see this person with a gun?"

"Yes."

It went on for more than an hour, slow, methodical questioning, Cruz's tone sometimes paternal, as if he were talking to a toddler. But he was a cerebral, patient detective, and he knew what he needed to write a successful affidavit. Finally, police were building, word by word, what they needed to get inside Your Black Muslim Bakery.

"Are these dangerous people?" Cruz asked the man as if no one had ever contemplated the question before.

"They are," he replied.

It all meant that for the first time in nearly four decades police were going to fully and unambiguously confront the Beys. There would be no calls to come down to the police department to talk. No appeasement. Police were going to batter down doors and make arrests. Not even the investigation of Yusuf Bey's rapes of young girls had gotten inside the bakery compound. But these investigations would.

But it was taking day after day to get ready for it.

Six days after their interview with the car owner, Cruz and Basa asked to see him again. They had more pictures of men believed to be Fourth's soldiers and more questions about them. They also wanted his help identifying other buildings in the bakery compound and understanding more about Fourth's movements and his weapons. They recorded another slow and deliberate conversation with the man.

Likewise, detectives on the torture case were working methodically, writing in great detail and cross-referencing Cruz's information. Cruz had culled files and built a list for the judge of all the times that police had encountered the Beys in confrontational situations, often with weapons. He identified thirty-five incidents of "violent felony activity" involving cult members over a thirteen-year period. Few had resulted in serious investigations, let alone arrests.

As the warrants were prepared, other cops were working on plans to raid the bakery compound. It would require a massive strike force of more than two hundred officers drawn from a half dozen agencies. The Beys were suspected of having plenty of weapons and men not afraid to use them; the contempt that cult members bore for police was legendary. The cops had to prepare for the likelihood of an urban battle, perhaps even a siege.

Later, when it was obvious that the warrant preparation and raid planning over the last two weeks of July had lacked a sense of urgency and simply taken too long, somber-faced men, their collars adorned with brass stars, would say that police couldn't just rush into the bakery and start handcuffing people. They needed time to prepare. They weren't dealing with just any set of criminals. They were preparing to take down the Beys, and they wanted to ensure that convictions and prison sentences would be the end result. They needed time, they said, so there would be no more violence, no more deaths. But the result of their thoroughness would soon result in the very thing they were desperate to avoid.

———

Bailey wrote on a gray ten-year-old laptop that he lugged everywhere; often he just opened an e-mail and dashed off a few paragraphs he then sent to the *Post*'s composer, who assembled the paper's eight tabloid pages on Thursday afternoons and nights. Other than an array of small flags from the countries he had visited—Iran, Vietnam, Caribbean nations—that he kept on his desk, Bailey's small office overlooking Fourteenth Street was as austere as his writing. Bailey did not write eloquent prose. He wrote in jabs, and his report about Fourth was no different. It was a string of declarative sentences. They lacked attribution and subtlety.* First-year journalism students could have done better. The story read as if Saleem Bey simply dictated his concerns and Bailey took them all down like a stenographer. It was perhaps five hundred words long and not very good. It would be surprising if it took Bailey longer than thirty minutes to write it. It probably took less.

But had that story of staccato sentences appeared in the *Oakland Post,* it certainly would have gotten people's attention. As poorly written as it was, it did spell out that Fourth was seeking all sorts of political help to stop the bankruptcy. If the police officers, busy tapping out affidavits and making plans to raid Your Black Muslim Bakery, had read it, there is little question that they would have moved faster. Certainly, a flurry of phone calls would have been made, warning Barbara Lee and Ron Dellums that Fourth was suspected in violent crimes. It also seems likely that police would have increased surveillance on Fourth and his men. Bailey's story could have changed things.

But the publisher of the *Post,* Paul Cobb, wouldn't run it.

First Cobb told Bailey that the story lacked attribution, which it did. Bailey called Saleem, but after getting that phone call from Fourth warning him to shut up, Saleem was more adamant than ever that his name not appear in print. Bailey then called an Oakland lawyer whom Saleem had con-

*Paul Cobb has restricted access to Bailey's story about Your Black Muslim Bakery and Yusuf Bey IV since 2007. The author is one of the few people outside the *Oakland Post* to have read that story. Cobb allowed the author to read it on the afternoon of Saturday, February 23, 2008, in the composing room of the *Oakland Post.* The author was in the company of the oral historian Lani Silver, a member of the Chauncey Bailey Project. Cobb would not allow copies of the story to be made or notes taken. Silver died in January 2009.

sulted about his effort to join the bankruptcy case. The lawyer confirmed the facts in the story, and when Bailey asked him if he could attribute the information to him by name, the lawyer said yes. Bailey made changes to the story to reflect that the facts in it were confirmed by the lawyer. But when shown the edited version, Cobb still said no. It was not as if he had high journalistic standards. He didn't. But Cobb knew the Beys.

Bailey called Saleem and told him that he was having a hard time getting the story into print but that he would keep trying. Saleem understood without Bailey having to say it directly. Cobb, like so many others, was afraid.

26

What the Hell Is This?

"For rarely are sons similar to their fathers:
most are worse, and a few are better."
—HOMER

Fourth's new problem was this article he'd been told would soon be printed in the *Oakland Post*. No reporter had called him, but he had been told Saleem was the source and to expect it to be quite negative. He seethed at the prospect of such disrespect. Saleem had obviously told Chauncey Bailey a bucket of lies. Bailey was a devil. Look at how he had slandered Yusuf Bey four years earlier, repeating in the *Oakland Tribune* all the lies that the devil police told about his raping children.

But what made Bailey more of a devil to Fourth was that he was a Black man who was not working for his people. In Fourth's world, where racial hatred skewed everything, Bailey was against him merely because he wasn't clearly for him. And not being for someone so obviously destined by God to uplift the deaf, dumb, and blind Negroes made him a devil.

Sometimes, when he was troubled or deep in contemplation of his own power, Fourth watched a video recording of his Daddy's three-hour funeral. He loved and missed his father, who even with all his horrors had understood some of how the world worked. Little of that, though, had passed to the son. The packed church and splendor of the ceremony served to confirm what a great man Yusuf Bey had been. Fourth liked to see himself and other young soldiers drilling in sparkling white suits and blood-red bow ties.

In late July, he slipped the funeral tape in the VCR in his bedroom above the bakery and summoned a bunch of the men to watch it with him, Broussard, Mackey, and Lewis among them.

The drilling scene ended and for a moment the camera panned the crowd and paused on a handsome, middle-aged man in a dark suit and glasses. Fourth grabbed a remote and paused the tape.

"That's the motherfucker right there who killed my dad," Fourth said, pointing at the screen.

Wait. Hadn't his father been sick and died in the hospital? one of them asked.

Yeah, Fourth said, *but that motherfucker wrote stuff that slandered Daddy.*
Someone asked his name.

"Chauncey Bailey, the fucking reporter."

It didn't make a lot of sense, so Broussard tried to listen closely to Bey IV's logic, if it could be called that.

Yusuf Bey's death from cancer (they never admitted Bey had AIDS), Fourth insisted, had been hastened by the stress of the child-rape charges pending against him. Bailey added to that stress by writing articles for the *Tribune* that were slanderous to Daddy. Under Black Muslim law Daddy was entitled to bed any female he wished, and since Allah created women to submit to men in the first place, anything he did to force their submission was acceptable. The devil's laws didn't apply. Reporting that they did was slander.

Broussard wanted to make sure he understood. The articles in the newspaper killed Fourth's Daddy?

"Indirectly," Fourth answered. "Stress will eat you up."

Then Fourth told the others what he'd recently learned about Bailey.

"Man, as a matter of fact, that motherfucker's writing against us right now," he said. "He's against us, talking shit against us."

They went back to watching more of the funeral, but seeing Chauncey Bailey on the video had started Fourth scheming over just what he could do about him.

On July 25, a week after detectives first interviewed the man who knew about the inner workings of the bakery, police started night surveillance on Fourth and the compound. If they were going to hit it, presumably with darkness as their ally, then they needed to know his nocturnal habits. The department's best street cops, known as the Targeted Enforcement Task Force—an elite unit that could follow Fourth's thumping Dodge Charger around Oakland without being noticed—got the assignment. Little did Fourth know that on June 27, as part of the torture investigation, police had slipped an electronic tracking device onto his car's undercarriage. It emitted a signal that allowed it to be mapped by a global-positioning system. But police needed more intelligence; they had to have eyes on who one of the cops called "that little fucker." Where did he go, who was with him, how many men? Did they appear armed? If so, with what kind of weapons? How many people lived in the compound? What time at night did everyone go to sleep? How many children were in there? How could they be protected in the very likely event that police would be met with gunfire? Those were just some of the questions to which answers were needed.

As street cops tailed Fourth, detectives finished writing their search-warrant affidavits, cross-referencing the murder and the kidnapping and torture investigations. The cops were tense. The operation against the Beys would be the biggest in the department's history. No one wanted to make a mistake that could get an officer killed or trigger a legal technicality that a defense lawyer would somehow later exploit. There seemed to be a nearly overwhelming dread of the unknown. Just how much firepower did the Beys have in there, and how willing were the soldiers to use it? Were they really willing to die for Fourth? One of the reasons that raid planners were so adamant about hitting the compound with an overpowering force was that all signs pointed to the fact that Fourth's followers were simply not afraid of the police. To justify those concerns, they needed to look no further than an encounter that had happened just a few weeks earlier.

Fourth had been pulled over in front of the bakery for speeding. When the patrol cop realized who it was, he immediately called for backup. Lots of it. Ten more officers arrived. Fourth was initially polite to the officer, nearly saccharine, as Mackey and Broussard sat in the car, watching him. They were allowed to get out and joined other men who had come outside and stood in a military formation just yards away, stone-faced, awaiting orders. As soon as Fourth was allowed out of the car, his attitude changed. "Look, it takes ten cops to give me a traffic ticket," he said loudly. He whispered something to Broussard, who in turn said something to Mackey, who disappeared inside the bakery. A few seconds later, several loud, high-caliber shots shattered the night from the back of the compound. The cops scrambled for cover, ducking beside cars, pressing themselves against buildings, just the response Fourth wanted. As he stood in front of his formation of soldiers, he cupped his hand to his ear as if he needed help hearing and said in a loud, mocking tone, "What was what? What was that?" as his men laughed. The cops got in their cars and left.

If Bey IV would order someone to shoot in the air just to antagonize and scare cops over a speeding ticket, what would he order them to do when police raiders burst through the bakery's doors?

The same cops who watched Fourth at night trained with SWAT teams during the day, preparing for the raid. Among the myriad problems they encountered were that the fortified ground-floor doors that led to the bakery's upstairs living quarters opened outward, toward the street. This intelligence came from a surprising source—Detective Sergeant Derwin Longmire, who had known Yusuf Bey, investigated Antar's murder, and become friendly with Fourth.

Rumors had been whispered around the department that Longmire was a Black Muslim, or at least a sympathizer, ever since he had begun talking with Yusuf Bey and other bakery members a decade earlier. His repeated interventions into the liquor-store investigation on Fourth's behalf hadn't helped, even though he would say he was acting on orders from two department commanders.

"There's no doubt about it," Longmire was an associate of the Beys, one lieutenant would eventually tell state Justice Department investigators. "It seems that he has some type of pipeline or communications with them," a sergeant would say. "They communicate with him regarding any type of police matter." Even the department's number-two commander, Assistant Chief Howard Jordan, believed that Longmire was an associate of the Beys.

Given that perception of Longmire, other cops were leery of letting him anywhere near the raid planning. They even drew up a fake operations plan describing a raid on an East Oakland drug house and left it out in plain sight, hoping it would explain the intense preparations under way.

Longmire's commander in the homicide unit, his close friend Lieutenant Ersie Joyner, who was deeply involved in planning the raid, thought that the perception of Longmire as a Black Muslim or a Bey sympathizer was enough that Longmire should avoid the operation for his own sake. That decision was "doing him a favor," Joyner later described it. But when Longmire found out, he responded angrily. He was a proud man, and his service in the department and his reputation meant a tremendous amount to him.

"What the hell is this? What is this shit all about?" he snapped.

He had gone out of his way to build a shaky bridge to the Beys for a moment just such as this, to give the department an advantage, and now there were guys who really thought he was a Black Muslim and a member of what was, in reality, a criminal gang?

Longmire knew those odd doors to the upper level of the bakery were going to be a problem for the SWAT teams. He was one of the few cops who had ever been inside the building and probably the only one who had ever been upstairs. He knew if those doors were hit with a battering ram, they wouldn't just snap open. The Beys might catch the cops in a logjam and start shooting. Longmire was angry and hurt that he wasn't sought out to help in the planning; the others knew that he knew more about the Beys than they did yet ignored the help he could provide based on an assumption. Finally, he got the planners to listen to him about the doors. Based on what he described, they were going to need another way to breach the bakery. SWAT planners decided the first officer at the door would have a chain saw instead of a rifle. He'd cut around the lock and pull the door open so others could storm inside.

To train for the raid, police rigged practice doors at an abandoned army base near Oakland's sprawling port. Again and again the officer with the chain saw sprang from the back of a truck, the saw roaring to life as he ran and cut loose a lock. He got it down to a few seconds. The whole operation seemed to depend on the ability to quickly breach the door.

Longmire's intelligence about the bakery helped. But the persistent rumors and perceptions of his bearing allegiances to the Beys were not going to go away.

On July 30, the pieces finally fell together.

Superior Court judges Allan Hymer and Thomas Reardon signed the warrants without hesitation. They included a caveat that surprise was crucial to success, waiving the basic requirement that police announce themselves before entering private property. The judges also allowed police to storm the compound at night. In effect, the raid would be a military operation. Two hundred officers would burst into the compound at 5:00 a.m. on August 1, 2007, ready to kill or be killed. Among the many elements of the plan was the staging of a fleet of ambulances a few blocks away, along with a trauma surgeon. Blood seemed certain. The squads that would race upstairs and burst into Fourth's living quarters were so large that no police vehicles could accommodate them. Commanders had to rent U-Haul moving vans in order to ferry all the raiders from a staging area several blocks south of the bakery on San Pablo Avenue.

Oakland police were finally and forcefully going to confront the Beys. But it was a city where few things ever seemed to go as planned, and on July 31, word trickled down through the ranks that the raid was being delayed for forty-eight hours.

Two senior SWAT commanders were on vacation—backpacking together in Yosemite National Park—and weren't due back for another two days. Oakland police chief Wayne Guy Tucker, a cautious former executive officer for the county sheriff's department who was despised by rank-and-file cops as a pencil-pushing, hand-wringing outsider, ordered the delay. Cops who had seen the bullet-riddled corpses of Odell Roberson and Michael Wills were incensed. It had been nearly three weeks since the Wills murder. It seemed like only a matter of time before the Beys killed again. SWAT team members were insistent that the raid go off as planned. The very nature of what SWAT cops did—maintaining a constant state of readiness to respond to emergency situations—meant they never had the luxury of waiting around until everything was just so, the way Tucker wanted. They went forward with whatever they had available whenever they were needed. The raid was big and complicated, but an experienced sergeant could run it, the cops complained; they didn't need captains and deputy chiefs. What kind of confidence was Tucker expressing about the real cops in the street by insisting that top commanders were needed? But to the officers who fumed over his decision, Tucker had never been a real cop; he was just some bureaucrat. He wanted things nice and tidy and wouldn't listen to anyone, nor would he attempt to reach his commanders on the camping trip and order them to return early.

Oakland had waited since the early seventies to confront the cult growing in its midst.

After all that time, what could delaying another forty-eight hours possibly hurt?

27

I Told Y'all It Was Gonna Be Big

*"Let me say right here, no one hates Black folks more
than Black folks. . . . Ninety-five percent of the murders
of Blacks are by other Blacks."*
—CHAUNCEY BAILEY, 2007

On Wednesday, August 1, 2007, on what should have been the morning that police raided the bakery, Fourth woke up and decided that he needed to kill Chauncey Bailey.

Not that he had any intention of actually pulling a trigger himself. That's what soldiers did. The satisfaction that Fourth derived from ending the lives of others came not from doing his own blood work but from ordering it done.

Fourth didn't know that Bailey couldn't get his story about the bakery published in the *Post* because Paul Cobb was afraid. No one had alerted him to *that* bit of intelligence.

He called Broussard and Mackey together and said that he was certain Bailey's story about him was going to be in Friday's paper and that it would hurt his ability to win further support to fight the bankruptcy or perhaps even get a bailout from the city government.

Somehow, Fourth thought that killing the messenger might still save the bakery.

"We got to take him out before he write that story."

He told Broussard and Mackey where the *Oakland Post* was and to go down there and stake out the building. When Bailey came out, they were to follow him home, check out the area, and then call Fourth. If all went well, they'd take care of business the next morning, Thursday, the day before the *Post* hit the streets.

Once they got downtown that afternoon, Mackey called the bakery and had Fourth describe the building at Franklin and Fourteenth to make sure they had the right one. Fourth was tense, his jaw tight, his tone brisk, a commander at work. It was obvious to others that he was up to something. He seemed ready to snap.

Broussard and Mackey had taken photos of Bailey with their phones from a freeze-frame of Yusuf Bey's funeral video, the one that had set off Fourth on this latest tangent, so they would recognize him when he came out of the building. After a few hours, Bailey hadn't emerged and Mackey and Broussard were growing impatient. But Fourth had been explicit. Wait for him and follow him home, then call the bakery.

They decided to get out and walk around to keep from nodding off. As Broussard paced up and down Franklin Street, he saw a dark-colored SUV parked nearby. He thought it might be Saleem Bey's and told Mackey, who called Fourth. Fourth hurried downtown.

Broussard was right; it did look like Saleem's SUV. Fourth craned his neck at the building across the street and said, "That motherfucker up there right now talking to him." Apparently the thought of Saleem and Bailey having a conversation about him set Fourth off even further. He stomped around, cursing, ranting, and then, turning to Broussard and Mackey, said, "We should get that motherfucker too." He meant Saleem. He gave them directions to Saleem's home and told them to get it done. Kill both of them, the reporter and the source.

But Fourth quickly reconsidered about Saleem, thinking of his sister and how she might react. Fourth didn't want to incur her wrath. "My sister [would] be trippin'" if her husband was killed, he told Broussard and Mackey. But was it just her response he wanted to avoid? If Saleem was killed, Fourth's sister obviously would have known who was responsible.

Fourth seemed confident that Bailey's murder, if done right, would be untraceable—just as he thought he wouldn't be held accountable for his other recent crimes. But kill Saleem? That was trickier. He let it go. Just keep waiting for the fucking reporter, he ordered Broussard and Mackey, and he went back to the bakery to await their call.

Finally, several hours later, around 5:30 p.m., Bailey emerged onto the street. Mackey, over by a bus stop on Fourteenth Street, saw him first; Broussard was on a parking deck on Franklin, across from the building, watching as Bailey headed directly for a bus that had just pulled over. Mackey and Broussard ran for their car, Mackey calling Fourth. Back at the bakery, Fourth paced and yelled into the phone. He'd been ranting about some reporter most of the day. Now he spoke loudly, repeating what had just been said to him: "He walking out?"

Broussard and Mackey followed the bus down Fourteenth Street, past the city public library and the boxy Rene C. Davidson Courthouse, then the western edge of Lake Merritt. Within five minutes, Bailey got off. The lazy motherfucker should have walked, Broussard said. They pulled over and watched him enter a gray stucco apartment building with plastic owls mounted atop the peaks of its roof.

After thirty minutes of waiting, they figured they'd found where he lived and drove back to the bakery, where Fourth remained edgy, demanding details. Were they sure? Yes.

He wanted them to ambush Bailey when he came out to go to work in the morning. Broussard saw that he finally had the leverage to get something out of Fourth. If he wanted Bailey dead, then it was time to cut through the bullshit and make good on his promise to share his knowledge about buying luxury cars and expensive suits and houses. Fourth would have to deliver on his vaunted and long-promised "credit hookup" scam if he wanted a journalist who worked downtown killed in broad daylight, the kind of hit that would obviously draw intense scrutiny.

During the year that Broussard had come and gone from Oakland, Fourth had made all those promises about teaching him the get-rich-quick games and fraud crimes that underpinned the Beys' finances. Fourth loved to bait Broussard with money, to lord it over him. It had been a conversation that began the first night that Broussard showed up looking for work, the talk of cars and suits and houses. The inequitable nature of life on San Pablo Avenue had both angered Broussard and kept him entranced. Fourth, in a sense, was the reincarnation of Noble Drew Ali in Chicago and, a few years later, W. D. Fard in Detroit, con men who foisted scam after scam on their followers: expensive membership cards, the requirement to wear suits that had to be bought through the temple, the requirement that to belong even the poorest of people had to fork over hefty tithes to the Nation. Elijah Muhammad had soared from a penniless Detroit drunk to a multimillionaire preaching the same thing.

But it wasn't promises of salvation that lured Broussard. It was money. Nothing more. He wanted to be like Fourth, "to get loans and not pay shit back."

Now, as they planned how to kill Bailey, Fourth promised and promised. "You gonna be taken care of, set for life. This gonna be big. This ain't gonna be forgotten. Y'all gonna be real soldiers for this one." As soon as the murder was over, Fourth said, he would take Broussard and Mackey to a person who arranged the fake IDs and credit scores. They had his word. Just kill that fucking reporter.

Fourth wanted to see where Bailey lived and make sure the hit was well planned, so they drove downtown shortly after midnight on August 2. Mackey and Broussard needed to re-create the tailing of the bus to find the apartment again. They parked across the street from Bailey's at 12:24 a.m.

The simplest plan was to catch Bailey as he emerged in the morning. A little taco stand was right across the street. The spotter could hide there. The gunman would be nearby, wearing a ski mask. Fourth had a set of walkie-talkies they could use. The spotter would send a chirp when Bailey stepped outside, and the shooter would run down the street before Bailey could go anywhere and blow him away. As the hit was going down, the spotter would run for the car and pick up the killer. They'd be gone in seconds.

Given Mackey's physical limitations from his bullet wounds, Broussard seemed like a better choice to do the running. "Dre, you gotta do it, man, it's nothing," Mackey said.

Fourth chimed in. "Yeah, you gotta do it, but you can't miss, man. Nothing far away. Get right up on him. If you miss and he survive, they coming for the bakery," insisting that Broussard get in tight, point-blank, and fire three times, just to be safe.

Much later, he would tell prosecutors that Fourth's instructions were akin to reminding Michael Jordan not to miss free throws. He didn't need to be told to make sure Bailey was dead.

They did several dry runs, Mackey watching the apartment, Broussard running from different points. They got it down. They figured that anyone on the street would be so scared at the sight of a man with a shotgun that they would try to save themselves rather than watch or intervene. After a little more than fifteen minutes, they took a circuitous route back to the bakery, driving past a Mexican restaurant where Fourth often ate. It was closed. Whether or not he had planned to go that way, Fourth would be talking about that restaurant again soon.

Once safely within the compound, the three of them went up to Fourth's room, where he gave Broussard the 12-gauge Mossberg that had been stolen from one of the liquor stores, the little shotgun's magazine brimming with shells containing loads of slugs and buckshot.

Cheryl Davis, a woman whom Fourth fancied as one of his multiple wives, had heard him barking orders on the phone all day and now waited for him in his bed. She could hear him out in the hall talking to the guys she knew as Ali and Catfish. They were up to something. Finally, she heard Fourth tell Ali to wake him up at 5:00 a.m. He never got up that early, and when he came into the bedroom she asked him why.

He said he needed to get up to pray.

Pray? He never got up to pray.

Where was he?

Broussard panicked. It was 7:12 a.m. He and Mackey had already lost Chauncey Bailey.

The bus. There was a bus right there in front of his building. He must have gotten on it. Broussard ran toward it, the shotgun tilted in his hands.

He tried the doors; the driver wouldn't open them. He ran alongside, cran-
ing to look in the windows, then at the street, then in the windows again,
his head swiveling.

Fuck. Where did Bailey go? Mackey had signaled Broussard, but when
Broussard ran to the building, Bailey had vanished.

The bus was a 40-line coach headed downtown with about fifty people
aboard. The driver slammed the accelerator and sped away, panicked. Her
heart raced, adrenaline nearly overrunning her. She got a few blocks away,
where it seemed safe, then pulled over. Her hands shook as she radioed
her dispatcher. There was a man wearing a mask carrying a shotgun, right
outside.

Everything was going wrong that morning. First, Fourth wouldn't
let them have the Charger; instead, he told them to take some bucket, a
beat-up minivan that belonged to a guy who did construction work around
the compound. Then they discovered that the walkie-talkies were dead;
they'd forgotten to charge them. They used cell phones instead. Now the
motherfucker was gone. Broussard jumped in the minivan. "He must be
walking," Mackey said. They had to find him.

Bailey had decided to skip the bus. It was a beautiful morning. He
looped around the lake. Plans were in the works to replace all the roads that
crossed there and rebuild the little bridges over the stream that flowed out
to the estuary and the bay. Physical progress in Oakland had long lagged.
What good, really, were bricks and mortar when the city couldn't keep
schools and libraries open or enough police on the street? What good was
it when the lack of decent programs to help poor people find jobs, or get
off drugs, or obtain counseling when they returned from prison, left Your
Black Muslim Bakery as what too many saw as the best alternative, one endorsed by mayors and members of Congress? Maybe the biblical quote atop
the *Post* was right. Those without vision would perish.

As Bailey strode along the lakeshore on a walkway offset from speeding
cars by a line of bright orange barriers, his story on the bakery must have
pressed on his mind. He didn't like taking no for an answer, even from Paul
Cobb. He had to get the story in the paper. He still believed the bakery
could help people if it ever got in the right hands. If he hadn't, he wouldn't
be pushing so hard to get the bankruptcy article printed. Bailey probably

didn't notice the white minivan passing on his left and the nineteen-year-old slouched in its passenger seat, scanning the walkway. What was one more junker in Oakland?

"There you go right there," Broussard said, glancing at the photo on his phone, then pointing at a man in a gray suit with a bag over his shoulder.

They'd caught up to Bailey as he neared Fourteenth Street and Lakeside Drive, near a cluster of governmental buildings: the courthouse, the library, the headquarters of Alameda County government. It was still early, but the streets were busy with people going to work, walkers, joggers.

Broussard told Mackey to slow down and he'd just hop out and do it right there. Then they could just peel off and get away. But Mackey disagreed. There were too many people.

"It's too hot," he said.

It was obvious where Bailey was going. All they had to do was find a better position up ahead and wait for him.

Bailey crossed Fourteenth Street and slipped in the side door of a McDonald's where he often bought coffee. A sixty-year-old homeless man named Tony Amos hung around there most mornings. Bailey usually chatted with him for a minute. There was something about Amos that he liked; even a street drinker could be a source. Bailey bought two coffees, handing Amos one. The transaction left Bailey with twenty-eight cents in his pants pocket. Bailey gulped his quickly; he needed to get to the office and put out a newspaper.

He hurried out the front door, crossed Jackson Street on Fourteenth, and walked briskly along the sidewalk next to a parking lot. Amos wandered behind him but couldn't keep up. Bailey was the one in a hurry. Amos had nowhere to be but a nearby bodega where he bought morning beers.

Parents with toddlers strapped in car seats pulled up at a child-care center across the street. Next to it, a window washer pushed a squeegee across rows of glass on an office building. A bus huffed along Fourteenth. As Bailey walked, his bag swung on his left shoulder in time with his strides. Nearby the city post office was coming slowly to life for the day. Next to it, the cars of government workers were beginning to fill a circular parking structure. A block away, a workman stood atop a building under construction, looking out at the street. Just down Fourteenth, a medical worker waited in front of the Hong Fook Health Center for someone to unlock the door. A woman who also worked there pulled up to the curb. Across the street, another woman walked briskly toward the Lake Merritt BART station to catch a train to San Francisco. It seemed like any other morning.

There he was, on the far sidewalk. They were running out of time; Bailey was just three blocks from his office. Mackey hung a hard right on Alice Street and stopped. Broussard pulled the black ski mask over his face and jumped out. He inched along the side of the child-care center and peeked around the corner. Bailey was right across the street now. Broussard broke into a run, his right index finger flicking off the shotgun's safety. It was 7:24 a.m.

Broussard went hard across the four lanes of traffic on Fourteenth Street, leveling the weapon. Bailey, it seemed, didn't see him until the last moment, only turning slightly and swinging his bag awkwardly when Broussard came upon him.

True to his orders, Broussard got close. The first shot hit Bailey's right shoulder, a copper slug ripping into his torso at a muzzle velocity of nearly 1,400 feet per second. It severed Bailey's trachea and esophagus, shredding the tops of both lungs before exiting behind his left shoulder.

Broussard racked the pump, an empty cartridge kicking away, another shell sliding into the chamber.

Bailey began to fall just off the sidewalk next to a small bush. The second round, a load of buckshot, tore into his abdomen, splintering his belt buckle, ripping him open.

Broussard turned and nearly broke into a run back across Fourteenth to where Mackey waited. Then he remembered his instructions.

"There ain't no coming back from this," Fourth had said. *Don't miss.* Three to be safe.

Shit. He'd only shot twice.

He turned back, his left hand racking the pump again. Another spent shell flicked away. Broussard stopped at Bailey's feet, dropping the muzzle about three or four feet from his head, and fired a load of buckshot.

It exploded into the left side of Bailey's face, destroying his cheek, his eye, and most of his forehead, opening a hole nearly eight inches long and four inches wide. The buckshot splattered pieces of his bone and brain onto the sidewalk and parking lot. Wadding from the shell blew into the back of his skull. The left cerebral hemisphere of his brain was gone.

Now Broussard ran back across Fourteenth Street. He left the two spent cartridges lying on the ground, one a red Hornady buckshot load, the other a green Remington stamped with the words "copper solid." Each, of course, bore the tiny, telltale imprint of the shotgun's firing pin on the primer pad of its brass base. Had Broussard scooped up the casings and disposed of them, the next forty-eight hours might have unfolded very differently. But no one had told him to do that. His orders were simple and explicit: Just make sure the fucking reporter was dead.

That, he'd done.

Broussard threw the shotgun into the open cargo door, slammed it, and jumped into the passenger seat, the van already speeding off, Mackey phoning Fourth to tell him the news. For a moment, silence covered the killing scene. There was remarkably little blood around the body—a sign of just how quickly Bailey's heart had stopped beating. But his remaining eye was locked with a gaze of absolute wide-open horror, suggesting that perhaps he had lingered for a few seconds and seen Broussard point the shotgun down at him for the third blast.

A bus went by on Fourteenth, passengers gaping out the windows at the man sprawled just off the sidewalk beside a scrubby bush, half his face gone. The woman who had just pulled up in front of her workplace had ducked below her dashboard, fumbling for her phone. Her coworker waiting at the door crouched and watched the gunman run across the street. The construction worker had recognized the three booms as reports from a large-caliber shotgun. He looked around an elevator shaft and saw the killer running with the weapon in his right hand. The window washer turned when he heard the first two shots and saw the masked man step away from Bailey, then return and fire into the prone man's face. The woman walking to BART hid behind a pickup truck in a small parking lot on Alice Street. The gunman ran right past her, turning to look into her face as he went by. On Fourteenth Street, Tony Amos ran back toward the McDonald's.

The wail of sirens shattered the brief quiet. Police converged from all directions, black-and-white patrol cars skidding to stops, cops reaching across their torsos for the radio microphones clipped to their lapels as they ran toward the body.

The first officer to get to Bailey saw that the grotesque wound to his head alone was fatal, but still checked for a rise and fall of his chest. Of course there wasn't one. He looked around, then reached into Bailey's bag and removed a copy of the *Post,* opened it, and gently spread the newspaper over what remained of Chauncey Bailey's face.

No sooner had Broussard and Mackey returned to the compound than Fourth announced he wanted to go see the scene of the shooting. But first Broussard handed him back the shotgun. Fourth took it, saw that the empty shell from Broussard's third shot was still in the chamber, and ejected it onto his bedroom floor, where it lay amid a scattering of live rounds and spent casings. Fourth reloaded the gun and put it in his closet, then he, Mackey, and Broussard went downstairs and piled into the Charger. When they got downtown, they found streets blocked off by dozens of police cars and television vans.

"Damn! Damn! I told y'all it was gonna be big," Fourth exclaimed. He was ecstatic.

They pulled over by Lake Merritt and got out. Fourth insisted that they leave their cell phones in the car. The government, he said, had secret ways, tricknology, of using phones to overhear conversations.

Once he thought they were clear, Fourth asked, "What happened? How did y'all do it?"

They told him.

"Ain't no way it can get connected back to me," Broussard boasted. It had been over in less than a minute. Mackey had taken off the van's license plates. Broussard had had a mask on. The only person who had seen him up close was dead. "Who can identify me? What can happen now? We good," he said.

A few blocks away at the scene, homicide Sergeant Derwin Longmire arrived at 7:58 a.m. Despite the help he'd given raid planners, he still wasn't going to be part of that operation. His job that week was to investigate any fresh killings. Now he had one.

Witnesses had seen the gunman flee to a waiting white van. There were two discharged shotgun shells near the body. Cases had started with far less. Soon Paul Cobb was there. He told Longmire a man had been unhappy about how Bailey had portrayed him in a recent feature story. Maybe he had done it. But later that day, Cobb called Chief Tucker and said Bailey had been writing a story about the Beys. Those who knew about the delayed raid flinched. They ordered a ballistics comparison between the firing-pin imprint on the shells found next to Bailey and those collected at the car shooting months earlier.

As Broussard, Mackey, and Fourth left the lake, Richard Lewis called. Where was everybody? They said they would pick him up and go to IHOP for breakfast.

When they sat down to eat, Fourth wouldn't shut up. He kept badgering Broussard. *How did he fall? What did he say?*

"What did the inside of his head look like?"

Broussard didn't answer. He thought Fourth was acting like an asshole, a guy who didn't have the balls to kill anyone himself. At least in his jubilation Fourth promised that rewards would be coming. They'd go see his credit man tomorrow.

"I love you guys," Fourth blurted.

But as Broussard slowly calmed down, the adrenaline in his body ebbing, he found himself oddly skeptical. If Fourth really did show him how to score bogus loans, how could Fourth then control him in the future? Did he really think that once Broussard got that kind of money he'd still be interested in Black Muslim bullshit and that dinky bakery?

When they got back to the compound, Fourth went back upstairs and flicked on his TV. There was a news story airing about the killing. He yelled for the woman who had spent the night with him. When she came over, he pointed at the screen, where a reporter stood in front of yellow crime-scene tape.

"That will teach them to fuck with me," he boasted.

———

Word spread rapidly about who was dead and what he'd been working on: Chauncey Bailey had been writing something about the Beys, and they'd killed him over it. Reporters were tripping over one another, working police sources. By midafternoon the day of the murder, they were even calling the bakery for Fourth's response. Flat denials of involvement in violence had been part of his radical faith since W. D. Fard's claims that Robert Harris had misunderstood the instructions in the booklet at the scene of James Smith's sacrificial murder. The Nation of Islam had insisted the Zebra Killers were framed. Yusuf Bey responded, "I didn't do it," when confronted with scientific evidence of rape.

Now if those media devils wanted a response, they'd get it: Fourth brazenly called a news conference to deny involvement in the killing. It was nearly surreal. He stood in front of the bakery near a mural of his father, wearing dark glasses and a scalding red bow tie atop a white shirt, and denied a crime he had not been charged with.

"For our name to be brought up in such a slanderous, negativity type way, of course it upsets us," he said rapidly, as if he were on speed. "I feel for Chauncey Bailey and what happened. I have never met him, but I've seen him around," he said. "There are homicides in Oakland every day. We need to clean the streets up. That's one thing we do, clean the streets up of violence. Oakland is a magnet for violence. Our job, for 45 years through our leader, Dr. Yusuf Bey, is to clean the streets up. I hope they get to the bottom of it and solve this problem." Fourth retreated inside the compound, confident his fortunes had turned.

Within a few hours, a criminalist finished the preliminary comparisons of the shotgun shells. The firing-pin imprints were identical. The same shotgun had fired both the shells found at the car shooting and the ones that killed Chauncey Bailey.

It was official. The forty-eight-hour delay in the raid on the bakery had cost Bailey his life.

28

I Shot Him

"Daddy would have died!"
—YUSUF BEY V, talking of how his father would have reacted to
police raiding Your Black Muslim Bakery

Whenever police went to the bakery, Bey men appeared on its roof. The threat of plunging fire was a serious concern to raid planners. If someone got up there with a rifle and started shooting, cops on the ground could be pinned down, killed. The only solution was for the police to get a higher position. Just down San Pablo Avenue, the Star Bethel Missionary Baptist Church towered over the Beys' compound, a perfect lair from which snipers could take out anyone atop the bakery. But the church's pastor refused to allow men with guns to pass through his sanctuary. The snipers couldn't get upstairs.

The pastor's unwillingness to help wasn't going to deter police, though. A little past midnight on August 3, the sniper team's sergeant went to a nearby fire station and asked for help. Under the pretext of an electrical fire, a hook-and-ladder truck was soon aside the church. The snipers disguised themselves in heavy turnout coats and fire helmets and trudged up a ladder, their weapons concealed. From the church's roof, all seemed quiet inside the compound. They could see Fourth's Dodge Charger behind the bakery.

The uncooperative pastor wasn't the only obstacle police faced. After Chief Tucker's postponement, they had returned the U-Haul trucks a day early. But when they tried to rent them again to carry the SWAT teams up San Pablo Avenue, the trucks were gone, rented to someone else. At the last minute, a lieutenant remembered he knew someone who worked for another rental company and raced there to lease other trucks, paying for them out of his own pocket. The combination of ingenuity and Keystone Kops scrambling defined the department. Individual officers could conquer problems on the street, but bureaucratic bungling lurked at every turn, none bigger, of course, than the fateful decision to delay the raid.

As the sniper team settled in on the church roof, police assembled a staging area in a grocery store parking lot a half mile south on San Pablo Avenue. It soon looked like a forward camp in a war zone. Tension seemed to grip everyone. If they had just hit the place on August 1, as planned, then Bailey wouldn't be dead and the media wouldn't be in hysterics. But the larger concern was whether the Beys were now prepared for an assault. A raid on August 1 would have been a surprise. A raid on August 3 could be a bloodbath.

But men at the bakery were quite capable of their own blunders. Broussard had told Fourth and Mackey that he thought the murder weapon could never be traced back to him and so returned the little shotgun to Fourth rather than ditching it. From Broussard's point of view, he had been masked and someone else now possessed the weapon. Who could say with certainty that he was the shooter? But on the evening of August 2, Fourth gave the murder gun back to Broussard and told him to use it to patrol the perimeter of the compound. Broussard, though, was exhausted. He went to his room, tossed the shotgun aside, and fell deeply asleep.

At 4:50 a.m., two Penske trucks raced up San Pablo Avenue, headlights piercing the North Oakland morning. At the same time, cops drove several large garbage trucks toward the compound from the other direction. They were to block the street so any Bey soldiers from the cold-water flats across from the bakery couldn't easily rally to the compound.* Toward the bakery's rear, two SWAT teams, the officers in body armor and carrying gas masks, crept slowly toward the duplex where Broussard and Mackey slept.

The trucks on San Pablo came to hard stops beneath the red star-and-crescent sign that had hung there for years. The first officer to jump from the trucks was the one carrying the chain saw meant to cut around the locks of the door leading upstairs. But as he did, pulling again and again on the saw's starter cord, it wouldn't roar to life. Two squads of raiders were now stacked up on the sidewalk with nowhere to go. Officers rushed forward with a battering ram, their only other option, and began to hammer the door, reverberations rising through the building. Upstairs, Fourth jumped from bed. In his closet were monitoring screens of security cameras throughout the compound. On them he could see the police outside. But it was too late to do anything. As the door finally collapsed and cops with rifles poured through the breach, Fourth ducked into the next room, where his two young sons slept with their mother, Alaia. Then he peeked down the stairs as officers raced upward.

As the lead cop neared the landing, he saw Fourth's unmistakable face glancing around the corner. The cop threw a flash-bang grenade and charged behind its explosion, his MP5 ready to fire. But rather than seeing Fourth run into the expected hail of bullets, he found him lying on the floor, clad in a tank top and brown boxer shorts, hands folded behind his head, crying and begging for his life. Rather than rallying his men, or even sacrificing himself, Fourth had burst into tears.

More stun grenades detonated, including one in the room where Alaia covered her children with her body. Police rushed in, pointing guns, yelling for her to not move. "Devils! Devils!" she screamed. Nearby a few men emerged from small rooms with their hands up. They were unarmed. No one had fired a shot.

At the duplex, raiders threw a flash-bang onto the porch, rammed open

---

*Somehow, police had failed to ask for access to those buildings across from the bakery in their search warrant applications, even though the weapons they sought could easily have been stashed there.

the door, and stormed inside. Another grenade went off. Shocked from sleep, Broussard grabbed the little shotgun from the floor and leaned out an open window. But he wasn't trying to shoot. Instead he pitched the gun toward the ground, where it landed fifteen feet from a cop. Then Broussard tried to run, but as he stepped from the room, screaming police rushed him. He slammed the door and went for the window again, but his pursuers kicked the door in, weapons trained on him. Broussard surrendered. With the little shotgun now in the hands of police, his boast that Bailey's murder couldn't be traced to him had evaporated in less than twenty-four hours.

In another bedroom, cops found Mackey on the floor, trying to reach under his bed. They flipped his mattress aside and found another shotgun, a sawed-off Remington 12-gauge, its barrel hacked down to fourteen inches, its stock removed. They cuffed Mackey and pushed him into a chair.

Across the Beys' compound, the drama ended in minutes. With nothing more than a few stun grenades, police had finally taken control of the Black Muslim citadel that had plagued Oakland for decades—albeit too late for Chauncey Bailey, Michael Will, and Odell Roberson.

The snipers lowered their rifles and filed down from the church roof. The garbage trucks roared away. Back at the staging area, commanders breathed again. In the midst of all the tension of the night, they hadn't forgotten to call all the local television stations and alert them that a large operation would happen before dawn in North Oakland. Now they let the camera crews creep closer to the bakery. On the surface, at least, it all looked like what mattered most to Tucker and his commanders: good publicity, a successful operation.

Upstairs at the bakery, in Fourth's bedroom—the same room where his father had raped children for so many years—adrenaline-charged cops laughed and clipped bow ties to their body armor and snapped victorious photos with their cell phones. Five men were rousted on the top floor, including Richard Lewis and one of Fourth's younger brothers. Fourth's children clung to their mother, crying. The handcuffed men were seated on the floor against a wall and given blankets. Fourth, his hands cinched together, watched as more cops, designated to cull for evidence, descended on his quarters. In short order, they found the spent shotgun shell he had ejected from the murder gun the morning before. Eventually, a ballistics report would show it had contained the same type of pellets and wadding found in Bailey's skull.

One by one, police led people in handcuffs from the bakery and duplex and into waiting patrol cars. They hauled each suspect away individually; there were no paddy wagons. Fourth wouldn't be given the chance to communicate with anyone, to plot anything.

At least not yet.

As police wandered freely through the compound, they discovered it was far from a fortress. The bakery itself was filthy. Rodent feces littered the floor, and rotting fish floated in a sink, giving off a gagging stench. More fish lay outside on a pile of melting ice. Garbage was strewn about; other sinks were heaped with unwashed pots and baking pans. Barrels of used kitchen grease sat out exposed; insects crawled over sacks of flour and sugar. Commanders ordered the walk-in freezers searched for bodies. All cops found was more rotten food.

Bullets and shell casings were everywhere. A mother lode of spent rifle and pistol cartridges and shotgun shells were found on the roof. Neighbors often complained about random gunfire. Here was the proof.

The end of Your Black Muslim Bakery was at hand. The deplorable conditions in the kitchen were enough to shut it down; to make sure, police had called in health department inspectors. Later that morning in downtown Oakland, the federal judge overseeing the bankruptcy would finally order the long-anticipated liquidation of bakery assets to satisfy creditors.

At the compound, Fourth, under heavy guard, was put in the back of a patrol car, a cop's hand on the back of his head as he slid through the door. For the kidnapping and torture of JoAnne alone, he faced life in prison with no parole. As the car drove away, other vehicles flanking it in escort, their lights flashing, the likelihood that Fourth would never return to San Pablo Avenue seemed overwhelming.

Fourth, though, thought far differently. He had every expectation that he would be released from custody within a few days. He hadn't shot anyone. He was technically arrested on a warrant for skipping court dates on the charges he had run over the nightclub bouncers in San Francisco. But his lawyer could take care of that. Police could hold him for seventy-two hours in the torture and murder investigations, but if the evidence remained as thin as he thought it was, he might even get out sooner. Mackey had taken the rifle used to kill Wills and Roberson and hidden it at a house Fourth owned in Richmond. Police would never recover it. If they had gotten rid of the shotgun used to kill Bailey, police wouldn't have had much evidence at all.

Allah must have been looking out for Fourth; how else could his good fortune of giving that gun back to Broussard just before the raid be explained? What if police had found it in Fourth's closet, where he kept it? Then he might be in a far more dire situation.

Derwin Longmire, the detective others kept out of the bakery raid because of suspicions he was a Black Muslim, was now deeply involved in its aftermath. Bailey's killing was his case. Broussard's possession of what tests soon confirmed was the murder weapon made him the chief suspect. Broussard's desperate attempt to rid himself of it showed a consciousness of guilt, as prosecutors say. Police already knew Fourth had stolen the little shotgun from one of the liquor stores he had attacked nearly two years earlier, the same gun police didn't bother to recover.

Plus, Broussard loosely matched the physical description—tall and lean—of the man people described shooting Bailey. Despite the killer's mask, witnesses had seen just enough of his skin to describe him as African American.

Getting the shooter wouldn't be the problem. But what about the others? Witnesses both outside Bailey's apartment and minutes later at the killing scene made it clear that there was someone else in the white van—a getaway driver. And if police knew one thing about the Beys, it was that everything flowed from the top. Yusuf Bey, then Antar, and then Fourth preached that Blacks had to think for themselves—but those who followed them lived under a rigid command structure. Soldiers didn't act without orders. If the Beys were responsible for Bailey's death, as everything suggested they were, then Fourth had to have ordered it. The question from the start of the investigation wasn't whether Fourth was the intellectual author of Bailey's assassination—a fact that made him as guilty as if he had fired the shotgun himself—but whether he would be aggressively investigated for it. In the harried culture of Oakland police murder investigations, those who ordered killings weren't often pursued—just shooters. Police didn't get extra credit for charging more than one person in the same slaying. They did what they had to do to consider a case solved and moved on.

At 9:55 a.m., Longmire, backed by Sergeant Louis Cruz, walked into interview room two of a police substation in East Oakland, where Fourth waited in a sweat suit he had been allowed to put on. The tears that had soaked his cheeks when he begged the SWAT cops not kill him a few hours earlier were gone; now he steeled himself with beliefs passed from W. D. Fard to Elijah Muhammad to Daddy to him. After Longmire recited a Miranda warning, he asked Fourth if he was willing to talk. Fourth had every legal right to say no, or at least to ask for a lawyer. But he was Yusuf Ali Bey IV. He could talk his way out of this; the cops didn't have shit on him. He could defeat their tricknology. Of that he was sure.

"Of course" he would talk, he said.

Within minutes, Fourth claimed that Broussard had admitted to him that he killed Bailey after learning independently that he was writing about the bakery. It was a solo act, an enterprise designed to show loyalty and ingenuity, Fourth claimed. Broussard had asked early the previous morning to borrow the white van; then, around 8 a.m., he had taken Fourth and Mackey downtown, saying he wanted to show them something. They drove by the crime scene, where they caught a glimpse of Bailey's corpse, then walked around by the lake. Broussard alluded to the fact that he had done something to someone, Fourth explained. It was only later, Fourth said, that he learned Bailey had been that someone. He even said he had planned to call Longmire and explain everything—be a responsible citizen—once he had figured it all out. But before he could, police raided the bakery.

That was his story.

The cops left, returning an hour later with a voice recorder. Now the real dance would start.

After some background questions, Longmire asked whether Fourth allowed guns in the compound.

"No guns are allowed in our premises. Period. Based on the fact that Dr. Yusuf Bey never allowed guns on the premises when he was here. My brother didn't, either. I wasn't going to change anything," he said.

The lies had begun, one atop the other.

Finally, Longmire said, "I am going to ask you, as I asked you before, do you suspect [Broussard] or anyone else being involved in Mr. Bailey's homicide?"

"I don't suspect anything, but from the evidence that I've gotten this morning, the shotgun being thrown out the window, the white van . . . it doesn't take, um, a rocket scientist to figure out, to put two and two together, but that's for the court."

Fourth's amalgam of lies, half-truths, and quarter-truths was, of course, laughable. But in his radical faith, which defied rational thought, he had been taught to believe in his own superiority. His truthful statement that Broussard had shot Bailey—but his lie that Broussard had acted alone—was obviously calculated to protect himself. If Broussard admitted, truthfully, that Fourth had ordered the hit, then Fourth would have already given police an alternative version.

In another interrogation room, down the hall from Fourth, Devaughndre Broussard had fallen asleep. The detectives, Longmire among them, left him alone for several hours, then went in and confronted him with the ballistics results. There are two official versions of what happened after Longmire shut the door. The first is the detective's block-lettered notes on two pages of plain white typing paper on which he wrote his version of Broussard's answers to his questions: "I grew up in S.F. Western Edition [*sic*]. Father lives in Richmond. I went back and Yusuf Bey IV gave me a job. He is a good brother."

Then there is what Broussard later told prosecutors about his initial in-

teraction with detectives. First, Broussard said, he waived his right to remain silent, but later he repeatedly told Longmire he had changed his mind
and wanted an attorney but was rebuffed. "You ain't getting no lawyer," he
claimed Longmire told him. "This ain't going away. You're going down for
this."

Broussard said he made several denials. Then, he said, Longmire told
him, "Fourth said you shot him."

While Broussard didn't consider himself much of a Muslim, he refused
to believe that Fourth, the man who preached brotherhood above all else,
who claimed it was a defiance of Allah to ever cooperate with police, would
snitch on him.

Longmire, he said, reached over and grabbed his thigh with one of his
bodybuilder's hands and squeezed.

"This is not going nowhere. You're gonna answer to this," Broussard
claimed Longmire said, squeezing harder. "I tried to scoot away from him,
but he had my thigh like that. I mean, he just squeezing that motherfucker
the hell apart." But still Broussard wouldn't admit anything. Nearly four
years later, Longmire would deny before a jury that he had squeezed Broussard's leg or done anything at all inappropriate, just as he had once testified
that he hadn't threatened to sic a "swarm of Muslims" on Alfonza Phillips's
girlfriend, Althea, when he interrogated her, as she claimed.

Now, obviously frustrated with Broussard, Longmire got up and went
back down the hall to Fourth, again with his recorder on.

This time Fourth made his story clearer. He said he asked Broussard,
"Did you get him?" and Broussard replied, "Yes, I did it."

Then Longmire asked him, "Yusuf, did you have anything to do with it?
Did you put him up to it at all?"

"Of course not."

Then Longmire had an idea. If Fourth ordered Broussard to "be truthful," would he?

Fourth said he might. Longmire wrote in his notes that his next investigative step would be to use Fourth to help confront Broussard and force his
confession. At 8:45 p.m., detectives brought Broussard into the interview
room where Fourth sat at a table.

Fourth had not, of course, been officially deputized or any such nonsense. But here was a man who had told police blatant lies about his involvement in a murder—involvement that was legally tantamount to firing
the shotgun himself. Now police had enlisted his aid in eliciting a confession from the shooter.

But the problem was that a truthful, complete confession would impli-
cate Fourth. Was that what detectives hoped would be the result? By using
him in this way, were they making Fourth effectively an agent of the police,
asked to use his sway as a religious leader over a follower? But Fourth, obviously, had a compelling self-interest in blocking exactly what defined the
mission of the police: to get the truth.

Longmire, Cruz, and Fourth went at Broussard together now, the audio
recorder turned off, but Broussard continued to deny that he had shot Bailey. After about fifteen minutes, Longmire gestured at Fourth and urged him
to "chime in" more. He did, and when he repeated his claim that the previous day, Broussard had said he'd killed Bailey on his own, Broussard jumped
at him. Fourth flinched, but he was otherwise "cool as an ice cube." Broussard would one day recall: "He's talking about [me], he told on me in front
of my face. That's fucked up. This nigga just told on me in front of my
face."

Broussard started to cry. At any moment he could have blurted out that
Fourth had ordered the killing and implicated them both. But he didn't.
Instead, he asked Longmire to let him speak with Fourth alone. So without
any way to record the ensuing conversation or even eavesdrop on it, the
detectives left. There was no place in the room to conceal a recording device, Longmire would eventually say, and if he had left one out in the open
Broussard and Fourth wouldn't have talked freely.

Using Fourth to bully Broussard with cops in the room was one thing.
But leaving them alone, unobserved and unrecorded, was entirely another.
Derwin Longmire would spend years explaining that he was not a bakery
member or sympathizer, that he wasn't Fourth's friend and protector, that
all he ever wanted was to put Fourth in jail. But his troubles were always
rooted in that assumption within the police department that he was a Black
Muslim and sympathetic to the Beys. He added to the suspicions with questionable actions—keeping a thin case file, not following up on evidence,

and communicating with Fourth and members of the Bey family, even referring to Fourth in his notes by his first name. Chief among them was giving Fourth and Broussard time to talk alone that night.

Others would later say it was good police work. Longmire would say
that without the decency he had shown the Beys over the years, Fourth
would not have told him Broussard shot Bailey, even if Fourth lied about all
the rest. Fourth, Longmire insisted, would never have spoken to any other
detective but him.*

When Broussard said he wanted to talk to Fourth in the absence of police, it was a now-or-never moment. Broussard was not going to crack if this
request wasn't granted, Longmire would say, so he let it happen. "Broussard
had asked for privacy and it didn't seem reasonable to me to leave a recording device," he would say. "I guess you could call it a tactic," one meant to
"get the truth."

What police would get was a snippet of the truth. The door shut behind
the detectives, and now Fourth had his chance. All those years of listening
to his father preach and cajole and order men around, telling them what to
think, what to do. All that rhetoric about Allah and duty and passing tests,
of sacrifice for the cause, of being a good, strong soldier. He had to draw on
it now and save himself.

Broussard tried to ask Fourth why he had given him up, but Fourth
started ranting.

"All you gotta do is say you did it, man, and we'll get you a lawyer and
you gonna get out and you gonna be safe. I'm gonna get you a good-ass
lawyer and you gonna walk," Fourth said.

Then came what Broussard would call "that religious shit."

"You gotta act upon your faith," Fourth said. Broussard had to be a
strong soldier for the cause, take the fall alone. He must accept that Allah
was testing him, pushing him. If he could just carry this burden, he would
be home in a year or two and Fourth would make him rich. He'd get paid.

---

*Fourth did, however, give a statement that same night to other detectives investigat-
ing the kidnapping and torture case in which JoAnne was the victim. He also spoke
with a prosecutor and inspector from the Alameda County District Attorney's Office,
repeating most of what he told Longmire.

All he had to do was be a true believer, be strong. He just had to say the bakery had nothing to do with the killing, that it was all his idea.

"Man had money. I had nothing," Broussard would say. "He was 21 years old, had a couple of houses [and] not Toyotas and Hondas, he had luxury cars. I can do this, this sacrifice . . . two years at the most. And I come home and be on easy street. I'm gonna have some money. Or I can say no, still be in jail for two years, and come home, struggle again.

"I'm like, OK, I can say I am a Muslim. It was all a game."

The detectives opened the door and peeked in. Broussard said through tears to give them another minute or two. They did, then came back and took Fourth away.

Longmire sat down. Everyone was tired. It was more than sixteen hours after the raid that morning. It was time to get it over with.

"OK, man, what happened?"

Broussard drew a breath.

"I shot him."

"Then what happened when you shot him?"

"He fell."

"And when he fell, what happened then?"

"I shot him again . . . and again."

"Did anybody instruct you or order you to do this?"

"No, sir."

29

Pow . . . Pow . . . *Poof!*

"They had the judges, the juries, the shotguns, the law—in
a word, power. But it was a criminal power to be feared but
not respected, and to be outwitted in any way whatever."
—JAMES BALDWIN, *The Fire Next Time*

But what about Fourth?

Broussard had said the magic words: "I shot him." Why he had didn't much matter. He'd said it, three little words of truth. In effect, they closed the case.

The rest of what he told Longmire was a thin, fictive concoction designed to do exactly what Fourth ordered him to do, sacrifice himself. It's what soldiers did. He had learned Bailey was writing "bad things" about Fourth and decided to kill him with a shotgun that he, Broussard, owned. He went downtown, followed him home, took the white van the next morning, smoked a cocaine-laced cigar called a blunt on the way, found Bailey, and blew him to bits.

Longmire recorded Broussard's story and took notes, then filed papers asking the district attorney to charge Broussard with murder.

Lies would sort themselves out. Maybe the kid would eventually flip, tell the full truth. But for now, those three little words, "I shot him," meant the murder of Chauncey Bailey was cleared.

And elsewhere at the police substation, other cops were making mistakes that might just enable Fourth to get away with ordering the killing.

Perhaps the biggest one involved Cheryl Davis, the woman who had observed Fourth's tension the day before the hit, then watched as he boasted shortly after Bailey's death that it would "teach them to fuck with me."

After being held for hours after the raid, Davis spoke at length with two detectives, telling a very different story from those Fourth and Broussard were spinning just down the hall. She had known Fourth for years and agreed to work at the bakery that summer to help him keep better track of the money. Their relationship turned physical as he pursued her as a plural wife. But she appeared to not be a true believer, and after being held for more than fifteen hours, she agreed to give the cops a formal statement.

Fourth had been complaining about Bailey earlier that week, she said.

"I believe [Bailey] was writing . . . a newspaper article about the bakery going into bankruptcy. . . . I guess some more information about Yusuf was going to be in that article and . . . he wasn't too happy about it," she said. "I overheard Yusuf talking about it. . . . He sounded like, upset, when they stated they was writing stuff about him. I kind of had a feeling that he was up to something," she said.

"Like what?" a detective asked.

"Um, like trying to assassinate Chauncey Bailey."

The next day, when she learned Bailey was dead, "it kind of added up."

She understood Fourth's immense ego; he could not stand the idea of being the subject of news reporting, she said. "The way he makes himself seem . . . Like he feels it's disrespectful to talk about him . . . what he's doing, who he is, what he stands for." Killing wasn't beyond him. "I think he was going to have someone do it."

"Based upon what you know of him and what you know of the bakery, could anyone have done that without his approval?" a detective asked.

"No."

She told them how Fourth huddled with Mackey and Broussard just outside his bedroom well after midnight on August 2 and then told Mackey to wake him up at 5:00 a.m., repeating his claim to her that he needed to rise early to pray. This was incredible evidence, but the detectives who interviewed her somehow filed their notes and the recording in the file for the Wills murder, not Bailey's, where they would sit undisturbed for more than a year.

Police would blame that misfiling on the chaos of trying to interrogate all the people detained in the raid. "There were so many moving parts, and there was not one person in charge," an Oakland police commander eventually said.

One of the detectives later claimed that what Davis had said wasn't relevant to the investigation of Bailey's killing, even though he had quoted Davis in his notes as saying, "I think [Fourth] had him killed." The detective who interviewed Davis would eventually say that he gave Longmire a brief verbal summary of her statement. There is no record of such a conversation in Longmire's case notes.

But what Davis told detectives "was obviously relevant" to Bailey's murder, the commander eventually admitted, and "there definitely was a mistake" in not bringing her statement to the front of the investigation.

What it showed was that police were not constructing a cohesive narrative of Bailey's killing, the first assassination of an American journalist over a domestic story in thirty-one years. It also showed that authorities lacked interest in diving too far into what was left of the Bey cult. If they could just get Fourth in the torture case, it would be all over. That's all they needed, murder orders be damned.

Another blunder by the police was the release that night of Antoine Mackey. One of the truths that Fourth used to buttress his lies was that Mackey had gone with him and Broussard to drive past the murder scene. It seemed clear that Mackey was the van driver. Since he was on felony probation, the gun found under his bed could have sent him to prison for several years. Mackey, unlike the others, though, refused to talk to detectives, and for reasons that have never been completely explained, he wasn't charged with weapons possession and was released.

But even with those mistakes, Fourth still made another clumsy error that should have immediately reinvigorated efforts to tie him to Bailey's murder. Just past 2:00 a.m., well after Broussard had said, "I shot him," a top prosecutor and an inspector from the district attorney's office arrived, and Fourth agreed to speak with them. It was routine for the DA's office to send a "call-out team" to interview suspects who had confessed to police they had committed murder. Broussard wouldn't talk, but Fourth, after lying his way through his conversations with Longmire and enjoying his incredible fortune in convincing Broussard to weave a web of deception around his confession, must have thought no one with a badge was his equal.

Assistant District Attorney Tom Rogers and Inspector Robert Chenault repeated many of the same questions Longmire had asked, but they kept circling back to where Fourth had been the night before the killing. Had he gone to Bailey's apartment? No. But he had been in the general area, he said, because it just happened to be the location of one of his favorite restaurants, the Mexican joint they had driven past on the way back to the bakery. *So you didn't go by Bailey's apartment?* they kept asking. *No,* he kept saying, they were there to go to the restaurant, but it was closed.

Then the men from the DA's office sprung the trap.

"We have other evidence saying exactly where you were that night," Rogers said. "We have a tracking device on your car."

Now Fourth panicked, his voice broke, and he struggled to form the words he needed to change his story. Yes, actually, Broussard *had* shown him Bailey's apartment just hours before the murder, but he hadn't told Fourth why and Fourth hadn't asked, he claimed. He hadn't told Longmire that fact, he said, so he'd thought it best to continue to deny it until they confronted him with the evidence.

The assistant district attorney and inspector left him sitting there, awash in more lies than he could remember.

But they didn't know about what Davis had told the other detectives. In the days ahead, top members of the DA's office, including District Attorney Tom Orloff, would make key decisions about the investigation, apparently without all the available information about Fourth's involvement in Bailey's murder.

And even while those decisions were being made, Fourth continued to incriminate himself. All anyone had to do was listen.

———

Shortly after arriving under heavy guard at the Santa Rita Jail in eastern Alameda County, Fourth started making collect calls to the woman he considered his first wife, Alaia Bey.

He was worried about his cell phone. Did the cops get it? No, she told him, she had concealed it in her clothing during the raid. "They didn't know I had it," she said, a fact that brought Fourth great relief. In a barely audible voice, he ordered her to erase all the text messages on it, calling those messages "evidence."

"Yes, sir," Alaia replied.

In four separate phone calls that day, he asked what Alaia knew about the other people taken in during the raid and said that he had seen Davis from a distance at the police station as she was shuttled between interrogation rooms. Knowing that she knew a lot about his activities before and after Bailey's murder, he was worried about what she might be telling the cops. Davis lived near the bakery, and Fourth told Alaia to send someone to her house and bring her back so he could speak to her. He waited a few minutes and called back, but Alaia said that the man she sent reported that Davis wasn't there. This obviously scared Fourth. "Ohhh shit," he responded.

He also wanted to know if anyone knew where Mackey was, expressing surprise when he was told that Mackey had been released from police custody.

He issued order after order, trying to rally support. He needed to fight back against the devils. After the raid, Alaia said, she had heard cops boast that they finally owned North Oakland. "They broke everything they could," she said.

"Disrespectful-ass devils," Fourth replied, obviously posturing for the recording. "We don't forgive and we don't forget. When they come for us, though, they gotta come with a whole army. As long as the prince of the bakery is still alive, everything stands. We ain't no Mafia. Man, all we do is bake bread. But it's all about God. They don't believe in the right one."

In more calls during Fourth's first few days in jail, Alaia told him that Broussard had phoned her repeatedly, asking where his lawyer was. Fourth told her to stop answering his calls, making a decision to cut his soldier loose. No help. No lawyer. Did Fourth somehow think that Broussard would remain loyal? Did he think so many lies had been told that the truth could never emerge? Broussard was on his own. Failing to take care of Broussard, even just emotionally, was a decision Fourth would come to regret.

Fourth also had no idea how close he might have been to escaping charges in the kidnapping and torture of JoAnne, if he could just somehow suppress his ego and stay silent.

On August 6, 2007, a hot, dry Monday four days after Chauncey Bailey's murder, the detectives investigating the kidnapping and torture were desperate to gather more evidence against Fourth. Since authorities were showing little interest in charging Fourth with Bailey's murder, that case had become paramount. But Rogers and others in the district attorney's office had told the detectives that the case still felt thin and that they might not be able to make the charges stick. Rogers, though, had an idea how to bolster it.

Joshua Bey and another torture suspect, Tamon Halfin, the one who had sat in the Crown Vic with JoAnne's mother and contemplated killing the cop, had also been arrested on August 2. Police hauled them and Fourth to a police station south of Oakland under the pretext of further interrogations. When these were over, they marched the men outside, but one of the detectives' cars had a flat tire. So they ushered the three men, all in jail jumpsuits and heavy shackles, back into the police station, put them into a small room, and told them to relax for a while. The tire would take some time to fix.

Fourth sat against the far wall at a metal table topped with white Formica. His red clothing signified his status as a prisoner in protective custody—he had snitched on Broussard. Halfin sat at the other end of the table, dressed in canary yellow. Joshua was seated across from them—also in the red of protective custody, apparently because his name was Bey.

As the door closed and they were left alone, it seemed to Fourth as if benevolent Allah had once again bestowed good fortune upon him. First the cops had let him be alone with Broussard; now he'd been left alone with Joshua and Halfin. Each of them leaned forward until their heads were but a few feet apart, voices dropping to whispers. All they had to do to get out of the torture case, Fourth insisted, was keep their mouths shut.

"She didn't see shit," he whispered of JoAnne. "If we don't say shit, they ain't got shit."

All they had to do, he repeated, was stay quiet.

In a little space hardly bigger than a closet, detectives smiled as they watched and listened to the feeds from the secret camera and microphones that were concealed in the room with Fourth and the others. The flat-tire ruse was working perfectly. Fourth's "She didn't see shit" comment clinched the torture case; it was devastating evidence.

But they might as well let them talk for a while, the detectives decided. In doing so, they were given an incredible picture of Fourth in full. There, in his red jumpsuit and shackles, with loyal followers seeming to cling to his every utterance, the scion of Your Black Muslim Bakery, one of the last believers in the divinity of W. D. Fard, revealed himself.

He seemed simply unable to stop himself from talking about murders.

"If they had found my phone, there was some evidence on my phone. There was text messages and shit," Fourth said. He expressed yet another relief, this one about the assault rifle used to kill Odell Roberson and Michael Wills: "I'm damn sure glad the guns were gone."

Fourth leaned even farther forward. So did the others, their shackles rattling.

"The gun they used. The night before [the raid] it was in my closet. The only reason I took it out was because I saw a van going back and forth in front of the gate and the brothers were scared, so I gave them a gun," he said. "The one they used."

Joshua leaned forward. "Which one? The shotty?"

"The shotty," Fourth replied, using their nickname for the little 12-gauge. "I had it in my closet the whole time after it happened, the shells and everything. I didn't even touch it since he did it. . . . I gave it back to Dre in case something happened. He never gave it back to me.

"But had that been in my room? OH . . ."

Soon he shifted the conversation to how he'd convinced Broussard to admit to the murder. The kid was a pawn, Fourth boasted, one willing to let himself be knocked over. Longmire, he claimed, had demanded Fourth give him someone to charge, or, in Fourth's words, "he was gonna blame it on the bakery." So, Fourth said, he'd pointed at Broussard and said, "That motherfucker did it."

If Joshua and Halfin were concerned that a similar fate awaited them in the kidnapping investigation, that Fourth would discard them too for his own self-interest, they didn't say anything. They sat rapt while Fourth bragged that Longmire was protecting him—"the reason they didn't pin the murder on me was Longmire."

Either that was true—as state investigators eventually alleged—or, as Longmire would doggedly claim, Fourth was simply a gullible moron who believed so much in his own power that he didn't know he was being played. The question would be debated in Oakland, and in courtrooms, for years.

Fourth claimed that the aftereffect of Bailey's murder was that the Beys would be more feared than ever. Mayor Dellums, he said, was going to be so scared he would give him whatever amount of money was demanded of the city. And he focused on another person high in the Oakland elite whom he also intended to target. That man, whose name wasn't mentioned, drove a Bentley, Fourth said, and had a lot of money. "I'm gonna make him give me $10,000. He probably thinks we're gonna kill him next."

Killing someone next, of course, implied that someone had been killed first. It could only mean Bailey.

Joshua asked him if he had been there when Bailey died, which Fourth flatly—and truthfully—denied: "Hell no. *Hell no.* You're not going to put me close. But we drove by there right after it happened."

He couldn't resist the temptation to reenact what he knew of the murder that he had ordered.

"That fool said, 'POW . . . POW . . . *POOF!*'" Fourth said, rolling his eyes back in his head and lifting his chin with the final word to demonstrate the third shot Broussard had fired, the load of buckshot directly into Bailey's face. "He a soldier for that shit!" Fourth laughed so hard that he gave himself a coughing fit.

"Where he shoot him at?" Joshua asked, grinning. "The head?"

"The *head!*" Fourth replied.

"With the fucking shotty?" Joshua asked, his eyes open widely, almost bulging.

But Fourth couldn't answer. He was laughing hysterically, leaning so close to the Formica tabletop that for a moment he nearly rested on it before straightening up as he again rolled his head and eyes back and repeated, *"POOF!"*

In the little closet, the detectives continued to listen intently. But when one of them later tried to interest homicide detectives in what Fourth had to say about Bailey's murder, he was rebuffed. Broussard had said, "I shot him." That was enough to close the case, and as far as they were concerned, they didn't need any damn tape of Fourth. Much later, Longmire and others would claim that the detective who said he had delivered the tape was a liar. Longmire would say he didn't know anything about it until he saw clips from it on the news.

By then, the impression that the person who had ordered Bailey's death was an untouchable Black Muslim radical would have taken deep root.

30

Captain Marvel, Come Help Us

"Silence is golden when you can't think of a good answer."
—MUHAMMAD ALI

Mayor Ronald Dellums insisted on speaking at Bailey's funeral. As he waited in the front row of a Catholic church in East Oakland accompanied by Congresswoman Barbara Lee, a line of people stretched from the vestibule and down the street. When Dellums stood and walked to the pulpit, he glanced at Chauncey Bailey Sr., ninety-one, who had made the trip from Iowa to bury his son the newspaper editor.

"Chauncey was often intense. Life as a journalist was a big part of who he was," Dellums said, looking down at Bailey's family, his sister, two half brothers, his son, Chauncey III, a slew of other relatives. "Chauncey Bailey, I want you to know all of us came here today in a tremendous gathering of community to say thank you for your service to the community."

Any mayor would have to address violence when eulogizing someone who had died so brutally. Few, though, could do it in a less meaningful way than Dellums. Even when presented with the sharp rhetorical devices like those that surrounded Bailey's assassination, he failed to be clear, convincing, or specific. For decades, the Beys had terrorized and victimized Oakland. Yet Dellums, who had cemented his legacy in Washington by defeating Ronald

Reagan over South Africa, who played such a large role in helping that nation overcome apartheid, couldn't challenge hate in his own city, or the conditions that enabled it.

But how could he now criticize the Beys without looking like a hypocrite for his support of them and also embarrassing Lee, former mayor Elihu Harris, Senator Don Perata, and the other politicians present who had supported and praised Your Black Muslim Bakery for so long?

Still, standing before a packed church, looking down at Bailey's father and son, the doddering mayor had to impart *something*.

"Allow me to say what needs to be said to this community," Dellums began. "We cannot fall prey to fear and cynicism. Do not allow them to grip us. We will change this community. We will change this world with optimism. We will not be conquered by fear. We will take back our community. We will commit. We will do this today. We cannot do this alone."

Dellums stopped and pointed skyward, his arm nearly brushing his gray Afro. "I wish there were superheroes, so we could put up a sign: 'Batman, come help us,' 'Captain Marvel, come help us.' But that's not going to happen. We are the superheroes, and we will do it by coming together."

References to Batman and Captain Marvel aside, Dellums's remarks were notable for their omissions.

Bailey was the first reporter slain in the United States in pursuit of a domestic story since 1976, when Don Bolles of the *Arizona Republic* died in a car bombing for which members of organized crime were convicted. Yet the mayor made no call for justice, no promise that his police force would perform a complete and thorough investigation of the killing of a journalist in his city and arrest all those responsible for it. Dellums probably didn't know then that police chief Wayne Tucker had ordered the forty-eight-hour delay in the raid on the bakery. Tucker was desperate to keep that decision a secret. But Dellums never seemed to have confidence in the department anyway, which was at the height of dysfunction under his watch. It is unlikely he had been briefed on the investigation at all or knew that misfiled reports and other shoddy work had already doomed it.

There was also not a bit of talk about the First Amendment implications of Bailey's killing, how his murder was so much bigger than him, no matter how far his career had fallen. It didn't matter that Bailey had worked for the lowly *Oakland Post*. It mattered that he had been writing a newspaper story and someone who hadn't wanted it published—who thought the facts in it might be detrimental to him—had ordered the writer killed to stop it. The simple facts of the crime gave Dellums bushels of rhetorical devices that he failed to draw from. Even after a mayoralty that was defined far more by endless esoteric babble than by accomplishment, Dellums likely never gave a speech that was emptier than what he said that day over Bailey's closed casket. Oakland's mayor was in no way Batman or Captain Marvel. He was no hero.

Neither was Paul Cobb, who, like Dellums, came bearing the hollowest of words. When he eulogized Bailey, the publisher exercised little restraint in glorifying a journalist whose story he wouldn't print (and still wouldn't, even with Fourth jailed).

"I want to make Chauncey's untimely forced exodus our genesis," Cobb said, "a renewed advocacy for investigative journalism. We should continue his legacy of not being afraid to call the wicked man wicked to the wicked man's face."

But, as Bailey had confided to people, that's exactly what Cobb had been—afraid to publish a story about Fourth.

"If we can't find something to die for, it's not worth it," Cobb said. "To the forces behind and connected to this assassination . . . it ain't over. You might have assassinated the messenger, but the message will prevail. . . . The world is going to find out what Chauncey and I were working on."

It would?

In the months ahead, Cobb would downplay the unpublished story on Fourth and the bankruptcy, insisting that what Bailey had *really* been investigating was police corruption and former mayor Jerry Brown, by then California's attorney general. But there was little record of Bailey digging for anything salient on cops or politicians, and it was well known that he lacked the patience and many of the skills to do so. The only thing he'd written that was remotely close was a story that Brown had destroyed public documents when he'd left the mayor's office—a flimsy, unattributed rehash of what daily newspapers had reported five months earlier. Yet Cobb would continually allude to deeper conspiracies behind the killing, suggesting that

Oakland police somehow knew of Fourth's plan and did nothing to stop it because they wanted Bailey silenced, an absurd claim.

He would seize on the fact that police told him a few hours after the murder that someone "stalked and targeted" Bailey as proof that something more sinister than Your Black Muslim Bakery was responsible. But the ideas that someone had stalked Bailey and that his killing was not a random, unplanned act were simple, obvious facts quickly deduced from witnesses, especially the bus driver who had seen a masked gunman outside Bailey's apartment, blocks from where he died minutes later. Cobb told police that Bailey had been working on a story about Fourth. He would claim later, though, that when asked what stories could have sparked a murder, he'd said Bailey was really investigating ties between the Beys and the department, another baseless statement. By not simply acknowledging that his editor had died because a twenty-one-year-old psychopath wanted to censor a rather straightforward story was a disservice to Bailey's career as a community journalist. Cobb tried to lionize Bailey—and thus himself and the *Post*—into far more than he was, effacing Bailey's true value to Oakland. Eventually, Cobb would propose so many conspiracy theories about the assassination that prosecutors came to regard him as a buffoon and refused to deal with him.

Saleem Bey went public about being Bailey's source for the unpublished bakery story four days after the murder, further undermining Cobb. It was all quite simple, Saleem said. Fourth learned of his conversations with Bailey and ordered the journalist killed.

"It was a known fact that I was the one speaking to the reporter. . . . It could've been me just as easily as it could've been him," Saleem told the *Tribune*. "I do feel bad about that, but he asked for that story over two years ago. He knew there was a bunch of stuff going on, and he knew that I knew all of it, so he asked me that when I was ready to speak, that I speak to him first. Everybody has known for years that these people were mad dogs biting people out on the street," he said. "I've been saying and showing all this evidence to all these people and it's like they just willfully look away. This thing should've been stopped well before it got to Chauncey."

Unlike Dellums and Cobb and others who seemed unable to understand the significance of Bailey's murder, not everyone failed to get it. A few days after Bailey was buried in Oakland, sixty people gathered in Detroit for a memorial service in the city where he had done his best work for more than a decade. It was where a far better testament to his death would be made than anything said in Oakland. Bailey's former editor at the *News,* Luther Keith, seized in one sentence the significance of the murder that Dellums and Cobb and others in Oakland did not.

"His death was an attack on what America stands for," Keith said.

Others far outside of Oakland also understood its significance.

A few days later, then Illinois senator Barack Obama appeared before the National Association of Black Journalists, which had gathered for its annual convention in Las Vegas. "I want to honor, and give my thoughts and prayers to, the family of Chauncey Bailey," the future president said to a burst of applause. He had been campaigning in Oakland a few days after the murder. "I was reading the reports of the senseless violence that had taken him from his family and his community and the outstanding work that he had done. It is a tragedy." Obama took out a condolence ad in the *Post* and later as president mentioned Bailey's death in an observance of World Press Freedom Day.

Speaking afterward to the same group of Black journalists, Obama's then Democratic rival, New York senator Hillary Rodham Clinton, made similar remarks. The *New York Times,* the *Washington Post,* the *Los Angeles Times,* and *Observer* magazine* in the United Kingdom all ran long stories about Bailey and Oakland. The international press-freedom group Reporters Without Borders repeatedly called for a larger investigation of Fourth's obvious involvement in the slaying. The Committee to Protect Journalists expressed outrage at the assassination, as did the Society of Professional

---

*The *Observer* piece was one of those that greatly exaggerated Bailey's journalistic standing, calling him "one of black America's most successful journalists," a vast overstatement.

Journalists and the top trade group for journalists in the world, Investigative Reporters and Editors.

But there were also underlying thoughts by some, including the late *Tribune* editor Bob Maynard's daughter, Dori, a former reporter who runs the Robert C. Maynard Institute for Journalism Education, that the killing didn't get as much media attention as it would have if Bailey had been a white reporter for a major metropolitan newspaper.

Unanswered questions about the Beys remained, too, as well as a lack of detailed reporting on the peculiar sort of Islam they practiced. Much of the journalism around the killing either identified them as Nation of Islam members or simply as Muslims, with no examination of their beliefs, lumping them in with the Sunnis and Shiites of Orthodox Islam.

What few people actually did was call for the type of all-out investigation of the killing that was demanded by the nature of its attack on the First Amendment. It didn't matter that Bailey was an aging reporter, his career sloping downward, or that the *Post* was a free-circulation weekly, or that he couldn't get a story published about a militant group in Oakland. His killing was bigger than that, bigger than him. Bailey's murder was an assault on the bedrock principle of a free press, as Luther Keith put it, the American way of life. It needed the type of attention that would change the way it was characterized and probed, the type of attention that would remove it from Oakland's provincial, hurried way of investigating killings, the haphazard culture of its overworked, understaffed homicide unit.

The person who could have ordered an immediate and full-force investigation of all those involved in Bailey's assassination was Alameda County District Attorney Thomas Jensen Orloff. Orloff sat behind a refurbished desk that had once belonged to Earl Warren when he held the office. Any comparisons to Warren, though, stopped there. In the first week of August 2007, Orloff could have said that the First Amendment wasn't going to get shredded on a street corner three blocks from his courthouse. He didn't. His reasons weren't even particularly sinister; perhaps they were even naive and an outgrowth of his own tepid persona.

Orloff was a tall, shy man with a long, narrow face who wore oversized glasses. He bore an aversion to publicity that could easily be taken as aloof or arrogant. "I've always been a very pensive person," he once said. The pensive prosecutor had worked nowhere else as a lawyer, joining the DA's office in 1969 straight from law school at Berkeley, jumping into trials. Except for undergraduate studies in Los Angeles at Occidental College, Orloff had never spent considerable time outside Alameda County, where his family had deep political roots.

He held a nonpartisan office for which only undisputed elections had been conducted for decades. Like a string of his predecessors, Orloff became DA when an incumbent resigned midterm and handpicked a successor. By 2007, he was a three-term politician who had never had to give a campaign speech in a contested race in his career. Orloff had risen through a parochial network of hard-drinking, cigar-chomping, good-old-boy white men who stuck photos of pinup girls on their office walls and boasted about how many niggers they'd put on death row. It was an office where a culture of racism, sexism, and anti-Semitism that had existed for decades behind a thin veil of courtroom propriety had only just begun to slowly fade. Among Orloff's first actions as DA was removing a white prosecutor from a case involving an African American defendant. During a trial break, the prosecutor had said loudly that "niggers" had mugged a colleague's mother the night before. When the defendant's public defender confronted him about his obvious racism, the prosecutor wouldn't back down. "Well, I don't care. That's what they are . . . niggers," he said.

It had never been suggested that Orloff condoned the long-ingrained attitudes that allowed a prosecutor to so brazenly express racism in a public courtroom. But there are also scant examples of him criticizing it, at least publicly. In his ninth-floor office at the Rene C. Davidson Courthouse near Lake Merritt, Orloff lit several cigars a day despite a state law that made it a misdemeanor offense to smoke in government buildings; he transferred an employee who complained of being made ill by his smoke. When a female prosecutor sued Orloff charging sex discrimination, several other women in the office testified in depositions that racism, sexism, and anti-Semitism continued to exist on his staff. Although the lawsuit was thrown out, it left Orloff tarnished. He continued to serve wistfully, shying from publicity, making pragmatic decisions on prosecutions, taking few risks. He didn't pursue political-corruption cases; he undertook few, if any, proactive investigations. He sat back chomping cigars and waited for police to bring him cases.

During the first weekend of August 2007, the Oakland police brought him Yusuf Bey IV and Devaughndre Broussard. Orloff had ordered the aggressive pursuit of Yusuf Bey for child rape four years earlier. The DNA didn't lie, and although Bey and his followers howled about persecution, there was little doubt that he would have been convicted had he lived. But like so many other Alameda County politicians, Orloff had done little else about the Beys. Perhaps the most glaring absence of action was when he didn't act independently after Oakland officials failed to ask for an investigation of how the Beys had fleeced taxpayers of one million dollars for their short-lived home-health-care businesses. What Orloff also didn't do was pursue headlines. He had no real ambition for other offices, it seemed. There was little public talk of his ever pursuing a judgeship. Going after the taxpayers' missing money would have grabbed media attention, especially since it involved the Beys, and it might have been fruitless. Why take the chance?

But now a reporter was dead, and his assassin's story about acting alone couldn't be believed. It was obvious others were involved.

As Orloff huddled with his staff the weekend after the murder, the first priority was to make certain Fourth didn't get out of jail. The secretly recorded video of him with Joshua and Tamon Halfin would soon see to that. But despite all the incriminating statements Fourth made on the recording about Bailey's murder, Orloff was uninterested in aggressively pursuing him. As he reviewed the cases, Orloff made the incredibly pragmatic decision that as long as the charges were solid against Fourth in the torture case, for which he faced life with no parole, there was no need to pursue him for Bailey's murder. They had Broussard. He was enough.

"My boss, Mr. O., is not interested in charging Yusuf Bev IV with conspiracy to commit murder," Orloff's chief prosecutor, Tom Rogers, told Oakland police homicide commander Lieutenant Ersie Joyner just days after Bailey died. The larger charge, though, was aiding and abetting—ordering the hit. What Mr. O. really wasn't interested in was going after the bigger case.

Joyner later claimed that the implication passed down from Orloff was clear: Don't devote resources to pursuing Fourth in Bailey's death. The pensive prosecutor had spoken, and no one challenged him. "If the aggravated kidnapping case did not exist . . . there'd be more effort put into seeing what you can develop with a chargeable, provable [murder] case against Bey. There's a marginal benefit to spending a lot of resources on a case that might not be provable," is how Orloff eventually explained his thinking.

Certainly, Dellums should and could have challenged him. A congressman who had organized an override of a foreign-policy veto by one of the most popular presidents in American history could browbeat a lightweight like the shy and pensive district attorney. But he didn't, perhaps because he was worried about stirring up too much political muck about the Beys. Police chief Tucker might have forced Orloff's hand too, or ordered police to continue investigating Fourth's involvement in Bailey's murder with or without Orloff's consent. But that might have drawn attention or caused leaks about his decision to delay the raid on the bakery. That wouldn't do. If Tucker served five years as Oakland police chief, his contract called for him to receive thirty thousand dollars a year in pension payments from the city for the rest of his life, in addition to the government pension he was already drawing from his long career as a deputy sheriff. Why do anything to jeopardize that?

None of it was going to bring back Chauncey Bailey anyway. Broussard would go down as the assassin, the bakery was boarded up, and the building was soon to be sold on orders of a federal judge. If Fourth wasn't held accountable for ordering the murder, well, that was just the way things went in Oakland.

There was only one person who could change any of it, but for what seemed like the longest time, he appeared to have no idea just how much power he held.

31

Why . . .

*"If the laws could speak for themselves, they would
complain of the lawyers in the first place."*
—LORD HALIFAX

As Oakland buried Chauncey Bailey, Devaughndre Broussard tried to understand what he'd done. He was in an isolation cell for twenty-three hours
a day, and with good reason. As with most of the other members of the
Bey cult locked up after the raid, jailers were taking no chances with him.
Broussard must have suspected, too, that his life was in danger. If Fourth
could somehow get him killed, there would be one less person who knew he
had ordered Bailey's assassination. That would leave only Mackey, who had
fled California for Georgia as soon as he was released from jail.

Being alone gave Broussard too much time to think. He would later say
that in the desperate, early days of his jailing, he tried to find the courage,
and the means, to kill himself.

As he pondered suicide and desperately sought again some sort of meaningful human connection, Broussard showed the near-pathetic portions of
his nature that seemed to make him so susceptible to Fourth's spiels about
brotherhood and solidarity. He remained as desperate to connect to something as the people in a Detroit ghetto had been eighty years earlier, who
found a little man of indistinguishable race at their door spinning tales

about their own country, preaching about better nutrition and, eventually, mad scientists and the end of the world.

Broussard began by writing a letter to the man he considered his father, Marcus Callaway.

> Yo Pops,
>
> I just want to holla at you cause I might not eva get to see you again. I really love you dad, so don't 4-get that. Man I ain't never get to see daylight again cuz of a bitch made nigger told on me. I'm go hold it down in here, you already know I am far from a punk, but I guess this how it go end for me, huh? Remember all the whooping I used to get cuz I used to fuck up. I guess it made me stronger not smarter. You should know you raised a man, ok? Can you believe this shit dad. I'm probably gonna grow old and die in the pen. My whole life is done with. It over dad at 19 yrs. Remember all the dreams I had. I was gonna make you real proud knowing I made it through all that shit. I just wish I could have done something great. I was good in damn near everything, huh. I am in the dorm where everybody fighting murder. It's hella stressful in here. I'm go really miss talking to you pops and that's 4 real. I learned a lot from you. Don't let DeMarcus* follow in my footsteps cuz he not ready 4 this. I'm here with a couple of folks I know from the city. Writing this letter is hard as fuck cause as I'm writing I remember all the good times we had. Im a go see you again 1 day. Remember Dad I love you.
>
> Love—Devaughndre M. Broussard

But what Broussard needed more than love was a decent criminal attorney—what Fourth had promised him for taking the fall. He kept phoning Alaia Bey asking in a little boy's voice when Fourth would send a lawyer. But that was a promise that Fourth had no intention of keeping, letting Broussard twist in the wind. Besides, Fourth had his own

*One of Callaway's sons.

problem—he'd finally been charged with kidnapping and torturing JoAnne. He needed a competent attorney of his own.

As Broussard became more and more desperate, he knew there were only a few people who could help him. Of them, none knew the justice system better than a relative on his mother's side, a career criminal in San Francisco's Fillmore District named Lester Hogan. Broussard affectionately called him "Unc." Hogan had urged Broussard to be wary of the Beys. When Broussard left the bakery in frustration, Hogan had warned him Fourth was using him and not to go back.

Now, Hogan picked up a collect call on the second ring.

"They got me for murder," Broussard said.

"They got you for murder? They got your fingerprints on something?" Hogan said, his voice rising.

"Man, yes. . . . I don't got nobody else to call," Broussard said.

"Boy, I told your stupid ass."

"I was being smart," Broussard replied. He burst into heavy sobs.

"You wasn't being smart. Quit crying, nigger! . . . You got to be cool. We gonna do something, man. Fuck. *I told you,* nigger, to leave them fucking Muslims alone. . . . Oh blood, I feel like beating your ass, nigger. Why you, why you can't listen to me, man?" Hogan said. "Did you admit to it?"

"I had to," Broussard replied.

"No, you didn't, you stupid-ass nigger!" Hogan screamed. "Fuck! Blood, what the fuck is wrong with you? It ain't nothing we can do now, nigger!"

"They said they gonna get a good lawyer for me," Broussard said.

"Who?"

"The Beys."

"Fuck that," Hogan yelled.

Without saying Fourth's name, he told Hogan that "the person who made the call" on the killing "told on me to my face."

Hogan apparently didn't understand him, because he said the detectives should have brought "in the motherfucker that sent you." He meant the person who sent him to kill Bailey.

"They did," Broussard said.

"So he told them that he sent you?"

"No, he told them that I did that out of my own will," Broussard said.

"Why? Why would you let another motherfucker send you to go do something, nigger, and them motherfuckers ain't did shit for you? Nothing, blood. They wasn't even taking care of you, so why would you risk yourself for somebody else? Why, my nigger?"

"I don't know," Broussard sobbed.

Hogan implored Broussard to stay silent, reject representation by a public defender, and wait for him, not Fourth, to "get a good lawyer."

Hogan did know a lawyer who would quickly agree to represent Broussard. That lawyer never turned down a case. Whether he met the definition of "good," though, was another question entirely.

To call attorney LeRue James Grim a bottom-feeder would imply that he inhabited the bottom of the legal system. It would also insult all the solo practitioners who troll courthouse hallways for teary-eyed grandmothers and live off reputations spread in bullpens and holding cells that they can get charges reduced, evidence thrown out, and deals cut for time served. But LeRue Grim, once described by a judge as possessing "absolute blindness to conflicts of interest and professional ethics," inhabited a place far beneath the world of even the most unscrupulous criminal lawyers. He worked and lived in a moldy three-room office above a bail-bonds shop across Bryant Street from the mammoth San Francisco Hall of Justice. One could always tell if he was in because his 1975 robin's-egg-blue Rolls-Royce, its winged Spirit of Ecstasy hood ornament long missing, would be parked nearby. A drug dealer had given him the car in exchange for services rendered. Grim was always scampering for a payday, promising his clients legal successes if they could just scrape together a small retainer. And people did it. Ten different lawyers might reject a case as baseless, but Grim would find some justification to accept payment—always in advance, preferably in cash. He was San Francisco's silver-tongued lawyer of last resort.

Grim also had perhaps one of the most sordid records of bar association discipline in Northern California for disservice to clients. Once, he strung along a poor and ignorant woman for seven years after accepting $2,500 to handle her son's appeal of a rape conviction, before finally admitting to her he had never filed the case. But that was far from his most infamous dealing with a client. Years earlier, Grim claimed that when he was sixty-three, the twenty-year-old wife of a murder defendant crawled in bed with him and the resulting sexual act occurred against his will because his erection was involuntary. A judge called Grim's argument preposterous but didn't think his conduct warranted disbarment, just a suspension.

Grim had successfully defended a member of Broussard's family on murder charges decades earlier and was the "good lawyer" Lester Hogan sought out to represent his desperate nephew. On the day he took Broussard's case, Grim was seventy-nine years old.

The first thing a competent criminal lawyer likely would have done when presented with an indigent client by a poor relative was seek court appointment to represent him. There would be legal research to conduct, briefs to write, private investigators to hire; it all required money. Broussard, dead broke, was eligible for a government-funded lawyer, a position for which Grim might have applied. But with that would come responsibilities— accounting for hours, billing, providing updates to judges. That meant that Grim would have to actually work the case, something that, despite his need for money, he was loath to undertake.

Before attending an unaccredited law school in the early sixties, Grim had been a dog trainer, specializing in Doberman pinschers; he often said that his best legal strength was preparing clients for testimony, likening it to his work with canines. That is just what he told Lester Hogan he would do for Devaughndre Broussard—teach him to speak better and overcome his stutter so that he could eventually tell a jury that he was not the man in the mask who had shot Chauncey Bailey three times at the corner of Fourteenth and Alice streets in downtown Oakland.

But Grim would learn that the case was far more complex than he told Hogan, and then, over the course of a few jail visits, Broussard that it was. It was as if Broussard could never get a break in life. Even when he had hit complete bottom, when he was facing life in prison without parole, ever, for a heinous slaying, fate dealt him arguably one of the worst lawyers imaginable. Broussard, alone, suicidal, desperate, didn't even have the sense to reject Grim's representation.

The entire basis of the charge was Broussard's confession. But had police obtained it legally? Could it be proven that Fourth was a de facto police agent who had made Broussard false promises, such as money and a manslaughter sentence, in exchange for admitting he'd pulled the trigger? Since police cannot promise a suspect a particular sentence or outcome in exchange for confessing—and certainly cannot promise monetary or other types of payment—neither can those acting on their behalf. And Fourth certainly would have promised Broussard anything to say he acted alone.

Prosecutors and Longmire would emphasize that Fourth had helped obtain the confession because Broussard had *asked* to speak to him alone. But Broussard made that request twenty-four minutes after Fourth joined Longmire in what Longmire described in his notes as an attempt of his design to use Fourth to "confront" Broussard and demand a confession. As those minutes unwound, Longmire gestured to Fourth and asked him, in a description Longmire would give in court, "to chime in." Fourth, of course, possessed every motive to convince Broussard to say he'd conceived and executed the crime entirely on his own. A competent criminal attorney would have seen the glaring soft spots in the confession that followed and challenged it. Or such a lawyer might have sought additional funds to hire an expert on interrogations.

But LeRue Grim was looking for other, more expedient ways to serve Broussard, especially once a judge ruled after a perfunctory preliminary hearing in November 2007 that ample probable cause existed to try him for Bailey's murder. Grim drove his Rolls-Royce back across the Bay Bridge to his San Francisco hovel, facing the daunting task of preparing a huge case for trial. He and his client needed a break.

Within a few days, Grim got a call from a producer at the CBS News show *60 Minutes*. Editors were interested in a piece about Bailey, recognizing, as many did outside Oakland, that his death was a story about the intersection of press freedoms and radical faith. Would Grim allow Broussard to be interviewed for national television? Grim gave an answer that few criminal lawyers would dare utter on behalf of a client charged with murder: yes.

Broussard would eventually say that Grim counseled him to lie in the interview. Grim would say he preferred the phrase "muddy the waters." Either way, Broussard intended to use the national spotlight to claim that he hadn't killed anybody. When he sat across a table from Anderson Cooper in a brightly lit jail room in early 2008, Broussard had practiced many times saying that Fourth had tricked and pressured him into confessing to a crime he now insisted he didn't commit.

The camera came on, and Broussard tried to control his stutter as he said that everything he'd told Longmire five months earlier was a lie—even the true parts, like pulling the trigger.

"I never heard about Chauncey Bailey. I never met him. I never seen him. The first time I heard about Chauncey Bailey was the night I got arrested," he said.

Cooper asked what Fourth had said during those six minutes.

"He was telling me how I was being tested by God. . . . He was saying that you gotta prove your loyalty or whatnot. He was saying that 'most times people don't realize when they being tested by God. I'm helping you out, I'm telling you that you being tested by God.'"

"Did you kill Chauncey Bailey?" Cooper asked.

"No."

For the first twenty minutes of his telephone conversation with Alaia Bey on February 24, 2008, the night Broussard's interview was broadcast, Fourth stayed calm, almost flippantly cool. But the more details she relayed to Fourth about the interview, things like "He says he's going to say who did it at his trial" and "He said you used his Islamic faith to get him to confess," the edgier Fourth's voice became.

"He's a good liar for a Negro. He's got a little finesse to it," Fourth admitted.

Fourth had long since convinced himself that, thanks to Allah's protection, he had escaped accountability for Bailey's killing. Broussard had said he did it alone, and that was that. Some relative had even gotten him a terrible old-man devil lawyer, another gift from Allah. The cops had cleaned it up; only shooters went down in Oakland, never the shot callers. And he was Yusuf Ali Bey IV; no one would dare tread on him. His phone calls to Alaia were often filled with dreamy talk of the future—at least in the moments he wasn't berating and belittling her, reminding her it was her duty to submit to him.

He'd beat the torture charge, then they'd open another bakery, with a youth center and a Black Muslim ministry. His jail time was simply part of Allah's plan to steel him for the challenges ahead. He was reading, praying, his days devoted to studying the Honorable Elijah Muhammad. He understood the devils' true nature now, and he often said he was more convinced than ever that the mother plane would soon obliterate them all anyway. In one call a few weeks before Broussard appeared on *60 Minutes,* he insisted that it had been recently spotted in the skies above Texas. Did Alaia understand that its bombs would burrow a mile into the earth and make a nuclear explosion look like a firecracker? He sometimes lectured Alaia about Yakub and how the devils had come into being. And his own life was the fulfillment of prophecy, he would insist. Sometimes his mother, Tammy, would take the phone and confirm everything he was saying. If he just prayed and placed all his faith in the teachings of W. D. Fard, he would survive his tests. "The devil is meant to trick and deceive. All his appearances are deceptive," Tammy reminded him. "You were born with a job to do, to help people."

But on the night Broussard went on *60 Minutes,* Fourth wasn't worried about helping people; he was suddenly worried that he might never get out of jail. What if Broussard finally broke and told the truth? Then what? The more he and Alaia talked, the more agitated he became, until he finally blew up.

"This motherfucker destroyed the whole organization," Fourth yelled. "They destroyed my father's 35-year business. If he didn't do that none of this would have happened. His stupidity jeopardized the whole thing." He was, of course, really talking about himself.

He told Alaia that he had to cut a deal: In exchange for a shorter sentence in the torture case, he would offer to testify against Broussard.

But if he cooperated with the *police* against one of his followers, he would lose all credibility with the others, she said.

But Fourth insisted that his people would remain with him regardless. It was all Broussard, he screamed into the phone. He had to be discredited, and those who had depended on the Beys for everything in their lives would understand that.

"What did he jeopardize, Alaia? They livelihood, right? They help, right? They safe haven, right? They chance, right? Come on now, you ain't talking to some little pussy. Don't think you are.

"I know what it is," he continued, the guilt within him apparently welling. "You probably think I did it." He meant Bailey's murder.

But Alaia was a true believer. He had her convinced that he had nothing to do with murders or torture. Everything was about devils, weak people who let him down, Allah's tests. Now, as he panicked about Broussard, knowing what Broussard could truthfully say about the Bailey murder, he tried to convince her that cutting a deal would not be the mortal sin of hypocrisy. He was desperate with fear.

Alaia, though, apparently still believed Broussard had killed Bailey alone. "But you're not part of it," she insisted.

Fourth was adamant that he needed to do something or else he would soon be on trial for Bailey's murder. "If they keep using me as a scapegoat, they are gonna be successful if I keep being quiet," he snapped. "When I'm charged what are you going to say?"

He had, of course, no bargaining chips. District Attorney Orloff had decided the torture case would be what put Fourth in prison for life without parole. Fourth could never be trusted as a witness anyway. There was nothing Fourth could do but wait to learn what Broussard and his old-man devil lawyer did. Like Broussard, Fourth spent twenty-three hours a day in a tiny cell, alone. He was, after all, already the most hated thing in jail, a snitch, for telling Longmire that Broussard had killed Bailey. He wouldn't last long out in the general population, no matter how powerful he perceived himself to be. All he could do was sit and sweat.

All the prayers he could make to Allah in all his hours alone couldn't change that.

32

My Life Is No Accident

"For 12 long years I lived within the narrow minded
confines of the 'straightjacket world' created by my strong
belief that Elijah Muhammad was a messenger direct from
God Himself, and my faith in what I now see to be
a pseudo-religious philosophy that he preaches. . . . I shall
never rest until I have undone the harm I did to so many
well-meaning, innocent Negroes who through my own
evangelistic zeal now believe in him even more fanatically
and more blindly than I did."
—MALCOLM X, letter to a friend, from Mecca, October 1964

Allah only rewarded strength. Those, like the Beys, who had never forsaken the teachings of W. D. Fard and Elijah Muhammad were spared the indignity of human weaknesses. Yusuf Bey had never wavered, not for a moment, not even when the devils ravaged him with lies and slander as his death approached. Like his Daddy, Fourth needed to rally his courage and hold fast. Devaughndre Broussard had told too many lies to ever be believed now. Fourth, though, had remained consistent about his innocence. He had gone on television within a few hours of Chauncey Bailey's slaying, denied involvement, and hadn't wavered since. He'd told police and the men from the DA's office that Broussard had admitted the killing to him. Fourth was not a snitch. Saving the bakery—Daddy's legacy and his own destiny—trumped street rules. Trying to testify at Broussard's trial, Fourth yelled at Alaia, was not about him, it was about the bakery. Broussard's lies on national television were just another test, all part of the prophecy. Fourth would remain strong.

How else could the events that were unfolding be explained? The devil was at work all around Fourth, unrelenting. But the devil was also Allah's tool. It had to be so. It was prophecy that Fourth would be betrayed. But Broussard was not alone in being Fourth's Judas. In order to prove his worth to Allah, Fourth also had to overcome the test of his own blood turning on him. Joshua Bey, like Broussard, had become a minion of the devils.

The torture case was crawling through an interminable preliminary hearing. Fourth, Fifth, Joshua, Tamon Halfin, and Richard Lewis, who had been arrested a month after the raid, all had their own lawyers, making the examination of even minor witnesses cumbersome and drawn out. It was also proving to be a scheduling nightmare. So it didn't surprise Fourth at first when one day Joshua wasn't present as a hearing began.

Then the prosecutor, a short, red-haired man, intoned simply, "The people call Joshua Bey."

What Fourth didn't know was that Joshua had secretly pleaded guilty in another courtroom to one count of kidnapping in exchange for a three-year sentence. His mother, Jane, had convinced him to cooperate with authorities and save himself from a life in prison. It was a bit more of her revenge for her savaged childhood, her son turning on two of Yusuf Bey's other offspring. But family tension was everywhere. Joshua was now a witness not only against Fourth but also against his half brother and first cousin, Fifth, whose mother was Nancy, Jane's sister.*

A courtroom door opened and Joshua, chains stretching from his ankles to his waist to his wrists, shuffled slowly to the witness stand in the open-toed slippers of a prisoner, a bailiff at his side.

"You're not a Bey anymore," Fifth yelled.

Joshua, his head swiveling on his long neck, looked like he would cry.

---

*The sisters' lawsuit over their childhood abuses had finally settled a few months earlier. Alameda County, the only remaining defendant, agreed to pay them, along with two other "Jane Doe" plaintiffs, under California laws meant to protect rape victims, fifty thousand dollars each while admitting no liability. Lawyers for the county, though, clearly said they had no doubt the victims were horribly abused by Yusuf Bey, as they alleged. But because they were not foster children, as their suit alleged, but under the legal guardianship of Alice, the county's responsibility was greatly reduced. The social workers who had visited the girls were there to check on Alice's aid eligibility, not the welfare of the girls, lawyers argued.

When he referred to Fourth as "my brother" in his testimony, Fourth shouted, "Don't say brother anymore, just say Yusuf."

Outside the courtroom, several of the Bey women screamed at Jane, calling her a devil, a traitor, a liar. Jane would do anything, they yelled, to destroy the Beys. She had told horrific lies against Yusuf Bey, and now look what her retarded bastard son was doing to Fourth and Fifth. Deputies and bailiffs pulled the women apart. Joshua, already in a red jumpsuit and a lockdown cell, was placed under extra security as a precaution against Fourth trying to have him killed.

Yet that was all merely a prologue to the tests Fourth now realized awaited him with Broussard. But he was a man of action, he told Alaia. Action, in fact, defined him. If he testified against Broussard, it would simply be an act to ensure the bakery's survival so that once he was out of jail he could continue helping people. What was gone, he acknowledged, was just a building. The essence of the bakery lived on in his heart and the hearts of others, especially the young men who in their day on San Pablo Avenue had saluted him as their commander in chief, who had deferentially called him "Brother Fourth." When he was free, another building could be found. Buildings were nothing compared to brotherhood. His men would come back, he insisted. They would be together again, stronger than before.

Unlike Fourth, LeRue Grim was weak.

He didn't file any legal motions attacking the charges against Broussard, a nearly rote undertaking when a defendant is held for trial after a preliminary hearing. Lawyers spent too much time filing frivolous motions just to churn out billings, Grim often said. That Lester Hogan and the rest of Broussard's family had not paid him anything had nothing to do with how he decided to proceed, Grim claimed. Motions and pretrial maneuvering were a waste of time. What Grim would do was prepare Broussard to testify in his own defense, he said, perhaps clean up his language, not say "motherfucker" and "shit" so often. Broussard was feral; Grim would work to domesticate him. If the jury liked him, if he was soft-spoken and humble and polite, if he looked at them when he said he didn't kill Bailey, Broussard would have a chance. He would tell the jury that he'd confessed only because a man who was his spiritual leader—essentially his minister—had told him to do it so that what was basically his church—the bakery—could stay open.

Broussard, of course, was the fall guy who wasn't really a fall guy. He'd blown Chauncey Bailey away. His confession claiming to have acted alone was flawed in that regard, but his three little words, "I shot him," were true. He'd pulled the trigger, then gotten caught with the murder weapon and admitted the crime. But Grim's strategy appeared to be to try to overcome those facts with lies, a daunting task. Broussard could say all he wanted that he wasn't the one who shot Bailey, but he'd thrown the murder weapon out the window, and he matched the physical description of the masked man seen by witnesses. Clarence Darrow might have made a persuasive argument against those facts, but wizened and tired LeRue Grim wasn't Clarence Darrow. Still, Broussard was entitled to the strongest possible defense, which Grim was incapable of providing. Broussard was essentially on his own.

But as the first anniversary of Bailey's killing approached, there were other factors at play. In late June, the group of disparate journalists working collectively as the Chauncey Bailey Project obtained a copy of the secretly recorded police video showing Fourth laughing about and mocking Bailey's murder and posted it on the Internet, also reporting the story in several newspapers and on television stations.

With sound enhancements and subtitles, the video made a stunning presentation.

"Pow . . . pow . . . *poof*," Fourth had said, throwing his head back before descending into fits of laughter. The video, which until then had been seen only by a few detectives and prosecutors, raised far more questions than it answered. Chief among them: Why hadn't authorities done more to hold Fourth accountable for the killing?

Grim, who had not yet been given the recording as discovery, immediately overstated its importance as he stood before television cameras under an array of bail-bonds signs near his office. "It exonerates my client," he blurted gleefully, as if he had somehow escaped the case. It obviously didn't. However, it did make it much clearer that Fourth thus far had escaped accountability. But District Attorney Tom Orloff still maintained that his priority was to convict Fourth on the torture case and again said publicly that he wasn't interested in expending resources to investigate Fourth for the murder.

Deep behind the scenes, however, Orloff finally prompted action. Two inspectors working with the lawyer assigned to prosecute Broussard began to quietly probe Bailey's killing anew, focusing on Fourth. Police commanders, meanwhile, reacting to the lingering suspicion that Sergeant Derwin Longmire was a Bey sympathizer and reports that the secretly recorded video was never mentioned in his case file, ordered an internal investigation of how he had handled Bailey's murder.

Four months later, the Chauncey Bailey Project reported that data from the tracking device hidden on Fourth's car showed it been parked outside Bailey's apartment less than seven hours before the murder. It also reported that phone records showed Fourth and Mackey exchanged several calls within minutes of the killing at the time the white van was speeding back to the compound. The *San Francisco Chronicle* followed a few weeks later with a report that the misfiled notes and recording of Cheryl Davis's interview had finally been found and turned over to Grim. Police acknowledged a serious mistake, fueling more questions about whether Longmire was simply sloppy or, as Fourth bragged on the secretly filmed video and in recorded jail phone calls, was his protector.

There was more. Longmire had spoken several times with Fourth in phone calls from jail. Fourth would call Alaia. Alaia would use three-way calling to connect Fourth to Longmire. Longmire didn't mention the calls in his case file. Nor did he mention that he sometimes exchanged text messages with Alaia and with Fourth's older sister, Jannah. Longmire would eventually claim the conversations were an investigative technique, that prosecutors and his homicide lieutenant had encouraged him to keep Fourth talking. But if that is true, it shows at best a major disconnect, because top officers in the police department had sought legal opinions of how they could stop Longmire from talking to Fourth on his own time on his personal phone. The lawyers concluded that Longmire had a First Amendment right to speak with whomever he chose.

In late October, Mayor Dellums, picking each word as if it were a footfall in a minefield, asked the state Justice Department to conduct a "concurrent, parallel investigation" to the internal-affairs investigation of the Bailey case. A few weeks later, the Chauncey Bailey Project revealed that police chief Wayne Tucker had ordered the forty-eight-hour delay of the raid on the bakery to accommodate the vacation schedules of his underlings. Tucker stumbled through an interview, at first saying there had been no delay, then reversing his position, saying there had. Police received another jolt a month later, when it was disclosed that Tucker had promoted a captain to lead the Internal Affairs Division who had once interfered with an internal-affairs investigation of his role in the beating of a suspect who later died. The city council, its members concerned about both the raid delay and the captain's promotion, scheduled a no-confidence vote, but Tucker resigned a few days before it could occur, forfeiting his prize thirty-thousand-dollar-a-year pension by failing to remain on the job for five years. His department, he admitted, had "made mistakes" in the Bailey case, leaving Fourth, "the one we want," uncharged.

Those mistakes were obvious. After a few months of reviewing evidence and tracking new leads, such as taking statements from Saleem Bey, Nisayah Yahudah, the former Sister Felicia, and members of Barbara Lee's staff, the district attorney's renewed investigation of the killing pointed directly to Fourth. By December, Deputy District Attorney Christopher Lamiero, who was leading the investigation, and his inspectors were confident that Fourth would be charged with ordering the killing—the legal equivalent of pulling the trigger himself. But each piece of that evidence had existed in the days and weeks following the killing, while the investigation foundered. Recollections had been fresher; cell-phone tower records had existed that could have pinpointed where Mackey was when he called Fourth minutes after the shooting. Fourth's phone contained text messages he had feared police finding. There was simply a lot of evidence of his involvement that had been overlooked.

All of the leads the investigators now followed also could have been followed by LeRue Grim. But he had barely examined the hundreds of pages of police documents that had been turned over to him so he could prepare a competent defense for Devaughndre Broussard. They sat in boxes scattered around his musty office, compact discs of jail phone calls and police interviews strewn about. If prosecutors weren't already concerned that Broussard might have grounds to appeal a potential conviction because of Grim's ineffective representation, they should have been. The old lawyer often said he was planning on starting an investigation as soon as he could find time to get organized and decide where to begin. He routinely allowed journalists* access to those records, which he later admitted to a judge in open court, earning a stern rebuke.

But Grim occasionally pulled on a stained brown overcoat and drove his Rolls to Oakland to see his client. Broussard had stewed in an isolation cell for eighteen months, receiving few visitors. Finally, he would say, with all that time to think, he came to realize how Fourth had used and abandoned him. Still, all it would have taken to keep his loyalty, he would one day say, was if Fourth "had hollered at me." He could have accepted not getting a lawyer, he said, since Fourth had gone down in the torture case and the bakery had closed. But he could not take the fact he had been completely abandoned. All Fourth might have needed to do was send a message by word of mouth through the jails and courthouses until Broussard heard that his leader passed on a "What's up" or a "Stay strong, brother" to him. But the silence had broken him down.

Grim was trying to stall the scheduling of a trial date as long as he could. At one short hearing in February 2009, he sat beside Broussard in the jury box of a crowded courtroom beneath a high, tiled ceiling, dreading, he would say, having to give the judge an update on his preparations. It was then that Broussard leaned close to the old man's ear and said softly, "I know about them other murders."

He meant Wills and Roberson.

Grim turned to face his client.

"Get at the DA," Broussard said.

He meant for Grim to go to Lamiero and begin negotiating a deal.

---

*Including the author.

For three weeks, though, Broussard heard nothing from his lawyer. He fumed and decided that he would fire Grim as soon as he went back to court. The old man was a snake. Even a public defender would be better. Then one morning, guards yanked him from his cell and put him on a bus headed for court. Broussard thought it was "a dry run," a scheduling error. He didn't have an appearance scheduled. But instead of a courtroom, guards whisked Broussard to a jury deliberation room on the courthouse's fourth floor. He had no idea what was going on. A door opened, and there was little LeRue Grim with Lamiero, who was nearly six feet five, towering over him. Grim had negotiated a deal with the prosecutor without talking to Broussard. Only now did he lay it out for his client. If Broussard would plead guilty to killing Bailey and tell everything about how the assassination happened—how it had been ordered, who had helped him—plus everything he knew about the other two murders, he would get a sentence of far less duration than what he faced if convicted by a jury, in all likelihood life without parole.

Grim whispered a few sentences of encouragement and handed Broussard a pen.

Broussard didn't hesitate in signing. He had finally seized the core message of the Black Muslim faith. He had done something for himself. At a few minutes past 10:00 a.m., Lamiero fiddled with a voice recorder, placing it on a table in front of Broussard and then leaning over to make sure it was turned on and capturing every word.

Broussard started talking. It took him two days to tell all that had happened.

Grim would say it had been his plan all along to simply wait out Broussard, to give him time to realize that "Mr. Yusuf the Fourth and Mr. Mackey were not his friends." It had been his plan all along, Grim boasted, to wait for his client to say such words.

Lester Hogan's initial call to LeRue Grim had proven to be of incredible benefit to Broussard. Grim, possibly the worst lawyer available, had landed his nephew a remarkable plea bargain. "I told them to make me a deal I couldn't refuse and they did," Grim said. "They wanted to clear the whole thing up." But it was far less his doing than a combination of the failure of authorities to pursue charges against Fourth from the start and the fact that Broussard could help clear the unsolved killings of Roberson and Wills.

Broussard's agreement was equally important to District Attorney Orloff, the pensive prosecutor. He, too, would say that the path to charging Fourth led through waiting for Broussard to serve him up. Patience, he and others in authority would say, had led to solving the Roberson and Wills killings.

Left unsaid by all, of course, was what would have happened if Broussard had remained silent, if he had gotten that "stay strong" from Fourth, if he had been hollered at with that sense of brotherhood for which he yearned. Would the case being built against Fourth before Broussard turned against him have been strong enough to convict him of Bailey's murder? And what about Mackey? He had never been investigated for his role in Bailey's slaying. Until Broussard implicated him in all three murders, it appeared likely he would escape charges, at least until he killed again.

A few weeks after Broussard turned state's evidence, Department of Justice investigators concluded that Detective Sergeant Derwin Longmire had intentionally compromised his investigation of Chauncey Bailey's murder, a finding Longmire adamantly denied and fought fiercely. The police department placed Longmire on paid suspension and moved to fire him under California's byzantine civil-service rules—an effort that fizzled when Longmire's lawyer picked apart the state's reasoning. Longmire went back to work as a uniformed patrol sergeant, a position to which he had been transferred before his suspension. His story, though, was not finished.

Fourth read a lot in his isolation cell. Alaia sent books by Elijah Muhammad to the jail. But he wanted more than Black Muslim literature. He asked for W.E.B. DuBois's *The Souls of Black Folk* and other texts. He had a Qur'an and a Bible, and he copied long passages from them in his own hand, trying to decipher what prophecy held for him. He also began writing what he described to Alaia as a crime-prevention plan for Oakland that he would use after his release and assumption of his role as a civic leader of Oakland.

But the guards took it. "The devils keep fucking with me," he said. And they were. Even locked down, Fourth remained an extremely dangerous prisoner. Broussard and Joshua had turned on him. Even far away in a Central Valley prison, Alfonza Phillips must have lived in constant fear of a shiv.

The phone was Fourth's lifeline, his only outlet other than visits, since he wasn't allowed to mingle with others on his cellblock. He called Alaia and Tammy daily, often ordering Alaia to use the three-way calling feature of her cell phone to get his supporters and followers on the line. He ranted, raved, shouted, demanded. He was still *Yusuf Ali Bey IV*, damn it. He wanted a Web site dedicated to his pending freedom. He wanted money raised for his defense. He wanted submission from his wife, mother, sister, brothers.

But there were moments when he was calm.

"I have learned more in this year than I have the rest of my life," he told his mother in a long conversation.

"God is going to be merciful. The most important thing is to learn. You're in God's grace," Tammy replied.

His jailing, Fourth insisted, was "God forcing me to find out my purpose. In order to fulfill prophecy you have to know your purpose."

Fourth knew his purpose was to continue what W. D. Fard had taught his messenger, Elijah Muhammad, who had in turn relayed it to the faithful, including Yusuf Bey. Daddy had, in turn, taught Fourth to be strong and decisive. That was the mission. Nothing else. His radical faith was absolute.

If he had been told that the concoction of that faith had begun eighty years earlier, in a cell forty miles away at San Quentin, a space not much bigger than the one he now occupied, he would have dismissed it. That's what the faithful always had done to any challenge of W. D. Fard's divinity. Allah had journeyed from Mecca to save the lost Tribe of Shabazz in the Wilderness of North America. Those who wavered, who accepted anything less than the fact that the Asiatic Black Man was the cream of the planet earth, the master-of-the-universe race, was a dupe. Only the weak followed versions of Islam in which Caucasians and Jews were not regarded as devils, skunks of the earth created by Yakub.

Elijah Muhammad had taught that all answers could be found in the Old Testament, and it was there that Fourth found the prophecy that assured him his release from jail would come soon. Fourth was Joseph in the book of Genesis, he told his mother, the eleventh son of Jacob betrayed by his brothers and sold into slavery. The other Beys hated him because he was Daddy's favorite, just as Joseph's brothers had hated him.

"Do you see how similar to this our family is? Mommy," he said, "I am the Joseph one."

His detractors, like Saleem, "are fulfilling the parts that have to be fulfilled and they don't even know it. I haven't done anything to justify what they are doing to me. That's the part of the scripture that has to be fulfilled."

Tammy warned him, though, that "the devil gets a hold on people" and that not all that was happening to him—or was about to happen to him—was prophecy. It could also be a result of his own doing. "There is good and evil. There is right and wrong. There is no mystery God. It is that simple."

Fourth, though, said he was convinced that God had destined his future. He was simply God's instrument, God's hand. He would soon leave jail and rise to power in a way similar to how Joseph rose after he interpreted the pharaoh's dreams, saw an approaching famine, and advised the pharaoh to store grain.

Like Joseph, it was others who meant him harm, not God. His faith was absolute.

"Nothing is going to change," he told Tammy. "Why did God design a set day for the destruction if he thought people were going to be hunky dory and just believe?"

Until that destruction came—until the mother plane launched its bombers—he was destined to rise to power, he said, and he would rule what remained, a beautiful kingdom filled only with believers.

Still, Tammy told him that she believed he had some free will to recognize his faults and change behaviors. She knew her son was far from perfect, although she often proclaimed his innocence. "If you do the same things you are going to have the same results."

For the Beys, though, the same results meant surviving, if not prospering, in Oakland. How many people had died and how many children had been raped because of them? How many people had Yusuf Bey exploited so he could have wealth and power and sex and make people fear him? Yusuf Bey had preached violence and hatred and greed and told Fourth that he was a prince, the scion who would rise in succession. Antar was just a placeholder, although he'd served a purpose in removing Waajid. Perhaps Fourth had angered God with his youthful escapades, but look what had happened. He had gone to jail in San Francisco, where God had intended for him to meet Richard Lewis, who had sent Broussard to him. Now Broussard was a test. Fourth's Malcolm X. But like Elijah Muhammad, Fourth would survive. As soon as he had completed God's lessons and shown enough strength, the jail door would open.

"You are going to come out and be better for it," Tammy said. "I hate you had to get it this way."

"I know, Mommy. If you can't go through the fire you can't get shaped. It is better to get it this way than to not get it at all. . . . My life is no accident."

There he was correct. His life was no accident. Neither was his faith. The society that now worked through its flawed laws and imperfect courts to put him in prison for life had only itself to blame for the terror that Fourth and his fellow believers had inflicted upon it. The backlash against centuries of enslavement of Africans and the subhuman treatment of their descendants had seen to that. The stick figure hanging from a noose that Elijah Muhammad had ordered displayed in all the Nation of Islam's mosques, the symbol of the boyhood lynching of his friend Albert Hamilton, showed that some could never forget, or forgive. Neither could Yusuf Bey forget the stories of cotton fields his parents brought west from East Texas along with the story of a Negro burned to death as white people gathered in the square of a horrible place called Greenville and cheered. Some wounds were too deep to heal.

Alameda County was good to its grand juries, and the one that heard nearly a week of testimony in the Roberson, Wills, and Bailey murders was treated no differently. It concluded its work before noon on a shining late-April Wednesday in a bland office building on the edge of Lake Merritt. On another shining day near the lakeshore almost two years earlier, Chauncey Bailey had walked right past that building in the final minutes of his life.

Before any indictments were announced, the jurors were treated to a catered lunch across the street at the courthouse. The eighteen men and women, who had heard so much sordid testimony about the Beys from Devaughndre Broussard, Cheryl Davis, and others, were treated to steaming trays of barbecued pork. Obviously, the devil was mocking Fourth by serving his accusers swine.

The indictments handed up later that afternoon contained few shocks. Word had leaked that Broussard had agreed to cooperate, and Grim had provided copies of the transcript of his two-day session with prosecutors the month before to anyone who wanted a copy. News coverage that he had gotten his young client such a favorable deal—a set term of twenty-five years for killing Roberson and Bailey in cold blood—was sure to be good for business.

Likewise, Orloff was pleased with the indictments of Yusuf Bey IV and Antoine Mackey, although he let Lamiero make the understated announcement. Fourth faced three counts of murder for ordering Roberson, Wills, and Bailey killed. Mackey also faced three counts for killing Wills and helping Broussard kill Bailey and Roberson.

"He said, 'We gotta stop him before he write that story,'" is how Broussard described Fourth's assassination order.

For the first time in its long history in Oakland, someone in the Bey cult was going to be tried for serious crimes.

The charges came close to breaking Fourth, alone in his little cell, a whole new chapter of his saga beginning. The bakery was gone and many of his men had scattered. But he still had others who believed in him, the way he believed in himself.

He rallied his faith that God still had a plan for him.

It's an Analogy?

Fourth was far from finished with his schemes.

Shortly after 9:00 p.m. on March 12, 2010, nearly a year after Fourth and Antoine Mackey were indicted for the murders of Chauncey Bailey, Michael Wills, and Odell Roberson, district attorney's inspectors and cops pulled over a car near downtown Oakland. With guns drawn, they forced the driver, a man who once professed to be Fourth's "number one soldier," to the ground, wrapping handcuffs around his wrists. On the car's dashboard was an envelope stuffed with transcripts from three witness interviews in the Bailey killing that prosecutors had turned over to Fourth's lawyer. Now, written in the margins of the documents, in Fourth's neat hand, was what authorities soon described as "a hit list." In the year since Devaughndre Broussard had turned on him, Fourth had become convinced that his way out of triple murder charges was to have more people killed.

The targets included Cheryl Davis, the woman to whom he had bragged about Bailey's killing. Fourth's "Ohhh shit" lament that he made on his first day in jail, when he learned that she couldn't be found, showed that he knew the devastating level of testimony she could give. But if she wasn't around to tell jurors how Fourth had boasted about the murder, his chances of an acquittal would be much greater. And if she was dead, Fourth presumed, other witnesses would obviously be much more reluctant to testify.

The man assigned to kill Davis professed love and loyalty to his jailed leader that few exceeded. Gary Larue Popoff, who sometimes went by the name Rasoul Bey, wore the block letters YBMB in a tattoo on his right shoulder. He had once told Fourth, his junior by nearly twenty years, "There is nothing I won't do for you."

In many way, Popoff epitomized the people the Beys had exploited for decades. He had drifted in and out of the bakery and various state prisons for most of his adult life, struggling with drug addictions and mental illnesses. He suffered from schizophrenia and anti-social personality disorder and was bipolar. "Gary is clever and wily," a manipulator of high order, his brother once wrote to a judge, begging for help as his aging parents prepared for Popoff to be once again released from prison. Despite being adopted by a middle-class family, Popoff had found solace only at Your Black Muslim Bakery, a place where, his relatives eventually conceded, he was at least away from them. After he was released from one of his many prison terms, Fourth phoned him from jail. Popoff vowed not to be incarcerated again unless it was "the will of Allah."

But only he, Fourth, could be God's oracle, he told Popoff. "The will of Allah will be transferred to you through me," Fourth said. "If you don't hear it from me, that means the work of Allah is not ready yet. You have to trust me. I have a lot of enemies out there."

Fourth met regularly in jail with his attorney, Lorna Patton Brown, who had represented Yusuf Bey against the child-rape charges several years earlier. Brown was the wife of a Berkeley veterinarian; she had graduated from law school in her forties and built a career as a court-appointed criminal defense lawyer specializing in capital cases and had occasionally served as a substitute judge. Although Fourth was eligible for the death penalty for ordering the three murders, prosecutors had decided not to pursue it, apparently not wanting to make Fourth a martyr, a decision that was made weeks after Brown took the case. Brown stayed on anyway—she had been defending Fourth in San Francisco court for running down the strip-club bouncers, and she knew her young client well. She was, in effect, the family lawyer.

Sometime shortly before Popoff's arrest, Fourth wrote notes in the margins of Brown's transcript of Cheryl Davis's police interview, and Brown, in the words of an investigator, "smuggled the written communication and materials" out of the jail. Brown, when questioned by inspectors, said she met a member of the Bey family on a street corner and handed over an envelope containing the marked-up transcripts, which were quickly passed on to Popoff.

Authorities learned about the plot when Fourth bragged about it and another prisoner alerted guards. Inspectors, by then, had been listening intently to recordings of Fourth's phone calls and visits and knew he was doing all he could to keep people from testifying against him. But all his scheming did was cost him his lawyer. Shortly after Popoff's arrest, Brown appeared at a hastily arranged hearing before a judge, who told her to "cease all communication and contact with Mr. Bey effective immediately" and ordered her to resign from the case. She did. Authorities, though, didn't charge Fourth with plotting against Davis, wanting to do nothing that would slow the murder trial, which would be delayed anyway because Fourth would need a new lawyer. Popoff returned to prison for again violating parole. Brown eventually moved to resign from the practice of law, but as of this writing, in September 2011, the State Bar Association has yet to take action, and the possibility that she could still be charged with a crime remains. She has yet to talk publicly about her role in Fourth's schemes. Lawyers who know Brown have defended her integrity, but her apparent involvement in the scheme remains one of the most bizarre developments in Fourth's story.

To replace Brown, the assigning judge called one of the most unflappable defense lawyers in the Bay Area and asked him to take Fourth as a client. White-haired Gene Guy Peretti had been a member of the bar for thirty-three years and was so Romanesque in appearance that he looked at times as if he were carved from marble. Throughout his career, Peretti had represented people who had committed gruesome crimes—including a woman who beat her sister to death with a crowbar and dismembered her with a circular saw. Lawyers, especially those who make their living representing indigent defendants by court appointment, don't turn down direct requests from judges. Peretti—calm, cerebral, thoughtful—took the case. But Fourth seemed to want a yeller, a fist-pounder, an advocate brimming with righteous indignation that Yusuf Ali Bey IV, scion of Your Black Muslim Bakery, was being prosecuted for crimes he didn't commit. He would spend the next two years often demonstrably annoyed with Peretti's style.

The defense was not the only side switching attorneys. Christopher Lamiero, who led the DA's investigation of Bailey's killing and who had successfully prosecuted Richard Lewis in the kidnapping and torture case, declined to try Fourth himself. Rather, that work went to Melissa Krum, an ambitious lawyer known for a razor wit and limitless sarcasm. Tall and stately, Krum would force a tremendous indignity on Fourth during the trial—he would be repeatedly maligned by *a woman,* one who wore flashy heels to extend her height, who paced back and forth before the defense table right in front of him and tinged her questions about him with a smoldering contempt.

Then there was the judge.

Thomas Mathew Reardon, an impatient if not quick-tempered former prosecutor, was known for cutting off attorneys and questioning witnesses himself and occasionally storming off the bench and slamming the door to his chambers behind him, which he did when defense lawyers began to nitpick the process by which prospective jurors were randomly selected.

In his off hours, Reardon fostered his passion for acting and theater, taking leads in local productions of *The Music Man* and *Chicago,* belting out show tunes. The judge once told an interviewer that he had little trouble playing flimflam artists like *Chicago*'s Billy Flynn, a sleazy lawyer, a "fast talking ne'er-do-well who's trying to put something over on people." He reveled, too, in playing *The Music Man*'s scamming antagonist, Harold Hill. "The con-man aspect of it comes to me kind of naturally," Reardon said of the Hill role. In other words, the judge knew a huckster when he saw one, which, like he sang as Hill, spelled trouble with a capital T, not for the fictional people of River City, Iowa, but for Yusuf Ali Bey IV.

It had been Reardon who, while sentencing Richard Lewis to a life term, had dubbed Fourth's bungling crew that kidnapped and tortured JoAnne "the gang that couldn't shoot straight," after the old Jimmy Breslin novel. As the fourth day of jury selection ended in *People v. Bey and Mackey,* Fourth suddenly began snapping at Reardon for making the gang comment several months earlier. Fourth wouldn't know Jimmy Breslin from Jimmy Buffett, but he knew what a gang was, and equating the Beys to one was a sign of high disrespect, he tersely informed Reardon. He would, he said, prefer someone else to preside over the case. Reardon, he was certain, couldn't be impartial, not after such a slur: "I don't think, personally, you can be fair in this case."

Reardon paused, a hand rising to rub his eyes, and said slowly, as if he were speaking to a child, "I didn't mean the Bloods and the Crips."

Sitting beside Fourth, Peretti looked for a moment as if he might be ill. It was the second consecutive day that Fourth made spontaneous, caustic remarks to Reardon. A day earlier, frustrated that Peretti wasn't aggressively grilling prospective jurors, Fourth had announced loudly that he wanted to fire Peretti and represent himself. This seemed not to upset Peretti as much as it did Mackey's lawyer, Gary Sirbu, who was forced to contemplate a triple murder defense with Fourth as his de facto co-counsel.

But now, as Reardon picked his words carefully to answer the gang question, Fourth seemed to lose his smugness.

Peretti would not submit a formal motion seeking Reardon's replacement. He also talked Fourth out of representing himself. It was all a prologue, anyway. The curtain had not yet risen, and when it did neither Reardon, Fourth, Krum, Peretti, Sirbu, nor even Mackey would be the star of the drama entitled *People v. Yusuf Bey IV and Antoine Mackey.*

No, that role could fall to only one person: Devaughndre Monique Broussard.

Broussard had grown a beard that wrapped under his chin, leaving his upper lip bare. He held his head high when, dressed in a red jumpsuit and chains, he shuffled into Reardon's aged, cavernous courtroom shortly before noon on March 24, 2011. Fourth chose that day to wear his best suit, a cream-colored Armani, and his first bow tie of the trial. No, Peretti insisted tiredly outside of court, Fourth's choice of neckwear had nothing to do with intimidating his chief accuser. He simply wanted to dress well. But, Peretti said, Fourth was "outraged" that Broussard had built a plea deal on a foundation of lies that he was now reciting for jurors.

Melissa Krum had strategically put Broussard on early in her lengthy prosecution, which would stretch over two months and require more than seventy witnesses. It was a simple strategy: No matter how poorly he did, she would have plenty of time to rebuild her case.

Around the courtroom several of Fourth's brothers and other men from the bakery stared icily at Broussard as he slowly spelled his name for the court reporter. LeRue Grim sat alone in a row of seats reserved for court personnel as Broussard took the stand, but he soon left, not to return. Grim had cut the deal; now Broussard had to live up to it alone. Before he was gone, though, Grim said Broussard had asked him to counsel Marcus Callaway and members of his family to stay away from court. He feared a confrontation with the Beys.

After a few questions about his arriving at the bakery four and a half years earlier, Krum asked Broussard if he recognized the man he kept referring to in a hurried cadence as "Yusuf-Bey-the-fourth." Broussard smiled widely as if to say "Got you, motherfucker" and lifted a chained hand slightly, the sharp jabbing point of his index finger aborted by the chain padlocking his handcuffs to the one wrapping his waist.

It was not, by any means, easy testimony for Broussard to provide or for the jury of seven women and five men to understand. He stammered badly, telling Krum that first day that he didn't know how to respond to even her simplest queries.

Why did unrelated men at the bakery call each other "brother"? she asked.

"I can't find the words to answer the question," he replied.

Finally, here was the public display of Broussard's damaged human existence. He would eventually calm himself, find words, and parry with defense lawyers, but all of his time on the stand would simply be an exposition, as if the lawyers on both sides were carnival barkers calling people to a pathetically sad freak show.

When Reardon sent jurors to lunch, Broussard remained on the witness stand, his eyes closed, rocking front to back and mumbling to himself, perhaps in prayer. During breaks in his testimony he did the same thing repeatedly, especially when the judge ushered the lawyers into his chambers for what became longer and longer disputes over legal objections. Fourth and Mackey just sat and stared at him with what seemed like growing amazement, as Broussard, chin tucked down, prattled and rocked, his eyes squeezed shut.

On the second day of his testimony, Krum finally got Broussard to the murders, taking him, first, slowly through his killing of Odell Roberson. There was Broussard, taking the gun from Mackey, whirling, yelling for Roberson to freeze, then the bullets ripping through face and chest. When Krum asked him what happened next, though, Broussard burst into laughter, turning to his left and trying to bury his face in his sleeve. But he couldn't quite raise his chained arm high enough, and his grin remained exposed as he struggled to compose himself. Jurors rolled their eyes and looked away. Juror number six, an older African American woman who wore long skirts every day, bit her lower lip and looked as if she would cry.

Months later, speaking through the glass of a tiny jail visiting room, Broussard would tell me he had laughed because he found Krum's question ridiculously obvious. "He fell. What do you think he did? I wasn't laughing in the sense that the murder was funny."

But Broussard managed to keep a straight face when he described what happened to Bailey. Fourth "wanted us to kill him. He was concerned about what he was writing."

He went on to describe hunting down Bailey, shooting him twice, turning to run, then going back to stand over the dying journalist.

"Where did you aim?" Krum asked, looking away.

"At his face."

Yet despite his often strange behavior, Broussard frequently demonstrated that underestimating his intelligence was a mistake. This became especially apparent when Peretti and Mackey's lawyer, Gary Sirbu, cross-examined him, a process during which Broussard seemed to take keen delight in frustrating his foes. Sirbu, a veteran of more than forty-five years of defense work and a passionate advocate for the rights of indigent criminal defendants, experienced that when he tried to question Broussard about why Fourth would want Roberson killed. Broussard was suddenly able to find the words.

"The impression I had of Yusuf Bey IV [was that] if somebody would do something to his, he would do something to theirs," Broussard said. "Here's this guy [Roberson] that is continuously around the neighborhood or the area to where [Fourth] be at daily, and he was just walking around, and I thought of it in context of a person who's hungry or who's starving and there's a rabbit around or a bunch of rabbits—well, shit, there go a rabbit, you can go get one."

What Broussard meant was that Fourth talked a lot about revenge but didn't act on it even though Roberson—the rabbit—was always around the bakery asking for free fish sandwiches, an easy target.

Sirbu, though, was perplexed, a situation for which he could hardly be blamed.

"There are rabbits, go get one?" he asked.

"Yeah," Broussard answered.

"What does that mean? I don't understand."

Broussard started laughing, relishing the moment.

"Because you could kill the rabbits," he answered.

"So if you can't eat them, what do you do?" Sirbu asked, plunging deeper into the brambles where Broussard merrily led him.

"What do you mean, 'If you can't eat them?' That's how I was, you know, fried rabbit legs, so you know, you hungry, and you see rabbits around, get one."

"Oh, so, in other words, Mr. Roberson is who is supposed to go get a rabbit. Is that what you are saying?"

"Say what?" Broussard asked.

They went back and forth, Sirbu not understanding what Broussard meant at all, Broussard growing bolder, his voice rising, grinning widely, as he baffled Sirbu.

Finally Broussard presented his thesis again: "I was saying the way I was relaying it to myself is that, OK, if the person's hungry and/or starving and there is a bunch of rabbits around the area. So it shouldn't be nothing hold- ing you back from satisfying your hunger by just killing one of the rabbits so you can eat a rabbit."

"Instead of just asking for a fish sandwich, is that what you mean?"

As jurors giggled, Krum grabbed a legal pad, scrawling on it "it's an analogy" and shoved the note into Sirbu's hand. Just then, as Sirbu looked at the paper, perplexed, Reardon could take no more of it either.

"No, it has nothing to do with Mr. Roberson. You're confused," he said.

"It's an analogy?" Sirbu said, his eyes rising from the note to the judge.

"Yes," Reardon answered, painfully.

"Ohhhh," Sirbu said slowly as Broussard's grin turned into a smirk, a master of his own world.

But despite brief respites, most of the trial was tense and agonizing. Bailey's relatives sobbed when autopsy photos of him were flashed on a large screen, and when the secret video of Fourth laughing about the murder was played. Krum wrestled with a slew of reluctant witnesses, perhaps none more so than Cheryl Davis, who had been told of Fourth's plot to have her killed. She had blocked her time at the bakery out of her mind, she testified, and try as she might she could not recall the events surrounding Bailey's murder. It was completely transparent self-protection, but it was her testimony. She had blocked it, she said again and again.

Members of Fourth's family had been coming by her house, she said, harassing her. Once, during a break, as Davis walked out of the courtroom, Fourth turned and blatantly nodded to his brother, Fard, to follow her. In- spectors found Davis sitting in a chair, her head in her hands as Fard Bey sat nearby, staring at her menacingly. Later, Peretti described Davis as a terrible witness. He was right, but the recorded statement she had given to police the day after the murder was what mattered, not Davis's obvious reluctance and feigned memory loss on the stand. Even Fourth knew that, and as Rear- don slowly worked through the recording a few days later, ruling on which portions of it jurors could hear, Fourth began to make his own objections to the judge's decisions as Peretti nearly begged him to shut up. "When you go to law school and learn the evidence code, you get back to me," Reardon snapped at Fourth, who briefly suggested that he should be tried in absentia before quieting down.

The next day, Krum played Davis's statement—the one detectives misfiled directly after the murder—for the jurors. Perhaps it was then that their reasonable doubt vanished as they heard Davis quote Fourth as saying, "That will teach them to fuck with me." Or it might have happened when the case's former prosecutor, Christopher Lamiero, took the stand himself and, as Krum pitched him softball after softball, described how a bakery soldier named Dawud Bey, who was close to Fourth, had told him in an interview that Fourth said "I did what I had to do" about Bailey. Or maybe it happened as they watched the videotape of Fourth saying "Pow . . . pow . . . *poof!*" and then laughing hysterically.

The verdicts came on the ninth day of deliberations. Jurors convicted Fourth of ordering the three murders. They also found Mackey guilty of killing Bailey and Wills, but not Roberson—not because they believed his testimony that he wasn't there, but because they couldn't decide if Mackey knew what Broussard intended to do when he handed him the rifle. In essence, they couldn't pick between first-degree and second-degree murder.

Peretti said Fourth was "shocked" by the outcome. If he was, he must have been the only one. Krum had bombarded him with all of the bakery's recent history. The liquor-store attack and the kidnapping and torture of JoAnne were used to show how bakery soldiers blindly followed Fourth's orders.* His use of fake driver's licenses to steal cars was used to show that Broussard's testimony about being baited with credit scams rang true. Krum even found a photo of Fourth posing with a 9 mm pistol and an assault rifle and displayed it at length on a large television screen. Above the

---

*Sirbu, citing the fact that Mackey had not yet joined the bakery when those crimes occurred, made numerous objections that his client was unjustly being confronted with evidence of crimes he did not commit, calling it guilt by association. But Reardon rejected Mackey's request to be tried separately and told jurors they could consider the liquor-store and kidnapping cases against Mackey only as a way to understand how Fourth convinced others to follow his orders. Sirbu said Mackey will raise a vigorous appeal.

photo, Krum had written, in black letters, one of the more incredible things Fourth had told Detective Longmire on tape: "Guns aren't allowed on our premises, period."

Longmire testified twice, wearing dark suits rather than his patrol sergeant's blues. No, he didn't promise Fourth protection, he deadpanned. No, he didn't deny Broussard a lawyer. Fourth was simply a crook, and if he was stupid enough to think that a cordial detective who took his calls and asked how he was and was polite to his mother was thereby protecting him, so be it. Still, Longmire seemed nervous on the stand, almost flighty. The first time he testified, Krum took him through his brief tenure as head of the department's intelligence unit, and was about to have him tell the jury, in essence, that the bakery was a long-standing criminal enterprise (albeit one police did little about) when Peretti vigorously objected, claiming the bakery's long history had no direct bearing on the three murder charges his client faced. Reardon shepherded the lawyers into his chambers for nearly an hour as Longmire stared blankly from the witness chair and jurors grew restless. Finally the proceedings continued, but Krum's line of questioning had vanished. Peretti and Sirbu minimalized their cross-examinations, and Longmire's testimony ended so quickly that the trial was adjourned at mid-afternoon because Krum had no other witnesses queued up. Longmire didn't get the chance to publicly reaffirm himself as an honest cop—an opportunity he desperately wanted. But he also showed why his reputation for sloppiness and lack of thoroughness seemed well earned. At one point Krum asked him if he had subpoenaed Fourth's cell-phone records. Yes, Longmire answered. But when she asked him if he had performed any analysis of those records, a look of bewilderment appeared on his face as he said he was uncertain if he had examined them at all.

Toward the end of the three-month trial—after jurors had seen the secretly recorded video of Fourth, Joshua, and Tamon Halfin in the jail cell—Krum put Longmire back on the stand to again refute Fourth's boasts that he was being protected.

"Did you make him any promises?" she asked.

"No, ma'am," he replied.

In another legal proceeding, Longmire would eventually say the Bailey case caused him "a tremendous cost in respect. There are a lot of people that still are very skeptical of who I am. Prior to this I was a good guy and somebody that everybody didn't mind having their kids around. Now folks don't really know exactly what to believe about me."

Investigators for both the state justice department and the police department concluded that Longmire had compromised the case. But these inquiries as well were deemed so inadequate that police commanders were unable to make a clear determination of what exactly happened, and they eventually dropped the whole matter. Longmire continued to insist he wasn't a Black Muslim, as many of his fellow officers believed.

But it was a third, separate examination of ten of Longmire's unsolved murder cases ordered by police commanders that provided greater context to his work, as well as the department and perhaps Oakland itself. The investigating officer, a by-the-book lieutenant who took over command of the homicide unit, concluded that Longmire did sloppy work in all ten instances, included failing to turn in evidence for crime-lab analysis. Each case, as an attorney put it, contained "significant errors or holes." Longmire, though, said the standards used to scrutinize those investigations were "completely subjective" and that his work was only examined "to take a great big swing at me." Longmire was sloppy, but he was sloppy within a dysfunctional department that policed a staggering city, one where the government mostly failed to serve a public in desperate need. He was simply one more broken cog in a production line that for years dumped people on the Beys' doorstep.

In 2010, Longmire sued Oakland in federal court, claiming among other things that a police department gag order on the Bailey case violated his First Amendment rights by failing to allow him to address swirling rumors about his loyalties and religious beliefs. A judge threw out most of the suit but allowed the First Amendment claim to go forward. In November 2011, after months of depositions, the judge threw out the rest of the suit, writing that Longmire had presented no evidence of real harm. Another suit that Longmire had filed in state court was still proceeding.

As Fourth's trial concluded, an alternative narrative began to creep through Oakland, fueled in part by Longmire's lawsuit: All's well that ends well. Fourth and Mackey were down for life. If Broussard hadn't confessed, none of the murders would have been solved. Former DA Orloff knew exactly what he was doing when he didn't order an immediate investigation of Fourth's role in the murder. Longmire, no matter how many lies Fourth and Broussard told him, extracted the magic words: "I shot him." That's all that was needed—after Broussard took a good, long stew—to eventually clear three homicides.

But that conclusion doesn't take several things into account, such as LeRue Grim's failure to wage an aggressive defense on behalf of his client, rather than waiting for Broussard to flip and cut a deal. What if Broussard had had a competent attorney who got the confession thrown out? Or what if Fourth had stayed silent in the jail cell as the hidden camera rolled? What if Broussard had remained devoted to Fourth and not talked, a possibility that he insisted in testimony was not out of the question. If Fourth, in turn, had just remained loyal to him—if he had passed on a "What's up?" or a "Stay strong" through the jail grapevine—if he had been true to the concepts of brotherhood and loyalty he preached, Broussard would have stayed silent, he insisted. And given his search for acceptance in life, he might have.

"The bond was strong, like, 'You my dude,'" Broussard said. "But they [Fourth and Mackey] broke the contract we had," and only then did he figure it was all a lie—that it had been all along.

But suppose, then, that in the name of brotherhood, Broussard didn't flip. Would there have ever been a complete accounting of—and full justice for—Bailey's murder? Given that there was no aggressive investigation of the whole crime in the beginning, the only reasonable answer is no.

Lost in the revising narrative, too, was the simple concept that the First Amendment deserved better. Orloff, who had retired as DA, was replaced by a far more outgoing and confident prosecutor named Nancy O'Malley, who had worked her way up to being his chief assistant. O'Malley spoke bluntly after the verdicts, saying what Orloff and others such as Oakland mayor Ron Dellums and police chief Wayne Tucker should have said four years earlier, expressing what she called an "abiding conviction that violence against a free voice of the press will not be tolerated in our community or our society."

Reardon sentenced Fourth and Mackey in August 2011 to life terms with no chance of parole. Michael Wills's mother and Bailey's former wife both spoke tearfully as Fourth looked away.

Fourth had written a statement that he asked Peretti to read. The lawyer complied after making it very clear that the words were his client's, not his:

> I would like the people to know that this case has never been about truth and justice. It has been about perception and politics. Although I know I am innocent of the crimes of which I've been convicted, I do apologize to my family and to the families of the victims for not making wiser decisions and allowing this to have occurred on my watch. I will not rest until I find out those who are truly responsible for setting this operation up. For years, there have been elements out there trying to destroy the institution of Your Black Muslim Bakery, and although they have been successful temporarily, I know and believe that truth and righteousness always triumphs in the end. Although my physical freedom may be taken away for a time, my mind will always be free and I will continue to help those in need. Once again, I apologize to my family and the families of those who lost their lives senselessly.

"Didn't Mr. Grim tell you I was coming?" I said into a tiny slit in the window of a jail visiting room to Devaughndre Broussard. For a moment he was silent, just shaking his head side to side.

"Well, you know how he is," I said, smiling though the glass.

Broussard laughed knowingly, and I settled into a battered plastic chair.

For more than a year I had been mentioning to Grim that I intended to interview his client, once the trial was over. Now, a week after the verdicts, Broussard stared intently at me.

I was there, ostensibly, I told him, to write a newspaper story about his thoughts on the verdicts. But I also wanted to get another sense of Broussard, especially after some of the bizarreness of his testimony. He was, I found, eager to talk, but also abundantly willing to say what he thought people might expect him to say. "I don't expect them to forgive me," he said of his victims' families, looking straight through the glass at me, our eyes locked. "But I hope they hear me. It was morally wrong."

He didn't have to say anything, of course. Reardon would soon sentence him to the twenty-five-year term that was predetermined by the plea bargain. All the sorrow in the world wasn't going to shave a minute off Broussard's prison time, just as a lack of remorsefulness couldn't add to it. But did he mean a word of what he said? During the trial, Peretti had called Broussard an accomplished liar, which was obviously true. Why should now be any different?

Our conversation turned to the bakery, and Broussard allowed as how he had let Fourth mess with his "mind state" and how both he and Richard Lewis had reached "the wrong conclusion" in thinking that the bakery would give them a decent life.

"I took what Yusuf Bey IV said to be Islam. It wasn't," Broussard said. Now, he said, he had been reading the Holy Qu'ran during those long, lonely hours in his isolation cell and was planning to use his prison time to continue to educate himself about religion even after all that had happened to him. He wanted to become an imam, he said, but one who drew influences from both Orthodox Islam and Christianity to craft his own faith.

"Now I have time to read the Holy Qu'ran beginning to end and come up with my own conclusions," he said, bending slightly to speak through the slot at the bottom of the window.

He didn't know I was coming, yet his apology for the murders and his claims that he was seeking peaceful spirituality both seemed well rehearsed, as if he had just been waiting for the chance to say them, perfecting his lines. Three years earlier I had gone to another jail and interviewed Fourth after obtaining a copy of the secret video recording of him laughing about Bailey's murder. Fourth's lies that day had been more transparent than Broussard's were now: He said he knew the cops were watching, and he made up things to deceive them. That was how he tried to explain away the video.

"Did you order anyone to kill Chauncey Bailey," I had asked Fourth.

"Of course not," he had answered.

There could be no such confrontation with Broussard. He spun what we discussed forward, toward his future and his creating some new belief system for himself. Surely, Broussard insisted, he could become a better religious teacher than any of the Beys had been. Just wait and see, he said, what with all the time he had ahead of him to study and pray, and—I thought, finishing his sentence in my mind—to scheme just like so many decades earlier W. D. Fard had spent time in prison, scheming how he would use his own religious distortions to enrich himself. Look at all that Fard had wrought, I thought, staring through the glass again at a man who had killed two people on the street in the name of the salvation Fard peddled door to door in Detroit's ghettos. Broussard may have dismissed Fourth's, and thus Fard's, version of Islam, but he was, as Krum had told jurors several times, a sociopath, a demon, who sure had been willing to blow people away in its name when he had the chance.

I wanted to know more, but visiting time is short, and before I could ask Broussard to further define his religious ideas, a door opened behind him and a guard motioned to him to step out. We stood and said brief good-byes, my doubts about his sincerity rising.

When he moved through the tiny door, Broussard looked back for an instant, raising his head slightly as the guard put a hand in the small of his back. As he disappeared from my view, I could hear him laughing.

Acknowledgments

In January 2009, the writer Lisa Catherine Harper and her husband, the art director Kory Heinzen, joined my wife and me for dinner at our home. The occasion, ostensibly, was the celebration of the completion of my master's thesis a year earlier, for which Harper had been my adviser. But I also wanted to get her input on whether to immediately try to turn the thesis—an account of my time as a reporter covering Atlantic City, New Jersey—into a publishable book, or to start another project: a book about the Bey cult of Black Muslims in Oakland and the murder of Chauncey Bailey. At that point, I had been investigating and writing about Bailey's killing and the Beys for more than a year. Go for the immediate story, Harper said; write the Bailey book. The next day my friend and former city editor at the *Atlantic City Press,* Kevin Shelly, said the same thing. Atlantic City could wait. I am grateful to both Harper and Shelly for their wise counsel and friendship. My agent at the Jean V. Naggar Literary Agency, Elizabeth Evans, and editor at Crown, Jenna Ciongoli, have never wavered in their support of this project, and I am indebted to them for their passion and guidance. Thanks also to Kimberly Cameron and her staff at Kimberly Cameron and Associates, where Evans worked at the beginning of the project. Also, thanks to Dyana Messina, Julie Cepler, and Mark Birkey for their work on the project. Thanks to Patty Sullivan for the cover photo, to Nick Lammers at the Bay Area News Group for the photos of Chauncey Bailey and Yusuf Bey that he provided, and to Karl Mondon for his jacket photo and help in providing other photos for the book.

Thanks also to the Alameda County District Attorney's Office for providing the photograph of Yusuf Bey IV that had been entered into evidence at his murder trial. I am especially indebted to Karl Evanzz, author of the

368 Acknowledgments

seminal biography of Elijah Muhammad, *The Messenger,* for the draft card of Wallace Fard. I am also grateful to Evanzz for being generous with his time and advice, especially concerning Fard's identity.

Nate Gartrell, who had been my student when I taught in the journalism department at San Francisco State University, proved himself to be an able researcher, especially about the Zebra murders, and I am grateful for his constant work on this project. Ali Winston, whom I met through the University of California, Berkeley, Graduate School of Journalism, also provided research, especially on FBI files concerning W. D. Fard, and I am grateful for his help. Thanks also to Tyler Curtis, another former student, for his research assistance.

Thanks to Matt Krupnick for his stellar copy editing of early drafts and to K. G. Schneider and Kevin Shelly for their critical assessments of parts of those drafts, and to Andy Raskin for his help in drafting the proposal for the book.

Without the other members of the Chauncey Bailey Project's core reporting team—Mary Fricker, Bob Butler, Josh Richman, A. C. Thompson, and G. W. Schulz—this book would not have been possible. Their dedication and single-minded pursuit of the complete story of Chauncey Bailey's assassination and the Beys of Oakland were extraordinary. The same can be said for the project's editors and administrators: Robert Rosenthal, Sandy Close, Dori Maynard, Kevin Keane, Pete Wevurski, Mike Oliver, Michael Maitre, Martin G. Reynolds, Michelle Fitzhugh-Craig, Neil Henry, Bruce B. Brugman, Linda Jue, Pamela Turntine, and our legal counsel, Duffy Carolyn. Other journalists who worked on the project to whom I am indebted include Cecily Burt, Paul T. Rosynsky, Cliff Parker, Michael Stoll, Angela Hill, Harris Rashid, L. A. Chung, Tamerlin Drummond, Kristin Bender, Harry Harris, Roland De Wolk, Judy Campbell, Kevin Westin, the late Lani Silver, Gene Durnell, Karl Mondon, Ray Chavez, Jane Tyska, Laura Oda, D. Ross Cameron, Will Evans, Carrie Ching, and Ethan Harp. Thanks also to the journalism students who worked on the project, including Andrew Palma, Lisa Pickoff White, Rhyen Coombs, Marnette Federis, Lucie Schwartz, Robert Lewis, Marguerite Davenport, Nick Kusnetz, and Robin Urevich. The Bailey Project also had outside support, both journalistic and financial. I am grateful to Brant Houston, formally of Investigative Reporters and Editors, for his advice on databases and his encouragement, and to Eric Newton of the Knight Foundation, the Society of Professional Journalists, the Newspaper Guild, and the California Endowment for their generous support of our work.

Without the support of MediaNews Chairman W. Dean Singleton and the publishers of his Bay Area papers during the run of the Bailey Project, John Armstrong, David Rounds, and Mac Tully, we would have been able to accomplish little.

At the *San Francisco Chronicle,* Jaxon Vanderbeken and Matthai Kuruvila did excellent work covering Bailey's killing and its aftermath, and their constant competition brought an even greater urgency to our work.

Lowell Bergman, Rob Gunnison, and Zachery Stauffer at the University of California, Berkeley, Graduate School of Journalism and its Investigative Reporting Program provided me video of hours of interviews with Nadar Bey, and I am deeply grateful to them. I am also grateful to Stauffer for a copy of his excellent short film about Chauncey Bailey's murder, *A Day Late in Oakland.*

The novelist Lewis Buzbee and the nonfiction writers Nick Krieger and Alex Abramovich were generous with their advice in navigating the publishing world, and I am grateful to them. So was the novelist Steven Gore, who, as a private investigator retired from the Alameda County Public Defender's Office, also provided me with analysis of the county's criminal justice system. I am also grateful to Harper, Buzbee, Lowell Cohn, and Aaron Shurin for their tutelage at the University of San Francisco when I was a graduate student there.

I am grateful to the staffs at the Oakland, San Francisco, and Berkeley public libraries and to the research staffs at the Oakland African-American Museum and Library, the University of Chicago, the University of Michigan, the New York Public Library's Schomberg Center for Research in Black Culture, the University of California, Berkeley, Bancroft Library, and the Graduate Theological Union in Berkeley, for their assistance. Thanks especially to Veronica Martinez at the *Oakland Tribune* library, and to Linda Cullpepper, librarian at the *Detroit News,* for her assistance in accessing Chauncey Bailey's card file there, containing summaries of his many, many stories.

At the Alameda County District Attorney's Office, the primary prosecutors of the Beys, Melissa Krum, Christopher Lamiero, and David Lim, were never too busy to answer questions and explain trial procedures even at the height of case work. I am grateful to them for their patience and kindness.

Notes

Killing the Messenger is a book primarily about people who wish not to be its subject. Yusuf Bey IV and members of his cadre believe they are above journalistic scrutiny or attempts at explanation. Also, many of its subjects—W. D. Fard, Elijah Muhammad, Yusuf Bey, and Chauncey Bailey—are dead. What we have of their lives—what tells their stories—are vast written accounts, from books to FBI files to myriad documents. The bulk of this book is sourced through records—indictments, court transcripts, depositions, police reports, birth and death certificates. Especially in part 4, I am sourced through law-enforcement documents, recordings of police interviews, and, in the case of Devaughndre Broussard and Bey IV, scores of recorded telephone calls they made from jail that were digitally recorded. I am also fortunate as a journalist to have observed hundreds of hours of criminal court proceedings in which they and others were defendants. I have posted as many source documents as possible on my Web site, Thomaspeele.com, especially those not easily available to the public, such as the Devaughndre Broussard proffer statement and Oakland Police Sergeant Derwin Longmire's defense in disciplinary proceedings.

I have also conducted interviews, sometimes with people who have requested not to be fully identified. Some were with Oakland police officers who were subject to a department-wide gag order during the time this book was being written. Others were members of law enforcement working elsewhere or members of the legal profession who asked not to have information directly attributed to them because of ongoing prosecutions and litigation, requests I mostly honored. Others, such as people in North Oakland who lived near Your Black Muslim Bakery, simply remain afraid of the Beys—even those, like Bey IV, who are unlikely to ever see a day outside a jail or prison for the remainder of their lives. References to those interviews in the notes provide as much identifying information as possible while honoring those requests.

The following abbreviations are used in the notes.

Business
Your Black Muslim Bakery: YBMB

Courts
Superior Court of the State of California, County of Alameda: ACSC
Superior Court of the State of California, County of San Francisco: SFSC
United States Bankruptcy Court, Northern District of California: USBCNDC
United States District Court, Northern District of California: USDCNDC

Government agency
Alameda County Department of Environmental Health: ACDEH

Journalistic cooperative
The Chauncey Bailey Project: CBP

Law-enforcement agencies
Alameda County District Attorney's Office: ACDAO
Alameda County Sheriff's Office: ACSO
Oakland Police Department: OPD
San Francisco Police Department: SFPD
Santa Barbara Police Department: SBPD

News service
Associated Press

Periodicals
Chicago Defender: CD
Contra Costa Times: CCT
Detroit Free Press: DFP
Detroit News: DN
Detroit Times: DT
East Bay Express: EBX
East Bay Monthly: EBM
Final Call: FC
Los Angeles Herald-Examiner: LAHE
Los Angeles Times: LAT
Muhammad Speaks: MS
New York Times: NYT
Oakland Post: OP
Oakland Tribune: OT
San Francisco Chronicle: SFC
San Francisco Examiner: SFE
San Francisco Sun Reporter: SFSR
San Jose Mercury News: SJMN
Village Voice: VV

INTRODUCTION: A MURMUR OF GROWING INTENSITY

xviii "the community and other like communities": Investigative Reporters and Editors, "The Arizona Project," http://www.ire.org/history/arizonaproject.html#Bolles _history.

xviii "was an attack on the American way of life": "Commentary: In Detroit, Some Note Absences at Bailey Service," CBP, http://www.chaunceybaileyproject.org/2007/ 08/17/in-detroit-some-note-absences-at-bailey-service/.

PROLOGUE: THAT WILL TEACH THEM . . .

3 He took a moment: ACSO, Coroner's Report No. 2007-02208.

3 "The only men a lot of Blacks see": Mark Cooley, interview with the author, April 13, 2010, Modesto, CA.

4 "get it down and get it in": Martin G. Reynolds, interview with the author, May, 5 2010, Oakland, CA.

4 stuffed a jury summons in his pants: OT, December 9, 2007.

4 he wanted those closest to him: Cooley interview.

5 Paul Cobb . . . spike it: OPD, Case No. 07-059842, notes, Sergeant D. Longmire.

6 he'd written about a handful: SFSR, February 2, 1974, "Charges of Police Harassment in Muslim Shooting Incident"; April 6, 1974, "Operation Zebra: Huge Manhunt Yields No Arrests"; April 27, 1974, "Operation 'Zebra': Police Captain Claims It's Not Racial"; May 18, 1974, "Muhammad Is 'Doing More for Blacks Than Any Ball Player.'"

7 the Black Muslims' basic beliefs: The author is informed by Karl Evanzz, *The Messenger: The Rise and Fall of Elijah Muhammad* (New York: Pantheon Books, 1999); Claude Andrew Clegg, *An Original Man: The Life and Times of Elijah Muhammad* (New York: St. Martin's Press, 1997); and Steven Tsoukalas, *The Nation of Islam: Understanding the "Black Muslims"* (Phillipsburg, NJ: P & R, 2001).

7 "tricknology": *True Solutions,* November 19, 2002. Soul Beat television, Oakland, CA. Yusuf Bey's weekly television show, shown on the Soul Beat cable television channel in Oakland, was a shoestring affair, filmed without episode numbers or other identifiers. The few episodes that the author was able to obtain are identified only by broadcast date.

7 The devils were "snakes": Ibid.

7 "We don't turn no other cheek": *True Solutions,* November 19, 2002.

10 highest educational achievement was: SBPD, Case No. 411911 (Scott homicide). (Case file includes Joseph H. Stephens's cosmetology certificate.)

10 But in *East Bay Express* stories: "The Sinister Side of Yusuf Bey's Empire," EBX, November 13, 2002.

10 Bruises and cuts frequently appeared: *Jane Does v. Yusuf Ali Bey,* ACSC, Case No. RG03105036, depositions.

10 all received public assistance: Ibid.

13 "That will teach them": OPD, Case No. 07-059842, recorded statement of person referred to in the text as Cheryl Davis.

1. THERE GOES LUCIFER

14 the rat shit–flecked kitchen floor: ACDEH, inspection notes and embargo notice, YBMB, August 3, 2007.

15 "I have no alternative": MS, April 1962.

15 The correct interpretations: The author is informed by dozens of hours of Yusuf Bey IV's recorded jail telephone calls.

15 called for Hitleresque mass slaughters: NYT, January 11, 1994.

16 a woman who had borne: Alameda County recorded documents: birth certificates, numbers 6005-2737, 18961-000379, 19561-002588, 1199861002580, 18661-000138, 6005-03571, 19261-001414, and 6005-3453, each identified in the text "Tammy" as the mother. Paternity on the certificates is either blank or lists Yusuf Bey. The author has not identified the children listed in the documents to protect the identity of "Tammy," a victim of abuse.

16 lived in constant terror: *Jane Does v. Yusuf Ali Bey,* ACSC, Case No. RG03105036.

16 "the prince of the bakery": ACSO, recorded jail phone call 853O20AV, August 5, 2007.

17 "There goes Lucifer": North Oakland residents, interviews with the author in 2009. Interview subjects, fearing members of the Bey cult remaining in Northern California, asked not to be identified by name.

17 Bey's soldiers frequently attacked: Oakland police officers, interviews with the author between 2008 and 2011. The officers asked not to be identified by name or rank, citing a department gag order on the Chauncey Bailey case and also fear of reprisal from department commanders.

17 clip-on bow ties on the blood-speckled: Ibid.

18 drew his *superbia* from the fealty: The author is informed on this point from dozens of Yusuf Bey IV's jail phone calls in which he discussed his followers; *People v. Yusuf Ali Bey (IV) and Antoine A. Mackey,* ACSC, Testimony of Dawud Bey, Dept. 10, April 13, 2011.

18 he ordered them to salute: Ibid.

18 punks beating up other punks: Oakland police officers, interviews with the author.

18 police department was chronically understaffed: "Understaffed Oakland Department Behind Other Cities in Solving Homicides," CBP, December 28, 2008.

18 the job was simply about: Oakland police officers, interviews with the author.

19 "Everything related to the bakery": Police Sergeant Derwin Longmire, Predis-

ciplinary Response, OPD, July 9, 2009. This 60-page document, written by Long-mire's lawyer, Michael Rains, lays out Longmire's argument against his proposed 2009 firing on administrative charges that he intentionally compromised the investigation of Chauncey Bailey's murder. Under California law, it is a confidential personnel re-cord and not publicly available. A copy was obtained by the author.

20 **So Brown paid a visit to:** "Politicians Bowed to Bey," SFC, January 27, 2008.

21 **"You have a God in you":** *True Solutions,* November 19, 2002.

21 **Bey made a show of visiting:** "The Door to Salvation?" EBM, March 1995.

21 **"damn Jews and faggots":** *True Solutions,* November 19, 2002.

22 **While prophecy dictated his divinity:** ACSD, recorded jail phone call 751U102G.v08, July 5, 2008.

22 **But Fourth was beginning to understand:** Ibid.

22 **leader of his people:** Ibid.

23 **Apocalypse eventually wiped the devils:** Ibid.

2. YOU'RE A BAKER?

25 **potential multiple wives:** Yusuf Bey IV states this in dozens of jail phone calls heard by the author.

25 **Fourth forked over $150:** *People vs. Yusuf A. Bey (IV),* SFSC, Case No. 2264607, Preliminary Hearing Transcript.

25 **Fourth found power in forcing:** ACSO, recorded jail phone call CH1U10YX, December 17, 2007.

26 **"The fuck we get for $150?":** *People v. Bey,* Preliminary Hearing Transcript. Nearly all of chapter two describing events at the New Century Theater relies on the preliminary hearing transcript and examination of witnesses Charles F. Johnson, Jeffrey Johnson, Hakeem Khalad Marshal, Raymond Alan Vega, and SFPD Sergeant Timothy F. Flaherty.

26 **made his living dealing with rubes:** Ibid.

26 **"Keep an eye on the girls":** Ibid.

26 **"No slappin' ass":** Ibid.

26 **Her eyes caught the floor manager's:** Ibid.

27 **pushing him toward the door:** Ibid.

27 **A maelstrom of blows followed:** Ibid.

27 **The bouncers held the doors:** Ibid.

27 **"We already called the cops":** Ibid.

27 **a bouncer walked outside:** Ibid.

27 **his fists clenched in a bizarre:** Ibid.

28 **"You're a baker?":** Ibid.

28 **Fourth drove his fist squarely:** Ibid.

28 skidding to a stop: Ibid.

28 "I got something for you": Ibid.

28 to fire imaginary pistol shots: Ibid.

28 One of the bouncers laughed: Ibid.

29 "Let's go. Let's go": Ibid.

29 Police Sergeant Tim Flaherty was patrolling: Ibid.

29 *nothing like dealing with a bunch:* Ibid.

29 but now he was right: Ibid.

29 He landed between two: Ibid.

29 clipped his leg and spun: Ibid.

29 slowly flexing his fingers and toes: Ibid.

30 *What a mess:* Ibid.

30 "There's the BMW right there": Ibid.

30 Flaherty saw it slowly moving: Ibid.

30 a handcuff cinching hard: Ibid.

30 The ID card said Yusuf: Ibid.

31 keep his mouth shut: Ibid.

31 Fourth had the BMW key: Ibid.

31 often preached about his preference: *True Solutions,* November 19, 2002.

31 a football standout: "Man Acquitted in S.F. Slaying Held in Kidnap Tied to Muslim Bakery," SFC, October 18, 2007.

32 Send some strong brothers: *People v. Devaughndre Broussard,* ACSC, Case No. 157043, Proffer Statement.

3. AN ANGUISHED LIFE

33 He tried to divert his eyes: SFPD, Case No. 05-231428, narrative.

33 Devaughndre Monique Broussard: San Francisco County recorded documents: birth certificate no. 18738010351. Monique is Broussard's middle name. In some references and law enforcement Web sites listing him as an inmate, it has been abbreviated to Moniq.

33 splattered the kid's face: Ibid.

34 an outbound two-car: Ibid.

34 He had a red Magic Marker: Ibid.

34 handcuffed the bloody young man: Ibid.

34 Former supervisor Tony Hall: KGO-TV San Francisco, August 24, 2007, evening newscast.

34 Police scooped him up: *People v. Devaughndre Broussard,* SFSC, Case No. 2242731.

34 the judge gave him a year: Ibid.

34 "That punk should have": KGO-TV San Francisco.

35 police had arrested his mother: SFPD, Case No. 051013511.

35 She would eventually have: San Francisco County recorded documents: birth certificate for Devaughndre Broussard, *People v. Aundra Dixon,* SFPC, Case No. 120525; *Alameda County Court v. Aundra R. Dixon,* ACSC, Case No. RF03122966; and *Alameda County Department of Child Support Services v. Aundra Reniece Dixon,* ACSC, Case No. 07-00392. All identify children born to Aundra Dixon.

35 "She has had an anguished life": *People v. Aundra Dixon,* SFPC, Case No. 120525, Declaration of Jasper L. Monti.

35 Dixon returned to jail: "Bailey Killing Figure Had Troubled Youth," OT, June 22, 2008.

35 Dixon soon became pregnant: Ibid.

35 shooting a woman: *People v. Dixon.*

35 he loved Broussard as if: OT, June 22, 2008.

36 Callaway gave him: Ibid.

36 Then Aundra Dixon got out: Ibid.

36 "He never was out": Ibid.

37 To finance the household: SFPD, Case No. 051013511.

37 Dixon's mother suffered: SFPD, Incident Report No. 060153990.

37 Dixon called police and reported: SFPD, Incident Report No. 050252013.

37 police in San Mateo County: *People v. Yusuf Ali Bey (IV) and Antoine A. Mackey,* ACSC, Case No. 160939-A/B, Trial Testimony of Devaughndre Broussard, Dept. 10, March 21, 2011.

37 someone anonymously reported child abuse: SFPD, Incident Report No. 051013511.

37 This time, Dixon returned: California Department of Corrections and Rehabilitation, Identification Information System, Inmate History, Aundra R. Dixon.

37 Broussard liked to tell people: *People v. Devaughndre Broussard,* ACSC, Case No. 157043, Proffer Statement. Hereinafter referred to as "Broussard Proffer."

38 "What you gonna do?": Ibid.

38 "Go back to the 'hood": Ibid.

38 "I know this dude": Ibid.

38 "What's happening, my brother?": Ibid.

38 "Them Muslims, they're militant": Ibid.

39 "Are y'all still hiring?": Ibid.

39 It was the Wednesday-night meeting: Ibid.

39 The doors to salvation: EBM, March 1995.

39 a stone-faced man told him: Broussard Proffer.

40 as if they were new recruits: Ibid.

40 "You want to see": Ibid.

40 and had walked into a boot camp: Ibid.

41 "You gotta know it's more": Ibid.

41 **credit ratings that would allow:** Ibid.

41 **"We from the 'hood":** Ibid.

41 **"I'm with them Muslims now":** "Bailey Killing Figure Had Troubled Youth," OT, June 22, 2009.

42 **an empty space in a dirty:** Broussard Proffer.

42 **"You know what I'm":** OT, June 22, 2009.

4. LOVE YE ONE ANOTHER

45 **From June 12, 1926, to May 27, 1929:** Federal Bureau of Investigation, files on Wallace Fard (containing San Quentin Prison and LAPD records). In November 2010, the FBI released files on Fard from the Detroit, Chicago, Los Angeles, Portland, and San Francisco field offices and the FBI national headquarters in response to a Freedon of Information Act request that heavily censored files first released on Fard in the 1980s and '90s be reviewed for reconsideration of censoring.

46 **It was Ford's third:** FBI files containg Fard's San Quentin Prison and LAPD records.

46 **Ford was five feet six inches:** Ibid.

46 **When his son was born:** Ibid.

46 **Six years later, Ford told:** Ibid.

46 **Ford completed a draft card:** Registration card no. 70, precinct 401, Los Angeles, California, June 5, 1917. United States, Selective Service System, World War I Selective Service System Draft Registration Cards 1917–1918. Washington, D.C.: National Archives and Records Administration. MI509, 4582 rolls. An electronic copy of the card was first provided to the author by the journalist and author Karl Evanzz.

46 **Ford identified his place:** Ibid.

47 **Ford also listed his birthday:** Ibid.

47 **Ali favored:** Juan Williams and Quinton Hosford Dixie, *This Far by Faith: Stories from the African-American Religious Experience* (New York: William Morrow, 2003).

47 **a member of the Ancient Egyptian Arabic Order:** Peter Lamborn Wilson, *Sacred Drift: Essays on the Margins of Islam* (San Francisco: City Light Books, 1993).

47 **"not strayed after the strange Gods":** Susan Nance, "Mystery of the Moorish Science Temple: Southern Blacks and American Alternative Spirituality in 1920s Chicago," *Religion and American Culture* 12, no. 2 (summer 2002): 123–66.

48 **Their true religion was not Christianity:** Ibid.

48 **Jesus was not God's son:** Wilson, *Sacred Drift*.

48 **"Go ahead. Getting Negroes to convert":** Keith Moore, *Moorish Circle 7: The Rise of the Islamic Faith Among Blacks in America and Its Masonic Origins* (Bloomington, IN: AuthorHouse, 2005).

48 Another Ali myth concerned the founding: Wilson, *Sacred Drift.*

49 Noble Drew Ali was born: Ibid.

49 Around 1912, Drew began: Nance, "Mystery of the Moorish Science Temple."

49 in 1913 in Newark: Wilson, *Sacred Drift.*

49 Dowling claimed that during: Ibid.

50 Drew plagiarized Dowling: Ibid.

50 He soon changed the name: Nance, "Mystery of the Moorish Science Temple."

51 By casting his story around Canaan: Ibid.

51 white Christians, especially antebellum Southerners: Stephen R. Haynes, *Noah's Curse: The Biblical Justification of American Slavery* (Oxford: Oxford University Press, 2007).

51 Africans were "wicked and depraved": Ibid.

51 Ali claimed the dilemma proved: Wilson, *Sacred Drift.*

51 "to Americanize the Oriental": Ibid.

52 "a thought of Allah": Ibid.

52 He began selling his flock: Ibid.

52 Ali ordered his followers: Nance, "Mystery of the Moorish Science Temple."

53 and sales of products like: Wilson, *Sacred Drift.*

53 As prophet, he deemed it: Ibid.

53 In 1929, a fourteen-year-old: "Cult Leader Lured Girls to His Harem," CD, March 23, 1929.

53 Sheik Claude Greene-Bey, had long: Wilson, *Sacred Drift.*

54 a janitor heard two shots: Ibid.

54 "hold on, keep the faith": Ibid.

55 It didn't take Ford long: Wilson, *Sacred Drift*; Karl Evanzz, *The Messenger: The Rise and Fall of Elijah Muhammad* (New York: Pantheon Books, 1999).

55 In a matter of days: Wilson, *Sacred Drift*; Evanzz, *The Messenger*; FBI file on Wallace Fard.

55 Ford-El made a move: Wilson, *Sacred Drift.*

55 A gun battle followed: Ibid.

5. THE FORCES OF HELL

57 a written directive the French military: "The Crisis," May 1919, *Documents of War,* collected by W. E. Burghardt DuBois. See also Tyler Stovall, *Paris Noir: African Americans in the City of Lights* (New York: Houghton Mifflin, 1996).

57 "The increasing number of Negroes": "The Crisis," *Documents of War.*

58 "on how they should conduct themselves": David Allan Levine, " 'Expecting the Barbarians': Race Relations and Social Control, Detroit, 1915–1925" (PhD diss., University of Chicago Department of History, 1970).

58 "America has to do a whole lot": Ibid.

58 "If one race [is] inferior": *Plessy v. Ferguson,* 163 U.S. 537 (1896), reprinted in Gloria J. Browne-Marshall, *Race, Law, and American Society: 1607 to Present* (New York: Routledge, Taylor & Francis Group, 2007).

59 "Justice Harlan: come get": Browne-Marshall, *Race, Law, and American Society.*

59 "decrees that it shall not": "The Crisis," *Documents of War,* May 1919.

59 So many Negroes left South Carolina: Levine, " 'Expecting the Barbarians.' "

59 "There's been lots of darkies": Ibid.

60 in Memphis, where its national edition: Arna Bontemps and Jack Conroy, *Anyplace but Here* (Columbia: University of Missouri Press, 1997).

60 "Please do write at once": Ibid.

60 "I have been here all my life": Ibid.

60 an agent in Cincinnati who prowled: Levine, " 'Expecting the Barbarians.' "

61 As the Model T became a national craze: Ibid.

62 "A corrupt orientalism": Ibid.

62 the Negro population of Detroit: Ibid.

62 "True friends of the Negro": *Dearborn Independent,* December 21, 1921.

63 Despite the organized recruiting: Levine, " 'Expecting the Barbarians.' "

63 The *Detroit News* called a plan: Levine, " 'Expecting the Barbarians.' "

64 frequent causes of Negro deaths: Jamie Hart, *African Americans, Health Care, and the Reproductive Freedom Movement in Detroit, 1918–1945* (Ann Arbor: University of Michigan, 1998).

64 Negroes found themselves in a factory's: Richard Walter Thomas, *From Peasant to Proletarian: The Formation and Organization of the Black Industrial Working Class in Detroit, 1915–1945* (Ann Arbor: University of Michigan, 1976).

65 the Detroit Urban League offered classes: Levine, " 'Expecting the Barbarians.' "

65 "Those damn Southern niggers": Ibid.

66 "The growth of the Ku Klux Klan": "Wizard in Vigorous Defense of Ku Klux," NYT, October 13, 1921.

66 "It has been charged": Ibid.

66 A man dressed as Santa Claus: Levine, " 'Expecting the Barbarians.' "

66 "Nigger! You are being watched": Ibid.

67 More than one hundred ten variations: Ibid.

67 His attempt to move: Ibid.

68 "Niggers! Niggers! Get the niggers": Ibid.

68 "Doctor," the chief of police asked: Ibid.

68 "Did the defendants shoot": Ibid.

70 "Is everything this man saw": Ibid.

70 "I am sick of this talk about an innocent": http://law2.umkc.edu/faculty/projects/ftrials/sweet/Darrowsumm1.html.

70 "I don't give a damn": Levine, " 'Expecting the Barbarians.' "

71 "I do not believe in the law": Clarence Darrow, Closing Argument, *People v.*

Ossian Sweet, available at http://law2.umkc.edu/faculty/projects/ftrials/sweet/Darrowsumm1.html.

72 **"Your part in the Sweet verdict":** Levine, "'Expecting the Barbarians.'"

72 **their one and true path away from misery:** Karl Evanzz, *The Messenger: The Rise and Fall of Elijah Muhammad* (New York: Pantheon Books, 1999).

6. I AM THE SUPREME RULER OF THE UNIVERSE

73 **Robert Harris would claim:** "Leader of Cult Admits Slaying at Home Altar," DFP, November 21, 1932.

73 **"The non-believer shall be stabbed":** Karl Evanzz, *The Messenger: The Rise and Fall of Elijah Muhammad* (New York: Pantheon Books, 1999).

73 **"Aliker alump," Harris yelled:** "Cult Leader Pleads Guilty," DN, November 25, 1932.

73 **Harris's children, Arsby, nine:** "Voodoo Slayer Admits Plotting Death of Judges," DFP, November 22, 1932.

74 **"My name is Karriem":** Ibid.

74 **"I told him I had been commanded":** Ibid.

75 **the butchering of a faith healer:** "Leader of Cult Admits Slaying at Home Altar," DFP, November 21, 1932.

75 **"Like this," Karriem said:** "500 Join March to Ask Voodoo King's Freedom," DFP, November 25, 1932.

75 **The Evangelista killings would remain:** "Voodoo Slayer Admits Plotting Death of Judges," DFP, November 22, 1932.

76 **A pamphlet entitled "The Secret Rituals":** Evanzz, *The Messenger.*

76 **The mayor, two judges:** "Leader of Cult Called Insane," DN, November 22, 1932.

76 **Wencel told his colleagues:** "Leader of Cult Admits Slaying at Home Altar," DFP, November 21, 1932.

77 **Miller's unbylined story:** Ibid.

77 **the assumption that Harris practiced voodoo:** A prominent University of Michigan sociologist, Erdmann Beynon, wrote the first scholarly article of Nation of Islam members in 1939 and, based largely on interviews with police, entitled it "The Voodoo Cult Among Negro Migrants in Detroit."

77 **he, too, had been attending:** "Leader of Cult Called Insane," DN, November 22, 1932.

78 **the "Negro lunatic":** "Negro Leaders Open Fight to Break Voodoo's Grip," DFP, November 24, 1932.

78 **The mayor said he looked:** "Marked for Death by Cult," DT, November 22, 1932.

79 **Gladys Smith was twenty-one:** Ibid.

79 "We sent the family to live": Ibid.

79 Ivey wrote to their relatives: "Leader of Cult Called Insane," DN, November 22, 1932.

80 " 'We are all Muslims now' ": "Marked for Death by Cult," DT, November 22, 1932.

80 "I can prove from records": Ibid.

80 "It's lucky for her": Ibid.

80 Ugan Ali demanded to see: "Raided Temple Bares Grip of Voodoo in City," DFP, November 23, 1932.

81 About fifty men sat in chairs: Ibid.

81 "The walls are covered": Ibid.

81 Yes, Ali was his teacher: Ibid.

82 In almost every answer: Ibid.

82 "He was just an ordinary member": "Negro Leaders Open Fight to Break Voodoo's Grip," DT, November 23, 1932.

82 "a hydra of jungle fanaticism": "Negro Leaders Open Fight to Break Voodoo's Grip," DFP, November 24, 1932.

83 "Asiatic trend among Negro dole recipients": " 'Asiatic' Trend of Negroes Is Cited," DT, November 22, 1932.

83 referred to Karriem repeatedly: "Harris, Cult Leader, Faces Court on Friday," DN, November 24, 1932.

83 Fard was a fakir: DN, November 24, 1932.

83 "I am Wallace Fard Muhammad": "Negro Leaders Open Fight to Break Voodoo's Grip," DFP, November 24, 1932.

84 "I am the supreme ruler": Ibid.

7. TRICKNOLOGY

85 The cops called for an ambulance: "Voodoo Killer Tries to Flee from Police," DT, November 23, 1932.

86 The small man, lean and olive-skinned: Karl Evanzz, *The Messenger: The Rise and Fall of Elijah Muhammad* (New York: Pantheon Books, 1999).

86 W. D. Fard from the Holy City: Ibid.

86 "After the meal he began to talk": Erdmann Doane Beynon, "The Voodoo Cult Among Negro Migrants in Detroit," *American Journal of Sociology* 43, no. 6 (May 1938): 894–907.

87 "We all wanted him": Ibid.

87 "headaches, chills, grippe, hay fever": Ibid.

87 "You were lost": Evanzz, *The Messenger.*

87 "My name is W. D. Fard": Ibid.

88 "The Bible tells you": Ibid.

88 "After I heard that sermon": Ibid.

89 "Why does the devil keep": Ibid.

89 "Me and my people": Ibid.

89 Studies later found: Ibid.

90 He also parroted the apocalyptic: William Maesen, "Watchtower Influences on Black Muslim Eschatology: An Exploratory Story," *Journal for the Scientific Study of Religion* 9, no. 4 (winter 1970): 321–25.

90 He also tapped a children's book: Evanzz, *The Messenger.*

90 Yakub took 59,999 Asiatics: Ibid.

91 "Slay four, stab them through": Ibid.

91 a smallish, light-skinned Georgian: Ibid.

91 he attended a Moorish Science Temple: Ibid.

91 "I know who you are": Steven Tsoukalas, *The Nation of Islam: Understanding the "Black Muslims"* (Phillipsburg, NJ: P & R, 2001).

92 "I recognized him": Ibid.

92 "the most powerful Black man": Ibid.

92 "He used to teach me": Evanzz, *The Messenger.*

92 he had witnessed the lynching: Ibid.

93 naming him "Supreme Minister": Ibid.

93 "The name 'Poole' was never": Elijah Muhammad, *Message to the Blackman in America* (Atlanta: Messenger Elijah Muhammad Propagation Society, 1965).

93 what he said was the Muslim name: Evanzz, *The Messenger.*

93 "My sweet savior": Federal Bureau of Investigation, file on W. D. Fard.

94 "Give the little babies milk": Evanzz, *The Messenger.*

95 Karriem appeared in court: "Harris, Cult Slayer, Faces Court Friday," DN, November 25, 1932.

95 "This whole business is": "Raided Temple Bares Grip of Voodoo in City," DFP, November 23, 1932.

95 "confined to the ignorant": "500 Join March to Ask Voodoo King's Freedom," DFP, November 25, 1932.

95 "Still digging out": Ibid.

95 "apparently not driven to his sinister": "Voodoo Chief Held Unfound," DFP, November 30, 1932.

95 "This voodooism is an extremely dangerous": "Pastors Decry Growth of Cult Practices Here," DFP, November 28, 1932.

96 But Fard's bond to Elijah: Evanzz, *The Messenger.*

96 "It was a racket": Claude Andrew Clegg, *An Original Man: The Life and Times of Elijah Muhammad* (New York: St. Martin's Press, 1997).

8. THERE WILL BE PLENTY OF BLOODSHED

97 **Authorities would search fruitlessly:** Karl Evanzz, *The Messenger: The Rise and Fall of Elijah Muhammad* (New York: Pantheon Books, 1999).

98 **showed that he possessed:** Taylor Branch, *Pillar of Fire: America in the King Years, 1963–1965* (New York: Simon & Schuster, 1998).

98 **"preach(es) a gospel of hate":** *The Hate That Hate Produced,* PBS, available at http://www.archive.org/details/PBSTheHateThatHateProduced.

98 **"The government of the United States":** Ibid.

98 **"Are there any good white people?":** Ibid.

99 **"isn't down in the ground":** Malcolm X and George Breitman, *Malcolm X Speaks: Selected Speeches and Statements* (New York: Grove Weidenfeld, 1965).

99 **"Anybody can sit":** Ibid.

99 **Men were required to join:** Evanzz, *The Messenger.*

99 **Elijah demanded that the government:** Ibid.

100 **Yet Elijah had made a pilgrimage:** Ibid.

100 **One American Muslim leader:** Edward E. Curtis IV, *Black Muslim Religion in the Nation of Islam, 1960–1975* (Chapel Hill: University of North Carolina Press, 2006).

100 **"The Muslim Cult of Islam":** Federal Bureau of Investigation, file on Wallace Fard.

100 **The FBI spent countless resources:** Ibid.

101 **"Black Muslim Founder Exposed as a White:"** LAHE, July 28, 1963.

101 **It began when two white patrolmen:** Branch, *Pillar of Fire.*

101 **Two other Muslims ran:** Ibid.

101 **Weese killed him:** Ibid.

101 **Inside the mosque:** Ibid.

102 **"We shot your brothers":** Ibid.

102 **moved one of his hands "menacingly":** Ibid.

102 **"I don't care what color":** Manning Marable, *Malcolm X, A Life of Reinvention* (New York: Viking, 2011).

102 **"There's already been one bloodbath":** Robert E. Terrill, *Malcolm X, Inventing Radical Judgment* (East Lansing: Michigan State University Press, 2004).

102 **"Every one of the Muslims":** Marable, *Malcolm X.*

102 **"We are not going out":** Terrill, *Malcolm X, Inventing Radical Judgment.*

103 **"It would have been more safe":** "L.A. Was Like Nazi Germany or Algiers," MS, June 1962.

103 **Malcolm claimed that God was responsible:** Terrill, *Malcolm X, Inventing Radical Judgment.*

104 **"L.A. frame-up trial":** "Say Los Angeles Grand Jury Bypasses Negroes," MS, August 31, 1963.

105 Q: "Couldn't you have apprehended": Ibid.

105 "As you may now know": Ibid.

106 In a speech at a race-relations: "Mayor Wants Black Press Muzzled, Backs Cops' Role," MS, August 15, 1962.

106 Every male member of every: Marable, *Malcolm X.*

9. YOU DON'T HATE PEOPLE ENOUGH

107 got his beautician's license in 1957: SBPD, Case No. 441911. (License application is included in police file.)

107 "They did top work": Ali Omar, interview with the author, March 4, 2008.

108 Joseph had served in the desegregated: Joseph H. Stephens's service records were lost in a 1973 fire at the National Personnel Records Center in St. Louis.

108 Someone brought a copy of *Muhammad Speaks:* "Reciting Some of the History of the Nation of Islam," FC, March 9, 2010.

109 Billy was discussing an article: Ibid.

109 "My mother told me": Ibid.

109 "We had never heard anything": Ibid.

110 "I declare to you that Allah": "Build Own Society," MS, August 9, 1964.

110 "Just why do you want": Ibid.

111 They raised the sign above Lee Street: Brenda Huey, *The Blackest Land, The Whitest People: Greenville, Texas* (Bloomington, IN: AuthorHouse, 2006).

111 Apologists claimed "the blackest land": Ibid.

111 in a part of Greenville all those: Ibid.

112 was born in Greenville on March 1: Texas Department of Vital Statistics, birth certificate no. 098284, Theron Hancil Stephens.

112 William, born in Georgia in 1840: 1910 U.S. Census, Justice Precinct 1, Hunt County, Texas, T623_1647; p. 2A: Enumeration District 118. Twelfth Census of the United States, 1900. Washington, D.C.: National Archives and Records Administration. T623, 1854 rolls.

112 The mob dragged Smith: Huey, *The Blackest Land.*

112 Then someone yelled, "Burn him": Ibid.

112 "Burning of the Negro Smith": Ibid.

112 the county sheriff said he doubted: Ibid.

113 Joseph, was born in Greenville: Alameda County recorded documents: death certificate no. 3200361000616, Yusuf Bey. Bey's death certificate identifies his place of birth.

113 "out of his cotton-pickin' mind": *True Solutions,* November 26, 2002.

114 Theron quickly found work: *Ruth Stephens v. (Theron) Hancil Stephens,* ACSC, Case No. 237350, complaint for divorce.

114 The local newspaper ran: Omar interview.

115 that he started making: Ibid.

115 Twice, Cadillacs registered to his mother: SBPD, Case No. 441911. Oxnard Police and Fire department reports on the car files are included in the SBPD file.

116 He and Billy were brothers-in-law: Ibid.

116 "must reap the punishment": Ibid.

116 "You better know what you want": Ibid.

117 "I guess you know": Ibid.

117 The gunman favored: Ibid.

118 "All indications are this was": Ibid.

118 "I wouldn't go up there": Ibid.

119 Other Muslims said it was: Ibid.

120 Billy became irate: Ibid.

120 "Stephens was advised": Ibid.

120 But it all kept coming back: Ibid.

120 "Mrs. Stephens would not answer": Ibid.

10. DETROIT OF THE WEST

125 The city's Black population had increased: Robert O. Self, *American Babylon: Race and the Struggle for Postwar Oakland* (Princeton, NJ: Princeton University Press, 2003).

125 "Detroit of the West": Ibid.

125 More than sixty thousand migrants: Ibid.

126 "members of the Caucasian race": Ibid.

126 "Oakland has the second largest": "Oakland Police Inquiry Hears Brutality Charge," SFC, January 6, 1950.

126 "that there is reasonable cause": California Assembly Interim Committee on Crime and Corrections, Report on the Oakland Police Department, April 1950.

126 their skin color made them targets: Ibid.

127 "Boy, you're lying": "Oakland Police Inquiry," SFC, January 7, 1950.

127 Patrolman Spencer Amundsen noticed Hines: "Civil Rights Prober Has One-Sided Testimony, Paves Way for Police Defense," OT, January 6, 1950.

128 "That's the boy. You help him": Interview with Geraldine Bowers McConnell, Earl Warren Oral History Project, Views and Episodes, Regional Oral History Office, University of California, Berkeley.

129 "There is no final answer": Gayle B. Montgomery and James W. Johnson, *One Step from the White House: The Rise and Fall of Senator William F. Knowland* (Berkeley: University of California Press, 1998).

129 **who saw Northern Negroes:** Robert A. Caro, *The Years of Lyndon Johnson: Master of the Senate* (New York: Alfred A. Knopf, 2002).

130 **"a city planner's version of the seventh":** "The Story of Oakland, California," *Ramparts,* February 1966.

130 **A full 47 percent of city residents:** Ibid.

130 **substantiated** *all forty-nine claims:* Ibid.

130 **"I come from Oakland, shitbox":** Ibid.

131 **"They thought we were rooty-poots":** Ali Omar, interview with the author, March 4, 2008.

131 **Joseph wore a little two-part mustache:** Bay Area Television Archive, J. Paul Leonard Library, San Francisco State University, http://www.library.sfsu.edu/about/collections/sfbatv/index.php.

131 **on Pine Street in West Oakland:** Omar interview.

132 **Billy and Joseph both competed:** "Bey's Second Wife Was a Confidant of Chauncey Bailey's," SFC, December 30, 2007.

132 **In the winter of 1971–72:** "Gang War Over Dope," OT, January 7, 1972.

132 **At 10:15 p.m. on November 14:** "Little Girl 'Executed' by Gunman," OT, November 15, 1971.

132 **a Muslim husband and wife:** "Man Slain, Wife Shot in Home," OT, January 4, 1972.

133 **the Stephens brothers each read:** Askia Muhammad, "Recipe for Mayhem in Your Black Muslim Bakery," op-ed, OT, August 16, 2007.

133 *This is how we will do things:* Ibid.

133 **money from mosques and associated businesses:** Karl Evanzz, *The Messenger: The Rise and Fall of Elijah Muhammad* (New York: Pantheon Books, 1999).

134 **run a mosque in Las Vegas:** Muhammad, "Recipe for Mayhem."

134 **the kind of vicious violence Elijah's enforcers:** Manning Marable, *Malcolm X, A Life of Reinvention* (New York: Viking, 2001).

135 **Bey needed to employ three:** KPIX, May 21, 1971. Available at J. Paul Leonard Library Bay Area Television Archive, San Francisco State University, http://www.library.sfsu.edu/about/collections/sfbatv/index.php.

135 **"We use natural products":** Ibid.

136 **in a two-story brick building:** Building Structure and Object Record No. 1533, 5826–38, San Pablo Ave., Oakland, California Natural Resources Agency, Department of Parks and Recreation.

136 **another, younger Black man:** Mark Cooley, interviews with the author, March 6 and April 13, 2011, Modesto, CA.

11. NO GOOD CAUSE SHALL LACK A CHAMPION

137 "Yo-u-u-u sk-sk-sk ip-ip-ip-ed one": Mark Cooley, interviews with the author, March 6 and April 13, 2011, Modesto, CA.

137 Cooley, was often in the backseat: Ibid.

137 Even as a youngster: Ibid.

139 Chauncey Wendell Bailey Jr. was born: Alameda County recorded documents: Certificate of Live Birth.

139 needed more space than they could find: Ibid.

139 "Down in Alabama": SFC, November 14, 1957.

139 that city's first African American residents: OT, September 13, 2002.

139 a cross had been burned: Ibid.

139 "Being young children we became friends": Lorelei Waqia, written remembrance prepared for the author, September 29, 2010.

140 long hours alone in the Hayward: Cooley interviews.

140 "If you don't like this": Robin Hardin, interviewed in Zachary Stauffer, *A Day Late in Oakland* (documentary film).

140 "No medication": Cooley interviews.

141 "Too long have others spoken": African-American Newspapers and Periodicals, Wisconsin State Historical Society, http://www.wisconsinhistory.org/libraryarchives/aanp/freedom/.

141 "The black tail": "Black Press Leader Makes History in Washington, D.C.," SFSR, March 16, 1974.

12. GENERATE A CAUSE FOR ARREST

142 The first victim was a young: "A Night of Murder, Two Women Slain," SFE, October 22, 1973. One victim was Quita Hauge, the other's slaying is unrelated.

142 dumped south of downtown: Ibid.

142 "You should have seen": *People v. Jesse Lee Cooks, Larry Craig Green, Manuel Moore, and J. C. X Simon,* Court of Appeal of the State of California, First Appellate District, Division Two, Case No. A010750, decision affirming convictions.

142 "break necks, punch out eyes": Ibid.

143 Cooks had started boasting: Ibid.

143 Cooks immediately joined Mosque 26: Ibid.

143 His pink shirt was blood soaked: "Rare Witness Pleases Both Sides at Zebra Trial," SFE, May 14, 1975.

144 Manney employed Green: "Peripheral Glimpse for Jury of Two More Zebra Murders," SFE, June 6, 1975.

144 Green kept a journal: *People v. Cooks.*

145 "Why does Muhammad or any Muslim": Ibid.

145 "Wallace D. (Fard) is making": "Zebra Jury Told of Muslim Changes," SFE, December 4, 1975.

145 kept a binder of papers: *People v. Cooks.*

145 Manuel Moore, another of the men: Ibid.

146 its leaders included Yusuf Bey: The author is sourced on Bey's involvement in the East Bay murders by current and former members of law enforcement familiar with investigations of the killings and intelligence gathered on Bey both before and after his death and identifying his North Oakland compound, and before that the Oakland mosque he helped to form, as a staging area for the series of slayings. It is not known if Bey directly committed any of the killings himself.

146 A run of seemingly random murders: "30 Victims of Cult in Eastbay," OT, May 2, 1974.

147 a woman with gruesome hack wounds: Ibid.

147 In Oakland and Berkeley, the shooters: Ibid.

147 The Black Muslim triggerman: Ibid.

147 "need for acceptance": California Board of Prison Terms, Transcript of Parole Consideration Hearing of Russell Lang, Avenal, CA, October 11, 2006.

147 It "was that strong": Ibid.

148 "It definitely was a racial crime": California Board of Prison Terms, Transcript of Parole Consideration. Hearing of Larry Pratt, Vacaville, CA. December 23, 2009.

148 On Friday, January 25, 1974: OT, January 26, 1974.

148 "generate a cause for arrest": "Muslim-Police Clash Trial Has Quiet End," OT, September 4, 1977.

149 One of the cops who approached the van: "Bail Is Reduced for Black Muslims," OT, January 30, 1974.

149 grabbed for Cooper's revolver: OT, February 1, 1974.

149 would later cite too many "gaps": Ibid.

150 Anyone of color "should be tired": "Muslim Off Critical List," SFE, January 28, 1974.

150 After Muhammad's meeting: Prentice Earl Sanders and Bennett Cohen, *The Zebra Murders: A Season of Killing, Racial Madness, and Civil Rights* (New York: Arcade, 2006).

150 The next day, Monday: "Defendant Changes His Zebra Story," SFE, November 3, 1975.

150 Over the next six hours: "Four More Street Killings, Toll Is 10 in Two Months," SFE, January 29, 1974.

151 The young man staggered: "Gunmen Slay Four in S.F.—Sacrifice Rites?" OT, January 29, 1974.

152 The next day, newspapers reported: "Blood Cult Hint in SF Murders," OT, January 30, 1974.

152 Privately, though, police leaked: Ibid.

152 "The chilling account, pieced together": "Huge Hunt for SF Killers, Report of 'Sect' Murders," SFC, January 30, 1974.

152 "Police said the victims": Ibid.

153 Among the men they stopped: "Blacks in Big Black Cars Fear Hassle on Streets," SFE, January 31, 1974.

153 "In light of recent events": Ibid.

153 "Charges of Police Harassment": "Charges of Police Harassment in Muslim Shooting Incident," SFSR, February 2, 1974.

154 The San Francisco killers didn't strike: "Another Senseless Street Killing," SFE, April 2, 1974.

154 "We're not going to stop": "Slugs Link Shootings in 'Zebra' Case," SFC, April 16, 1974.

154 Bailey made an astonishing revelation: "Operation Zebra: Huge Manhunt Yields No Arrests," SFSR, April 6, 1974.

155 *Sun Reporter* carried an unbylined story: "Cabbie Shot in Oakland," SFSR, April 13, 1974.

155 car he had parked nearby: *People v. George Foreman and Larry Williams*, ACSC, Case No. 57930-6A/B, written statement of Alameda County deputy district attorney Richard Conti.

155 "George Foreman is an extremely dangerous": Ibid.

156 San Francisco Police finally made arrests: "Seven Zebra Arrests! 'Death Angels' Cult," SFE, May 1, 1974.

156 A breathless front-page story: OT, May 2, 1974.

13. A BOY IN SEASIDE

158 The little girl cut her pinky: *Jane Does 1, 2, 3, et al., v. Yusuf Ali Bey, County of Alameda, et al.*, ACSC, Case No. RG0310536, Deposition of Jane Doe 2. Hereinafter referred to as "Jane Doe 2 Deposition."

158 But instead of school: Ibid.

159 She held her bloody pinky: Ibid.

159 "Brother Bey, Brother Bey": Ibid.

159 Bey began grinding against her: Ibid.

159 Afterward, Bey approached Nancy: *Jane Does 1, 2, 3, et al., v. Yusuf Ali Bey, County of Alameda, et al.*, ACSC, Case No. RG0310536, Deposition of Jane Doe 1. Hereinafter referred to as "Jane Doe 1 Deposition."

160 "You better not tell anyone": Ibid.

160 he wanted them to be molded: Ibid.

160 A family court judge approved: *Jane Does 1, 2, 3, et al. v. Yusuf Ali Bey, County of Alameda, et al.* Order Appointing Guardian, February 22, 1979, included in case file. The author has omitted from this note the names of the children listed in the order to protect their anonymity.

161 **For years, beginning as early:** Karl Evanzz, *The Messenger: The Rise and Fall of Elijah Muhammad* (New York: Pantheon Books, 1999).

161 **Elijah even suggested that:** Manning Marable, *Malcolm X, A Life of Reinvention* (New York: Viking, 2011).

162 **took control of the Nation:** Ibid.

162 **His father, Theron Stephens:** *People v. Theron Stephens,* ACSC, Case No. 37286, April 27, 1965. Report summary; see also transcript of preliminary hearing.

162 **he'd had sex hundreds of times:** Ibid.

162 **A man who rapes, beats, and humiliates:** Dr. Stephen M. Raffle, interview with the author, July 21, 2010, Kentfield, CA.

163 **He started raping her:** Jane Doe 1 Deposition.

163 **He broke her will through heinous:** Ibid. See also *People v. Yusuf Bey,* ACSC, Case No. 479904, and OPD Incident Report No. 02-058831, June 20, 2002, Follow-up Investigation Report, J. Salada.

163 **Rather, Alice was Bey's enabler:** Jane Doe 1 Deposition.

163 **"He doesn't do anything":** Ibid.

165 **When he returned to Oakland:** OT and CBP, April 9, 2008.

165 **"Brother Bey! What are you doing?":** Ibid.

165 **"I couldn't believe what":** Ibid.

166 **He'd been shot in the head:** ACSO, Coroner's Report No. 86-1316.

166 **Vincent called a social worker:** *Jane Does 1, 2, 3, et al. v. Yusuf Ali Bey, County of Alameda, et al.*

166 **The social worker went to the compound:** Ibid.

166 **"The children appeared to be healthy":** Ibid.

167 **Nancy became pregnant first:** Jane Doe 1 Deposition.

167 *You better say a boy:* Ibid.

167 **No paternity was identified:** Alameda County, CA, recorded documents: birth certificate no. 6005-1668. The author has omitted the name of the child from the title of the document to protect the anonymity of the mother as a rape and abuse victim.

168 **the investigating social worker had called:** Jane Doe 1 Deposition.

168 *A boy in Seaside,* **Nancy replied:** Ibid.

169 **Nancy had her second baby:** Jane Doe 1 and 2 Depositions.

169 **"Daddy didn't do half":** ACSO, recorded jail phone call 3CIU19MG, March 12, 2008.

169 **"Slaves, we were just slaves":** Jane Doe 1 Deposition.

169 **"Ninety-nine percent of black folks":** *True Solutions,* November 19, 2002.

169 **"You can't put no price on slavery":** Ibid.

170 **"Mr. Bey gave me instructions":** *Jane Does 1, 2, 3, et al. v. Yusuf Ali Bey, County of Alameda, et al.,* deposition of woman identified in the text as "Alice."

170 **"It is the will of Allah":** Jane Doe 1 Deposition.

170 **Their mother was white:** Ibid.

171 "I have foster kids": Ibid.

171 "People who was there": Ibid.

14. TOTALLY LUDICROUS

172 On February 15, 1994: "Two More Candidates Join Mayoral Contest," OT, February 16, 1994.

173 "If people want change": Ibid.

173 "We don't even have one": "Bey Calls for Basic Changes," OT, June 6, 1994.

174 "They have no concern for us": Ibid.

174 "If you're not in the soup": "Fur Flying in Race for Mayor," OT, May 29, 1994.

174 "Quite a few," Bey replied: "Stormy Oakland Election Ahead, Broadcaster Has Contentious Views," SJMN, February 24, 1994.

174 Shortly after he announced: "The Sinister Side of Yusuf Bey's Empire," EBX, November 13, 2002.

174 Abaz Bey heated a butter knife: Ibid.

174 One Muslim yelled he would gladly: Ibid.

175 "This is money that could": "Candidate Set to Post Bail for 'Adopted Sons,'" OT, March 10, 1994.

175 Mohammed even destroyed the Nation's historical: Manning Marable, *Malcolm X, A Life of Reinvention* (New York: Viking, 2011).

176 "went in there to Germany": "Divided by a Diatribe: College Speech Ignites Furor Over Race," NYT, December 29, 1993.

176 "Kill the women . . . kill the children . . .": Ibid.

176 saying he took issue: "Farrakhan Repudiates Speech for Tone, Not for Anti-Semitism," NYT, February 4, 1994.

176 he booked Muhammad for a rally: "Controversial Muslim Leader Coming to Town," OT, April 15, 1994.

178 "Our babies are used to seeing": "Thousands Hear Khalid Muhammad," OP, May 18, 1994.

178 "You don't need": Ibid.

178 "Mr. Rabbi, when you challenge us": Ibid.

178 "positive and very informative": "Candidate Bey Slams 'Hypocrites,'" OT, May 15, 1994.

179 "They live in glass houses": Ibid.

179 On September 1, 1994: "Son, 21, Slain Over 'Nothing,' Bey Says," OT, September 2, 1994.

180 He was high on cocaine: ACSO, Coroner's Report No. 9402235.

180 **"One of you motherfuckers knows"**: "The Sinister Side of Yusuf Bey's Empire," EBX, November 13, 2002.

180 **"a loving warrior"**: "Yusuf Bey's Son Mourned at Rites," OT, September 9, 1994.

180 **"a little street thug"**: "The Sinister Side of Yusuf Bey's Empire," EBX, November 13, 2002.

180 **Akbar's tattoos included:** ACSO, Coroner's Report No. 9402235.

181 **Among those who helped him:** "Politicians Bowed to Bey; Bakery Founder Was a Formidable Presence on Oakland's Rough Streets, and Local Leaders Paid Him Respect," SFC, January 27, 2008.

181 **That there were enough questions:** OT and CBP, December 31, 2007, "How Oakland's $1 Million Loan Vanished into Bakery's Sham Firm"; January 1, 2008, "E.M. Heath Attempts to Borrow Away Debt"; January 2, 2008, "Political, Racial Pressure Pays Off for Bakery."

181 **The Beys—particularly Nadar Bey:** Ibid.

15. AN INSTRUMENT OF COMMUNITY UNDERSTANDING

183 **Bey had raped one of his own:** *Jane Does 1, 2, 3, et al. v. Yusuf Ali Bey, County of Alameda, et al.,* ACSC, Case No. RG0310536, Deposition of Jane Doe 1. Hereinafter referred to as "Jane Doe 1 Deposition."

185 **"Few Black Detroiters Shop Black"**: "Few Black Detroiters Shop Black," DN, October 28, 1981.

185 **"Have a newspaper. Read the newspaper"**: Lorelei Waqia, interview with the author, April 22, 2010, Oakland, CA.

185 **There was at least one newsroom fight:** "Slain Journalist's Decades-Long Career in News Spanned Globe," OT, August 3, 2007.

185 **"I don't think 'abrasive' is a bad word"**: Mark Cooley, interview with the author, March 6, 2010, Modesto, CA.

185 **"You don't like black reporters"**: "In Detroit, Some Note Absences at Bailey Service," http://www.chaunceybaileyproject.org/2007/08/17/in-detroit-some-note-absences-at-bailey-service/, August 17, 2007.

186 **"We didn't listen to music"**: Zachary Stauffer, *A Day Late in Oakland* (documentary film).

186 **he volunteered to create a weekly:** Ibid.

187 **His coffin was laid on a caisson:** "Elaborate Funeral for Mobster," AP, August 29, 1986.

187 **The son of parents who had emigrated:** Maynard Institute, "Robert C. Maynard: Life and Legacy," http://mije.org/robertmaynard.

187 **"an instrument of community understanding"**: Ibid.

188 making him the first African American: Ibid.

188 "This country cannot be the country": Ibid.

189 The more well known he became: Martin G. Reynolds, interview with the author, May 5, 2010, Oakland, CA.

16. THE EVIL OLD MAN IS DEAD

191 Nancy knew there was something: *Jane Does 1, 2, 3, et al. v. Yusuf Ali Bey, County of Alameda, et al.*, ACSC, Case No. RG0310536, Deposition of Jane Doe 1. Hereinafter referred to as "Jane Doe 1 Deposition."

191 Yusuf Bey was still raping: Ibid.

192 when her daughter was eighteen: Ibid.

192 On June 2, 2002: OPD, Case No. 02-058831, investigative follow-up report.

192 He took the case and bore: Ibid.

192 Over the course of several interviews: Ibid.

193 But Bey also had AIDS: The author's source is a person with definitive knowledge of Bey's HIV status who asked not to be identified.

193 Bey dodged giving the DNA sample: OPD, Case No. 02-058831, investigative follow-up report.

193 Finally the tension eased: OPD, Case No. 02-058831, investigative follow-up report.

193 On September 20, 2002, Yusuf Bey surrendered: "Court Date for Muslim Leader; Oakland Businessman Faces Sex Charges," SFC, September 21, 2002.

194 "You only scratched the surface": OPD, Case No. 02-058831, investigative follow-up report.

194 More women called and said: Ibid.

194 Then the crowd began to applaud: Martin G. Reynolds, interview with the author, May 5, 2010, Oakland, CA; see also OT, September 22, 2002.

194 caused women's groups to aggressively rebuke: OT, October 15, 2002.

195 his bail increased from fifty thousand: OT, July 15, 2003.

195 "I didn't do it": OPD, Case No. 02-058831, June 20, 2002.

195 "I want you to understand": "Bakery Leader Defiant in Sermons After Arrest," SFC, December 23, 2007.

196 Chuck Johnson, yielded to Bey's demands: "How Official Oakland Kept the Bey Empire Going," EBX, November 20, 2002.

196 Bailey confided to the *East Bay Express*'s: Zachary Stauffer, *A Day Late in Oakland* (documentary film), trailer. Also "The Killing of a Journalist," VV, August 3, 2007.

196 "Mr. media man . . . you seem": Ibid.

197 the diseases ravaging his body: OT, July 15, 2003.

197 Bey died on September 30, 2003: Alameda County recorded documents: death certificate no. 3200361000616, Yusuf Bey.

198 Jane, Nancy, and others had sued him: *Jane Does 1, 2, 3, et al. v. Yusuf Ali Bey, County of Alameda, et al.,* ACSC, Case No. RG03105036.

198 "The evil old man is dead": "Even in His Death Yusuf Bey Is Lionized as an Elder Statesmen Rather Than Branded as a Thug," EBX, October 8, 2003.

17. WE HAVE ENEMIES

201 a man who managed the bakery's: OT, March 19, 2004.

201 "We have enemies": "Dignity, Diligence, Scandal,"LAT, December 30, 2003.

202 Waajid was raised a Pentecostal: "Muslim Bakery Leader Confirmed Dead," OT, August 14, 2004.

202 "I get the opportunity to work": "Aljawwaad's Brief Reign as Bakery CEO Ended in Tragedy," CBP, September 8, 2008.

203 The next day, bakery members reported: OT, March 19, 2004.

204 a document that stated the directors: *Your Black Muslim Bakery, Inc., debtor,* USBCNDC, Case No. 06-41991. The document that stated directors appointed Antar Bey president is included in the file.

204 when Farieda Bey, Yusuf Bey's legal wife: *Farieda Bey v. Antar Bey, Your Black Muslim Bakery, et al.,* ACSC, Case No. RG04165951, July 16, 2004.

205 He even commissioned an artist: The painting was recovered after the YBMB building was sold in 2007.

205 Soon after Waajid disappeared: USBCNDC, Case No. 06-41991.

206 But whoever killed Waajid Aljawwaad: "Muslim Bakery Leader Confirmed Dead," OT, July 21, 2004.

206 Given the body's decay: Ibid.

206 a cut just above where his right eye: Ibid.

207 John Bey left his Montclair home: "John Muhammad Bey," CBP, June 19, 2008.

207 as soon as he recovered: Ibid.

207 Jane and Nancy had sued Yusuf Bey's estate: *Jane Does 1, 2, 3, et al. v. Yusuf Ali Bey, County of Alameda, et al.,* ACSC, Case No. RG03105036.

208 As summer faded into autumn: *People v. Alfonza Alvon Phillips,* Court of Appeal of the State of California, First Appellate District, Case No. A120183.

208 It sounded to her like it was Fourth: Ibid.

208 On the night of October 25, 2005: OPD, Case No. 05-067098.

208 Alfonza Phillips was a small man: *People v. Phillips.*

209 people stopped at a traffic light: OPD, Case No. 05-067098.

209 One witness would say he entered: Ibid.

18. A SWARM OF MUSLIMS

210 Antar was one of five men: "Police Seek Motive in Bey Killing; Officers Say It Was Attempted Carjacking or an Assassination," SFC, October 27, 2005.

210 where only about one: "Understaffed Oakland Department Behind Other Cities in Solving Homicides," OT, CBP, December 28, 2008.

211 Some homicide detectives put in: Public Employee Salaries, *San Jose Mercury News,* http://www.mercurynews.com/salaries/bay-area.

211 "Having these rights in mind": ACSC, Case No. 531971, Preliminary Hearing Transcript.

211 Sometimes, when he wore: *Derwin Longmire v. City of Oakland, Howard Jordan, Sean Whent, et al.,* USDCNDC, Case No. C 10-01465 JSW, Deposition of Derwin Longmire. Hereinafter referred to as "Longmire Deposition."

211 Longmire began going to the bakery: Sergeant Derwin Longmire, Predisciplinary Response, OPD. Hereinafter referred to as "Longmire Disciplinary Response."

211 a little nervous, thinking "shit": Ibid.

212 walking into dark places: Ibid.

212 one constantly building a network: Ibid.

212 "Where [Oakland Police] have fallen": Ibid.

212 Keeping detailed case files: Longmire Deposition; *Derwin Longmire v. City of Oakland, Howard Jordan, Sean Whent, et al.,* USDCNDC, Case No. C 10-01465 JSW, Deposition of Ersie Joyner (hereinafter referred to as "Joyner Deposition"); *People v. Yusuf Ali Bey IV and Antoine A. Mackey,* ACSC, Case No. 160939-A/B, Trial Testimony of Derwin Longmire, Dept. 10, May 3, 2011.

212 he was among the best interrogators: Joyner Deposition.

213 He was obsessed with guns: *People v. Bey and Mackey.*

213 Tammy took cash from the bakery: ACSO, recorded jail phone call 890820AW, August 9, 2007.

214 a phone call from one of his: *People v. Alfonza Alvon Phillips,* Court of Appeal of the State of California, First Appellate District, Case No. A120183.

214 "I shot the Muslim": Ibid.

214 He got his grand: Ibid.

215 she would later claim: "Police Interview Tapes Under Scrutiny in Antar Bey Trial," OT, October 30, 2007.

215 "I haven't slapped a young Black": Ibid.

215 "a swarm of Muslims": Ibid.

215 The thought of Bey soldiers: Ibid.

215 Althea would testify that: Ibid.

215 Police charged Phillips with Antar's murder: *People v. Phillips.*

216 It was Fourth: The author is informed here by a person with direct knowledge of the circumstances regarding Phillips's motive in shooting Antar Bey. Yusuf Bey IV's involvement in Antar Bey's murder is also articulated in Alfonza Phillips's appeal of his murder conviction (in *People v. Phillips*), although Phillips, in this appeal, continued to deny shooting Antar Bey. The appeal was denied.

217 **A short while later, they marched:** *People v. Yusuf Ali Bey (IV), Demetrius Harvey, Donald Cunningham, Dyamen Namer Williams, Jamall Robinson, Ajuwon Muhammad, Kahlil Ali Raheem, Tamon Oshun Halfin, James Watts,* ACSC, Case No. 514516A/B/C/D/E/F, Preliminary Hearing Transcript.

217 **Cunningham wore a dark fedora:** Surveillance video of the attack on New York Market charged in *People v. Bey, Harvey, Cunningham, et al.* was played during the trial in *People v. Bey and Mackey.*

217 **As he did, one of them waved:** Ibid.

218 **allowing them to take the issue:** Ibid.

218 **A few blocks away, the men hit:** Ibid.

219 **it was on the news all over:** KTVU, November 25, 2005.

219 **She'd just lost Antar:** OPD, Case No. 05-075886/05-075887.

219 **Sergeant Longmire had made a strong impact:** Longmire Deposition.

220 **Deputy Police Chief Howard Jordan:** Ibid.

220 **some cops secretly harbored the belief:** Ibid.

220 *Nothing,* **Arotzarena snapped:** OPD, Case No. 05-075886/05-075887, investigative follow-up report.

220 **"I received a call from Sgt. D. Longmire":** Ibid.

221 **"I met with DC Jordan":** Ibid.

221 **Then, at 11:25 a.m.:** Ibid.

222 **"In the Black community":** KTVU, December 2, 2005.

19. I GOT HELLA FLAWS

223 **said he was the cousin:** *People v. Devaughndre Broussard,* ACSC, Case No. 531971, Proffer Statement. Hereinafter referred to as "Broussard Proffer."

223 **He wouldn't even take a Muslim name:** Ibid.

223 **entitled "The Twenty-four Rules":** *People v. Yusuf Ali Bey (IV) and Antoine A. Mackey,* ACSC, Case No. 160939-A/B, Closing Argument of Deputy Alameda County District Attorney Melissa Krum, Dept. 10, May 19, 2011.

224 **Lewis had helped rob:** *People v. Richard Lewis and Chad Dias,* SFSC, Case No. 2207628.

224 **The kid had immediately lunged:** Broussard Proffer.

224 **"the credit hookup":** Ibid.

224 **"Fuck the white man":** A person who lived in the neighborhood of the bakery described Bey as saying this in the 1990s. The person, like others the author interviewed in North Oakland, asked not to be identified.

225 **He thought of Muslims:** Ibid.

225 **"It's a cause":** Ibid.

225 **"I got hella flaws":** *People v. Yusuf Ali Bey (IV) and Antoine A. Mackey,* ACSC, Case No. 160939-A/B, Testimony of Devaughndre Broussard, Dept. 10, April 4, 2011. Hereinafter referred to as "Broussard Testimony."

225 **Broussard considered his San Francisco probation:** Ibid.

226 **As an adolescent:** *People v. Richard Lewis,* ACSC, Case No. 549951D, Testimony of Yusuf Bey V, Dept. 10, March 22, 2010. Hereinafter referred to as "Bey V Testimony."

226 **his mother let Joshua make:** *People v. Richard Lewis,* ACSC, Case No. 549951D, Testimony of Joshua Bey, Dept. 10, March 17, 2010. Hereinafter referred to as "Joshua Bey Testimony."

226 **He wore gold caps and grills:** Ibid.

227 **the bread wasn't even wrapped right:** Bey V Testimony.

227 **stopping when he stopped:** This observation was made by prosecutor Melissa Krum during the trial of *People v. Bey and Mackey.*

227 **The spoils included a used 2002 Mercedes:** "Judge Rules Fraud Evidence OK in Bey Murder Trial," OT, December 17, 2010.

227 **he used another forged driver's license:** "Bey IV's Rap Sheet Spans Range of Criminal Charges," CBP, October 19, 2007.

228 **Using stolen notary stamps:** "Bailey Suspects, Associates Left Behind $6 Million Trail of Bad Loans," OT, August 2, 2009.

228 **Finally, Broussard got in his face:** Broussard Proffer.

228 **"Take me to the side":** Ibid.

228 **"feel the brotherly love":** *People v. Broussard* trial testimony.

229 **Broussard's relief didn't arrive:** Broussard Proffer.

229 **At one assignment, Broussard:** Ibid.

230 **"Anybody who fucks up":** Ibid.

20. THE GANG THAT COULDN'T SHOOT STRAIGHT

231 **Your Black Muslim Bakery filed for Chapter 11:** *Your Black Muslim Bakery, Inc., debtor,* USBCNDC, Case No. 06-41991.

231 **With the creditors' collection attempts:** Ibid.

232 **Weapons were all around:** OPD, Case Nos. 07-059842 and 07-053064, recorded statements of victim of car shooting.

232 **Richard Lewis had beaten:** SFC, May 3, 2007.

233 **he was interested in one of Johnny's:** ACSO, recorded jail phone call 1J1S10AD, January 19, 2008.

233 **He had recently suffered:** *People v. Yusuf Ali Bey (IV) and Antoine A. Mackey,*

ACSC, Case No. 160939-A/B, Testimony of Johnny Antone, Dept. 10, April 13, 2011.

233 **Fifth would eventually testify:** *People v. Richard Lewis,* ACSC, Case No. 549951D, Testimony of Yusuf Bey V, Dept. 10, March 22, 2010. Hereinafter referred to as "Bey V Testimony."

233 **On the night of May 17, 2007:** Ibid.

233 **Fourth then found Fifth and Lewis:** Ibid.

234 **JoAnne had reason to worry:** *People v. Richard Lewis,* ACSC, Case No. 549951D, Testimony of kidnapping and torture victim referred to as "JoAnne," Dept. 10, March 9, 2010. Hereinafter referred to as "Lewis Victim Testimony."

234 **but she hadn't gotten a clean look:** Ibid.

235 **"Where the fuck's Tim":** Ibid.

235 **it had a long, curved blade:** *People v. Richard Lewis,* ACSC, Case No. 549951D, Testimony of Joshua Bey, Dept. 10, March 17, 2010. Hereinafter referred to as "Joshua Bey Testimony."

235 **he was going to shove:** Lewis Victim Testimony.

236 **Back out in the street:** Ibid.

236 **"a real police car":** Ibid.

237 **Fourth would admonish Halfin:** *People v. Yusuf Ali Bey IV, Tamon Oshun Halfin, Joshua Bey, Yusuf Bey V, and Richard Lewis,* ACSC, Case No. 531990A-E, video of Bey IV, Joshua Bey, and Halfin talking in jail cell.

237 **Joshua, in his panicked flight:** Joshua Bey Testimony.

237 **a judge would give them:** *People v. Richard Lewis,* ACSC, Case No. 549951D, Dept. 10, December 10, 2010, remark of Superior Court Judge Thomas Reardon during sentencing.

21. CRAZY-ASS HITTERS

238 **On May 11, 2007, a San Francisco cop:** *People v. Devaughndre Broussard,* SFSC, Case No. 2242731, supplemental report, performance on probation.

238 **he saw a black Charger crawling:** *People v. Devaughndre Broussard,* ACSC, Case No. 531971, Proffer Statement. Hereinafter referred to as "Broussard Proffer."

239 **"Don't trip," Lewis replied:** Ibid.

239 **Fourth told Broussard that the doors:** Ibid.

239 **He would try the bakery:** Ibid.

240 **"You can put a bowtie on a pig":** The author found the article containing this quote in the SFSC files on the Zebra murders (*People v. Jesse Lee Cooks, Larry Craig Green, Manuel Moore, and J. C. X Simon,* SFSC, Case No. 88244-01). The headline is "Islam's Unpredictable Fringe." The story is undated and lacks the name of the publication and author. The story mentions that the Zebra trial is ongoing, and a small

portion of a United Press International story on the same page identified Gerald Ford as U.S. president, meaning the story ran sometime after August 9, 1974.

240 **San Francisco police suspected Mackey:** "Viciousness Marks Mackey's History," OT, April 30, 2009.

240 **He became a registered sex offender:** *Antoine Arlus Mackey, through his mother and natural guardian, v. City and County of San Francisco, et al.,* SFSC, Case No. 421-900, Deposition of Antoine Mackey, January 13, 2005.

240 **"I just feel crazy":** Ibid.

241 **"thick as thieves":** *People v. Broussard* trial testimony.

241 **Fourth called them his:** *People v. Yusuf Ali Bey IV, Tamon Oshun Halfin, Joshua Bey, Yusuf Bey V, and Richard Lewis,* ACSC, Case No. 531990A-E, video of Bey IV, Joshua Bey, and Halfin talking in a jail cell.

241 **why, Broussard wondered:** Broussard Proffer.

242 **Broussard wondered, what good:** Ibid.

242 **"Do you know who":** Ibid.

242 **"And he's just like walkin' around?":** Ibid.

243 **At midnight on July 6:** Ibid.

243 *Might as well get this done*: Ibid.

244 **"Guess what? I got this":** Ibid.

244 **Others hit his face:** ACSO, Coroner's Report No. 2007-01971.

22. WE SHOULD NOT BECOME THE EVIL THAT WE DEPLORE

245 **They began to push to convert:** *Your Black Muslim Bakery, Inc., debtor,* US-BCNDC, Case No. 06-41991, Motion to Convert.

246 **The man who still pushed:** ACDAO, Case No. 157043.

246 **Saleem Bey had been born:** ACSO, Concealed Weapon Initial Application, Ali Saleem Bey, September 29, 2005.

246 **applied for a concealed-weapon:** Ibid.

246 **they told him it seemed:** ACDAO, Case No. 157043.

248 **"Run Ron, run":** "Dellums May Face Big Reality Check," SFC, October 9, 2005.

248 **Dellums had also once tried:** "2 Muslims in Court Row," OT, May 11, 1972.

249 **"I am writing":** ACDAO, Case No. 157043.

249 **"spiral out of control":** "Congress Approves $40 Billion Anti-Terror Package; Senate Endorses Use of Force Against Terrorists," AP, September 14, 2001.

249 **"One of the clergy members said":** "Uphill Bid to Oust Lone Dissenter," LAT, December 2, 2001.

250 **"always advocating on behalf of poor people":** "Storm Greets Lone Dissenter in Vote to Broaden Bush's Powers," LAT, September 18, 2001.

250 **On July 11, 2007, Fourth:** ACDAO, Case No. 157043.

250 **He had known Lee's director:** *People vs. Yusuf Ali Bey (IV) and Antoine A. Mackey,* ACSC, Case No. 160939-A/B, Testimony of Leslie Littleton, Dept. 10, April 26, 2011. Hereinafter referred to as "Littleton Testimony."

251 **to talk with her and Lee's:** Ibid.

251 **"I am well acquainted":** ACDAO, Case No. 157043. A copy of the letter is included in the file.

251 **"It's a pretty standard letter":** Littleton Testimony.

23. CONVENIENT BUT NOT TRUE

253 **Broussard knew the difference:** *People v. Devaughndre Broussard,* ACSC, Case No. 531971, Proffer Statement. Hereinafter referred to as "Broussard Proffer."

253 **"Open the back gate":** Ibid.

253 **It was 3:12 a.m. on July 12:** ACDAO, Case No. 157043.

253 **Broussard watched as Mackey and Fourth:** Broussard Proffer.

254 **"I knocked one down":** *People v. Yusuf Ali Bey (IV) and Antoine A. Mackey,* ACSC, Case No. 160939-A/B, Testimony of Devaughndre Broussard, Dept. 10, April 4, 2011. Hereinafter referred to as "Broussard Testimony."

254 **"Go see for yourself":** Ibid.

254 **a thirty-six-year-old sous-chef:** "Michael J. Wills Jr., a Short Biography of Wills," CBP, June 19, 2008.

254 **been giving Mackey lessons:** Broussard Proffer.

255 **tore into his upper back:** *People v. Yusuf Ali Bey (IV) and Antoine A. Mackey,* ACSC, Case No. 160939-A/B, Testimony of Dr. Thomas Rogers, Dept. 10, April 21, 2011.

255 **the cartoon character Elmer Fudd:** Broussard Proffer.

255 **"It's good!":** Ibid.

256 **They had to be responsible:** OPD, Case Nos. 07-053064 and 07-054096.

256 **Fourth had ordered the retaliatory destruction:** Ibid.

256 **"the guys from the bakery":** Ibid.

257 **they seemed taken aback:** *People v. Richard Lewis,* ACSC, Case No. 549951D, Testimony of Frank Gyson, Dept. 10, March 4, 2010.

257 **thanks largely to Joshua's dropped cell phone:** OPD, Case No. 07-039206.

258 **were investigating more than 1,200:** "Did Cops Drag Feet in Bakery Probe?" OT, October 11, 2007.

258 **"We watched hella Mafia movies":** Broussard Proffer.

258 **I whacked one, I smacked one:** Ibid.

258 **"We got a devil":** Ibid.

259 **"until they got greedy":** Ibid.

259 **"in that little box":** OPD, Case No. 07-059842, recorded statement of person referred to in the text as Cheryl Davis.

259 **Larry Green, Manuel Moore, J. C. Simon:** California Board of Prison Terms, Parole Consideration Hearing of Larry Green, Vacaville, CA, September 11, 2009; California Board of Prison Terms, Parole Consideration Hearing of Manuel Moore, Blythe, CA, January 24, 2010; California Board of Prison Terms, Parole Consideration Hearing of J. C. X Simon, Vacaville, CA, November 11, 2007; California Board of Prison Terms, Parole Consideration Hearing of Jesse Cooks, San Diego, CA, April 26, 2011.

259 **"The doctrine of the Nation of Islam":** California Board of Prison Terms, Parole Consideration Hearing of Larry Green.

24. HIGHLY QUESTIONABLE CIRCUMSTANCES

262 **he somehow agreed to try:** "Black Media War: Tribune Reporter Hopes to Start a Station to Compete with Oakland's Soul Beat," EBX, November 12, 2003.

262 **He gave Johnson a $15,000:** Ibid.

262 **Bailey then began his evening newscast:** Ibid.

262 **But Bailey wasn't finished:** Ibid.

262 **What Bailey did "wasn't ethical":** Ibid.

263 **But the extra work:** Alameda County recorded documents: federal lien tax no. 454488608. The lien shows that Bailey was nearly $15,000 in debt to the IRS at the time of his death.

263 **Bailey had sold his 1974 Mercedes-Benz:** California Department of Motor Vehicles, Report on Investigation No. 03B20345, Chauncey Wendell Bailey.

263 **Instead, he took out his frustration:** Ibid.

264 **A handwriting expert determined:** Ibid.

264 **He called a DMV media-relations officer:** Ibid.

264 **"extraordinary and disturbing interaction":** Ibid.

264 **He'd broken the deal:** Martin G. Reynolds, interview with the author, May 5, 2010, Oakland, CA.

265 **"He's a known journalist":** "Ex-*Tribune* Writer to Lead *Oakland Post*," OT, June 16, 2007.

265 **The litigation, he claimed:** "Ink-Stained Hell; San Francisco DA Puts Oakland Publisher on the Hook for His Predecessor's Dumping in Hunter's Point," EBX, February 7, 2007.

266 **As the summer of 2007 dawned:** ACDAO, Case No. 157043.

25. ARE THESE DANGEROUS PEOPLE?

268 **"Anybody out to get Your Black Muslim Bakery":** "Sermons Exhorted Bakery 'Soldiers' to Act," SFC, January 29, 2008.

268 **He'd broken the rules:** *People v. Richard Lewis,* ACSC, Case No. 549951D, Testimony of Richard Lewis, Dept. 10, March 29, 2010.

269 **"There should be no reason":** "Sermons Exhorted Bakery 'Soldiers' to Act," SFC, January 29, 2008.

269 **"How in the hell can you":** Ibid.

270 **Farieda Bey, his father's legal wife:** Ibid.

270 **She thought seriously about telling:** ACDAO, Case No. 157043.

270 **It had to end:** Ibid.

271 **Saleem told Bailey was that he couldn't:** Ibid.

271 **They even discussed whether Bailey:** Ibid.

272 **Bailey also believed deeply:** Mark Cooley, interviews with the author, March 6 and April 13, 2010, Modesto, CA.

273 **Just as they did, in walked a woman:** *People v. Yusuf Ali Bey (IV) and Antoine A. Mackey,* ACSC, Case No. 160939-A/B, Testimony of Ali Saleem Bey, Dept. 10, April 10, 2011. Hereinafter referred to as "Saleem Bey Testimony."

273 **He quickly concocted a cover story:** Ibid.

274 **After Saleem left, Bailey told Yahuda:** ACDAO, Case No. 157043. Yahuda has vehemently denied telling anyone at the bakery that Bailey was working on a story about it and Bey IV. "Chauncey told a lot of people he was working on a story about the bakery," she told *San Francisco Chronicle* religion writer Matthai Kuruvila in 2007. "There's no way in the world I'd want to harm him." She claimed in that interview, the only one she has given about Bailey's killing, that he had told other people at a Black business expo in Oakland a few months earlier that he was working on a story about the bakery, but she could not recall who those people were.

274 **word had already reached his wife:** Saleem Bey Testimony.

274 **Saleem panicked and phoned Bailey:** "Bey's Second Wife Was Confidant of Chauncey Bailey's," SFC, December 30, 2007.

274 **"These dudes are killers":** Ibid.

274 **"Keep my name out of your mouth":** Ibid.

274 **Plans were slowly coming together:** OPD, Case Nos. 07-054096, 07-053064, and 07-039206.

275 **Lieutenant Ersie Joyner, a talented street cop:** Ibid.

275 **On July 17, five days after the Wills killing:** OPD, Case Nos. 07-054096 and 07-053064, Search Warrant Affidavit. OPD, Case Nos. 07-054096, 07-053064, and 07-039206, recorded interviews with informant.

275 **He'd seen Fourth with a gun:** Ibid.

275 **All of Fourth's bodyguards carried guns:** Ibid.

276 **"They smart and they stupid":** Ibid.

276 **It went on for more:** Ibid.

276 **"Are these dangerous people?":** Ibid.

277 He identified thirty-five incidents: OPD, Case Nos. 07-054096, 07-053064, and 07-039206, Search Warrant Affidavit.

279 Cobb, like so many others: ACDAO, Case No. 157043.

26. WHAT THE HELL IS THIS?

281 "That's the motherfucker right there": *People v. Devaughndre Broussard*, ACSC, Case No. 531971, Proffer Statement. Hereinafter referred to as "Broussard Proffer."

281 *that motherfucker wrote stuff:* Ibid.

281 "Indirectly," Fourth answered: Ibid.

281 "Man, as a matter of fact": Ibid.

282 police started night surveillance: OPD, Case Nos. 07-054096, 07-053064, and 07-039206.

282 Little did Fourth know: OPD, Case No. 07-039206.

283 "Look, it takes ten cops": *People v. Yusuf Ali Bey (IV) and Antoine A. Mackey,* ACSC, Case No. 160939-A/B, Testimony of Sgt. Kyle Thomas, Dept. 10, April 25, 2011.

283 "What was what? What was that?": Ibid.

283 This intelligence came from a surprising: Sergeant Derwin Longmire, Predisciplinary Response, OPD. Hereinafter referred to as Longmire, Predisciplinary Response.

283 Rumors had been whispered: Ibid. Also see *Derwin Longmire v. City of Oakland, Howard Jordan, Sean Whent, et al.,* USDCNDC, Case No. C 10-01465 JSW, Deposition of Derwin Longmire.

283 "There's no doubt about it": Longmire, Predisciplinary Response.

283 "It seems that he has some type": Ibid.

283 Even the department's number-two commander: *Derwin Longmire v. City of Oakland, Howard Jordan, Sean Whent, et al.,* USDCNDC, Case No. C 10-01465 JSW, Deposition of Howard Jordan.

283 other cops were leery of letting him: Longmire, Predisciplinary Response.

284 "doing him a favor": Ibid.

284 "What the hell is this?": Ibid.

284 Longmire knew those odd doors: Ibid.

284 Longmire was angry and hurt: Ibid.

284 SWAT planners decided the first: Ibid.

285 Superior Court judges Allan Hymer: OPD, Case Nos. 07-054096, 07-053064, and 07-039206.

285 Two hundred officers would burst: Ibid.

285 word trickled down through the ranks: "Delayed Raid Likely Cost Chauncey Bailey His Life," OT, December 16, 2008.

285 Oakland police chief Wayne Guy Tucker: Ibid.

285 SWAT team members were insistent: Ibid.

286 nor would he attempt to reach: Ibid.

27. I TOLD Y'ALL IT WAS GONNA BE BIG

287 He called Broussard and Mackey together: *People v. Devaughndre Broussard,* ACSC, Case No. 531971, Proffer Statement. Hereinafter referred to as "Broussard Proffer."

287 "We got to take him out": Ibid.

288 Mackey called the bakery: Ibid.

288 It was obvious to others: Ibid.

288 He thought it might be: Ibid.

288 "That motherfucker up there": Ibid.

288 "My sister [would] be trippin'": Ibid.

289 around 5:30 p.m., Bailey emerged: Ibid.

289 "He walking out?": OPD, Case No. 07-059842, recorded statement of person referred to in the text as Cheryl Davis.

289 Broussard and Mackey followed the bus: Broussard Proffer.

290 "to get loans and not pay": Ibid.

290 "You gonna be taken care of": Ibid.

290 They parked across the street: OPD, Case No. 07-059842, tracking device report.

290 "Dre, you gotta do it": Broussard Proffer.

291 "Yeah, you gotta do it": Ibid.

291 Fourth's instructions were akin: Ibid.

291 he gave Broussard the sawed-off: Ibid.

291 she heard Fourth tell Ali: OPD, Case No. 07-059842.

292 when Broussard ran to the building: Broussard Proffer.

292 "He must be walking": Ibid.

293 "There you go right there": Ibid.

293 The transaction left Bailey: ACSO, Coroner's Report No. 2007-02208.

294 swinging his bag awkwardly: Broussard Proffer.

294 It severed Bailey's trachea: ACSO, Coroner's Report No. 2007-02208.

294 Broussard stopped at Bailey's feet: Broussard Proffer.

294 a hole nearly eight inches long: ACSO, Coroner's Report No. 2007-02208.

295 a red Hornady buckshot load: OPD, Case No. 07-059842.

296 and gently spread the newspaper: Ibid.

296 ejected it onto his bedroom floor: Ibid.

296 "Damn! Damn! I told y'all": Broussard Proffer.

296 "What happened?": Ibid.

296 "Ain't no way it can get": Ibid.

296 Longmire arrived at 7:58 a.m.: OPD, Case No. 07-059842.

297 "What did the inside of his head": Broussard Proffer.

297 They'd go see his credit man: Ibid.

297 "That will teach them": OPD, Case No. 07-059842, recorded statement of person referred to in the text as Cheryl Davis.

298 "For our name to be brought": KTVU evening newscast, August 2, 2007.

298 The same shotgun had fired: OPD, Case No. 07-059842.

28. I SHOT HIM

299 But the church's pastor refused: Oakland police officers, interviews with the author in 2008 and 2009. The officers asked not to be identified, citing a department gag order on the Bailey murder.

299 the sniper team's sergeant went: Ibid.

300 on the evening of August 2: People v. Devaughndre Broussard, ACSC, Case No. 531971, Proffer Statement. Hereinafter referred to as "Broussard Proffer."

301 pulling again and again: Oakland police officers, interviews.

301 Then he peeked down the stairs: Ibid.

301 found him lying on the floor: Ibid.

301 "Devils! Devils": ACSO, recorded jail phone call 841F10FM, August 4, 2007.

302 he pitched the gun toward the ground: Broussard Proffer.

302 They flipped his mattress aside: OPD, Case No. 07-059842.

303 Rodent feces littered the floor: ACDEH, Inspection Notes and Embargo Notice, YBMB.

303 Commanders ordered the walk-in freezers: OPD, Case No. 07-059842.

303 the federal judge overseeing the bankruptcy: Your Black Muslim Bakery, Inc., debtor, USBCNDC, Case No. 06-41991.

304 hidden it at a house: Devaughndre Broussard, interview with the author, June 16, 2011, Oakland, CA.

304 What if police had found it: People v. Yusuf Ali Bey IV, Tamon Oshun Halfin, Joshua Bey, Yusuf Bey V, and Richard Lewis, ACSC, Case No. 531990A-E, video of Bey IV, Joshua Bey, and Halfin talking in jail cell.

304 witnesses had seen just enough: OPD, Case No. 07-059842.

305 At 9:55 a.m., Longmire, backed: Ibid.

305 "Of course" he would talk: Ibid.

305 Fourth claimed that Broussard had admitted: Ibid.

306 "No guns are allowed in": OPD, Case No. 07-059842, first recorded statement of Yusuf Bey IV.

306 "it doesn't take, um, a rocket scientist": Ibid.

306 "I grew up in S.F. Western Edition": OPD, Case No. 07-059842.

307 "You ain't getting no lawyer": Broussard Proffer.

307 "I tried to scoot away": Ibid. Sgt. Derwin Longmire testified at Bey IV and Mackey's murder trial that he did not squeeze Broussard's leg and that Broussard did not ask for a lawyer.

307 "Did you get him?": OPD, Case No. 07-059842, first recorded statement of Yusuf Bey IV.

307 "Yusuf, did you have anything": Ibid.

308 Longmire gestured at Fourth: *People v. Devaughndre Broussard,* ACSC, Case No. 531971, Preliminary Hearing Transcript.

308 "cool as an ice cube": *People v. Broussard* trial testimony.

308 "He's talking about [me]": ACSO, recorded jail phone call 841F10F2, August 4, 2007.

308 he asked Longmire to let him speak: Broussard Proffer.

308 There was no place in the room: *People v. Yusuf Ali Bey (IV) and Antoine A. Mackey,* ACSC, Case No. 160939-A/B, Testimony of Sgt. Derwin Longmire, Dept. 10, April 14, 2007. Hereinafter referred to as "Longmire Testimony."

308 Longmire would spend years explaining: *Derwin Longmire v. City of Oakland, Howard Jordan, Sean Whent, et al.,* USDCNDC, Case No. C 10-01465 JSW, Deposition of Derwin Longmire.

309 the decency he had shown the Beys: Ibid.

309 "Broussard had asked for privacy": Longmire Testimony.

309 "All you gotta do is say": Broussard Proffer.

309 "that religious shit": Ibid.

310 "Man had money. I had nothing": Ibid.

310 "I'm like, OK, I can say": Ibid.

310 "OK, man, what happened?": OPD, Case No. 07-059842, recorded statement of Devaughndre Broussard.

310 "Did anybody instruct you": Ibid.

29. POW . . . POW . . . *POOF!*

311 a thin, fictive concoction: OPD, Case No. 07-059842.

311 filed papers asking the district attorney: Ibid.

312 Davis spoke at length: Ibid.

312 "I believe [Bailey] was writing": Ibid.

312 "Um, like trying to assassinate": Ibid.

312 "The way he makes himself seem": Ibid.

312 This was incredible evidence: SFC, December 8, 2007.

313 "There were so many moving parts": Ibid.

313 "I think [Fourth] had him killed": OPD, Case No. 07-059842.

313 **The detective who interviewed Davis:** Ibid.

313 **There is no record of such:** Ibid.

313 **"was obviously relevant":** SFC, December 8, 2007.

314 **Had he gone to Bailey's apartment?:** ACDAO, Case No. 157043.

314 **"We have other evidence":** Ibid.

315 **"They didn't know I had it":** ACSO, recorded jail phone call 841F10FF, August 4, 2007.

315 **"Ohhh shit":** ACSO, recorded jail phone call 841F10FH, August 4, 2007.

315 **"Disrespectful-ass devils":** ACSO, recorded jail phone call 841F10FM, August 4, 2007.

316 **but one of the detectives' cars:** *People v. Yusuf Ali Bey IV, Tamon Oshun Halfin, Joshua Bey, Yusuf Bey V, and Richard Lewis,* ACSC, Case No. 531990A-E, video of Bey IV, Joshua Bey, and Halfin talking in a jail cell.

317 **"She didn't see shit":** Ibid.

317 **it was devastating evidence:** *People v. Yusuf Ali Bey IV, Tamon Oshun Halfin, Joshua Bey, Yusuf Bey V, and Richard Lewis,* ACSC, Case No. 531990A-E, Statement of Judge Thomas Reardon, Dept. 10, August 21, 2009.

317 **"If they had found my phone":** *People v. Bey, Halfin, et al.,* video.

317 **"Which one? The shotty?":** Ibid.

318 **"I'm gonna make him give me":** Ibid.

318 **"Hell no":** Ibid.

318 **"That fool said":** Ibid.

318 **"Where he shoot him at?":** Ibid.

319 *"POOF!":* Ibid.

30. CAPTAIN MARVEL, COME HELP US

320 **a line of people stretched:** OT, August 9, 2007.

320 **"Chauncey was often intense":** "Mayor Ron Dellums Speaks During Chauncey Bailey's Funeral," http://www.youtube.com/watch?v=yjvyNLR3qW8.

321 **"Allow me to say what needs":** Ibid.

321 **"I wish there were superheroes":** Ibid.

322 **"I want to make Chauncey's untimely":** OT, August 9, 2007.

322 **"If we can't find something":** Ibid.

322 **Brown had destroyed public documents:** Articles concerning Brown's records as Oakland mayor were written when he'd left the mayor's office and appeared in the *Contra Costa Times* and *Oakland Tribune* on March 19, 2007: "Brown's Mayoral Files Missing: Oakland Aides Took Some; Legal Questions Raised."

323 **He would seize on the fact:** http://www.youtube.com/watch?v=vFEDJaW8M74 &feature=related.

323 "It was a known fact": OT, August 7, 2007.

324 "His death was an attack": "Commentary: In Detroit, Some Note Absences at Bailey Service," http://www.chaunceybaileyproject.org/2007/08/17/in-detroit-some-note-absences-at-bailey-service/.

324 "I want to honor": CBP, April 30, 2009, audio recording of Obama's remarks.

326 "I've always been a very pensive person": "D.A.: A Man of Conviction and Reflection, Orloff Tries to Carve His Own Niche as Meehan's Successor," SJMN, January 22, 1995.

326 the prosecutor had said loudly: "Jury Rigged?" EBX, May 4, 2005.

326 When a female prosecutor sued Orloff: Ibid.

327 "My boss, Mr. O., is not interested": Sergeant Derwin Longmire, Predisciplinary Response, OPD.

328 "If the aggravated kidnapping case": "DA Not Planning to Expand Bailey Case," CBP, July 3, 2008.

31. WHY . . .

329 he tried to find the courage: *People v. Yusuf Ali Bey (IV) and Antoine A. Mackey,* ACSC, Case No. 160939-A/B, Testimony of Devaughndre Broussard, Dept. 10, April 4, 2011. Hereinafter referred to as "Broussard Testimony."

330 a letter to the man he considered: ACDAO, Case No.157043. A copy of the letter is in the case file.

331 "They got me for murder": ACSO, recorded jail phone call 841F10F2, August 4, 2007.

331 "Boy, I told your stupid ass": Ibid.

331 *"No, you didn't, you stupid-ass"*: Ibid.

332 "No, he told them that I did": Ibid.

332 "absolute blindness to conflicts of interest": State Bar Court of California, *Matter of LeRue J. Grim,* Case Nos. 94-0-17544-EEB and 94-0-19001-EEB.

333 before finally admitting to her: Ibid.

333 when he was sixty-three: Ibid.

334 Could it be proven that Fourth: The author is informed on this point by Chauncey Bailey Project interviews conducted with University of San Francisco Law School professor Richard Leo.

334 Broussard made that request: OPD, Case No. 07-059842, investigative follow-up report.

334 once a judge ruled after a perfunctory: OT, November 22, 2007.

335 Broussard would eventually say: Broussard Testimony.

335 "I never heard about Chauncey Bailey": CBS News, *60 Minutes,* February 24, 2008.

335 "He was telling me how": Ibid.

335 "He says he's going to say": ACSO, recorded jail phone call 2O1U1099, February 24, 2008.

335 "He's a good liar for a Negro": Ibid.

336 he was more convinced than ever: ACSO recorded jail phone call 6H1U110E, June 17, 2008.

336 "The devil is meant": ACSO recorded jail phone call 7L1U104Z.v08, July 21, 2008.

336 "This motherfucker destroyed": ACSO, recorded jail phone call 2O1U1099, February 24, 2008.

337 "What did he jeopardize, Alaia?": Ibid.

337 "If they keep using me": Ibid.

32. MY LIFE IS NO ACCIDENT

339 "The people call Joshua Bey": "Surprise Guilty Plea in Kidnapping Case," OT, February 2, 2008.

339 Joshua had secretly pleaded guilty: Ibid.

339 "You're not a Bey anymore": Ibid.

340 "Don't say brother anymore": Ibid.

340 several of the Bey women: Ibid.

340 The essence of the bakery lived on: *People v. Yusuf Ali Bey (IV) and Antoine A. Mackey,* ACSC, Case No. 160939-A/B, Testimony of Dawud Bey, Dept. 10, April 13, 2011.

341 police video showing Fourth laughing: OT, June 18, 2008; CBP, June 18, 2008.

341 "It exonerates my client": Ibid.

342 lingering suspicion that Sergeant Derwin Longmire: "Secret Video Raises Questions About Bakery Leader's Role in Bailey Killing," OT, October 25, 2008; CBP, October 25, 2008.

342 It also reported that phone records: Ibid.

342 The *San Francisco Chronicle* followed: "Piece of Puzzle Surfaces; D.A. Now Has Missing Account of Bakery Leader's Comings and Goings in the Hours Before and After the Killing," SFC, December 7, 2008.

343 "concurrent, parallel investigation:": "Dellums Requests State Investigation of Police Handling of Bailey Investigation," OT, October 31, 2008.

343 who had once interfered: "Documents Point to Oakland Police Cover-Up," OT, January 22, 2009.

343 but Tucker resigned: "Bailey 'Mistakes' Added to Police Chief's Decision to Step Down," OT, January 27, 2009.

344 "had hollered at me": *People v. Yusuf Ali Bey (IV) and Antoine A. Mackey,* ACSC,

Case No. 160939-A/B, Testimony of Devaughndre Broussard, Dept. 10, April 10, 2011. Hereinafter referred to as "Broussard Testimony."

344 **"I know about them other murders"**: Broussard Testimony, April 4, 2011.

345 **Broussard heard nothing from his lawyer**: Ibid.

345 **"a dry run"**: Ibid.

345 **to make sure it was turned on**: *People v. Devaughndre Broussard*, ACSC, Case No. 531971, Proffer Statement.

345 **"Mr. Yusuf the Fourth"**: LeRue Grim, interview with the author, April 23, 2011, San Francisco, CA.

345 **"I told them"**: Ibid.

346 **Department of Justice investigators concluded**: "Putting Longmire on Bailey Case Was a Mistake, Jordan Admits," OT, April 14, 2009.

346 **an effort that fizzled**: "Longmire Returning to Duty After OPD Declines to Discipline Officer," OT, October 21, 2009.

346 **He asked for W.E.B. DuBois's**: ACSO, recorded jail phone call 2L1U1089, February 21, 2008.

347 **"The devils keep fucking with me"**: ACSO, recorded jail phone call 6U1U101E.v08, June 30, 2008.

347 **"I have learned more in this year"**: ACSO, recorded jail phone call 881U106M, August 8, 2008.

347 **"God is going to be merciful"**: Ibid.

347 **"God forcing me to find out"**: Ibid.

348 **"Do you see how similar"**: Ibid.

348 **"Why did God design a set day"**: Ibid.

349 **"You are going to come out"**: Ibid.

349 **"I know, Mommy"**: Ibid.

EPILOGUE

351 **"number one soldier"**: ACSO, recorded jail phone call no. 1B1S10J1v.09. January 11, 2009.

351 **"a hit list"**: *People vs. Yusuf Ali Bey (IV)*, ACSC, Case No. 531966, declaration of Inspector Kathleen Boyovich.

352 **Gary Larue Popoff**: California Department of Corrections and Rehabilitation, summary of revocation hearing and decision, Gary L. Popoff, no. F09604.

352 **"There is nothing"**: Ibid.

352 **"Gary is clever"**: *People vs. Gary L. Popoff*, ACSC, Case No. 157706, letter of J. Richard Popoff.

352 **"the will of Allah"**: ACSO, recorded jail phone call 1B1S10J1.v.09. January 11, 2009.

352 **"The will of Allah will be"**: Ibid.

353 **"smuggled the written communication"**: *People vs. Yusuf Ali Bey (IV)*, ACSC, Case No. 531966, declaration of Inspector Kathleen Boyovich.

353 **Brown eventually moved to resign:** "Lawyer in Chauncey Bailey Case Is Resigning from Practicing Law," OT, November 17, 2010.

354 **"fast talking ne'er-do-well"**: The Cool as Hell Theatre Show, http://www.coolashelltheatre.com/podcasts/ "Thomas Reardon, a real life criminal judge, says playing a con man comes naturally to him in the *Music Man.*"

355 **"I don't think, personally"**: *People v. Yusuf Ali Bey (IV) and Antoine A. Mackey*, ACSC, Case No. 160939-A/B, remarks of Yusef Bey IV, Dept. 10, February 10, 2011.

355 **"I didn't mean"**: *People v. Yusuf Ali Bey (IV) and Antoine A. Mackey*, ACSC, Case No. 160939-A/B, remarks of Judge Thomas M. Reardon, Dept. 10, February 10, 2011.

356 **"I can't find the words"**: *People v. Yusuf Ali Bey (IV) and Antoine A. Mackey*, ACSC, Case No. 160939-A/B, Testimony of Devaughndre Broussard, Dept. 10, March 24, 2011.

357 **"He fell"**: Devaughndre Broussard, interview with the author, June 16, 2011, Oakland, CA.

357 **"wanted us to kill him"**: *People v. Yusuf Ali Bey (IV) and Antoine A. Mackey*, ACSC, Case No. 160939-A/B, Testimony of Devaughndre Broussard, Dept. 10, March 28, 2011.

357 **"Where did you aim?"**: Ibid.

357 **"At his face"**: Ibid.

358 **"The impression I had"**: *People v. Yusuf Ali Bey (IV) and Antoine A. Mackey*, ACSC, Case No. 160939-A/B, Testimony of Devaughndre Broussard, Dept. 10, April 6, 2011. Note to reader: The dialogue exchange between Broussard and Gary Sirbu that concludes with Sirbu saying "Ohhhh" all occurred during Broussard's testimony of April 6, 2011.

359 **she could not recall:** *People v. Yusuf Ali Bey (IV) and Antoine A. Mackey*, ACSC, Case No. 160939-A/B, Testimony of person referred to in the text as Cheryl Davis, Dept. 10, April 21, 2011.

359 **"When you go to law school"**: *People v. Yusuf Ali Bey (IV) and Antoine A. Mackey*, ACSC, Case No. 160939-A/B, remark by Judge Thomas M. Reardon, Dept. 10, April 26, 2011.

360 **"I did what I had to do"**: *People v. Yusuf Ali Bey (IV) and Antoine A. Mackey*, ACSC, Case No. 160939-A/B, Testimony of Christopher Lamiero, Dept. 10, April 27, 2011.

360 **Peretti said Fourth was "shocked"**: Postverdict comments by Gene Peretti to media, June 9, 2011.

361 **"Guns aren't allowed"**: OPD, Case No. 07-059842, recorded statement of Yusuf Bey IV.

361 **Fourth was simply:** *People v. Yusuf Bey (IV) and Antoine A. Mackey,* ACSC, Case No. 160939-A/B, Trial Testimony of Derwin Longmire, Dept. 10, April 14, 2011.

361 **Finally the proceedings continued:** Ibid.

361 **"Did you make him any promises?":** *People v. Yusuf Ali Bey (IV), and Antoine Mackey,* ACSC, Case No. 160939-A/B, Trial Testimony of Derwin Longmire, Dept. 10, May 3, 2011.

362 **"a tremendous cost":** *Derwin Longmire v. City of Oakland, Howard Jordan, Sean Whent, et al.,* USDCNDC, Case No. C 10-01465 JSW, Deposition of Derwin Longmire. Hereinafter referred to as "Longmire Deposition."

362 **Investigators for both the state justice:** *Derwin Longmire v. City of Oakland, Howard Jordan, Sean Whent, et al.,* USDCNDC, Case No. C 10-01465 JSW, Depositions of Sean Whent and Jeffery Isreal.

362 **"significant errors or holes":** Longmire Deposition.

363 **"What's up":** *People v. Yusuf Ali Bey (IV) and Antoine A. Mackey,* ACSC, Case No. 160939-A/B, Testimony of Devaughndre Broussard, Dept. 10, April 4, 2011.

363 **"The bond was strong":** Ibid.

364 **"abiding conviction":** Alameda County District Attorney Nancy O' Malley, remarks at press conference, Oakland CA, June 9, 2011.

364 **"I would like the people to know":** *People v. Yusuf Ali Bey (IV) and Antoine A. Mackey,* ACSC, Case No. 160939-A/B, sentencing hearing statement of Yusuf Bey IV, read by Gene Peretti, Dept. 10, August 26, 2011.

Selected Bibliography

ARCHIVAL COLLECTIONS

Arthur C. Piepkorn Research Collection for "Profiles in Belief." Religious Bodies of the United States and Canada. Graduate Theological Union, Berkeley, CA.

Louis Wirth Papers. Special Collections Research Center. University of Chicago Library, Chicago.

Moorish Science Temple of America Collection. Manuscripts, Archives and Rare Books Division. Schomberg Center for Research in Black Culture. New York Public Library, New York.

BOOKS

Altman, Irwin, and J. Ginat. *Polygamous Families in Contemporary Society*. Cambridge: Cambridge University Press, 1996.

Armstrong, Karen. *A History of God: The 4000-Year Quest of Judaism, Christianity, and Islam*. New York: Ballantine Books, 1994.

Baldwin, James. *Another Country*. New York: Dial Press, 1962.

Baldwin, James. *The Fire Next Time*. New York: Dial Press, 1963.

Baldwin, James, and Sol Stein. *Native Sons: A Friendship That Created One of the Greatest Works of the Twentieth Century: Notes of a Native Son*. New York: One World/Ballantine Books, 2005.

Barboza, Steven. *American Jihad: Islam After Malcolm X*. New York: Image Books, 1995.

Bell, Derrick. *Faces at the Bottom of the Well: The Permanence of Racism*. New York: Basic Books, 1992.

Bennett, Lerone. *Before the Mayflower: A History of the Negro in America, 1619–1962*. Chicago: Johnson Publishing, 1962.

Bloom, Harold. *The American Religion: The Emergence of the Post-Christian Nation*. New York: Simon & Schuster, 1992.

Bontemps, Arna, and Jack Conroy. *Anyplace but Here*. Columbia: University of Missouri Press, 1997. (Originally published as *They Seek a City* in 1966.)

Branch, Taylor. *At Canaan's Edge: America in the King Years, 1965–1968.* New York: Simon & Schuster, 2006.

Branch, Taylor. *Parting the Waters: America in the King Years, 1954–1963.* New York: Simon & Schuster, 1988.

Branch, Taylor. *Pillar of Fire: America in the King Years, 1963–1965.* New York: Simon & Schuster, 1998.

Breitman, George. *The Last Year of Malcolm X: The Evolution of a Revolutionary.* New York: Pathfinder Press, 1992.

Browne-Marshall, Gloria J. *Race, Law, and American Society: 1607 to Present.* New York: Routledge, Taylor & Francis Group, 2007.

Caro, Robert A. *The Years of Lyndon Johnson: Master of the Senate.* New York: Alfred A. Knopf, 2002.

Clegg, Claude Andrew. *An Original Man: The Life and Times of Elijah Muhammad.* New York: St. Martin's Press, 1997.

Cleaver, Eldridge. *Soul on Ice.* New York: McGraw-Hill, 1968.

Curtis, Edward E., IV. *Black Muslim Religion in the Nation of Islam, 1960–1975.* Chapel Hill: University of North Carolina Press, 2006.

Douglass, Frederick. *Life and Times of Frederick Douglass.* Hartford, CT: Park Publishing, 1881.

Douglass, Frederick. *My Bondage and My Freedom.* New York: Miller, Orton and Mulligan, 1855.

Douglass, Frederick. *Narrative of the Life of Frederick Douglass, an American Slave.* Boston: Anti-Slavery Office, 1845.

DuBois, W.E.B. *The Souls of Black Folk.* Chicago: A.C. McClurg, 1903. Reprint, New York: Bantam Books, 1989.

Eliade, Mircea. *The Sacred and the Profane: The Nature of Religion.* New York: Harper & Row, 1961.

Ellison, Ralph. *Invisible Man.* New York: Random House, 1952.

Eugenides, Jeffrey. *Middlesex.* New York: Farrar, Straus and Giroux, 2002.

Evanzz, Karl. *The Messenger: The Rise and Fall of Elijah Muhammad.* New York: Pantheon Books, 1999.

Fauset, Arthur Huff. *Black Gods of the Metropolis: Negro Religious Cults of the Urban North.* Philadelphia: University of Pennsylvania Press, 1944.

Fritze, Ronald H. *Invented Knowledge: False History, Fake Science and Pseudo-Religions.* London: Reaktion Books, 2009.

Gaines, Ernest J. *A Lesson Before Dying.* New York: Alfred A. Knopf, 1993.

Gardell, Mattias. *In the Name of Elijah Muhammad: Louis Farrakhan and the Nation of Islam.* Durham, NC: Duke University Press (1996).

Garvey, Marcus. *Selected Writings and Speeches of Marcus Garvey.* Mineola, NY: Dover Publications, 2004.

Gates, Henry Louis. *Colored People: A Memoir.* New York: Alfred A. Knopf, 1994.

Genovese, Eugene D. *Roll, Jordan, Roll: The World the Slaves Made.* New York: Random House, 1972.

Gomez, Michael Angelo. *Black Crescent: The Experience and Legacy of African Muslims in the Americas.* Cambridge: Cambridge University Press, 2005.

Goodman, James. *Stories of Scottsboro.* New York: Pantheon Books, 1995.

Haddard, Yvonne Yazbeck, and John L. Esposito, eds. *Muslims on the Americanization Path?* New York: Oxford University Press, 1988.

Hakim, Nasir Makr. *Is Elijah Muhammad the Offspring of Noble Drew Ali & Marcus Garvey?* Phoenix: Messenger Elijah Muhammad Propagation Society Publications, 2006.

Hakim, Nasir Makr. *They Thought They Were Followers of Elijah Muhammad.* Phoenix: Messenger Elijah Muhammad Propagation Society Publications, 2006.

Harper, Michael S., and Anthony Walton. *Every Shut Eye Ain't Asleep: An Anthology of Poetry by African Americans Since 1945.* Boston: Little, Brown, 1994.

Hawkins, Homer C., and Richard W. Thomas. *Blacks and Chicanos in Urban Michigan.* Lansing: Michigan History Division, Michigan Department of State, 1979.

Haynes, Stephen R. *Noah's Curse: The Biblical Justification of American Slavery.* Oxford: Oxford University Press, 2007.

HoSang, Daniel Martinez. *Racial Propositions: Ballot Initiatives and the Making of Postwar California.* Berkeley: University of California Press, 2010.

Howard, Clark. *Zebra: The True Account of the 179 Days of Terror in San Francisco.* New York: R. Marek Publishers, 1979.

Huey, Brenda. *The Blackest Land, the Whitest People: Greenville, Texas.* Bloomington, IN: AuthorHouse, 2006.

Irving, Washington. *Selected Prose.* New York: Rinehart, 1950.

Jacobs, Harriet A. *Incidents in the Life of a Slave Girl.* Boston, 1861.

Kahaner, Larry. *AK-47: The Weapon That Changed the Face of War.* Hoboken, NJ: John Wiley & Sons, 2007.

Lemann, Nicholas. *The Promised Land: The Great Black Migration and How It Changed America.* New York: Alfred A. Knopf, 1991.

Leo, Richard A. *Police Interrogation and American Justice.* Cambridge, MA: Harvard University Press, 2008.

Lincoln, C. Eric. *The Black Muslims in America.* Boston: Beacon Press, 1973.

Lofton, John. *Denmark Vesey's Revolt: The Slave Plot That Lit a Fuse to Fort Sumter.* Kent, OH: Kent State University Press, 1983.

Lomax, Louis E. *When the Word Is Given: A Report on Elijah Muhammad, Malcolm X, and the Black Muslim World.* New York: Signet Books, 1963.

Lukman. *The Black Muslim Manifesto from Inside the Belly of the Beast.* Bloomington, IN: AuthorHouse, 2009.

Magida, Arthur J. *Prophet of Rage: A Life of Louis Farrakhan and His Nation.* New York: Basic Books, 1996.

Major, Reginald. *A Panther Is a Black Cat.* New York: William Morrow, 1971.

Marable, Manning. *Malcolm X: A Life of Reinvention.* New York: Viking, 2011.

Montgomery, Gayle B., and James W. Johnson. *One Step from the White House: The Rise and Fall of Senator William F. Knowland.* Berkeley: University of California Press, 1998.

Moon, Elaine Latzman. *Untold Tales, Unsung Heroes: An Oral History of Detroit's African American Community, 1918–1967.* Detroit: Wayne State University Press, 1994.

Moore, Keith. *Moorish Circle 7: The Rise of the Islamic Faith Among Blacks in America and Its Masonic Origins.* Bloomington, IN: AuthorHouse, 2005.

Morrow, Alvin. *Breaking the Curse of Willie Lynch: The Science of Slave Psychology.* Florissant, MO: Rising Sun Publications, 2003.

Moses, Wilson Jeremiah. *Black Messiahs and Uncle Toms: Social and Literary Manipulations of a Religious Myth.* University Park: Pennsylvania State University Press, 1993.

Moses, Wilson Jeremiah. *Classical Black Nationalism: From the American Revolution to Marcus Garvey.* New York: New York University Press, 1996.

Muhammad, Elijah. *Blood Bath: The True Teaching of Malcolm X.* Phoenix: Messenger Elijah Muhammad Propagation Society Publications, 1992.

Muhammad, Elijah. *Christianity Versus Islam: When Worlds Collide.* Phoenix: Messenger Elijah Muhammad Propagation Society Publications, 2002.

Muhammad, Elijah. *Divine Sayings of the Honorable Elijah Muhammad, Messenger of Allah.* Phoenix: Messenger Elijah Muhammad Propagation Society Publications, 2002.

Muhammad, Elijah. *The Fall of America.* Chicago: Nation of Islam, 1973.

Muhammad, Elijah. *The Flag of Islam.* Chicago: Nation of Islam, 1974.

Muhammad, Elijah. *The God-Science of Black Power.* Phoenix: Messenger Elijah Muhammad Propagation Society Publications, 2002.

Muhammad, Elijah. *History of the Nation of Islam.* Phoenix: Messenger Elijah Muhammad Propagation Society Publications, 1994.

Muhammad, Elijah. *How to Eat to Live.* Atlanta: Messenger Elijah Muhammad Propagation Society Publications, 1967.

Muhammad, Elijah. *Message to the Blackman in America.* Atlanta: Messenger Elijah Muhammad Propagation Society Publications, 1965.

Muhammad, Elijah. *The Mother Plane.* Phoenix: Messenger Elijah Muhammad Propagation Society Publications, 1992.

Muhammad, Elijah. *The True History of Master Fard Muhammad.* Phoenix: Messenger Elijah Muhammad Propagation Society Publications, 1996.

Muhammad, Elijah. *Yakub: The Father of Mankind.* Phoenix: Messenger Elijah Muhammad Propagation Society Publications, 2002.

Parish, Peter J. *Slavery: History and Historians.* New York: Harper & Row, 1989.

Pearson, Hugh. *The Shadow of the Panther: Huey Newton and the Price of Black Power in America.* Reading, MA: Addison-Wesley Publishing, 1994.

Redding, J. Saunders. *They Came in Chains: Americans from Africa.* Philadelphia: Lippincott, 1950.

Remnick, David. *King of the World: Muhammad Ali and the Rise of an American Hero.* New York: Random House, 1998.

Roberts, Gene, and Hank Kilbanoff. *The Race Beat: The Press, the Civil Rights Struggle, and the Awakening of a Nation.* New York: Alfred A. Knopf, 2006.

Sanders, Prentice Earl, and Bennett Cohen. *The Zebra Murders: A Season of Killing, Racial Madness, and Civil Rights.* New York: Arcade, 2006.

Self, Robert O. *American Babylon: Race and the Struggle for Postwar Oakland.* Princeton, NJ: Princeton University Press, 2003.

Singer, Margaret Thaler. *Cults in Our Midst.* San Francisco: Jossey-Bass, 2003.

Storr, Anthony. *Feet of Clay: Saints, Sinners, and Madmen: A Study of Gurus.* New York: Free Press, 1996.

Stovall, Tyler. *Paris Noir: African Americans in the City of Lights.* New York: Houghton Mifflin, 1996.

Sugue, Thomas J. *Sweet Land of Liberty: The Forgotten Struggle for Civil Rights in the North.* New York: Random House, 2008.

Thernstrom, Stephan, and Abigail M. Thernstrom. *America in Black and White: One Nation, Indivisible.* New York: Simon & Schuster, 1997.

Tsoukalas, Steven. *The Nation of Islam: Understanding the "Black Muslims."* Phillipsburg, NJ: P & R, 2001.

Van Deburg, William L. *Modern Black Nationalism: From Marcus Garvey to Louis Farrakhan.* New York: New York University Press, 1997.

White, Vibert L. *Inside the Nation of Islam: A Historical and Personal Testimony by a Black Muslim.* Gainesville: University Press of Florida, 2001.

Wilkerson, Isabel. *The Warmth of Other Suns: The Epic Story of America's Great Migration.* New York: Random House, 2010.

Wilson, Peter Lamborn. *Drift: Essays on the Margin of Islam.* San Francisco: City Lights Books, 1993.

Williams, Juan, and Quinton Hosford Dixie. *This Far by Faith: Stories from the African-American Religious Experience.* New York: William Morrow, 2003.

Wright, Kai. *The African American Experience: Black History and Culture Through Speeches, Letters, Editorials, Poems, Songs, and Stories.* New York: Black Dog & Leventhal, 2009.

X, Malcolm, and Alex Haley. *The Autobiography of Malcolm X.* New York: Ballantine Books, 1973.

X, Malcolm, and George Breitman. *Malcolm X Speaks: Selected Speeches and Statements.* New York: Grove Weidenfeld, 1965.

COURT RECORDS

California Appellate Court Cases

People v. Jesse Lee Cooks, Larry Craig Green, Manuel Moore, and J.C. X Simon. Court of Appeal of the State of California, First Appellate District, Division Two. Case No. A010750.

People v. Alfonza Alvon Phillips. Court of Appeal of the State of California, First Appellate District, Division Two. Case No. A120183.

California Bar Court Cases

Matter of discipline, LeRue J. Grim, Bar No. 37485. State Bar Court of California. Case Nos. 94-0-17544-EEB and 94-0-19001-EEB.

California Civil Court Cases

Alameda County Court v. Aundra R. Dixon. Superior Court of the State of California, County of Alameda. Case No. RF03122966.

Alameda County Department of Child Support Services v. Aundra Reniece Dixon. Superior Court of the State of California, County of Alameda. Case No. 07-00392.

Estate of Antar Yusuf Bey. Superior Court of the State of California, County of Alameda. Case No. RP06271660. Petition for Probate.

Farieda Bey v. Antar Bey. Superior Court of the State of California, County of Alameda. Case No. RG04156295. Request for Restraining Order.

Farieda Bey v. Antar Bey, Your Black Muslim Bakery, et al. Superior Court of the State of California, County of Alameda. Case No. RG04165951.

City and County of San Francisco v. Antoine A. Mackey. Superior Court of the State of California, County of San Francisco. Case No. FCS-06-339919.

Jane Does 1, 2 and 3, et al., v. Yusuf Ali Bey, County of Alameda, et al. Superior Court of the State of California, County of Alameda. Case No. RG03105036.

Antoine Arlus Mackey, through his mother and natural guardian, v. City and County of San Francisco, et al. Superior Court of the State of California, County of San Francisco. Case No. 421-900.

Montgomery Ward & Co., Inc. v. Yusuf Bey, et al. Superior Court of the State of California, County of Alameda. Case No. 329319.

Ruth Stephens v. (Theron) Hancil Stephens (Divorce). Superior Court of the State of California, County of Alameda. Case No. 237350.

California Criminal Court Cases

People v. Akbar Bey. City of Oakland Municipal Court. Case No. 387530.

People v. Akbar Bey. City of Oakland Municipal Court. Case No. 121325.

People v. Dahood Sharieff Bey, Basheer Fard Muhammad, Ajuwon Fardjamaal Muhammad, and Jonathan Moore. Superior Court of the State of California, County of Alameda.

People v. Yusuf A. Bey (IV). Superior Court of the State of California, County of San Francisco. Case No. 2264607.

People v. Yusuf A. Bey (V). Superior Court of the State of California, County of Alameda. Case No. 526347.

People v. Yusuf Ali Bey (IV). Superior Court of the State of California, County of Alameda. Case No. 213954.

People v. Yusuf Ali Bey (IV). Superior Court of the State of California, County of Alameda. Case No. 531966.

People v. Yusuf Ali Bey (IV). Superior Court of the State of California, County of Contra Costa. Case No. 01-124788-1-001.

People v. Yusuf Ali Bey (IV) and Tamon Halfin. Superior Court of the State of California, County of Alameda. Case No. 549951 A&B.

People v. Yusuf Ali Bey IV, Tamon Oshun Halfin, Joshua Bey, Yusuf Bey V, and Richard Lewis. Superior Court of the State of California. Case No. 531990A-E.

People v. Yusuf Ali Bey (IV), Demetrius Harvey, Donald Cunningham, Dyamen Namer Williams, Jamall Robinson, Ajuwon Muhammad, Kahlil Ali Raheem, Tamon Oshun Halfin, and James Watts. Superior Court of the State of California, County of Alameda. Case No. 514516A/B/C/D/E/F.

People v. Yusuf Ali Bey (IV) and Antoine A. Mackey. Superior Court of the State of California, County of Alameda. Case No. 160939-A/B.

People v. Yusuf Bey. Superior Court of the State of California, County of Alameda. Case No. 479904.

People v. Devaughndre Broussard. Superior Court of the State of California, County of San Francisco. Case No. 2242731.

People v. Devaughndre Broussard. Superior Court of the State of California, County of Alameda. Case No. 531971.

People v. Marlon Campbell, aka Amir Isanazim Wadi. Superior Court of the State of California, County of Alameda. Case No. 156260.

People v. Marlon Campbell, aka Amir Isanazim Wadi. Superior Court of the State of California, County of Alameda. Case No. 157466.

People v. Jesse Lee Cooks, Larry Craig Green, Manuel Moore, and J.C. X Simon. Superior Court of the State of California, County of San Francisco. Case No. 88244-01.

People v. Maurice Anthony Cotton, aka Jason Peterson, and Marlon Campbell, aka Amir Isa Nazim Wadi. Superior Court of the State of California, County of Alameda. Case No. 535505.

People v. Aundra Dixon. Superior Court of the State of California, County of San Francisco. Case No. 892963.

People v. Aundra Dixon. Superior Court of the State of California, County of San Francisco. Case No. 165100-1653287.

People v. Aundra R. Dixon. Superior Court of the State of California, County of San Francisco. Case Nos. 120525 and 126577.

People v. George Foreman and Larry Williams. Superior Court of the State of California, County of Alameda. Case No. 57930-6A/B.

People v. Tamon Halfin. Superior Court of the State of California, County of Alameda. Case No. 532643.

People v. Randy Harvey. Superior Court of the State of California, County of Alameda. Case No. 157139.

People v. Antonique Johnson. Superior Court of the State of California, County of San Francisco. Case No. 2115898-190052.

People v. Richard Lewis. Superior Court of the State of California, County of Alameda. Case No. 549951D.

People v. Richard Lewis and Chad Dias. Superior Court of the State of California, County of San Francisco. Case No. 2207628.

People v. Antoine Mackey. Superior Court of the State of California, County of San Francisco. Case No. 2209041.

People v. Antoine Mackey. Superior Court of the State of California, County of San Francisco. Case No. 02264127.

People v. Antoine Mackey and Isiain Johnson-Marin. Superior Court of the State of California, County of San Francisco. Case Nos. 2226567 and 2226568.

People v. Antoine Mackey and Terry Luckett. Superior Court of the State of California, County of San Francisco. Case Nos. 2272627 and 2272632.

People v. Ajuwon Fardjamaal Muhammad. Superior Court of the State of California, County of Alameda. Case No. 515967.

People v. Alfonza Alvon Phillips. Superior Court of the State of California, County of Alameda. Case No. 154053.

People v. Theron Stephens. Superior Court of the State of California, County of Alameda. Case No. 37286.

People v. Dyamen Namer Williams. Superior Court of the State of California, County of Alameda. Case No. 517864.

Federal Court Cases

Derwin Longmire v. City of Oakland, Howard Jordan, Sean Whent, et al. United States District Court, Northern District of California. Case No. C 10-01465 JSW.

Your Black Muslim Bakery, Inc., debtor. United States Bankruptcy Court, Northern District of California. Case No. 06-41991.

DISSERTATIONS AND THESES

Belding, Marc. "Racial Discrimination in Detroit: A Spatial Analysis of Racism." Wayne State University, 1969. Master's thesis.

Hart, Jamie. "African Americans, Health Care, and the Reproductive Freedom Movement in Detroit, 1918–1945." University of Michigan, 1988. PhD dissertation.

Kalinski, Peter. "Through the Vestibule: Assimilation and the Great Migration to Detroit: 1915–1925." Wayne State University, 2000. Master's thesis.

Levine, David Alan. "'Expecting the Barbarians': Race Relations and Social Control, Detroit, 1915–1926." University of Chicago, 1970. PhD dissertation.

Miles, Norman Kenneth. "Home at Last: Urbanization of Black Migrants in Detroit, 1916–1929." University of Michigan, 1978. PhD dissertation.

Thomas, Richard Walter. "From Peasant to Proletarian: The Formation and Organization of the Black Industrial Working Class in Detroit, 1915–1945." University of Michigan, 1976. PhD dissertation.

DOCUMENTARY

Zachary Stauffer. *A Day Late in Oakland.* 2008.

FREEDOM OF INFORMATION ACT REQUEST

Federal Bureau of Investigation. File on Wallace D. Fard, released to author under Freedom of Information Act Request No. 1139714-000. November 20, 2009.

GOVERNMENT DOCUMENTS

Federal Government Documents

U.S. Census data, National Archives.

U.S. Draft registration data, National Archives.

California State Government Documents

California Department of Justice. Transcript of interview of Oakland assistant police chief Howard Jordan. February 19, 2009.

California State Assembly Interim Committee on Crime and Corrections. Report on the Oakland Police Department. April 1950.

California State Board of Prison Terms. Transcript of Parole Consideration Hearing of Jesse Cooks, San Diego, CA. April 26, 2011.

California State Board of Prison Terms. Transcript of Parole Consideration Hearing of Larry Green, Vacaville, CA. September 11, 2009.

California State Board of Prison Terms. Transcript of Parole Consideration Hearing of Russell Lang, Avenal, CA. October 11, 2006.

California State Board of Prison Terms. Transcript of Parole Consideration Hearing of Manuel Moore, Blythe, CA. January 24, 2010.

California State Board of Prison Terms. Transcript of Parole Consideration Hearing of J.C. X Simon, Vacaville, CA. November 11, 2007.

California State Department of Corrections and Rehabilitation, Identification Information System, Aundra R. Dixon.

California State Department of Motor Vehicles. Report on Investigation No. 03B20345, Chauncey Wendell Bailey.

California State Natural Resources Agency, Department of Parks and Recreation. Building Structure and Object Record No. 1533: 5826-38, San Pablo Ave., Oakland.

Texas Government Documents

Birth certificates.

California City and County Government Documents

Alameda County Department of Environmental Health. Inspection Notes and Embargo Notice: Your Black Muslim Bakery, 5832 San Pablo Ave., Oakland, CA. August 3, 2007.

Alameda County recorded documents: birth, death, and marriage certificates.

Oakland Police Department Internal Affairs Division to Acting Police Chief Howard Jordan (memorandum). April 17, 2009.

Sergeant Derwin Longmire to Oakland Police Department (predisciplinary response). July 9, 2009.

INTERVIEWS

Nadar Bey. Various dates, Berkeley, CA. (Interviews conducted by students of the Investigative Reporting Program, University of California, Berkeley, Graduate School of Journalism.)

Devaughndre Broussard. June 16, 2011. Oakland, CA.

Mark Cooley. March 6 and April 13, 2010. Modesto, CA.

LeRue Grim, April 23, 2010. San Francisco, CA.

Dave Newhouse. April 23, 2010. Oakland, CA.

Dr. Stephen M. Raffle. July 21, 2010. Kentfield, CA.

Martin G. Reynolds. May 5, 2010. Oakland, CA.

Lorelei Waqia. April 22, 2010. Oakland, CA.

JOURNAL ARTICLES

Ansari, Zafar Ishaq. "Aspects of Black Muslim Theology." *Studia Islamica,* no. 53 (1981): 137–76.

Berg, Herbert, "Elijah Muhammad: An African American Muslim Mufassir?" *Arabica* 45, no. 3 (1998): 320–46.

Beynon, Erdmann Doane. "The Voodoo Cult Among Negro Migrants in Detroit." *American Journal of Sociology* 43, no. 6 (May 1938): 894–907.

Brown, Lee P. "Black Muslims and the Police." *Journal of Criminal Law, Criminology, and Police Science* 56, no. 1 (March 1965): 119–26.

Gomez, Michael. "Muslims in Early America." *Journal of Southern History* 60, no. 4 (November 1994): 671–710.

Howard, John. "The Social Basis of Organized Political Defiance: A Comparison of the Black Muslims, the John Birch Society, and the American Communist Party." *Western Political Quarterly* 18, no. 3 (supp.) (September 1965): 35–36.

Kaplan, Howard M. "The Black Muslims and the Negro American's Quest for Communion: A Case Study in the Genesis of Negro Protest Movements." *British Journal of Sociology* 20, no. 2 (June 1969): 164–76.

Maesen, William. "Watchtower Influences on Black Muslim Eschatology: An Exploratory Story." *Journal for the Scientific Study of Religion* 9, no. 4 (winter 1970): 321–25.

Mamiya, Lawrence H. "From Black Muslim to Bilalian: The Evolution of a Movement." *Journal for the Scientific Study of Religion* 21, no. 2 (June 1982): 138–152.

McNall, Scott Grant. "The Sect Movement." *Pacific Sociological Review* 6, no. 2 (autumn 1963): 60–64.

Nance, Susan. "Mystery of the Moorish Science Temple: Southern Blacks and American Alternative Spirituality in 1920s Chicago." *Religion and American Culture* 12, no. 2 (summer 2002): 123–66.

Nance, Susan. "Respectability and Representation: The Moorish Science Temple, Morocco, and Black Public Culture in 1920s Chicago." *American Quarterly* 54, no. 4 (December 2002): 623–59.

Pritchard, Robert L. "California Un-American Activities Investigations: Subversion on the Right?" *California Historical Society Quarterly* 49, no. 4 (December 1970): 309–27.

LAW-ENFORCEMENT RECORDS

Alameda County District Attorney's Office. Case No. 157043 (Chauncey Bailey homicide).

Alameda County Sheriff's Office. Coroner's investigative reports.

Alameda County Sheriff's Office. Recorded jail phone calls.

Alameda County Sheriff's Office. Case No. 07-015789 (kidnapping of Jane Doe #1 and Jane Doe #2, torture of Jane Doe #1).

Alameda County Sheriff's Office. Ali Saleem Bey concealed weapon initial application, September 29, 2005.

Oakland Police Department. Case No. 07-039206 (kidnapping of Jane Doe #1 and Jane Doe #2, torture of Jane Doe #1).

Oakland Police Department. Case No. 05-067098 (Antar Yusuf Bey homicide).

Oakland Police Department. Case No. 06-108485 (car shooting).

Oakland Police Department. Case No. 07-059842 (Chauncey Bailey homicide).

Oakland Police Department. Case No. 05-075886/05-075887 (liquor store vandalism).

Oakland Police Department. Case No. 07-054096 (Michael Wills homicide).

Oakland Police Department. Case No. 07-053064 (Odell Roberson Jr. homicide).

Oakland Police Department. Case No. 07-003071 (Yusuf Bey IV petty theft, Yusuf Bey V illegal firearm possession).

Oakland Police Department. Case No. 80-66370 (Yusuf Bey).

Oakland Police Department. Case No. 81-23354 (Yusuf Bey).

Oakland Police Department. Case No. 96-032294 (Yusuf Bey).

Oakland Police Department. Case No. 02-058831 (Yusuf Bey).

San Francisco Police Department. Case No. 050523109 (Aundra Dixon).

San Francisco Police Department. Case No. 051013511 (Aundra Dixon).

San Francisco Police Department. Case No. 060153990 (Aundra Dixon).

San Francisco Police Department. Case No. 060364539 (Aundra Dixon).

San Francisco Police Department. Case No. 060730203 (Aundra Dixon).

San Francisco Police Department. Case No. 070202678 (Aundra Dixon).

San Francisco Police Department. Case No. 051231428 (Devaughndre Broussard).

San Francisco Police Department. Case No. 051232222 (Devaughndre Broussard).

San Francisco Police Department. Case No. 050252013 (Devaughndre Broussard).

San Francisco Police Department. Case No. 050523109 (Devaughndre Broussard).

San Francisco Police Department. Case No. 05123142/051231428 (Devaughndre Broussard).

Santa Barbara Police Department. Case No. 411911, (Wendell and Birdie Mae Scott homicides).

Union City (CA) Police Department. Case No. 050625034 (Yusuf Bey IV).

NEWS SERVICE

Associated Press

NEWSPAPERS AND PERIODICALS

Contra Costa Times
Chicago Defender
Crisis
Detroit Free Press
Detroit News

Detroit Times
East Bay Express
East Bay Monthly
Final Call
Los Angeles Herald-Examiner
Los Angeles Times
Muhammad Speaks
New York Times
Oakland Post
Oakland Tribune
Ramparts magazine
San Francisco Chronicle
San Francisco Examiner
San Francisco Sun Reporter
San Jose Mercury News
Village Voice

TELEVISION NEWSCASTS

KGO-TV San Francisco, evening newscasts
KTVU-TV Oakland, evening newscasts
CBS News, *60 Minutes*

WEB SITES

Chauncey Bailey Project: http://www.chaunceybaileyproject.org/.

Closing Argument of Clarence Darrow in the Case of *People v. Ossian Sweet et al.:* http://law2.umkc.edu/faculty/projects/ftrials/sweet/Darrowsumm1.html.

Earl Warren Oral History Project. Earl Warren: Views and Episodes. Regional Oral History Office, University of California, Berkeley: http://content.cdlib.org/view?docId=ft9f59p1z7&brand=calisphere.

The Hate That Hate Produced. Internet Archive: http://www.archive.org/details/PBSTheHateThatHateProduced.

Investigative Reporters and Editors: http://www.ire.org/.

J. Paul Leonard Library Bay Area Television Archive at San Francisco State University: http://www.library.sfsu.edu/about/collections/sfbatv/index.php.

Robert C. Maynard Institute for Journalism Education: http://mije.org/robertmaynard.

San Jose Mercury News. Public Employee Salaries: http://www.mercurynews.com/salaries/bay-area; http://www.archive.org/details/PBSTheHateThatHateProduced.

YouTube:

http://www.youtube.com.

http://www.youtube.com/watch?v=yjvyNLR3qW8 (Oakland Mayor
Ronald V. Dellums's speech at Chauncey Bailey funeral).

http://www.youtube.com/watch?v=vFEDJaW8M74 (Oakland Post publisher
Paul Cobb discussing Chauncey Bailey murder).

http://www.youtube.com/watch?v=bvZLLuyv1rI (Malcolm X speech at First
Baptist Chuch, Los Angeles, on shooting of Ronald X Stokes).

Index

ABOUT THE AUTHOR

THOMAS PEELE was born in New York City. He is a digital investigative reporter for the Bay Area News Group, which publishes daily newspapers in Northern California, including the *Contra Costa Times,* the *Oakland Tribune,* and the *San Jose Mercury News.* He is also a lecturer in the Graduate School of Journalism at the University of California, Berkeley. In the fall of 2007, Peele became the lead reporter for the Chauncey Bailey Project, a consortium of news-gathering organizations, freelance journalists, educators, and students working to investigate the murder of *Oakland Post* editor Chauncey Bailey. Peele's many honors include the McGill Medal for Journalistic Courage and the Investigative Reporters and Editors Tom Renner Award for investigating organized crime. He lives in Northern California. His website is Thomaspeele.com.